The Ultimate

Hamilton Beach

Air Fryer

COOKBOOK

MANY ADVICES AND 500 AIR FRYER RECIPES TO IMPRESS YOUR GUESTS WITH ORIGINAL AND TASTY IDEAS

KEVIN BAILEY

Warning-Disclaimer: The purpose of this book is to educate and entertain. The author or publisher does not guarantee that anyone following the techniques, suggestions, tips, ideas, or strategies will become successful. The author and publisher shall have neither liability or responsibility to anyone with respect to any loss or damage caused, or alleged to be caused, directly or indirectly by the information contained in this book.

CONTENTS

INTRODUCTION

How Does the Hamilton Beach Air Fryer Work

Air fryers heat food by convection air is heated to 320-400 degrees Fahrenheit and passed around your food at high speed to heat it and give it a crispy exterior. It browns food by a process known as the Maillard reaction, a chemical reaction that occurs between amino acids and reducing sugars. With air fryers, your food is not submerged in oil. All you need is to coat whatever it is you're trying to heat with a thin layer of oil, place it in the air fryer's basket, set the timer and temperature regulator, and you're good to go.

The Advantages of Your Hamilton Beach Air Fryer

1. Remove Fat from Food

Air fryers use very little oil to cook. Even air fryers can cook food without oil. Foods cooked in other cooking methods contain high fat. As a result, food cooked in all these ways is not healthy. Many manufacturers claim that their air fryer removes up to 95% fat from fried foods.

Moreover, the air fryer cooks using very little oil compared to the traditional frying method. While many recipes require 3 cups of oil to cook in the traditional frying method, only 1 teaspoon of oil is required to cook the same recipe in an air fryer. However, the taste of food does not change much.

Air fryers use a special type of technology to remove excess fat from food that traps fat from food and stores it under the air fryer basket. Various experiments have shown that air fryers can cook delicious fried foods like the traditional frying method with very little oil. Which makes the food delicious and healthy at the same time.

2. To Lose Weight

Traditional fried foods not only contain extra fat but also extra calories. Excess calories will increase your weight. So if you want to lose weight, you should avoid fried foods. However, food cooked through an air fryer is extra calorie-free. Because air fryers use very little oil to cook fried food. With an air fryer, you can lose weight without avoiding fried foods.

3. Easy to Use and Clean

Air fryers are much easier to use. Most air fryers have a touch control system. Through which the temperature and time of the air fryer can be set very easily. However, many affordable air fryers have a knob control system. Air fryers can also be easily controlled through these. Air fryers are not only easy to use, but they are also very easy to clean. Because most air fryer baskets, trays, pans are dishwasher safe. As a result, they can be easily cleaned using soap and hot water. These must be thoroughly dried before re-using the air fryer.

Moreover, cooking in an air fryer does not require much oil. This makes it less messy and makes the cleaning process easier. Cooking in a drip fryer requires more oil so they are more dirty. An air fryer is much easier to clean than a drip fryer.

4. Safe to Use

Air fryers are much safer to use than other cooking utensils. The air fryer keeps the user safe from hot elements and hot oil. Sprinkling oil while cooking in a drip fryer is a regular occurrence. This can lead to accidents such as burning hands while cooking in a drip fryer. But there is no possibility of such an accident in an air fryer.

Moreover, most air fryers have cool-touch handles. Which will keep your hands safe from heated material. This allows you to cook safely in an air fryer. Modern air fryers have an automatic shut-off system. This automatically shuts off the air fryer when the cooking time is over. So there is no fear of burning food.

5. Use Little to No Oil to Cook Food

Cooking in traditional deep fryers often takes up to a gallon of oil. But it takes just one tablespoon of oil to cook any recipe in an air fryer. Moreover, many recipes can be cooked without oil.

There are several benefits to cooking in low oil. First of all, you need a little oil to cook in the air fryer so you don't have to spend extra money to buy cooking oil. Second, foods cooked with less oil are healthier. This is because foods cooked in low oil do not contain extra calories and fat. Third, the air fryer can be cooked with less oil so its baskets are not oily. Which makes it much easier to clean. Deep fryers on the other hand require a lot of oil to cook so it is very oily. Which makes the deep fryer very difficult to clean.

6. Take Little Space

Air fryers are usually small in size. As a result, they do not require much space in the kitchen. These are much smaller than other kitchen appliances. Air fryers are usually slightly larger than a coffee maker and smaller than a toaster oven. However, air fryers of different sizes are available in the market. You can buy small-size air fryers for small families and big-size air fryers for big families. All types of air fryers, small or large, do not require much space to be placed on the countertop.

Tips and Tricks on Using Your Hamilton Beach Air Fryer

1. Preheat Your Hamilton Beach Air Fryer

For a proper, it a normal practice that any cooking item should be preheated. Most air fryers recommend that the air fryer should be preheated to ensure even cooking. Often I do it, sometimes I don't do it, and my meal is still good. And in case your air fryer is without preheat feature, simply turn it to the desired temperature and allow it to run for about 3 minutes before bringing adding the food.

2. Use Oil For Food COOKED in the Hamilton Beach Air Fryer

I like using oil for certain food to make them crisp, but some foods don't always need it. If your diet has some fat on it (dark meat chicken, ground beef, fatty cuts of meat, etc.) so you really don't need oil. I use vegetable oil (like my Breakfast Air Fried Potatoes) and any dried seafood, Like the Crispy Air Fryer Fish).

3. Grease Your Hamilton Beach Air Fryer

Container Even if your food does not need oil, do take a moment to at least grease your air fryer container. I grease mine by rubbing or brushing a little bit of oil on the bottom of the grates. This will make sure the diet isn't going to stay on it.

4. Never Use Aerosol Spray Cans in Your Hamilton Beach Air Fryer

The Aerosol spray cans (such as Pam and related brands) are known to cause chipping in many Air Fryer containers. The aerosol cans contain toxic chemicals that don't match with the covering on most of the containers.

5. Don't Overload the Basket

If you want your fried food to turn out to be fresh, you'll want to make sure you don't congest the refrigerator. Placing too much food in the bowl will keep the food from stretching and browning. Cook your food in containers or invest in a larger air fryer to make sure this doesn't happen.

6. Shake the Basket During Frying Wings and Other Food

When frying small items such as chicken wings and French fries, shake the basket every few minutes to ensure uniform cooking, sometimes, instead of throwing, use a pair of silicone kitchen pins to flip over larger items

When you open the basket to shake, the air fryer will stop for a while, but it will continue frying the food at the same temperature when you return to the container.

Hints on Cleaning Baked on Grease from the Hamilton Beach Air Fryer

1) The most stubborn and irritating thing that can get stuck in an air fryer is the baked-on grease. The best way to ensure that the grease doesn't accumulate too much is to clean it after every use, if you do that, cleaning your air fryer should be quick and easy. Here's how to go about cleaning the grease out of your air fryer.

2) Unplug the air fryer and let it cool - Make sure the air fryer is off, unplugged and cool before beginning to clean it. These all sound obvious but taking a second to be sure that its ready will help you avoid hurting yourself or damaging the device.

3) Clean the basket and pans - In many air fryers, the removable baskets and pans are dishwasher safe. If this is the case, simply put the basket and pans into the dishwasher and let the dishwasher clean them for you. If not, you can simply soak the basket and pans in hot, soapy water for 10-15 minutes then gently scrub any food particles off with a non-abrasive sponge or towel. Finally, give the basket and pans a quick rinse and dry with a towel before putting them back in the air fryer. Check the manufacturer's instructions to see if the removable parts are dishwasher safe.

4) Clean the heating element - To clean the heating element, turn the air fryer upside down and wipe it down with a towel or non-abrasive sponge.

5) Clean the inside of the air fryer - Use a soft cloth or paper towels to wipe out any visible grease or food debris from the inside of the air fryer. Next, use a soft cloth, a non-abrasive sponge or a soft-bristled brush soaked in hot water with dish soap to gently scrub the bottom and sides of the inside of the air fryer.

6) Wipe down the outside of the air fryer - Grease does not just build up on the inside of the air fryer, it can also accumulate on the outside. After every use, wipe the outside of the air fryer down with a soft towel soaked in hot, soapy dishwater.

Sesame Orange Chicken

Servings: 2
Cooking Time: 9 Minutes

Ingredients:

- 1 pound boneless, skinless chicken breasts, cut into cubes
- salt and freshly ground black pepper
- ¼ cup cornstarch
- 2 eggs, beaten
- 1½ cups panko breadcrumbs
- vegetable or peanut oil, in a spray bottle
- 12 ounces orange marmalade
- 1 tablespoon soy sauce
- 1 teaspoon minced ginger
- 2 tablespoons hoisin sauce
- 1 tablespoon sesame oil
- sesame seeds, toasted

Directions:

1. Season the chicken pieces with salt and pepper. Set up a dredging station. Put the cornstarch in a zipper-sealable plastic bag. Place the beaten eggs in a bowl and put the panko breadcrumbs in a shallow dish. Transfer the seasoned chicken to the bag with the cornstarch and shake well to completely coat the chicken on all sides. Remove the chicken from the bag, shaking off any excess cornstarch and dip the pieces into the egg. Let any excess egg drip from the chicken and transfer into the breadcrumbs, pressing the crumbs onto the chicken pieces with your hands. Spray the chicken pieces with vegetable or peanut oil.
2. Preheat the air fryer to 400°F.
3. Combine the orange marmalade, soy sauce, ginger, hoisin sauce and sesame oil in a saucepan. Bring the mixture to a boil on the stovetop, lower the heat and simmer for 10 minutes, until the sauce has thickened. Set aside and keep warm.
4. Transfer the coated chicken to the air fryer basket and air-fry at 400°F for 9 minutes, shaking the basket a few times during the cooking process to help the chicken cook evenly.
5. Right before serving, toss the browned chicken pieces with the sesame orange sauce. Serve over white rice with steamed broccoli. Sprinkle the sesame seeds on top.

Thai Turkey And Zucchini Meatballs

Servings: 4
Cooking Time: 12 Minutes

Ingredients:

- 1½ cups grated zucchini,
- squeezed dry in a clean kitchen towel (about 1 large zucchini)
- 3 scallions, finely chopped
- 2 cloves garlic, minced
- 1 tablespoon grated fresh ginger
- 1 tablespoon finely chopped fresh cilantro
- zest of 1 lime
- 1 teaspoon salt
- freshly ground black pepper
- 1½ pounds ground turkey (a mix of light and dark meat)
- 2 eggs, lightly beaten
- 1 cup Thai sweet chili sauce (spring roll sauce)
- lime wedges, for serving

Directions:

1. Combine the zucchini, scallions, garlic, ginger, cilantro, lime zest, salt, pepper, ground turkey and eggs in a bowl and mix the ingredients together. Gently shape the mixture into 24 balls, about the size of golf balls.
2. Preheat the air fryer to 380°F.
3. Working in batches, air-fry the meatballs for 12 minutes, turning the meatballs over halfway through the cooking time. As soon as the meatballs have finished cooking, toss them in a bowl with the Thai sweet chili sauce to coat.
4. Serve the meatballs over rice noodles or white rice with the remaining Thai sweet chili sauce and lime wedges to squeeze over the top.

Crispy Duck With Cherry Sauce

Servings: 2

Cooking Time: 33 Minutes

Ingredients:

- 1 whole duck (up to 5 pounds), split in half, back and rib bones removed
- 1 teaspoon olive oil
- salt and freshly ground black pepper
- Cherry Sauce:
- 1 tablespoon butter
- 1 shallot, minced
- ½ cup sherry
- ¾ cup cherry preserves 1 cup chicken stock
- 1 teaspoon white wine vinegar
- 1 teaspoon fresh thyme leaves
- salt and freshly ground black pepper

Directions:

1. Preheat the air fryer to 400°F.
2. Trim some of the fat from the duck. Rub olive oil on the duck and season with salt and pepper. Place the duck halves in the air fryer basket, breast side up and facing the center of the basket.
3. Air-fry the duck for 20 minutes. Turn the duck over and air-fry for another 6 minutes.
4. While duck is air-frying, make the cherry sauce. Melt the butter in a large sauté pan. Add the shallot and sauté until it is just starting to brown – about 2 to 3 minutes. Add the sherry and deglaze the pan by scraping up any brown bits from the bottom of the pan. Simmer the liquid for a few minutes, until it has reduced by half. Add the cherry preserves, chicken stock and white wine vinegar. Whisk well to combine all the ingredients. Simmer the sauce until it thickens and coats the back of a spoon – about 5 to 7 minutes. Season with salt and pepper and stir in the fresh thyme leaves.
5. When the air fryer timer goes off, spoon some cherry sauce over the duck and continue to air-fry at 400°F for 4 more minutes. Then, turn the duck halves back over so that the breast side is facing up. Spoon more cherry sauce over the top of the duck, covering the skin completely. Air-fry for 3 more minutes and then remove the duck to a plate to rest for a few minutes.
6. Serve the duck in halves, or cut each piece in half again for a smaller serving. Spoon any additional sauce over the duck or serve it on the side.

Southern-style Chicken Legs

Servings: 6

Cooking Time: 20 Minutes

Ingredients:

- 2 cups buttermilk
- 1 tablespoon hot sauce
- 12 chicken legs
- ½ teaspoon salt
- ½ teaspoon pepper
- 1 teaspoon paprika
- ½ teaspoon onion powder
- 1 teaspoon garlic powder
- 1 cup all-purpose flour

Directions:

1. In an airtight container, place the buttermilk, hot sauce, and chicken legs and refrigerate for 4 to 8 hours.
2. In a medium bowl, whisk together the salt, pepper, paprika, onion powder, garlic powder, and flour. Drain the chicken legs from the buttermilk and dip the chicken legs into the flour mixture, stirring to coat well.
3. Preheat the air fryer to 390°F.
4. Place the chicken legs in the air fryer basket and spray with cooking spray. Cook for 10 minutes, turn the chicken legs over, and cook for another 8 to 10 minutes. Check for an internal temperature of 165°F.

Honey Lemon Thyme Glazed Cornish Hen

Servings: 2

Cooking Time: 20 Minutes

Ingredients:

- 1 (2-pound) Cornish game hen, split in half
- olive oil
- salt and freshly ground black pepper
- ¼ teaspoon dried thyme
- ¼ cup honey
- 1 tablespoon lemon zest

- juice of 1 lemon
- 1½ teaspoons chopped fresh thyme leaves
- ½ teaspoon soy sauce
- freshly ground black pepper

Directions:

1. Split the game hen in half by cutting down each side of the backbone and then cutting through the breast. Brush or spray both halves of the game hen with the olive oil and then season with the salt, pepper and dried thyme.
2. Preheat the air fryer to 390°F.
3. Place the game hen, skin side down, into the air fryer and air-fry for 5 minutes. Turn the hen halves over and air-fry for 10 minutes.
4. While the hen is cooking, combine the honey, lemon zest and juice, fresh thyme, soy sauce and pepper in a small bowl.
5. When the air fryer timer rings, brush the honey glaze onto the game hen and continue to air-fry for another 3 to 5 minutes, just until the hen is nicely glazed, browned and has an internal temperature of 165°F.
6. Let the hen rest for 5 minutes and serve warm.

Chicken Wellington

Servings: 2
Cooking Time: 31 Minutes

Ingredients:

- 2 (5-ounce) boneless, skinless chicken breasts
- ½ cup White Worcestershire sauce
- 3 tablespoons butter
- ½ cup finely diced onion (about ½ onion)
- 8 ounces button mushrooms, finely chopped
- ¼ cup chicken stock
- 2 tablespoons White Worcestershire sauce (or white wine)
- salt and freshly ground black pepper
- 1 tablespoon chopped fresh tarragon
- 2 sheets puff pastry, thawed
- 1 egg, beaten
- vegetable oil

Directions:

1. Place the chicken breasts in a shallow dish. Pour the White Worcestershire sauce over the chicken coating both sides and marinate for 30 minutes.
2. While the chicken is marinating, melt the butter in a large skillet over medium-high heat on the stovetop. Add the onion and sauté for a few minutes, until it starts to soften. Add the mushrooms and sauté for 5 minutes until the vegetables are brown and soft. Deglaze the skillet with the chicken stock, scraping up any bits from the bottom of the pan. Add the White Worcestershire sauce and simmer for 3 minutes until the mixture reduces and starts to thicken. Season with salt and freshly ground black pepper. Remove the mushroom mixture from the heat and stir in the fresh tarragon. Let the mushroom mixture cool.
3. Preheat the air fryer to 360°F.
4. Remove the chicken from the marinade and transfer it to the air fryer basket. Tuck the small end of the chicken breast under the thicker part to shape it into a circle rather than an oval. Pour the marinade over the chicken and air-fry for 10 minutes.
5. Roll out the puff pastry and cut out two 6-inch squares. Brush the perimeter of each square with the egg wash. Place half of the mushroom mixture in the center of each puff pastry square. Place the chicken breasts, top side down on the mushroom mixture. Starting with one corner of puff pastry and working in one direction, pull the pastry up over the chicken to enclose it and press the ends of the pastry together in the middle. Brush the pastry with the egg wash to seal the edges. Turn the Wellingtons over and set aside.
6. To make a decorative design with the remaining puff pastry, cut out four 10-inch strips. For each Wellington, twist two of the strips together, place them over the chicken breast wrapped in puff pastry, and tuck the ends underneath to seal it. Brush the entire top and sides of the Wellingtons with the egg wash.
7. Preheat the air fryer to 350°F.
8. Spray or brush the air fryer basket with vegetable oil. Air-fry the chicken Wellingtons for 13 minutes. Carefully turn the Wellingtons over. Air-fry for another 8 minutes. Transfer to serving plates, light a candle and enjoy!

Chicken Hand Pies

Servings: 8
Cooking Time: 10 Minutes Per Batch

Ingredients:

- ¾ cup chicken broth
- ¾ cup frozen mixed peas and carrots
- 1 cup cooked chicken, chopped
- 1 tablespoon cornstarch
- 1 tablespoon milk
- salt and pepper
- 1 8-count can organic flaky biscuits
- oil for misting or cooking spray

Directions:

1. In a medium saucepan, bring chicken broth to a boil. Stir in the frozen peas and carrots and cook for 5minutes over medium heat. Stir in chicken.
2. Mix the cornstarch into the milk until it dissolves. Stir it into the simmering chicken broth mixture and cook just until thickened.
3. Remove from heat, add salt and pepper to taste, and let cool slightly.
4. Lay biscuits out on wax paper. Peel each biscuit apart in the middle to make 2 rounds so you have 16 rounds total. Using your hands or a rolling pin, flatten each biscuit round slightly to make it larger and thinner.
5. Divide chicken filling among 8 of the biscuit rounds. Place remaining biscuit rounds on top and press edges all around. Use the tines of a fork to crimp biscuit edges and make sure they are sealed well.
6. Spray both sides lightly with oil or cooking spray.
7. Cook in a single layer, 4 at a time, at 330°F for 10minutes or until biscuit dough is cooked through and golden brown.

Chicken Parmesan

Servings: 4
Cooking Time: 11 Minutes

Ingredients:

- 4 chicken tenders
- Italian seasoning
- salt
- ¼ cup cornstarch
- ½ cup Italian salad dressing
- ¼ cup panko breadcrumbs
- ¼ cup grated Parmesan cheese, plus more for serving
- oil for misting or cooking spray
- 8 ounces spaghetti, cooked
- 1 24-ounce jar marinara sauce

Directions:

1. Pound chicken tenders with meat mallet or rolling pin until about ¼-inch thick.
2. Sprinkle both sides with Italian seasoning and salt to taste.
3. Place cornstarch and salad dressing in 2 separate shallow dishes.
4. In a third shallow dish, mix together the panko crumbs and Parmesan cheese.
5. Dip flattened chicken in cornstarch, then salad dressing. Dip in the panko mixture, pressing into the chicken so the coating sticks well.
6. Spray both sides with oil or cooking spray. Place in air fryer basket in single layer.
7. Cook at 390°F for 5minutes. Spray with oil again, turning chicken to coat both sides. See tip about turning.
8. Cook for an additional 6 minutes or until chicken juices run clear and outside is browned.
9. While chicken is cooking, heat marinara sauce and stir into cooked spaghetti.
10. To serve, divide spaghetti with sauce among 4 dinner plates, and top each with a fried chicken tender. Pass additional Parmesan at the table for those who want extra cheese.

Jerk Chicken Drumsticks

Servings: 2
Cooking Time: 20 Minutes

Ingredients:

- 1 or 2 cloves garlic
- 1 inch of fresh ginger
- 2 serrano peppers, (with seeds if you like it spicy, seeds removed for less heat)
- 1 teaspoon ground allspice
- 1 teaspoon ground nutmeg
- 1 teaspoon chili powder

- ½ teaspoon dried thyme
- ½ teaspoon ground cinnamon
- ½ teaspoon paprika
- 1 tablespoon brown sugar
- 1 teaspoon soy sauce
- 2 tablespoons vegetable oil
- 6 skinless chicken drumsticks

Directions:

1. Combine all the ingredients except the chicken in a small chopper or blender and blend to a paste. Make slashes into the meat of the chicken drumsticks and rub the spice blend all over the chicken (a pair of plastic gloves makes this really easy). Transfer the rubbed chicken to a non-reactive covered container and let the chicken marinate for at least 30 minutes or overnight in the refrigerator.
2. Preheat the air fryer to 400°F.
3. Transfer the drumsticks to the air fryer basket. Air-fry for 10 minutes. Turn the drumsticks over and air-fry for another 10 minutes. Serve warm with some rice and vegetables or a green salad.

Southern-fried Chicken Livers

Servings: 4
Cooking Time: 12 Minutes

Ingredients:

- 2 eggs
- 2 tablespoons water
- ¾ cup flour
- 1½ cups panko breadcrumbs
- ½ cup plain breadcrumbs
- 1 teaspoon salt
- ½ teaspoon black pepper
- 20 ounces chicken livers, salted to taste
- oil for misting or cooking spray

Directions:

1. Beat together eggs and water in a shallow dish. Place the flour in a separate shallow dish.
2. In the bowl of a food processor, combine the panko, plain breadcrumbs, salt, and pepper. Process until well mixed and panko crumbs are finely crushed. Place crumbs in a third shallow dish.
3. Dip livers in flour, then egg wash, and then roll in panko mixture to coat well with crumbs.
4. Spray both sides of livers with oil or cooking spray. Cooking in two batches, place livers in air fryer basket in single layer.
5. Cook at 390°F for 7minutes. Spray livers, turn over, and spray again. Cook for 5 more minutes, until done inside and coating is golden brown.
6. Repeat to cook remaining livers.

Tandoori Chicken Legs

Servings: 2
Cooking Time: 30 Minutes

Ingredients:

- 1 cup plain yogurt
- 2 cloves garlic, minced
- 1 tablespoon grated fresh ginger
- 2 teaspoons paprika
- 2 teaspoons ground coriander
- 1 teaspoon ground turmeric
- 1 teaspoon salt
- ¼ teaspoon ground cayenne pepper
- juice of 1 lime
- 2 bone-in, skin-on chicken legs
- fresh cilantro leaves

Directions:

1. Make the marinade by combining the yogurt, garlic, ginger, spices and lime juice. Make slashes into the chicken legs to help the marinade penetrate the meat. Pour the marinade over the chicken legs, cover and let the chicken marinate for at least an hour or overnight in the refrigerator.
2. Preheat the air fryer to 380°F.
3. Transfer the chicken legs from the marinade to the air fryer basket, reserving any extra marinade. Air-fry for 15 minutes. Flip the chicken over and pour the remaining marinade over the top. Air-fry for another 15 minutes, watching to make sure it doesn't brown too much. If it does start to get too brown, you can loosely tent the chicken with aluminum foil, tucking the ends of the foil under the chicken to stop it from blowing around.
4. Serve over rice with some fresh cilantro on top.

Simple Buttermilk Fried Chicken

Servings: 4

Cooking Time: 27 Minutes

Ingredients:

- 1 (4-pound) chicken, cut into 8 pieces
- 2 cups buttermilk
- hot sauce (optional)
- 1½ cups flour*
- 2 teaspoons paprika
- 1 teaspoon salt
- freshly ground black pepper
- 2 eggs, lightly beaten
- vegetable oil, in a spray bottle

Directions:

1. Cut the chicken into 8 pieces and submerge them in the buttermilk and hot sauce, if using. A zipper-sealable plastic bag works well for this. Let the chicken soak in the buttermilk for at least one hour or even overnight in the refrigerator.
2. Set up a dredging station. Mix the flour, paprika, salt and black pepper in a clean zipper-sealable plastic bag. Whisk the eggs and place them in a shallow dish. Remove four pieces of chicken from the buttermilk and transfer them to the bag with the flour. Shake them around to coat on all sides. Remove the chicken from the flour, shaking off any excess flour, and dip them into the beaten egg. Return the chicken to the bag of seasoned flour and shake again. Set the coated chicken aside and repeat with the remaining four pieces of chicken.
3. Preheat the air fryer to 370°F.
4. Spray the chicken on all sides with the vegetable oil and then transfer one batch to the air fryer basket. Air-fry the chicken at 370°F for 20 minutes, flipping the pieces over halfway through the cooking process, taking care not to knock off the breading. Transfer the chicken to a plate, but do not cover. Repeat with the second batch of chicken.
5. Lower the temperature on the air fryer to 340°F. Flip the chicken back over and place the first batch of chicken on top of the second batch already in the basket. Air-fry for another 7 minutes and serve warm.

Buttermilk-fried Drumsticks

Servings: 2

Cooking Time: 25 Minutes

Ingredients:

- 1 egg
- ½ cup buttermilk
- ¾ cup self-rising flour
- ¾ cup seasoned panko breadcrumbs
- 1 teaspoon salt
- ¼ teaspoon ground black pepper (to mix into coating)
- 4 chicken drumsticks, skin on
- oil for misting or cooking spray

Directions:

1. Beat together egg and buttermilk in shallow dish.
2. In a second shallow dish, combine the flour, panko crumbs, salt, and pepper.
3. Sprinkle chicken legs with additional salt and pepper to taste.
4. Dip legs in buttermilk mixture, then roll in panko mixture, pressing in crumbs to make coating stick. Mist with oil or cooking spray.
5. Spray air fryer basket with cooking spray.
6. Cook drumsticks at 360°F for 10minutes. Turn pieces over and cook an additional 10minutes.
7. Turn pieces to check for browning. If you have any white spots that haven't begun to brown, spritz them with oil or cooking spray. Continue cooking for 5 more minutes or until crust is golden brown and juices run clear. Larger, meatier drumsticks will take longer to cook than small ones.

Fiesta Chicken Plate

Servings: 4

Cooking Time: 15 Minutes

Ingredients:

- 1 pound boneless, skinless chicken breasts (2 large breasts)
- 2 tablespoons lime juice
- 1 teaspoon cumin
- ½ teaspoon salt
- ½ cup grated Pepper Jack cheese
- 1 16-ounce can refried beans

- ½ cup salsa
- 2 cups shredded lettuce
- 1 medium tomato, chopped
- 2 avocados, peeled and sliced
- 1 small onion, sliced into thin rings
- sour cream
- tortilla chips (optional)

Directions:

1. Split each chicken breast in half lengthwise.
2. Mix lime juice, cumin, and salt together and brush on all surfaces of chicken breasts.
3. Place in air fryer basket and cook at 390°F for 15 minutes, until well done.
4. Divide the cheese evenly over chicken breasts and cook for an additional minute to melt cheese.
5. While chicken is cooking, heat refried beans on stovetop or in microwave.
6. When ready to serve, divide beans among 4 plates. Place chicken breasts on top of beans and spoon salsa over. Arrange the lettuce, tomatoes, and avocados artfully on each plate and scatter with the onion rings.
7. Pass sour cream at the table and serve with tortilla chips if desired.

Turkey-hummus Wraps

Servings: 4

Cooking Time: 7 Minutes Per Batch

Ingredients:

- 4 large whole wheat wraps
- ½ cup hummus
- 16 thin slices deli turkey
- 8 slices provolone cheese
- 1 cup fresh baby spinach (or more to taste)

Directions:

1. To assemble, place 2 tablespoons of hummus on each wrap and spread to within about a half inch from edges. Top with 4 slices of turkey and 2 slices of provolone. Finish with ¼ cup of baby spinach—or pile on as much as you like.
2. Roll up each wrap. You don't need to fold or seal the ends.
3. Place 2 wraps in air fryer basket, seam side down.
4. Cook at 360°F for 4minutes to warm filling and melt cheese. If you like, you can continue cooking for 3 more minutes, until the wrap is slightly crispy.
5. Repeat step 4 to cook remaining wraps.

Chicken Chimichangas

Servings: 4

Cooking Time: 10 Minutes

Ingredients:

- 2 cups cooked chicken, shredded
- 2 tablespoons chopped green chiles
- ½ teaspoon oregano
- ½ teaspoon cumin
- ½ teaspoon onion powder
- ¼ teaspoon garlic powder
- salt and pepper
- 8 flour tortillas (6- or 7-inch diameter)
- oil for misting or cooking spray
- Chimichanga Sauce
- 2 tablespoons butter
- 2 tablespoons flour
- 1 cup chicken broth
- ¼ cup light sour cream
- ¼ teaspoon salt
- 2 ounces Pepper Jack or Monterey Jack cheese, shredded

Directions:

1. Make the sauce by melting butter in a saucepan over medium-low heat. Stir in flour until smooth and slightly bubbly. Gradually add broth, stirring constantly until smooth. Cook and stir 1 minute, until the mixture slightly thickens. Remove from heat and stir in sour cream and salt. Set aside.
2. In a medium bowl, mix together the chicken, chiles, oregano, cumin, onion powder, garlic, salt, and pepper. Stir in 3 to 4 tablespoons of the sauce, using just enough to make the filling moist but not soupy.
3. Divide filling among the 8 tortillas. Place filling down the center of tortilla, stopping about 1 inch from edges. Fold one side of tortilla over filling, fold the two sides in, and then roll up. Mist all sides with oil or cooking spray.

4. Place chimichangas in air fryer basket seam side down. To fit more into the basket, you can stand them on their sides with the seams against the sides of the basket.
5. Cook at 360°F for 10 minutes or until heated through and crispy brown outside.
6. Add the shredded cheese to the remaining sauce. Stir over low heat, warming just until the cheese melts. Don't boil or sour cream may curdle.
7. Drizzle the sauce over the chimichangas.

Peachy Chicken Chunks With Cherries

Servings: 4
Cooking Time: 16 Minutes

Ingredients:

- ⅓ cup peach preserves
- 1 teaspoon ground rosemary
- ½ teaspoon black pepper
- ½ teaspoon salt
- ½ teaspoon marjoram
- 1 teaspoon light olive oil
- 1 pound boneless chicken breasts, cut in 1½-inch chunks
- oil for misting or cooking spray
- 10-ounce package frozen unsweetened dark cherries, thawed and drained

Directions:

1. In a medium bowl, mix together peach preserves, rosemary, pepper, salt, marjoram, and olive oil.
2. Stir in chicken chunks and toss to coat well with the preserve mixture.
3. Spray air fryer basket with oil or cooking spray and lay chicken chunks in basket.
4. Cook at 390°F for 7minutes. Stir. Cook for 8 more minutes or until chicken juices run clear.
5. When chicken has cooked through, scatter the cherries over and cook for additional minute to heat cherries.

Chicken Cutlets With Broccoli Rabe And Roasted Peppers

Servings: 2
Cooking Time: 10 Minutes

Ingredients:

- ½ bunch broccoli rabe
- olive oil, in a spray bottle
- salt and freshly ground black pepper
- ⅔ cup roasted red pepper strips
- 2 (4-ounce) boneless, skinless chicken breasts
- 2 tablespoons all-purpose flour*
- 1 egg, beaten
- ⅓ cup seasoned breadcrumbs*
- 2 slices aged provolone cheese

Directions:

1. Bring a medium saucepot of salted water to a boil on the stovetop. Blanch the broccoli rabe for 3 minutes in the boiling water and then drain. When it has cooled a little, squeeze out as much water as possible, drizzle a little olive oil on top, season with salt and black pepper and set aside. Dry the roasted red peppers with a clean kitchen towel and set them aside as well.
2. Place each chicken breast between 2 pieces of plastic wrap. Use a meat pounder to flatten the chicken breasts to about ½-inch thick. Season the chicken on both sides with salt and pepper.
3. Preheat the air fryer to 400°F.
4. Set up a dredging station with three shallow dishes. Place the flour in one dish, the egg in a second dish and the breadcrumbs in a third dish. Coat the chicken on all sides with the flour. Shake off any excess flour and dip the chicken into the egg. Let the excess egg drip off and coat both sides of the chicken in the breadcrumbs. Spray the chicken with olive oil on both sides and transfer to the air fryer basket.
5. Air-fry the chicken at 400°F for 5 minutes. Turn the chicken over and air-fry for another minute. Then, top the chicken breast with the broccoli rabe and roasted peppers. Place a slice of the provolone cheese on top and secure it with a toothpick or two.
6. Air-fry at 360° for 3 to 4 minutes to melt the cheese and warm everything together.

Jerk Turkey Meatballs

Servings: 7

Cooking Time: 8 Minutes

Ingredients:

- 1 pound lean ground turkey
- ¼ cup chopped onion
- 1 teaspoon minced garlic
- ½ teaspoon dried thyme
- ¼ teaspoon ground cinnamon
- 1 teaspoon cayenne pepper
- ½ teaspoon paprika
- ½ teaspoon salt
- ⅛ teaspoon black pepper
- ¼ teaspoon red pepper flakes
- 2 teaspoons brown sugar
- 1 large egg, whisked
- ⅓ cup panko breadcrumbs
- 2⅓ cups cooked brown Jasmine rice
- 2 green onions, chopped
- ¾ cup sweet onion dressing

Directions:

1. Preheat the air fryer to 350°F.
2. In a medium bowl, mix the ground turkey with the onion, garlic, thyme, cinnamon, cayenne pepper, paprika, salt, pepper, red pepper flakes, and brown sugar. Add the whisked egg and stir in the breadcrumbs until the turkey starts to hold together.
3. Using a 1-ounce scoop, portion the turkey into meatballs. You should get about 28 meatballs.
4. Spray the air fryer basket with olive oil spray.
5. Place the meatballs into the air fryer basket and cook for 5 minutes, shake the basket, and cook another 2 to 4 minutes (or until the internal temperature of the meatballs reaches 165°F).
6. Remove the meatballs from the basket and repeat for the remaining meatballs.
7. Serve warm over a bed of rice with chopped green onions and spicy Caribbean jerk dressing.

Pecan Turkey Cutlets

Servings: 4

Cooking Time: 12 Minutes

Ingredients:

- ¾ cup panko breadcrumbs
- ¼ teaspoon salt
- ¼ teaspoon pepper
- ¼ teaspoon dry mustard
- ¼ teaspoon poultry seasoning
- ½ cup pecans
- ¼ cup cornstarch
- 1 egg, beaten
- 1 pound turkey cutlets, ½-inch thick
- salt and pepper
- oil for misting or cooking spray

Directions:

1. Place the panko crumbs, ¼ teaspoon salt, ¼ teaspoon pepper, mustard, and poultry seasoning in food processor. Process until crumbs are finely crushed. Add pecans and process in short pulses just until nuts are finely chopped. Go easy so you don't overdo it!
2. Preheat air fryer to 360°F.
3. Place cornstarch in one shallow dish and beaten egg in another. Transfer coating mixture from food processor into a third shallow dish.
4. Sprinkle turkey cutlets with salt and pepper to taste.
5. Dip cutlets in cornstarch and shake off excess. Then dip in beaten egg and roll in crumbs, pressing to coat well. Spray both sides with oil or cooking spray.
6. Place 2 cutlets in air fryer basket in a single layer and cook for 12 minutes or until juices run clear.
7. Repeat step 6 to cook remaining cutlets.

Philly Chicken Cheesesteak Stromboli

Servings: 2

Cooking Time: 28 Minutes

Ingredients:

- ½ onion, sliced
- 1 teaspoon vegetable oil
- 2 boneless, skinless chicken breasts, partially frozen and sliced very thin on the bias (about 1 pound)
- 1 tablespoon Worcestershire sauce
- salt and freshly ground black pepper

- ½ recipe of Blue Jean Chef pizza dough (see page 229), or 14 ounces of store-bought pizza dough
- 1½ cups grated Cheddar cheese
- ½ cup Cheese Whiz® (or other jarred cheese sauce), warmed gently in the microwave
- tomato ketchup for serving

Directions:

1. Preheat the air fryer to 400°F.
2. Toss the sliced onion with oil and air-fry for 8 minutes, stirring halfway through the cooking time. Add the sliced chicken and Worcestershire sauce to the air fryer basket, and toss to evenly distribute the ingredients. Season the mixture with salt and freshly ground black pepper and air-fry for 8 minutes, stirring a couple of times during the cooking process. Remove the chicken and onion from the air fryer and let the mixture cool a little.
3. On a lightly floured surface, roll or press the pizza dough out into a 13-inch by 11-inch rectangle, with the long side closest to you. Sprinkle half of the Cheddar cheese over the dough leaving an empty 1-inch border from the edge farthest away from you. Top the cheese with the chicken and onion mixture, spreading it out evenly. Drizzle the cheese sauce over the meat and sprinkle the remaining Cheddar cheese on top.
4. Start rolling the stromboli away from you and toward the empty border. Make sure the filling stays tightly tucked inside the roll. Finally, tuck the ends of the dough in and pinch the seam shut. Place the seam side down and shape the Stromboli into a U-shape to fit in the air-fry basket. Cut 4 small slits with the tip of a sharp knife evenly in the top of the dough and lightly brush the stromboli with a little oil.
5. Preheat the air fryer to 370°F.
6. Spray or brush the air fryer basket with oil and transfer the U-shaped stromboli to the air fryer basket. Air-fry for 12 minutes, turning the stromboli over halfway through the cooking time. (Use a plate to invert the stromboli out of the air fryer basket and then slide it back into the basket off the plate.)
7. To remove, carefully flip stromboli over onto a cutting board. Let it rest for a couple of minutes before serving. Slice the stromboli into 3-inch pieces and serve with ketchup for dipping, if desired.

Chicken Rochambeau

Servings: 4

Cooking Time: 20 Minutes

Ingredients:

- 1 tablespoon butter
- 4 chicken tenders, cut in half crosswise
- salt and pepper
- ¼ cup flour
- oil for misting
- 4 slices ham, ¼- to ⅜-inches thick and large enough to cover an English muffin
- 2 English muffins, split
- Sauce
- 2 tablespoons butter
- ½ cup chopped green onions
- ½ cup chopped mushrooms
- 2 tablespoons flour
- 1 cup chicken broth
- ¼ teaspoon garlic powder
- 1½ teaspoons Worcestershire sauce

Directions:

1. Place 1 tablespoon of butter in air fryer baking pan and cook at 390°F for 2minutes to melt.
2. Sprinkle chicken tenders with salt and pepper to taste, then roll in the ¼ cup of flour.
3. Place chicken in baking pan, turning pieces to coat with melted butter.
4. Cook at 390°F for 5minutes. Turn chicken pieces over, and spray tops lightly with olive oil. Cook 5minutes longer or until juices run clear. The chicken will not brown.
5. While chicken is cooking, make the sauce: In a medium saucepan, melt the 2 tablespoons of butter.
6. Add onions and mushrooms and sauté until tender, about 3minutes.
7. Stir in the flour. Gradually add broth, stirring constantly until you have a smooth gravy.
8. Add garlic powder and Worcestershire sauce and simmer on low heat until sauce thickens, about 5minutes.

9. When chicken is cooked, remove baking pan from air fryer and set aside.
10. Place ham slices directly into air fryer basket and cook at 390°F for 5minutes or until hot and beginning to sizzle a little. Remove and set aside on top of the chicken for now.
11. Place the English muffin halves in air fryer basket and cook at 390°F for 1 minute.
12. Open air fryer and place a ham slice on top of each English muffin half. Stack 2 pieces of chicken on top of each ham slice. Cook at 390°F for 1 to 2minutes to heat through.
13. Place each English muffin stack on a serving plate and top with plenty of sauce.

Gluten-free Nutty Chicken Fingers

Servings: 4
Cooking Time: 10 Minutes

Ingredients:

- ½ cup gluten-free flour
- ½ teaspoon garlic powder
- ¼ teaspoon onion powder
- ¼ teaspoon black pepper
- ¼ teaspoon salt
- 1 cup walnuts, pulsed into coarse flour
- ½ cup gluten-free breadcrumbs
- 2 large eggs
- 1 pound boneless, skinless chicken tenders

Directions:

1. Preheat the air fryer to 400°F.
2. In a medium bowl, mix the flour, garlic, onion, pepper, and salt. Set aside.
3. In a separate bowl, mix the walnut flour and breadcrumbs.
4. In a third bowl, whisk the eggs.
5. Liberally spray the air fryer basket with olive oil spray.
6. Pat the chicken tenders dry with a paper towel. Dredge the tenders one at a time in the flour, then dip them in the egg, and toss them in the breadcrumb coating. Repeat until all tenders are coated.
7. Set each tender in the air fryer, leaving room on each side of the tender to allow for flipping.
8. When the basket is full, cook 5 minutes, flip, and cook another 5 minutes. Check the internal temperature after cooking completes; it should read 165°F. If it does not, cook another 2 to 4 minutes.
9. Remove the tenders and let cool 5 minutes before serving. Repeat until all the tenders are cooked.

Sweet Chili Spiced Chicken

Servings: 4
Cooking Time: 43 Minutes

Ingredients:

- Spice Rub:
- 2 tablespoons brown sugar
- 2 tablespoons paprika
- 1 teaspoon dry mustard powder
- 1 teaspoon chili powder
- 2 tablespoons coarse sea salt or kosher salt
- 2 teaspoons coarsely ground black pepper
- 1 tablespoon vegetable oil
- 1 (3½-pound) chicken, cut into 8 pieces

Directions:

1. Prepare the spice rub by combining the brown sugar, paprika, mustard powder, chili powder, salt and pepper. Rub the oil all over the chicken pieces and then rub the spice mix onto the chicken, covering completely. This is done very easily in a zipper sealable bag. You can do this ahead of time and let the chicken marinate in the refrigerator, or just proceed with cooking right away.
2. Preheat the air fryer to 370°F.
3. Air-fry the chicken in two batches. Place the two chicken thighs and two drumsticks into the air fryer basket. Air-fry at 370°F for 10 minutes. Then, gently turn the chicken pieces over and air-fry for another 10 minutes. Remove the chicken pieces and let them rest on a plate while you cook the chicken breasts. Air-fry the chicken breasts, skin side down for 8 minutes. Turn the chicken breasts over and air-fry for another 12 minutes.
4. Lower the temperature of the air fryer to 340°F. Place the first batch of chicken on top of the second

batch already in the basket and air-fry for a final 3 minutes.

5. Let the chicken rest for 5 minutes and serve warm with some mashed potatoes and a green salad or vegetables.

Cornish Hens With Honey-lime Glaze

Servings: 2

Cooking Time: 30 Minutes

Ingredients:

- 1 Cornish game hen (1½–2 pounds)
- 1 tablespoon honey
- 1 tablespoon lime juice
- 1 teaspoon poultry seasoning
- salt and pepper
- cooking spray

Directions:

1. To split the hen into halves, cut through breast bone and down one side of the backbone.
2. Mix the honey, lime juice, and poultry seasoning together and brush or rub onto all sides of the hen. Season to taste with salt and pepper.
3. Spray air fryer basket with cooking spray and place hen halves in the basket, skin-side down.
4. Cook at 330°F for 30 minutes. Hen will be done when juices run clear when pierced at leg joint with a fork. Let hen rest for 5 to 10minutes before cutting.

Chicken Nuggets

Servings: 20

Cooking Time: 14 Minutes Per Batch

Ingredients:

- 1 pound boneless, skinless chicken thighs, cut into 1-inch chunks
- ¾ teaspoon salt
- ½ teaspoon black pepper
- ½ teaspoon garlic powder
- ½ teaspoon onion powder
- ½ cup flour
- 2 eggs, beaten
- ½ cup panko breadcrumbs
- 3 tablespoons plain breadcrumbs
- oil for misting or cooking spray

Directions:

1. In the bowl of a food processor, combine chicken, ½ teaspoon salt, pepper, garlic powder, and onion powder. Process in short pulses until chicken is very finely chopped and well blended.
2. Place flour in one shallow dish and beaten eggs in another. In a third dish or plastic bag, mix together the panko crumbs, plain breadcrumbs, and ¼ teaspoon salt.
3. Shape chicken mixture into small nuggets. Dip nuggets in flour, then eggs, then panko crumb mixture.
4. Spray nuggets on both sides with oil or cooking spray and place in air fryer basket in a single layer, close but not overlapping.
5. Cook at 360°F for 10minutes. Spray with oil and cook 4 minutes, until chicken is done and coating is golden brown.
6. Repeat step 5 to cook remaining nuggets.

Chicken Adobo

Servings: 6

Cooking Time: 12 Minutes

Ingredients:

- 6 boneless chicken thighs
- ¼ cup soy sauce or tamari
- ½ cup rice wine vinegar
- 4 cloves garlic, minced
- ⅛ teaspoon crushed red pepper flakes
- ½ teaspoon black pepper

Directions:

1. Place the chicken thighs into a resealable plastic bag with the soy sauce or tamari, the rice wine vinegar, the garlic, and the crushed red pepper flakes. Seal the bag and let the chicken marinate at least 1 hour in the refrigerator.
2. Preheat the air fryer to 400°F.
3. Drain the chicken and pat dry with a paper towel. Season the chicken with black pepper and liberally spray with cooking spray.

4. Place the chicken in the air fryer basket and cook for 9 minutes, turn over at 9 minutes and check for an internal temperature of 165°F, and cook another 3 minutes.

Buffalo Egg Rolls

Servings: 8

Cooking Time: 9 Minutes Per Batch

Ingredients:

- 1 teaspoon water
- 1 tablespoon cornstarch
- 1 egg
- 2½ cups cooked chicken, diced or shredded (see opposite page)
- ⅓ cup chopped green onion
- ⅓ cup diced celery
- ⅓ cup buffalo wing sauce
- 8 egg roll wraps
- oil for misting or cooking spray
- Blue Cheese Dip
- 3 ounces cream cheese, softened
- ⅓ cup blue cheese, crumbled
- 1 teaspoon Worcestershire sauce
- ¼ teaspoon garlic powder
- ¼ cup buttermilk (or sour cream)

Directions:

1. Mix water and cornstarch in a small bowl until dissolved. Add egg, beat well, and set aside.
2. In a medium size bowl, mix together chicken, green onion, celery, and buffalo wing sauce.
3. Divide chicken mixture evenly among 8 egg roll wraps, spooning ½ inch from one edge.
4. Moisten all edges of each wrap with beaten egg wash.
5. Fold the short ends over filling, then roll up tightly and press to seal edges.
6. Brush outside of wraps with egg wash, then spritz with oil or cooking spray.
7. Place 4 egg rolls in air fryer basket.
8. Cook at 390°F for 9minutes or until outside is brown and crispy.
9. While the rolls are cooking, prepare the Blue Cheese Dip. With a fork, mash together cream cheese and blue cheese.
10. Stir in remaining ingredients.
11. Dip should be just thick enough to slightly cling to egg rolls. If too thick, stir in buttermilk or milk 1 tablespoon at a time until you reach the desired consistency.
12. Cook remaining 4 egg rolls as in steps 7 and 8.
13. Serve while hot with Blue Cheese Dip, more buffalo wing sauce, or both.

Nashville Hot Chicken

Servings: 4

Cooking Time: 27 Minutes

Ingredients:

- 1 (4-pound) chicken, cut into 6 pieces (2 breasts, 2 thighs and 2 drumsticks)
- 2 eggs
- 1 cup buttermilk
- 2 cups all-purpose flour
- 2 tablespoons paprika
- 1 teaspoon garlic powder
- 1 teaspoon onion powder
- 2 teaspoons salt
- 1 teaspoon freshly ground black pepper
- vegetable oil, in a spray bottle
- Nashville Hot Sauce:
- 1 tablespoon cayenne pepper
- 1 teaspoon salt
- ¼ cup vegetable oil
- 4 slices white bread
- dill pickle slices

Directions:

1. Cut the chicken breasts into 2 pieces so that you have a total of 8 pieces of chicken.
2. Set up a two-stage dredging station. Whisk the eggs and buttermilk together in a bowl. Combine the flour, paprika, garlic powder, onion powder, salt and black pepper in a zipper-sealable plastic bag. Dip the chicken pieces into the egg-buttermilk mixture, then toss them in the seasoned flour, coating all sides. Repeat this

procedure (egg mixture and then flour mixture) one more time. This can be a little messy, but make sure all sides of the chicken are completely covered. Spray the chicken with vegetable oil and set aside.

3. Preheat the air fryer to 370°F. Spray or brush the bottom of the air-fryer basket with a little vegetable oil.

4. Air-fry the chicken in two batches at 370°F for 20 minutes, flipping the pieces over halfway through the cooking process. Transfer the chicken to a plate, but do not cover. Repeat with the second batch of chicken.

5. Lower the temperature on the air fryer to 340°F. Flip the chicken back over and place the first batch of chicken on top of the second batch already in the basket. Air-fry for another 7 minutes.

6. While the chicken is air-frying, combine the cayenne pepper and salt in a bowl. Heat the vegetable oil in a small saucepan and when it is very hot, add it to the spice mix, whisking until smooth. It will sizzle briefly when you add it to the spices. Place the fried chicken on top of the white bread slices and brush the hot sauce all over chicken. Top with the pickle slices and serve warm. Enjoy the heat and the flavor!

Poblano Bake

Servings: 4

Cooking Time: 11 Minutes Per Batch

Ingredients:

- 2 large poblano peppers (approx. 5½ inches long excluding stem)
- ¾ pound ground turkey, raw
- ¾ cup cooked brown rice
- 1 teaspoon chile powder
- ½ teaspoon ground cumin
- ½ teaspoon garlic powder
- 4 ounces sharp Cheddar cheese, grated
- 1 8-ounce jar salsa, warmed

Directions:

1. Slice each pepper in half lengthwise so that you have four wide, flat pepper halves.
2. Remove seeds and membrane and discard. Rinse inside and out.
3. In a large bowl, combine turkey, rice, chile powder, cumin, and garlic powder. Mix well.
4. Divide turkey filling into 4 portions and stuff one into each of the 4 pepper halves. Press lightly to pack down.
5. Place 2 pepper halves in air fryer basket and cook at 390°F for 10minutes or until turkey is well done.
6. Top each pepper half with ¼ of the grated cheese. Cook 1 more minute or just until cheese melts.
7. Repeat steps 5 and 6 to cook remaining pepper halves.
8. To serve, place each pepper half on a plate and top with ¼ cup warm salsa.

Thai Chicken Drumsticks

Servings: 4

Cooking Time: 20 Minutes

Ingredients:

- 2 tablespoons soy sauce
- ¼ cup rice wine vinegar
- 2 tablespoons chili garlic sauce
- 2 tablespoons sesame oil
- 1 teaspoon minced fresh ginger
- 2 teaspoons sugar
- ½ teaspoon ground coriander
- juice of 1 lime
- 8 chicken drumsticks (about 2½ pounds)
- ¼ cup chopped peanuts
- chopped fresh cilantro
- lime wedges

Directions:

1. Combine the soy sauce, rice wine vinegar, chili sauce, sesame oil, ginger, sugar, coriander and lime juice in a large bowl and mix together. Add the chicken drumsticks and marinate for 30 minutes.
2. Preheat the air fryer to 370°F.
3. Place the chicken in the air fryer basket. It's ok if the ends of the drumsticks overlap a little. Spoon half of the marinade over the chicken, and reserve the other half.
4. Air-fry for 10 minutes. Turn the chicken over and pour the rest of the marinade over the chicken. Air-fry for an additional 10 minutes.

5. Transfer the chicken to a plate to rest and cool to an edible temperature. Pour the marinade from the bottom of the air fryer into a small saucepan and bring it to a simmer over medium-high heat. Simmer the liquid for 2 minutes so that it thickens enough to coat the back of a spoon.
6. Transfer the chicken to a serving platter, pour the sauce over the chicken and sprinkle the chopped peanuts on top. Garnish with chopped cilantro and lime wedges.

Teriyaki Chicken Legs

Servings: 2
Cooking Time: 20 Minutes

Ingredients:

- 4 tablespoons teriyaki sauce
- 1 tablespoon orange juice
- 1 teaspoon smoked paprika
- 4 chicken legs
- cooking spray

Directions:

1. Mix together the teriyaki sauce, orange juice, and smoked paprika. Brush on all sides of chicken legs.
2. Spray air fryer basket with nonstick cooking spray and place chicken in basket.
3. Cook at 360°F for 6minutes. Turn and baste with sauce. Cook for 6 moreminutes, turn and baste. Cook for 8 minutes more, until juices run clear when chicken is pierced with a fork.

Peanut Butter-barbeque Chicken

Servings: 4
Cooking Time: 20 Minutes

Ingredients:

- 1 pound boneless, skinless chicken thighs
- salt and pepper
- 1 large orange
- ½ cup barbeque sauce
- 2 tablespoons smooth peanut butter
- 2 tablespoons chopped peanuts for garnish (optional)
- cooking spray

Directions:

1. Season chicken with salt and pepper to taste. Place in a shallow dish or plastic bag.
2. Grate orange peel, squeeze orange and reserve 1 tablespoon of juice for the sauce.
3. Pour remaining juice over chicken and marinate for 30minutes.
4. Mix together the reserved 1 tablespoon of orange juice, barbeque sauce, peanut butter, and 1 teaspoon grated orange peel.
5. Place ¼ cup of sauce mixture in a small bowl for basting. Set remaining sauce aside to serve with cooked chicken.
6. Preheat air fryer to 360°F. Spray basket with nonstick cooking spray.
7. Remove chicken from marinade, letting excess drip off. Place in air fryer basket and cook for 5minutes. Turn chicken over and cook 5minutes longer.
8. Brush both sides of chicken lightly with sauce.
9. Cook chicken 5minutes, then turn thighs one more time, again brushing both sides lightly with sauce. Cook for 5 moreminutes or until chicken is done and juices run clear.
10. Serve chicken with remaining sauce on the side and garnish with chopped peanuts if you like.

Crispy Chicken Parmesan

Servings: 4
Cooking Time: 12 Minutes

Ingredients:

- 4 skinless, boneless chicken breasts, pounded thin to ¼-inch thickness
- 1 teaspoon salt, divided
- ½ teaspoon black pepper, divided
- 1 cup flour
- 2 eggs
- 1 cup panko breadcrumbs
- ½ teaspoon dried oregano
- ½ cup grated Parmesan cheese

Directions:

1. Pat the chicken breasts with a paper towel. Season the chicken with ½ teaspoon of the salt and ¼ teaspoon of the pepper.

2. In a medium bowl, place the flour.
3. In a second bowl, whisk the eggs.
4. In a third bowl, place the breadcrumbs, oregano, cheese, and the remaining ½ teaspoon of salt and ¼ teaspoon of pepper.
5. Dredge the chicken in the flour and shake off the excess. Dip the chicken into the eggs and then into the breadcrumbs. Set the chicken on a plate and repeat with the remaining chicken pieces.
6. Preheat the air fryer to 360°F.
7. Place the chicken in the air fryer basket and spray liberally with cooking spray. Cook for 8 minutes, turn the chicken breasts over, and cook another 4 minutes. When golden brown, check for an internal temperature of 165°F.

Coconut Chicken With Apricot-ginger Sauce

Servings: 4
Cooking Time: 8 Minutes Per Batch

Ingredients:

- 1½ pounds boneless, skinless chicken tenders, cut in large chunks (about 1¼ inches)
- salt and pepper
- ½ cup cornstarch
- 2 eggs
- 1 tablespoon milk
- 3 cups shredded coconut (see below)
- oil for misting or cooking spray
- Apricot-Ginger Sauce
- ½ cup apricot preserves
- 2 tablespoons white vinegar
- ¼ teaspoon ground ginger
- ¼ teaspoon low-sodium soy sauce
- 2 teaspoons white or yellow onion, grated or finely minced

Directions:

1. Mix all ingredients for the Apricot-Ginger Sauce well and let sit for flavors to blend while you cook the chicken.
2. Season chicken chunks with salt and pepper to taste.
3. Place cornstarch in a shallow dish.
4. In another shallow dish, beat together eggs and milk.
5. Place coconut in a third shallow dish. (If also using panko breadcrumbs, as suggested below, stir them to mix well.)
6. Spray air fryer basket with oil or cooking spray.
7. Dip each chicken chunk into cornstarch, shake off excess, and dip in egg mixture.
8. Shake off excess egg mixture and roll lightly in coconut or coconut mixture. Spray with oil.
9. Place coated chicken chunks in air fryer basket in a single layer, close together but without sides touching.
10. Cook at 360°F for 4minutes, stop, and turn chunks over.
11. Cook an additional 4 minutes or until chicken is done inside and coating is crispy brown.
12. Repeat steps 9 through 11 to cook remaining chicken chunks.

Chicken Schnitzel Dogs

Servings: 4
Cooking Time: 10 Minutes

Ingredients:

- ½ cup flour
- ½ teaspoon salt
- 1 teaspoon marjoram
- 1 teaspoon dried parsley flakes
- ½ teaspoon thyme
- 1 egg
- 1 teaspoon lemon juice
- 1 teaspoon water
- 1 cup breadcrumbs
- 4 chicken tenders, pounded thin
- oil for misting or cooking spray
- 4 whole-grain hotdog buns
- 4 slices Gouda cheese
- 1 small Granny Smith apple, thinly sliced
- ½ cup shredded Napa cabbage
- coleslaw dressing

Directions:

1. In a shallow dish, mix together the flour, salt, marjoram, parsley, and thyme.

2. In another shallow dish, beat together egg, lemon juice, and water.
3. Place breadcrumbs in a third shallow dish.
4. Cut each of the flattened chicken tenders in half lengthwise.
5. Dip flattened chicken strips in flour mixture, then egg wash. Let excess egg drip off and roll in breadcrumbs. Spray both sides with oil or cooking spray.
6. Cook at 390°F for 5minutes. Spray with oil, turn over, and spray other side.
7. Cook for 3 to 5minutes more, until well done and crispy brown.
8. To serve, place 2 schnitzel strips on bottom of each hot dog bun. Top with cheese, sliced apple, and cabbage. Drizzle with coleslaw dressing and top with other half of bun.

Coconut Curry Chicken With Coconut Rice

Servings: 4
Cooking Time: 56 Minutes

Ingredients:

- 1 (14-ounce) can coconut milk
- 2 tablespoons green or red curry paste
- zest and juice of one lime
- 1 clove garlic, minced
- 1 tablespoon grated fresh ginger
- 1 teaspoon ground cumin
- 1 (3- to 4-pound) chicken, cut into 8 pieces
- vegetable or olive oil
- salt and freshly ground black pepper
- fresh cilantro leaves
- For the rice:
- 1 cup basmati or jasmine rice
- 1 cup water
- 1 cup coconut milk
- ½ teaspoon salt
- freshly ground black pepper

Directions:

1. Make the marinade by combining the coconut milk, curry paste, lime zest and juice, garlic, ginger and cumin. Coat the chicken on all sides with the marinade and marinate the chicken for 1 hour to overnight in the refrigerator.
2. Preheat the air fryer to 380°F.
3. Brush the bottom of the air fryer basket with oil. Transfer the chicken thighs and drumsticks from the marinade to the air fryer basket, letting most of the marinade drip off. Season to taste with salt and freshly ground black pepper.
4. Air-fry the chicken drumsticks and thighs at 380°F for 12 minutes. Flip the chicken over and continue to air-fry for another 12 minutes. Set aside and air-fry the chicken breast pieces at 380°F for 15 minutes. Turn the chicken breast pieces over and air-fry for another 12 minutes. Return the chicken thighs and drumsticks to the air fryer and air-fry for an additional 5 minutes.
5. While the chicken is cooking, make the coconut rice. Rinse the rice kernels with water and drain well. Place the rice in a medium saucepan with a tight fitting lid, along with the water, coconut milk, salt and freshly ground black pepper. Bring the mixture to a boil and then cover, reduce the heat and let it cook gently for 20 minutes without lifting the lid. When the time is up, lift the lid, fluff with a fork and set aside.
6. Remove the chicken from the air fryer and serve warm with the coconut rice and fresh cilantro scattered around.

Mediterranean Stuffed Chicken Breasts

Servings: 4
Cooking Time: 24 Minutes

Ingredients:

- 4 boneless, skinless chicken breasts
- ½ teaspoon salt
- ½ teaspoon black pepper
- ½ teaspoon garlic powder
- ½ teaspoon paprika
- ½ cup canned artichoke hearts, chopped
- 4 ounces cream cheese
- ¼ cup grated Parmesan cheese

Directions:

1. Pat the chicken breasts with a paper towel. Using a sharp knife, cut a pouch in the side of each chicken breast for filling.
2. In a small bowl, mix the salt, pepper, garlic powder, and paprika. Season the chicken breasts with this mixture.
3. In a medium bowl, mix together the artichokes, cream cheese, and grated Parmesan cheese. Divide the filling between the 4 breasts, stuffing it inside the pouches. Use toothpicks to close the pouches and secure the filling.
4. Preheat the air fryer to 360°F.
5. Spray the air fryer basket liberally with cooking spray, add the stuffed chicken breasts to the basket, and spray liberally with cooking spray again. Cook for 14 minutes, carefully turn over the chicken breasts, and cook another 10 minutes. Check the temperature at 20 minutes cooking. Chicken breasts are fully cooked when the center measures 165°F. Cook in batches, if needed.

Chicken Fried Steak With Gravy

Servings: 4

Cooking Time: 10 Minutes Per Batch

Ingredients:

- ½ cup flour
- 2 teaspoons salt, divided
- freshly ground black pepper
- ¼ teaspoon garlic powder
- 1 cup buttermilk
- 1 cup fine breadcrumbs
- 4 tenderized top round steaks (about 6 to 8 ounces each; ½-inch thick)
- vegetable or canola oil
- For the Gravy:
- 2 tablespoons butter or bacon drippings
- ¼ onion, minced (about ¼ cup)
- 1 clove garlic, smashed
- ¼ teaspoon dried thyme
- 3 tablespoons flour
- 1 cup milk
- salt and lots of freshly ground black pepper
- a few dashes of Worcestershire sauce

Directions:

1. Set up a dredging station. Combine the flour, 1 teaspoon of salt, black pepper and garlic powder in a shallow bowl. Pour the buttermilk into a second shallow bowl. Finally, put the breadcrumbs and 1 teaspoon of salt in a third shallow bowl.
2. Dip the tenderized steaks into the flour, then the buttermilk, and then the breadcrumb mixture, pressing the crumbs onto the steak. Place them on a baking sheet and spray both sides generously with vegetable or canola oil.
3. Preheat the air fryer to 400°F.
4. Transfer the steaks to the air fryer basket, two at a time, and air-fry for 10 minutes, flipping the steaks over halfway through the cooking time. This will cook your steaks to medium. If you want the steaks cooked a little more or less, add or subtract a minute or two. Hold the first batch of steaks warm in a 170°F oven while you cook the second batch.
5. While the steaks are cooking, make the gravy. Melt the butter in a small saucepan over medium heat on the stovetop. Add the onion, garlic and thyme and cook for five minutes, until the onion is soft and just starting to brown. Stir in the flour and cook for another five minutes, stirring regularly, until the mixture starts to brown. Whisk in the milk and bring the mixture to a boil to thicken. Season to taste with salt, lots of freshly ground black pepper and a few dashes of Worcestershire sauce.
6. Plate the chicken fried steaks with mashed potatoes and vegetables and serve the gravy at the table to pour over the top.

Lemon Sage Roast Chicken

Servings: 4

Cooking Time: 60 Minutes

Ingredients:

- 1 (4-pound) chicken
- 1 bunch sage, divided
- 1 lemon, zest and juice
- salt and freshly ground black pepper

Directions:

1. Preheat the air fryer to 350°F and pour a little water into the bottom of the air fryer drawer. (This will help prevent the grease that drips into the bottom drawer from burning and smoking.)
2. Run your fingers between the skin and flesh of the chicken breasts and thighs. Push a couple of sage leaves up underneath the skin of the chicken on each breast and each thigh.
3. Push some of the lemon zest up under the skin of the chicken next to the sage. Sprinkle some of the zest inside the chicken cavity, and reserve any leftover zest. Squeeze the lemon juice all over the chicken and in the cavity as well.
4. Season the chicken, inside and out, with the salt and freshly ground black pepper. Set a few sage leaves aside for the final garnish. Crumple up the remaining sage leaves and push them into the cavity of the chicken, along with one of the squeezed lemon halves.
5. Place the chicken breast side up into the air fryer basket and air-fry for 20 minutes at 350°F. Flip the chicken over so that it is breast side down and continue to air-fry for another 20 minutes. Return the chicken to breast side up and finish air-frying for 20 more minutes. The internal temperature of the chicken should register 165°F in the thickest part of the thigh when fully cooked. Remove the chicken from the air fryer and let it rest on a cutting board for at least 5 minutes.
6. Cut the rested chicken into pieces, sprinkle with the reserved lemon zest and garnish with the reserved sage leaves.

Chicken Tikka

Servings: 4

Cooking Time: 15 Minutes

Ingredients:

- ¼ cup plain Greek yogurt
- 1 clove garlic, minced
- 1 tablespoon ketchup
- 1 tablespoon extra-virgin olive oil
- 1 tablespoon lemon juice
- ½ teaspoon salt
- ½ teaspoon ground cumin
- ½ teaspoon paprika
- ¼ teaspoon ground cinnamon
- ½ teaspoon ground black pepper
- ½ teaspoon cayenne pepper
- 1 pound boneless, skinless chicken thighs

Directions:

1. In a large bowl, stir together the yogurt, garlic, ketchup, olive oil, lemon juice, salt, cumin, paprika, cinnamon, black pepper, and cayenne pepper until combined.
2. Add the chicken thighs to the bow and fold the yogurt-spice mixture over the chicken thighs until they're covered with the marinade. Cover with plastic wrap and place in the refrigerator for 30 minutes.
3. When ready to cook the chicken, remove from the refrigerator and preheat the air fryer to 370°F.
4. Liberally spray the air fryer basket with olive oil mist. Place the chicken thighs into the air fryer basket, leaving space between the thighs to turn.
5. Cook for 10 minutes, turn the chicken thighs, and cook another 5 minutes (or until the internal temperature reaches 165°F).
6. Remove the chicken from the air fryer and serve warm with desired sides.

Chicken Souvlaki Gyros

Servings: 4

Cooking Time: 18 Minutes

Ingredients:

- ¼ cup extra-virgin olive oil
- 1 clove garlic, crushed
- 1 tablespoon Italian seasoning
- ½ teaspoon paprika

- ½ lemon, sliced
- ¼ teaspoon salt
- 1 pound boneless, skinless chicken breasts
- 4 whole-grain pita breads
- 1 cup shredded lettuce
- ½ cup chopped tomatoes
- ¼ cup chopped red onion
- ¼ cup cucumber yogurt sauce

Directions:

1. In a large resealable plastic bag, combine the olive oil, garlic, Italian seasoning, paprika, lemon, and salt. Add the chicken to the bag and secure shut. Vigorously shake until all the ingredients are combined. Set in the fridge for 2 hours to marinate.
2. When ready to cook, preheat the air fryer to 360°F.
3. Liberally spray the air fryer basket with olive oil mist. Remove the chicken from the bag and discard the leftover marinade. Place the chicken into the air fryer basket, allowing enough room between the chicken breasts to flip.
4. Cook for 10 minutes, flip, and cook another 8 minutes.
5. Remove the chicken from the air fryer basket when it has cooked (or the internal temperature of the chicken reaches 165°F). Let rest 5 minutes. Then thinly slice the chicken into strips.
6. Assemble the gyros by placing the pita bread on a flat surface and topping with chicken, lettuce, tomatoes, onion, and a drizzle of yogurt sauce.
7. Serve warm.

Spinach And Feta Stuffed Chicken Breasts

Servings: 4

Cooking Time: 27 Minutes

Ingredients:

- 1 (10-ounce) package frozen spinach, thawed and drained well
- 1 cup feta cheese, crumbled
- ½ teaspoon freshly ground black pepper
- 4 boneless chicken breasts
- salt and freshly ground black pepper
- 1 tablespoon olive oil

Directions:

1. Prepare the filling. Squeeze out as much liquid as possible from the thawed spinach. Rough chop the spinach and transfer it to a mixing bowl with the feta cheese and the freshly ground black pepper.
2. Prepare the chicken breast. Place the chicken breast on a cutting board and press down on the chicken breast with one hand to keep it stabilized. Make an incision about 1-inch long in the fattest side of the breast. Move the knife up and down inside the chicken breast, without poking through either the top or the bottom, or the other side of the breast. The inside pocket should be about 3-inches long, but the opening should only be about 1-inch wide. If this is too difficult, you can make the incision longer, but you will have to be more careful when cooking the chicken breast since this will expose more of the stuffing.
3. Once you have prepared the chicken breasts, use your fingers to stuff the filling into each pocket, spreading the mixture down as far as you can.
4. Preheat the air fryer to 380°F.
5. Lightly brush or spray the air fryer basket and the chicken breasts with olive oil. Transfer two of the stuffed chicken breasts to the air fryer. Air-fry for 12 minutes, turning the chicken breasts over halfway through the cooking time. Remove the chicken to a resting plate and air-fry the second two breasts for 12 minutes. Return the first batch of chicken to the air fryer with the second batch and air-fry for 3 more minutes. When the chicken is cooked, an instant read thermometer should register 165°F in the thickest part of the chicken, as well as in the stuffing.
6. Remove the chicken breasts and let them rest on a cutting board for 2 to 3 minutes. Slice the chicken on the bias and serve with the slices fanned out.

Chicken Strips

Servings: 4

Cooking Time: 8 Minutes

Ingredients:

- 1 pound chicken tenders
- Marinade
- ¼ cup olive oil
- 2 tablespoons water
- 2 tablespoons honey
- 2 tablespoons white vinegar
- ½ teaspoon salt
- ½ teaspoon crushed red pepper
- 1 teaspoon garlic powder
- 1 teaspoon onion powder
- ½ teaspoon paprika

Directions:

1. Combine all marinade ingredients and mix well.
2. Add chicken and stir to coat. Cover tightly and let marinate in refrigerator for 30minutes.
3. Remove tenders from marinade and place them in a single layer in the air fryer basket.
4. Cook at 390°F for 3minutes. Turn tenders over and cook for 5 minutes longer or until chicken is done and juices run clear.
5. Repeat step 4 to cook remaining tenders.

Crispy Fried Onion Chicken Breasts

Servings: 2

Cooking Time: 13 Minutes

Ingredients:

- ¼ cup all-purpose flour*
- salt and freshly ground black pepper
- 1 egg
- 2 tablespoons Dijon mustard
- 1½ cups crispy fried onions (like French's®)
- ½ teaspoon paprika
- 2 (5-ounce) boneless, skinless chicken breasts
- vegetable or olive oil, in a spray bottle

Directions:

1. Preheat the air fryer to 380°F.
2. Set up a dredging station with three shallow dishes. Place the flour in the first shallow dish and season well with salt and freshly ground black pepper. Combine the egg and Dijon mustard in a second shallow dish and whisk until smooth. Place the fried onions in a sealed bag and using a rolling pin, crush them into coarse crumbs. Combine these crumbs with the paprika in the third shallow dish.
3. Dredge the chicken breasts in the flour. Shake off any excess flour and dip them into the egg mixture. Let any excess egg drip off. Then coat both sides of the chicken breasts with the crispy onions. Press the crumbs onto the chicken breasts with your hands to make sure they are well adhered.
4. Spray or brush the bottom of the air fryer basket with oil. Transfer the chicken breasts to the air fryer basket and air-fry at 380°F for 13 minutes, turning the chicken over halfway through the cooking time.
5. Serve immediately.

Maple Bacon Wrapped Chicken Breasts

Servings: 2

Cooking Time: 18 Minutes

Ingredients:

- 2 (6-ounce) boneless, skinless chicken breasts
- 2 tablespoons maple syrup, divided
- freshly ground black pepper
- 6 slices thick-sliced bacon
- fresh celery or parsley leaves
- Ranch Dressing:
- ¼ cup mayonnaise
- ¼ cup buttermilk
- ¼ cup Greek yogurt
- 1 tablespoon chopped fresh chives
- 1 tablespoon chopped fresh parsley
- 1 tablespoon chopped fresh dill
- 1 tablespoon lemon juice
- salt and freshly ground black pepper

Directions:

1. Brush the chicken breasts with half the maple syrup and season with freshly ground black pepper. Wrap three slices of bacon around each chicken breast, securing the ends with toothpicks.

2. Preheat the air fryer to 380°F.
3. Air-fry the chicken for 6 minutes. Then turn the chicken breasts over, pour more maple syrup on top and air-fry for another 6 minutes. Turn the chicken breasts one more time, brush the remaining maple syrup all over and continue to air-fry for a final 6 minutes.
4. While the chicken is cooking, prepare the dressing by combining all the dressing ingredients together in a bowl.
5. When the chicken has finished cooking, remove the toothpicks and serve each breast with a little dressing drizzled over each one. Scatter lots of fresh celery or parsley leaves on top.

Sweet-and-sour Chicken

Servings: 6
Cooking Time: 10 Minutes

Ingredients:

- 1 cup pineapple juice
- 1 cup plus 3 tablespoons cornstarch, divided
- ¼ cup sugar
- ¼ cup ketchup
- ¼ cup apple cider vinegar
- 2 tablespoons soy sauce or tamari
- 1 teaspoon garlic powder, divided
- ¼ cup flour
- 1 tablespoon sesame seeds
- ½ teaspoon salt
- ¼ teaspoon ground black pepper
- 2 large eggs
- 2 pounds chicken breasts, cut into 1-inch cubes
- 1 red bell pepper, cut into 1-inch pieces
- 1 carrot, sliced into ¼-inch-thick rounds

Directions:

1. In a medium saucepan, whisk together the pineapple juice, 3 tablespoons of the cornstarch, the sugar, the ketchup, the apple cider vinegar, the soy sauce or tamari, and ½ teaspoon of the garlic powder. Cook over medium-low heat, whisking occasionally as the sauce thickens, about 6 minutes. Stir and set aside while preparing the chicken.
2. Preheat the air fryer to 370°F.
3. In a medium bowl, place the remaining 1 cup of cornstarch, the flour, the sesame seeds, the salt, the remaining ½ teaspoon of garlic powder, and the pepper.
4. In a second medium bowl, whisk the eggs.
5. Working in batches, place the cubed chicken in the cornstarch mixture to lightly coat; then dip it into the egg mixture, and return it to the cornstarch mixture. Shake off the excess and place the coated chicken in the air fryer basket. Spray with cooking spray and cook for 5 minutes, shake the basket, and spray with more cooking spray. Cook an additional 3 to 5 minutes, or until completely cooked and golden brown.
6. On the last batch of chicken, add the bell pepper and carrot to the basket and cook with the chicken.
7. Place the cooked chicken and vegetables into a serving bowl and toss with the sweet-and-sour sauce to serve.

Chicken Chunks

Servings: 4
Cooking Time: 10 Minutes

Ingredients:

- 1 pound chicken tenders cut in large chunks, about 1½ inches
- salt and pepper
- ½ cup cornstarch
- 2 eggs, beaten
- 1 cup panko breadcrumbs
- oil for misting or cooking spray

Directions:

1. Season chicken chunks to your liking with salt and pepper.
2. Dip chicken chunks in cornstarch. Then dip in egg and shake off excess. Then roll in panko crumbs to coat well.
3. Spray all sides of chicken chunks with oil or cooking spray.
4. Place chicken in air fryer basket in single layer and cook at 390°F for 5minutes. Spray with oil, turn chunks over, and spray other side.
5. Cook for an additional 5minutes or until chicken juices run clear and outside is golden brown.

6. Repeat steps 4 and 5 to cook remaining chicken.

Pickle Brined Fried Chicken

Servings: 4
Cooking Time: 47 Minutes

Ingredients:

- 4 bone-in, skin-on chicken legs, cut into drumsticks and thighs (about 3½ pounds)
- pickle juice from a 24-ounce jar of kosher dill pickles
- ½ cup flour
- salt and freshly ground black pepper
- 2 eggs
- 1 cup fine breadcrumbs
- 1 teaspoon salt
- 1 teaspoon freshly ground black pepper
- ½ teaspoon ground paprika
- ⅛ teaspoon ground cayenne pepper
- vegetable or canola oil in a spray bottle

Directions:

1. Place the chicken in a shallow dish and pour the pickle juice over the top. Cover and transfer the chicken to the refrigerator to brine in the pickle juice for 3 to 8 hours.
2. When you are ready to cook, remove the chicken from the refrigerator to let it come to room temperature while you set up a dredging station. Place the flour in a shallow dish and season well with salt and freshly ground black pepper. Whisk the eggs in a second shallow dish. In a third shallow dish, combine the breadcrumbs, salt, pepper, paprika and cayenne pepper.
3. Preheat the air fryer to 370°F.
4. Remove the chicken from the pickle brine and gently dry it with a clean kitchen towel. Dredge each piece of chicken in the flour, then dip it into the egg mixture, and finally press it into the breadcrumb mixture to coat all sides of the chicken. Place the breaded chicken on a plate or baking sheet and spray each piece all over with vegetable oil.
5. Air-fry the chicken in two batches. Place two chicken thighs and two drumsticks into the air fryer basket. Air-fry for 10 minutes. Then, gently turn the chicken pieces over and air-fry for another 10 minutes. Remove the chicken pieces and let them rest on plate – do not cover. Repeat with the second batch of chicken, air-frying for 20 minutes, turning the chicken over halfway through.
6. Lower the temperature of the air fryer to 340°F. Place the first batch of chicken on top of the second batch already in the basket and air-fry for an additional 7 minutes. Serve warm and enjoy.

Parmesan Crusted Chicken Cordon Bleu

Servings: 2
Cooking Time: 14 Minutes

Ingredients:

- 2 (6-ounce) boneless, skinless chicken breasts
- salt and freshly ground black pepper
- 1 tablespoon Dijon mustard
- 4 slices Swiss cheese
- 4 slices deli-sliced ham
- ¼ cup all-purpose flour*
- 1 egg, beaten
- ¾ cup panko breadcrumbs*
- ⅓ cup grated Parmesan cheese
- olive oil, in a spray bottle

Directions:

1. Butterfly the chicken breasts. Place the chicken breast on a cutting board and press down on the breast with the palm of your hand. Slice into the long side of the chicken breast, parallel to the cutting board, but not all the way through to the other side. Open the chicken breast like a "book". Place a piece of plastic wrap over the chicken breast and gently pound it with a meat mallet to make it evenly thick.
2. Season the chicken with salt and pepper. Spread the Dijon mustard on the inside of each chicken breast. Layer one slice of cheese on top of the mustard, then top with the 2 slices of ham and the other slice of cheese.
3. Starting with the long edge of the chicken breast, roll the chicken up to the other side. Secure it shut with 1 or 2 toothpicks.
4. Preheat the air fryer to 350°F.

5. Set up a dredging station with three shallow dishes. Place the flour in the first dish. Place the beaten egg in the second shallow dish. Combine the panko breadcrumbs and Parmesan cheese together in the third shallow dish. Dip the stuffed and rolled chicken breasts in the flour, then the beaten egg and then roll in the breadcrumb-cheese mixture to cover on all sides. Press the crumbs onto the chicken breasts with your hands to make sure they are well adhered. Spray the chicken breasts with olive oil and transfer to the air fryer basket.
6. Air-fry at 350°F for 14 minutes, flipping the breasts over halfway through the cooking time. Let the chicken rest for a few minutes before removing the toothpicks, slicing and serving.

Italian Roasted Chicken Thighs

Servings: 6
Cooking Time: 14 Minutes

Ingredients:

- 6 boneless chicken thighs
- ½ teaspoon dried oregano
- ½ teaspoon garlic powder
- ½ teaspoon sea salt
- ½ teaspoon black pepper
- ¼ teaspoon crushed red pepper flakes

Directions:

1. Pat the chicken thighs with paper towel.
2. In a small bowl, mix the oregano, garlic powder, salt, pepper, and crushed red pepper flakes. Rub the spice mixture onto the chicken thighs.
3. Preheat the air fryer to 400°F.
4. Place the chicken thighs in the air fryer basket and spray with cooking spray. Cook for 10 minutes, turn over, and cook another 4 minutes. When cooking completes, the internal temperature should read 165°F.

Tortilla Crusted Chicken Breast

Servings: 2
Cooking Time: 12 Minutes

Ingredients:

- ⅓ cup flour
- 1 teaspoon salt
- 1½ teaspoons chili powder
- 1 teaspoon ground cumin
- freshly ground black pepper
- 1 egg, beaten
- ¾ cup coarsely crushed yellow corn tortilla chips
- 2 (3- to 4-ounce) boneless chicken breasts
- vegetable oil
- ½ cup salsa
- ½ cup crumbled queso fresco
- fresh cilantro leaves
- sour cream or guacamole (optional)

Directions:

1. Set up a dredging station with three shallow dishes. Combine the flour, salt, chili powder, cumin and black pepper in the first shallow dish. Beat the egg in the second shallow dish. Place the crushed tortilla chips in the third shallow dish.
2. Dredge the chicken in the spiced flour, covering all sides of the breast. Then dip the chicken into the egg, coating the chicken completely. Finally, place the chicken into the tortilla chips and press the chips onto the chicken to make sure they adhere to all sides of the breast. Spray the coated chicken breasts on both sides with vegetable oil.
3. Preheat the air fryer to 380°F.
4. Air-fry the chicken for 6 minutes. Then turn the chicken breasts over and air-fry for another 6 minutes. (Increase the cooking time if you are using chicken breasts larger than 3 to 4 ounces.)
5. When the chicken has finished cooking, serve each breast with a little salsa, the crumbled queso fresco and cilantro as the finishing touch. Serve some sour cream and/or guacamole at the table, if desired.

Apricot Glazed Chicken Thighs

Servings: 2

Cooking Time: 22 Minutes

Ingredients:

- 4 bone-in chicken thighs (about 2 pounds)
- olive oil
- 1 teaspoon salt
- ¼ teaspoon freshly ground black pepper
- ½ teaspoon onion powder
- ¾ cup apricot preserves 1½ tablespoons Dijon mustard
- ½ teaspoon dried thyme
- 1 teaspoon soy sauce
- fresh thyme leaves, for garnish

Directions:

1. Preheat the air fryer to 380°F.
2. Brush or spray both the air fryer basket and the chicken with the olive oil. Combine the salt, pepper and onion powder and season both sides of the chicken with the spice mixture.
3. Place the seasoned chicken thighs, skin side down in the air fryer basket. Air-fry for 10 minutes.
4. While chicken is cooking, make the glaze by combining the apricot preserves, Dijon mustard, thyme and soy sauce in a small bowl.
5. When the time is up on the air fryer, spoon half of the apricot glaze over the chicken thighs and air-fry for 2 minutes. Then flip the chicken thighs over so that the skin side is facing up and air-fry for an additional 8 minutes. Finally, spoon and spread the rest of the glaze evenly over the chicken thighs and air-fry for a final 2 minutes. Transfer the chicken to a serving platter and sprinkle the fresh thyme leaves on top.

Air-fried Turkey Breast With Cherry Glaze

Servings: 6

Cooking Time: 54 Minutes

Ingredients:

- 1 (5-pound) turkey breast
- 2 teaspoons olive oil
- 1 teaspoon dried thyme
- ½ teaspoon dried sage
- 1 teaspoon salt
- ½ teaspoon freshly ground black pepper
- ½ cup cherry preserves
- 1 tablespoon chopped fresh thyme leaves
- 1 teaspoon soy sauce*
- freshly ground black pepper

Directions:

1. All turkeys are built differently, so depending on the turkey breast and how your butcher has prepared it, you may need to trim the bottom of the ribs in order to get the turkey to sit upright in the air fryer basket without touching the heating element. The key to this recipe is getting the right size turkey breast. Once you've managed that, the rest is easy, so make sure your turkey breast fits into the air fryer basket before you Preheat the air fryer.
2. Preheat the air fryer to 350°F.
3. Brush the turkey breast all over with the olive oil. Combine the thyme, sage, salt and pepper and rub the outside of the turkey breast with the spice mixture.
4. Transfer the seasoned turkey breast to the air fryer basket, breast side up, and air-fry at 350°F for 25 minutes. Turn the turkey breast on its side and air-fry for another 12 minutes. Turn the turkey breast on the opposite side and air-fry for 12 more minutes. The internal temperature of the turkey breast should reach 165°F when fully cooked.
5. While the turkey is air-frying, make the glaze by combining the cherry preserves, fresh thyme, soy sauce and pepper in a small bowl. When the cooking time is up, return the turkey breast to an upright position and brush the glaze all over the turkey. Air-fry for a final 5 minutes, until the skin is nicely browned and crispy. Let the turkey rest, loosely tented with foil, for at least 5 minutes before slicing and serving.

Quick Chicken For Filling

Servings: 2

Cooking Time: 8 Minutes

Ingredients:

- 1 pound chicken tenders, skinless and boneless
- ½ teaspoon ground cumin
- ½ teaspoon garlic powder
- cooking spray

Directions:

1. Sprinkle raw chicken tenders with seasonings.
2. Spray air fryer basket lightly with cooking spray to prevent sticking.
3. Place chicken in air fryer basket in single layer.
4. Cook at 390°F for 4minutes, turn chicken strips over, and cook for an additional 4minutes.
5. Test for doneness. Thick tenders may require an additional minute or two.

Chicken Cordon Bleu

Servings: 2

Cooking Time: 16 Minutes

Ingredients:

- 2 boneless, skinless chicken breasts
- ¼ teaspoon salt
- 2 teaspoons Dijon mustard
- 2 ounces deli ham
- 2 ounces Swiss, fontina, or Gruyère cheese
- ⅓ cup all-purpose flour
- 1 egg
- ½ cup breadcrumbs

Directions:

1. Pat the chicken breasts with a paper towel. Season the chicken with the salt. Pound the chicken breasts to 1½ inches thick. Create a pouch by slicing the side of each chicken breast. Spread 1 teaspoon Dijon mustard inside the pouch of each chicken breast. Wrap a 1-ounce slice of ham around a 1-ounce slice of cheese and place into the pouch. Repeat with the remaining ham and cheese.
2. In a medium bowl, place the flour.
3. In a second bowl, whisk the egg.
4. In a third bowl, place the breadcrumbs.
5. Dredge the chicken in the flour and shake off the excess. Next, dip the chicken into the egg and then in the breadcrumbs. Set the chicken on a plate and repeat with the remaining chicken piece.
6. Preheat the air fryer to 360°F.
7. Place the chicken in the air fryer basket and spray liberally with cooking spray. Cook for 8 minutes, turn the chicken breasts over, and liberally spray with cooking spray again; cook another 6 minutes. Once golden brown, check for an internal temperature of 165°F.

Taquitos

Servings: 12

Cooking Time: 6 Minutes Per Batch

Ingredients:

- 1 teaspoon butter
- 2 tablespoons chopped green onions
- 1 cup cooked chicken, shredded
- 2 tablespoons chopped green chiles
- 2 ounces Pepper Jack cheese, shredded
- 4 tablespoons salsa
- ½ teaspoon lime juice
- ¼ teaspoon cumin
- ½ teaspoon chile powder
- ⅛ teaspoon garlic powder
- 12 corn tortillas
- oil for misting or cooking spray

Directions:

1. Melt butter in a saucepan over medium heat. Add green onions and sauté a minute or two, until tender.
2. Remove from heat and stir in the chicken, green chiles, cheese, salsa, lime juice, and seasonings.
3. Preheat air fryer to 390°F.
4. To soften refrigerated tortillas, wrap in damp paper towels and microwave for 30 to 60 seconds, until slightly warmed.
5. Remove one tortilla at a time, keeping others covered with the damp paper towels. Place a heaping tablespoon of filling into tortilla, roll up and secure with toothpick. Spray all sides with oil or cooking spray.
6. Place taquitos in air fryer basket, either in a single layer or stacked. To stack, leave plenty of space between

taquitos and alternate the direction of the layers, 4 on the bottom lengthwise, then 4 more on top crosswise.

7. Cook for 6minutes or until brown and crispy.
8. Repeat steps 6 and 7 to cook remaining taquitos.
9. Serve hot with guacamole, sour cream, salsa or all three!

Crispy "fried" Chicken

Servings: 4
Cooking Time: 14 Minutes

Ingredients:

- ¾ cup all-purpose flour
- ½ teaspoon paprika
- ¼ teaspoon black pepper
- ¼ teaspoon salt
- 2 large eggs
- 1½ cups panko breadcrumbs
- 1 pound boneless, skinless chicken tenders

Directions:

1. Preheat the air fryer to 400°F.
2. In a shallow bowl, mix the flour with the paprika, pepper, and salt.
3. In a separate bowl, whisk the eggs; set aside.
4. In a third bowl, place the breadcrumbs.
5. Liberally spray the air fryer basket with olive oil spray.
6. Pat the chicken tenders dry with a paper towel. Dredge the tenders one at a time in the flour, then dip them in the egg, and toss them in the breadcrumb coating. Repeat until all tenders are coated.
7. Set each tender in the air fryer, leaving room on each side of the tender to allow for flipping.
8. When the basket is full, cook 4 to 7 minutes, flip, and cook another 4 to 7 minutes.
9. Remove the tenders and let cool 5 minutes before serving. Repeat until all tenders are cooked.

Parmesan Chicken Fingers

Servings: 2
Cooking Time: 19 Minutes

Ingredients:

- ½ cup flour
- 1 teaspoon salt
- freshly ground black pepper
- 2 eggs, beaten
- ¾ cup seasoned panko breadcrumbs
- ¾ cup grated Parmesan cheese
- 8 chicken tenders (about 1 pound)
- OR
- 2 to 3 boneless, skinless chicken breasts, cut into strips
- vegetable oil
- marinara sauce

Directions:

1. Set up a dredging station. Combine the flour, salt and pepper in a shallow dish. Place the beaten eggs in second shallow dish, and combine the panko breadcrumbs and Parmesan cheese in a third shallow dish.
2. Dredge the chicken tenders in the flour mixture. Then dip them into the egg, and finally place the chicken in the breadcrumb mixture. Press the coating onto both sides of the chicken tenders. Place the coated chicken tenders on a baking sheet until they are all coated. Spray both sides of the chicken fingers with vegetable oil.
3. Preheat the air fryer to 360°F.
4. Air-fry the chicken fingers in two batches. Transfer half the chicken fingers to the air fryer basket and air-fry for 9 minutes, turning the chicken over halfway through the cooking time. When the second batch of chicken fingers has finished cooking, return the first batch to the air fryer with the second batch and air-fry for one minute to heat everything through.
5. Serve immediately with marinara sauce, honey-mustard, ketchup or your favorite dipping sauce.

Nacho Chicken Fries

Servings: 4
Cooking Time: 7 Minutes

Ingredients:

- 1 pound chicken tenders
- salt
- ¼ cup flour

- 2 eggs
- ¾ cup panko breadcrumbs
- ¾ cup crushed organic nacho cheese tortilla chips
- oil for misting or cooking spray
- Seasoning Mix
- 1 tablespoon chili powder
- 1 teaspoon ground cumin
- ½ teaspoon garlic powder
- ½ teaspoon onion powder

Directions:

1. Stir together all seasonings in a small cup and set aside.
2. Cut chicken tenders in half crosswise, then cut into strips no wider than about ½ inch.
3. Preheat air fryer to 390°F.
4. Salt chicken to taste. Place strips in large bowl and sprinkle with 1 tablespoon of the seasoning mix. Stir well to distribute seasonings.
5. Add flour to chicken and stir well to coat all sides.
6. Beat eggs together in a shallow dish.
7. In a second shallow dish, combine the panko, crushed chips, and the remaining 2 teaspoons of seasoning mix.
8. Dip chicken strips in eggs, then roll in crumbs. Mist with oil or cooking spray.
9. Chicken strips will cook best if done in two batches. They can be crowded and overlapping a little but not stacked in double or triple layers.
10. Cook for 4minutes. Shake basket, mist with oil, and cook 3 moreminutes, until chicken juices run clear and outside is crispy.
11. Repeat step 10 to cook remaining chicken fries.

Southwest Gluten-free Turkey Meatloaf

Servings: 8

Cooking Time: 35 Minutes

Ingredients:

- 1 pound lean ground turkey
- ¼ cup corn grits
- ¼ cup diced onion
- 1 teaspoon minced garlic
- ½ teaspoon black pepper
- ½ teaspoon salt
- 1 large egg
- ½ cup ketchup
- 4 teaspoons chipotle hot sauce
- ⅓ cup shredded cheddar cheese

Directions:

1. Preheat the air fryer to 350°F.
2. In a large bowl, mix together the ground turkey, corn grits, onion, garlic, black pepper, and salt.
3. In a small bowl, whisk the egg. Add the egg to the turkey mixture and combine.
4. In a small bowl, mix the ketchup and hot sauce. Set aside.
5. Liberally spray a 9-x-4-inch loaf pan with olive oil spray. Depending on the size of your air fryer, you may need to use 2 or 3 mini loaf pans.
6. Spoon the ground turkey mixture into the loaf pan and evenly top with half of the ketchup mixture. Cover with foil and place the meatloaf into the air fryer. Cook for 30 minutes; remove the foil and discard. Check the internal temperature (it should be nearing 165°F).
7. Coat the top of the meatloaf with the remaining ketchup mixture, and sprinkle the cheese over the top. Place the meatloaf back in the air fryer for the remaining 5 minutes (or until the internal temperature reaches 165°F).
8. Remove from the oven and let cool 5 minutes before serving. Serve warm with desired sides.

Teriyaki Chicken Drumsticks

Servings: 2

Cooking Time: 17 Minutes

Ingredients:

- 2 tablespoons soy sauce*
- ¼ cup dry sherry
- 1 tablespoon brown sugar
- 2 tablespoons water
- 1 tablespoon rice wine vinegar
- 1 clove garlic, crushed
- 1-inch fresh ginger, peeled and sliced
- pinch crushed red pepper flakes

- 4 to 6 bone-in, skin-on chicken drumsticks
- 1 tablespoon cornstarch
- fresh cilantro leaves

Directions:

1. Make the marinade by combining the soy sauce, dry sherry, brown sugar, water, rice vinegar, garlic, ginger and crushed red pepper flakes. Pour the marinade over the chicken legs, cover and let the chicken marinate for 1 to 4 hours in the refrigerator.
2. Preheat the air fryer to 380°F.
3. Transfer the chicken from the marinade to the air fryer basket, transferring any extra marinade to a small saucepan. Air-fry at 380°F for 8 minutes. Flip the chicken over and continue to air-fry for another 6 minutes, watching to make sure it doesn't brown too much.
4. While the chicken is cooking, bring the reserved marinade to a simmer on the stovetop. Dissolve the cornstarch in 2 tablespoons of water and stir this into the saucepan. Bring to a boil to thicken the sauce. Remove the garlic clove and slices of ginger from the sauce and set aside.
5. When the time is up on the air fryer, brush the thickened sauce on the chicken and air-fry for 3 more minutes. Remove the chicken from the air fryer and brush with the remaining sauce.
6. Serve over rice and sprinkle the cilantro leaves on top.

Chicken Flautas

Servings: 6

Cooking Time: 8 Minutes

Ingredients:

- 6 tablespoons whipped cream cheese
- 1 cup shredded cooked chicken
- 6 tablespoons mild pico de gallo salsa
- ⅓ cup shredded Mexican cheese
- ½ teaspoon taco seasoning
- Six 8-inch flour tortillas
- 2 cups shredded lettuce
- ½ cup guacamole

Directions:

1. Preheat the air fryer to 370°F.
2. In a large bowl, mix the cream cheese, chicken, salsa, shredded cheese, and taco seasoning until well combined.
3. Lay the tortillas on a flat surface. Divide the cheese-and-chicken mixture into 6 equal portions; then place the mixture in the center of the tortillas, spreading evenly, leaving about 1 inch from the edge of the tortilla.
4. Spray the air fryer basket with olive oil spray. Roll up the flautas and place them edge side down into the basket. Lightly mist the top of the flautas with olive oil spray.
5. Repeat until the air fryer basket is full. You may need to cook these in batches, depending on the size of your air fryer.
6. Cook for 7 minutes, or until the outer edges are browned.
7. Remove from the air fryer basket and serve warm over a bed of shredded lettuce with guacamole on top.

Asian Meatball Tacos

Servings: 4

Cooking Time: 10 Minutes

Ingredients:

- 1 pound lean ground turkey
- 3 tablespoons soy sauce
- 1 tablespoon brown sugar
- ½ teaspoon onion powder
- ½ teaspoon garlic powder
- 1 tablespoon sesame seeds
- 1 English cucumber
- 4 radishes
- 2 tablespoons white wine vinegar
- 1 lime, juiced and divided
- 1 tablespoon avocado oil
- Salt, to taste
- ½ cup Greek yogurt
- 1 to 3 teaspoons Sriracha, based on desired spiciness
- 1 cup shredded cabbage
- ¼ cup chopped cilantro
- Eight 6-inch flour tortillas

Directions:

1. Preheat the air fryer to 360°F.

2. In a large bowl, mix the ground turkey, soy sauce, brown sugar, onion powder, garlic powder, and sesame seeds. Form the meat into 1-inch meatballs and place in the air fryer basket. Cook for 5 minutes, shake the basket, and cook another 5 minutes. Using a food thermometer, make sure the internal temperature of the meatballs is 165°F.
3. Meanwhile, dice the cucumber and radishes and place in a medium bowl. Add the white wine vinegar, 1 teaspoon of the lime juice, and the avocado oil, and stir to coat. Season with salt to desired taste.
4. In a large bowl, mix the Greek yogurt, Sriracha, and the remaining lime juice, and stir. Add in the cabbage and cilantro; toss well to create a slaw.
5. In a heavy skillet, heat the tortillas over medium heat for 1 to 2 minutes on each side, or until warmed.
6. To serve, place a tortilla on a plate, top with 5 meatballs, then with cucumber and radish salad, and finish with 2 tablespoons of cabbage slaw.

Spicy Black Bean Turkey Burgers With Cumin-avocado Spread

Servings: 2
Cooking Time: 20 Minutes

Ingredients:

- 1 cup canned black beans, drained and rinsed
- ¾ pound lean ground turkey
- 2 tablespoons minced red onion
- 1 Jalapeño pepper, seeded and minced
- 2 tablespoons plain breadcrumbs
- ½ teaspoon chili powder
- ¼ teaspoon cayenne pepper
- salt, to taste
- olive or vegetable oil
- 2 slices pepper jack cheese
- toasted burger rolls, sliced tomatoes, lettuce leaves
- Cumin-Avocado Spread:
- 1 ripe avocado
- juice of 1 lime
- 1 teaspoon ground cumin
- ½ teaspoon salt
- 1 tablespoon chopped fresh cilantro
- freshly ground black pepper

Directions:

1. Place the black beans in a large bowl and smash them slightly with the back of a fork. Add the ground turkey, red onion, Jalapeño pepper, breadcrumbs, chili powder and cayenne pepper. Season with salt. Mix with your hands to combine all the ingredients and then shape them into 2 patties. Brush both sides of the burger patties with a little olive or vegetable oil.
2. Preheat the air fryer to 380°F.
3. Transfer the burgers to the air fryer basket and air-fry for 20 minutes, flipping them over halfway through the cooking process. Top the burgers with the pepper jack cheese (securing the slices to the burgers with a toothpick) for the last 2 minutes of the cooking process.
4. While the burgers are cooking, make the cumin avocado spread. Place the avocado, lime juice, cumin and salt in food processor and process until smooth. (For a chunkier spread, you can mash this by hand in a bowl.) Stir in the cilantro and season with freshly ground black pepper. Chill the spread until you are ready to serve.
5. When the burgers have finished cooking, remove them from the air fryer and let them rest on a plate, covered gently with aluminum foil. Brush a little olive oil on the insides of the burger rolls. Place the rolls, cut side up, into the air fryer basket and air-fry at 400°F for 1 minute to toast and warm them.
6. Spread the cumin-avocado spread on the rolls and build your burgers with lettuce and sliced tomatoes and any other ingredient you like. Serve warm with a side of sweet potato fries.

Herbed Cheese Brittle

Servings: 4
Cooking Time: 5 Minutes

Ingredients:

- ½ cup shredded Parmesan cheese
- ½ cup shredded white cheddar cheese
- 1 tablespoon fresh chopped rosemary
- 1 teaspoon garlic powder
- 1 large egg white

Directions:

1. Preheat the air fryer to 400°F.
2. In a large bowl, mix the cheeses, rosemary, and garlic powder. Mix in the egg white. Then pour the batter into a 7-inch pan (or an air-fryer-compatible pan). Place the pan in the air fryer basket and cook for 4 to 5 minutes, or until the cheese is melted and slightly browned.
3. Remove the pan from the air fryer, and let it cool for 2 minutes. Invert the pan before the cheese brittle completely cools but is semi-hardened to allow it to easily slide out of the pan.
4. Let the pan cool another 5 minutes. Break into pieces and serve.

Crab Rangoon Dip With Wonton Chips

Servings: 6
Cooking Time: 18 Minutes

Ingredients:

- Wonton Chips:
- 1 (12-ounce) package wonton wrappers
- vegetable oil
- sea salt
- Crab Rangoon Dip:
- 8 ounces cream cheese, softened
- ¾ cup sour cream
- 1 teaspoon Worcestershire sauce
- 1½ teaspoons soy sauce
- 1 teaspoon sesame oil
- ⅛ teaspoon ground cayenne pepper
- ¼ teaspoon salt
- freshly ground black pepper
- 8 ounces cooked crabmeat
- 1 cup grated white Cheddar cheese
- ⅓ cup chopped scallions
- paprika (for garnish)

Directions:

1. Cut the wonton wrappers in half diagonally to form triangles. Working in batches, lay the wonton triangles on a flat surface and brush or spray both sides with vegetable oil.
2. Preheat the air fryer to 370°F.
3. Place about 10 to 12 wonton triangles in the air fryer basket, letting them overlap slightly. Air-fry for just 2 minutes, shaking the basket halfway through the cooking time. Transfer the wonton chips to a large bowl and season immediately with sea salt. (You'll hear the chips start to spin around in the air fryer when they are almost done.) Repeat with the rest of wontons (keeping those fishing hands at bay!).
4. To make the dip, combine the cream cheese, sour cream, Worcestershire sauce, soy sauce, sesame oil, cayenne pepper, salt, and freshly ground black pepper in a bowl. Mix well and then fold in the crabmeat, Cheddar cheese, and scallions.
5. Transfer the dip to a 7-inch ceramic baking pan or shallow casserole dish. Sprinkle paprika on top and cover the dish with aluminum foil. Lower the dish into the air fryer basket using a sling made of aluminum foil (fold a piece of aluminum foil into a strip about 2-inches wide by 24-inches long). Air-fry for 11 minutes. Remove the aluminum foil and air-fry for another 5 minutes to finish cooking and brown the top. Serve hot with the wonton chips.

Okra Chips

Servings: 4
Cooking Time: 16 Minutes

Ingredients:

- 1¼ pounds Thin fresh okra pods, cut into 1-inch pieces
- 1½ tablespoons Vegetable or canola oil
- ¾ teaspoon Coarse sea salt or kosher salt

Directions:

1. Preheat the air fryer to 400°F.
2. Toss the okra, oil, and salt in a large bowl until the pieces are well and evenly coated.
3. When the machine is at temperature, pour the contents of the bowl into the basket. Air-fry, tossing several times, for 16 minutes, or until crisp and quite brown (maybe even a little blackened on the thin bits).
4. Pour the contents of the basket onto a wire rack. Cool for a couple of minutes before serving.

Kale Chips

Servings: 2
Cooking Time: 5 Minutes

Ingredients:

- 4 Medium kale leaves, about 1 ounce each
- 2 teaspoons Olive oil
- 2 teaspoons Regular or low-sodium soy sauce or gluten-free tamari sauce

Directions:

1. Preheat the air fryer to 400°F.
2. Cut the stems from the leaves (all the stems, all the way up the leaf). Tear each leaf into three pieces. Put them in a large bowl.
3. Add the olive oil and soy or tamari sauce. Toss well to coat. You can even gently rub the leaves along the side of the bowl to get the liquids to stick to them.
4. When the machine is at temperature, put the leaf pieces in the basket in one layer. Air-fry for 5 minutes, turning and rearranging with kitchen tongs once halfway through, until the chips are dried out and crunchy. Watch carefully so they don't turn dark brown at the edges.
5. Gently pour the contents of the basket onto a wire rack. Cool for at least 5 minutes before serving. The chips can keep for up to 8 hours uncovered on the rack (provided it's not a humid day).

Popcorn Chicken Bites

Servings: 2
Cooking Time: 8 Minutes

Ingredients:

- 1 pound chicken breasts, cutlets or tenders
- 1 cup buttermilk
- 3 to 6 dashes hot sauce (optional)
- 8 cups cornflakes (or 2 cups cornflake crumbs)
- ½ teaspoon salt
- 1 tablespoon butter, melted
- 2 tablespoons chopped fresh parsley

Directions:

1. Cut the chicken into bite-sized pieces (about 1-inch) and place them in a bowl with the buttermilk and hot sauce (if using). Cover and let the chicken marinate in the buttermilk for 1 to 3 hours in the refrigerator.
2. Preheat the air fryer to 380°F.
3. Crush the cornflakes into fine crumbs by either crushing them with your hands in a bowl, rolling them with a rolling pin in a plastic bag or processing them in a food processor. Place the crumbs in a bowl, add the salt, melted butter and parsley and mix well. Working in batches, remove the chicken from the buttermilk marinade, letting any excess drip off and transfer the chicken to the cornflakes. Toss the chicken pieces in the cornflake mixture to coat evenly, pressing the crumbs onto the chicken.
4. Air-fry the chicken in two batches for 8 minutes per batch, shaking the basket halfway through the cooking process. Re-heat the first batch with the second batch for a couple of minutes if desired.
5. Serve the popcorn chicken bites warm with BBQ sauce or honey mustard for dipping.

Muffuletta Sliders

Servings: 8
Cooking Time: 7 Minutes

Ingredients:

- ¼ pound thin-sliced deli ham
- ¼ pound thin-sliced pastrami
- 4 ounces low-fat mozzarella cheese, grated or sliced thin
- 8 slider buns
- olive oil for misting
- 1 tablespoon sesame seeds
- Olive Mix
- ¼ cup sliced black olives
- ½ cup sliced green olives with pimentos
- ¼ cup chopped kalamata olives
- 1 teaspoon red wine vinegar
- ¼ teaspoon basil
- ⅛ teaspoon garlic powder

Directions:

1. In a small bowl, stir together all the Olive Mix ingredients.
2. Divide the meats and cheese into 8 equal portions. To assemble sliders, stack in this order: bottom bun, ham, pastrami, 2 tablespoons olive mix, cheese, top bun.
3. Mist tops of sliders lightly with oil. Sprinkle with sesame seeds.
4. Cooking 4 at a time, place sliders in air fryer basket and cook at 360°F for 7 minutes to melt cheese and heat through.

Fried Apple Wedges

Servings: 4
Cooking Time: 9 Minutes

Ingredients:

- ¼ cup panko breadcrumbs
- ¼ cup pecans
- 1½ teaspoons cinnamon
- 1½ teaspoons brown sugar
- ¼ cup cornstarch
- 1 egg white
- 2 teaspoons water
- 1 medium apple
- oil for misting or cooking spray

Directions:

1. In a food processor, combine panko, pecans, cinnamon, and brown sugar. Process to make small crumbs.
2. Place cornstarch in a plastic bag or bowl with lid. In a shallow dish, beat together the egg white and water until slightly foamy.
3. Preheat air fryer to 390°F.
4. Cut apple into small wedges. The thickest edge should be no more than ⅜- to ½-inch thick. Cut away the core, but do not peel.
5. Place apple wedges in cornstarch, reseal bag or bowl, and shake to coat.
6. Dip wedges in egg wash, shake off excess, and roll in crumb mixture. Spray with oil.
7. Place apples in air fryer basket in single layer and cook for 5 minutes. Shake basket and break apart any apples that have stuck together. Mist lightly with oil and cook 4 minutes longer, until crispy.

Crunchy Tortellini Bites

Servings: 5
Cooking Time: 10 Minutes

Ingredients:

- 10 ounces (about 2½ cups) Cheese tortellini
- ⅓ cup Yellow cornmeal
- ⅓ cup Seasoned Italian-style dried bread crumbs
- ⅓ cup (about 1 ounce) Finely grated Parmesan cheese
- 1 Large egg
- Olive oil spray

Directions:

1. Bring a large pot of water to a boil over high heat. Add the tortellini and cook for 3 minutes. Drain in a colander set in the sink, then spread out the tortellini on a large baking sheet and cool for 15 minutes.
2. Preheat the air fryer to 400°F.
3. Mix the cornmeal, bread crumbs, and cheese in a large zip-closed plastic bag.
4. Whisk the egg in a medium bowl until uniform. Add the tortellini and toss well to coat, even along the

inside curve of the pasta. Use a slotted spoon or kitchen tongs to transfer 5 or 6 tortellini to the plastic bag, seal, and shake gently to coat thoroughly and evenly. Set the coated tortellini aside on a cutting board and continue coating the rest in the same way.

5. Generously coat the tortellini on all sides with the olive oil spray, then set them in one layer in the basket. Air-fry undisturbed for 10 minutes, gently tossing the basket and rearranging the tortellini at the 4- and 7-minute marks, until brown and crisp.

6. Pour the contents of the basket onto a wire rack. Cool for 5 minutes before serving.

Warm Spinach Dip With Pita Chips

Servings: 6

Cooking Time: 40 Minutes

Ingredients:

- Pita Chips:
- 4 pita breads
- 1 tablespoon olive oil
- ½ teaspoon paprika
- salt and freshly ground black pepper
- Spinach Dip:
- 8 ounces cream cheese, softened at room , Temperature: 1 cup ricotta cheese
- 1 cup grated Fontina cheese
- ½ teaspoon Italian seasoning
- ½ teaspoon garlic powder
- ¾ teaspoon salt
- freshly ground black pepper
- 16 ounces frozen chopped spinach, thawed and squeezed dry
- ¼ cup grated Parmesan cheese
- ½ tomato, finely diced
- ¼ teaspoon dried oregano

Directions:

1. Preheat the air fryer to 390°F.

2. Split the pita breads open so you have 2 circles. Cut each circle into 8 wedges. Place all the wedges into a large bowl and toss with the olive oil. Season with the paprika, salt and pepper and toss to coat evenly. Air-fry the pita triangles in two batches for 5 minutes each, shaking the basket once or twice while they cook so they brown and crisp evenly.

3. Combine the cream cheese, ricotta cheese, Fontina cheese, Italian seasoning, garlic powder, salt and pepper in a large bowl. Fold in the spinach and mix well.

4. Transfer the spinach-cheese mixture to a 7-inch ceramic baking dish or cake pan. Sprinkle the Parmesan cheese on top and wrap the dish with aluminum foil. Transfer the dish to the basket of the air fryer, lowering the dish into the basket using a sling made of aluminum foil (fold a piece of aluminum foil into a strip about 2-inches wide by 24-inches long). Fold the ends of the aluminum foil over the top of the dish before returning the basket to the air fryer. Air-fry for 30 minutes at 390°F. With 4 minutes left on the air fryer timer, remove the foil and let the cheese brown on top.

5. Sprinkle the diced tomato and oregano on the warm dip and serve immediately with the pita chips.

Beer Battered Onion Rings

Servings: 2

Cooking Time: 16 Minutes

Ingredients:

- ⅔ cup flour
- ½ teaspoon baking soda
- 1 teaspoon paprika
- 1 teaspoon salt
- ½ teaspoon freshly ground black pepper
- ¾ cup beer
- 1 egg, beaten
- 1½ cups fine breadcrumbs
- 1 large Vidalia onion, peeled and sliced into ½-inch rings
- vegetable oil

Directions:

1. Set up a dredging station. Mix the flour, baking soda, paprika, salt and pepper together in a bowl. Pour in the beer, add the egg and whisk until smooth. Place the breadcrumbs in a cake pan or shallow dish.

2. Separate the onion slices into individual rings. Dip each onion ring into the batter with a fork. Lift the onion ring out of the batter and let any excess batter drip

off. Then place the onion ring in the breadcrumbs and shake the cake pan back and forth to coat the battered onion ring. Pat the ring gently with your hands to make sure the breadcrumbs stick and that both sides of the ring are covered. Place the coated onion ring on a sheet pan and repeat with the rest of the onion rings.

3. Preheat the air fryer to 360°F.
4. Lightly spray the onion rings with oil, coating both sides. Layer the onion rings in the air fryer basket, stacking them on top of each other in a haphazard manner.
5. Air-fry for 10 minutes at 360°F. Flip the onion rings over and rotate the onion rings from the bottom of the basket to the top. Air-fry for an additional 6 minutes.
6. Serve immediately with your favorite dipping sauce.

Za'atar Garbanzo Beans

Servings: 6

Cooking Time: 12 Minutes

Ingredients:

- One 14.5-ounce can garbanzo beans, drained and rinsed
- 1 tablespoon extra-virgin olive oil
- 6 teaspoons za'atar seasoning mix
- 2 tablespoons chopped parsley
- Salt and pepper, to taste

Directions:

1. Preheat the air fryer to 390°F.
2. In a medium bowl, toss the garbanzo beans with olive oil and za'atar seasoning.
3. Pour the beans into the air fryer basket and cook for 12 minutes, or until toasted as you like. Stir every 3 minutes while roasting.
4. Remove the beans from the air fryer basket into a serving bowl, top with fresh chopped parsley, and season with salt and pepper.

Antipasto-stuffed Cherry Tomatoes

Servings: 12

Cooking Time: 9 Minutes

Ingredients:

- 12 Large cherry tomatoes, preferably Campari tomatoes (about 1½ ounces each and the size of golf balls)
- ½ cup Seasoned Italian-style dried bread crumbs (gluten-free, if a concern)
- ¼ cup (about ¾ ounce) Finely grated Parmesan cheese
- ¼ cup Finely chopped pitted black olives
- ¼ cup Finely chopped marinated artichoke hearts
- 2 tablespoons Marinade from the artichokes
- 4 Sun-dried tomatoes (dry, not packed in oil), finely chopped
- Olive oil spray

Directions:

1. Preheat the air fryer to 400°F.
2. Cut the top off of each fresh tomato, exposing the seeds and pulp. (The tops can be saved for a snack, sprinkled with some kosher salt, to tide you over while the stuffed tomatoes cook.) Cut a very small slice off the bottom of each tomato (no cutting into the pulp) so it will stand up flat on your work surface. Use a melon baller to remove and discard the seeds and pulp from each tomato.
3. Mix the bread crumbs, cheese, olives, artichoke hearts, marinade, and sun-dried tomatoes in a bowl until well combined. Stuff this mixture into each prepared tomato, about 1½ tablespoons in each. Generously coat the tops of the tomatoes with olive oil spray.
4. Set the tomatoes stuffing side up in the basket. Air-fry undisturbed for 9 minutes, or until the stuffing has browned a bit and the tomatoes are blistered in places.
5. Remove the basket and cool the tomatoes in it for 5 minutes. Then use kitchen tongs to gently transfer the tomatoes to a serving platter.

Fried Gyoza

Servings: 18
Cooking Time: 6 Minutes

Ingredients:

- 5 ounces Lean ground pork
- 2½ tablespoons Very thinly sliced scallion
- 1 tablespoon plus 2 teaspoons Minced peeled fresh ginger
- 1¼ teaspoons Toasted sesame oil
- ⅛ teaspoon Table salt
- ⅛ teaspoon Ground black pepper
- 18 Round gyoza or square wonton wrappers (thawed, if necessary)
- Vegetable oil spray

Directions:

1. Preheat the air fryer to 350°F .
2. Mix the ground pork, scallion, ginger, sesame oil, salt, and pepper in a bowl until well combined.
3. Set a bowl of water on a clean, dry surface or next to a clean, dry cutting board. Set one gyoza or wonton wrapper on that surface. Dip your clean finger in the water and run it around the perimeter of the gyoza wrapper or the edge of the wonton wrapper. Put about 1 ½ teaspoons of the meat mixture in the center of the wrapper.
4. For the gyoza wrapper, fold the wrapper in half to close, pressing the edge to seal, then wet the outside of the edge of both sides of the seam and pleat it into little ridges to seal.
5. For the wonton wrapper, fold it in half lengthwise to make a rectangle, then seal the sides together, flattening the packet a bit as you do.
6. Set the filled wrapper aside and continue making more in the same way. When done, generously coat them on all sides with vegetable oil spray.
7. Place the gyoza in the basket in one layer and air-fry undisturbed for 6 minutes, or until browned and crisp at the edges.
8. Use kitchen tongs or a nonstick-safe spatula to gently transfer the gyoza to a wire rack. Cool for only 2 or 3 minutes before serving hot.

Cherry Chipotle Bbq Chicken Wings

Servings: 2
Cooking Time: 12 Minutes

Ingredients:

- 1 teaspoon smoked paprika
- ½ teaspoon dry mustard powder
- 1 teaspoon dried oregano
- 1 teaspoon dried thyme
- ½ teaspoon chili powder
- 1 teaspoon salt
- 2 pounds chicken wings
- vegetable oil or spray
- salt and freshly ground black pepper
- 1 to 2 tablespoons chopped chipotle peppers in adobo sauce
- ⅓ cup cherry preserves ¼ cup tomato ketchup

Directions:

1. Combine the first six ingredients in a large bowl. Prepare the chicken wings by cutting off the wing tips and discarding (or freezing for chicken stock). Divide the drumettes from the win-gettes by cutting through the joint. Place the chicken wing pieces in the bowl with the spice mix. Toss or shake well to coat.
2. Preheat the air fryer to 400°F.
3. Spray the wings lightly with the vegetable oil and air-fry the wings in two batches for 10 minutes per batch, shaking the basket halfway through the cooking process. When both batches are done, toss all the wings back into the basket for another 2 minutes to heat through and finish cooking.
4. While the wings are air-frying, combine the chopped chipotle peppers, cherry preserves and ketchup in a bowl.
5. Remove the wings from the air fryer, toss them in the cherry chipotle BBQ sauce and serve with napkins!

Veggie Cheese Bites

Servings: 4

Cooking Time: 8 Minutes

Ingredients:

- 2 cups riced vegetables (see the Note below)
- ½ cup shredded zucchini
- ½ teaspoon garlic powder
- ¼ teaspoon black pepper
- ¼ teaspoon salt
- 1 large egg
- ¾ cup shredded cheddar cheese
- ⅓ cup whole-wheat flour

Directions:

1. Preheat the air fryer to 350°F.
2. In a large bowl, mix together the riced vegetables, zucchini, garlic powder, pepper, and salt. Mix in the egg. Stir in the shredded cheese and whole-wheat flour until a thick, doughlike consistency forms. If you need to, add 1 teaspoon of flour at a time so you can mold the batter into balls.
3. Using a 1-inch scoop, portion the batter out into about 12 balls.
4. Liberally spray the air fryer basket with olive oil spray. Then place the veggie bites inside. Leave enough room between each bite so the air can flow around them.
5. Cook for 8 minutes, or until the outside is slightly browned. Depending on the size of your air fryer, you may need to cook these in batches.
6. Remove and let cool slightly before serving.

Fried Bananas

Servings: 4

Cooking Time: 8 Minutes

Ingredients:

- ½ cup panko breadcrumbs
- ½ cup sweetened coconut flakes
- ¼ cup sliced almonds
- ½ cup cornstarch
- 2 egg whites
- 1 tablespoon water
- 2 firm bananas
- oil for misting or cooking spray

Directions:

1. In food processor, combine panko, coconut, and almonds. Process to make small crumbs.
2. Place cornstarch in a shallow dish. In another shallow dish, beat together the egg whites and water until slightly foamy.
3. Preheat air fryer to 390°F.
4. Cut bananas in half crosswise. Cut each half in quarters lengthwise so you have 16 "sticks."
5. Dip banana sticks in cornstarch and tap to shake off excess. Then dip bananas in egg wash and roll in crumb mixture. Spray with oil.
6. Place bananas in air fryer basket in single layer and cook for 4minutes. If any spots have not browned, spritz with oil. Cook for 4 more minutes, until golden brown and crispy.
7. Repeat step 6 to cook remaining bananas.

Eggplant Fries

Servings: 4

Cooking Time: 8 Minutes

Ingredients:

- 1 medium eggplant
- 1 teaspoon ground coriander
- 1 teaspoon cumin
- 1 teaspoon garlic powder
- ½ teaspoon salt
- 1 cup crushed panko breadcrumbs
- 1 large egg
- 2 tablespoons water
- oil for misting or cooking spray

Directions:

1. Peel and cut the eggplant into fat fries, ⅜- to ½-inch thick.
2. Preheat air fryer to 390°F.
3. In a small cup, mix together the coriander, cumin, garlic, and salt.
4. Combine 1 teaspoon of the seasoning mix and panko crumbs in a shallow dish.
5. Place eggplant fries in a large bowl, sprinkle with remaining seasoning, and stir well to combine.

6. Beat eggs and water together and pour over eggplant fries. Stir to coat.
7. Remove eggplant from egg wash, shaking off excess, and roll in panko crumbs.
8. Spray with oil.
9. Place half of the fries in air fryer basket. You should have only a single layer, but it's fine if they overlap a little.
10. Cook for 5minutes. Shake basket, mist lightly with oil, and cook 3 minutes longer, until browned and crispy.
11. Repeat step 10 to cook remaining eggplant.

Grilled Cheese Sandwich Deluxe

Servings: 4
Cooking Time: 6 Minutes

Ingredients:

- 8 ounces Brie
- 8 slices oat nut bread
- 1 large ripe pear, cored and cut into ½-inch-thick slices
- 2 tablespoons butter, melted

Directions:

1. Spread a quarter of the Brie on each of four slices of bread.
2. Top Brie with thick slices of pear, then the remaining 4 slices of bread.
3. Lightly brush both sides of each sandwich with melted butter.
4. Cooking 2 at a time, place sandwiches in air fryer basket and cook at 360°F for 6minutes or until cheese melts and outside looks golden brown.

Zucchini Fritters

Servings: 8
Cooking Time: 10 Minutes

Ingredients:

- 2 cups grated zucchini
- ½ teaspoon sea salt
- 1 egg
- ½ teaspoon garlic powder
- ¼ teaspoon onion powder
- ¼ cup grated Parmesan cheese
- ½ cup all-purpose flour
- ¼ teaspoon baking powder
- ½ cup Greek yogurt or sour cream
- ½ lime, juiced
- ¼ cup chopped cilantro
- ¼ teaspoon ground cumin
- ¼ teaspoon salt

Directions:

1. Preheat the air fryer to 360°F.
2. In a large colander, place a kitchen towel. Inside the towel, place the grated zucchini and sprinkle the sea salt over the top. Let the zucchini sit for 5 minutes; then, using the towel, squeeze dry the zucchini.
3. In a medium bowl, mix together the egg, garlic powder, onion powder, Parmesan cheese, flour, and baking powder. Add in the grated zucchini, and stir until completely combined.
4. Pierce a piece of parchment paper with a fork 4 to 6 times. Place the parchment paper into the air fryer basket. Using a tablespoon, place 6 to 8 heaping tablespoons of fritter batter onto the parchment paper. Spray the fritters with cooking spray and cook for 5 minutes, turn the fritters over, and cook another 5 minutes.
5. Meanwhile, while the fritters are cooking, make the sauce. In a small bowl, whisk together the Greek yogurt or sour cream, lime juice, cilantro, cumin, and salt.
6. Repeat Steps 2–4 with the remaining batter.

Grilled Ham & Muenster Cheese On Raisin Bread

Servings: 1
Cooking Time: 10 Minutes

Ingredients:

- 2 slices raisin bread
- 2 tablespoons butter, softened
- 2 teaspoons honey mustard
- 3 slices thinly sliced honey ham (about 3 ounces)
- 4 slices Muenster cheese (about 3 ounces)
- 2 toothpicks

Directions:

1. Preheat the air fryer to 370°F.
2. Spread the softened butter on one side of both slices of raisin bread and place the bread, buttered side down

on the counter. Spread the honey mustard on the other side of each slice of bread. Layer 2 slices of cheese, the ham and the remaining 2 slices of cheese on one slice of bread and top with the other slice of bread. Remember to leave the buttered side of the bread on the outside.

3. Transfer the sandwich to the air fryer basket and secure the sandwich with toothpicks.

4. Air-fry at 370°F for 5 minutes. Flip the sandwich over, remove the toothpicks and air-fry for another 5 minutes. Cut the sandwich in half and enjoy!!

Sweet Potato Chips

Servings: 4

Cooking Time: 10 Minutes

Ingredients:

- 2 medium sweet potatoes, washed
- 2 cups filtered water
- 1 tablespoon avocado oil
- 2 teaspoons brown sugar
- ½ teaspoon salt

Directions:

1. Using a mandolin, slice the potatoes into ⅛-inch pieces.
2. Add the water to a large bowl. Place the potatoes in the bowl, and soak for at least 30 minutes.
3. Preheat the air fryer to 350°F.
4. Drain the water and pat the chips dry with a paper towel or kitchen cloth. Toss the chips with the avocado oil, brown sugar, and salt. Liberally spray the air fryer basket with olive oil mist.
5. Set the chips inside the air fryer, separating them so they're not on top of each other. Cook for 5 minutes, shake the basket, and cook another 5 minutes, or until browned.
6. Remove and let cool a few minutes prior to serving. Repeat until all the chips are cooked.

Sweet Plantain Chips

Servings: 4

Cooking Time: 11 Minutes

Ingredients:

- 2 Very ripe plantain(s), peeled and sliced into 1-inch pieces
- Vegetable oil spray
- 3 tablespoons Maple syrup
- For garnishing Coarse sea salt or kosher salt

Directions:

1. Pour about ½ cup water into the bottom of your air fryer basket or into a metal tray on a lower rack in some models. Preheat the air fryer to 400°F.
2. Put the plantain pieces in a bowl, coat them with vegetable oil spray, and toss gently, spraying at least one more time and tossing repeatedly, until the pieces are well coated.
3. When the machine is at temperature, arrange the plantain pieces in the basket in one layer. Air-fry undisturbed for 5 minutes.
4. Remove the basket from the machine and spray the back of a metal spatula with vegetable oil spray. Use the spatula to press down on the plantain pieces, spraying it again as needed, to flatten the pieces to about half their original height. Brush the plantain pieces with maple syrup, then return the basket to the machine and continue air-frying undisturbed for 6 minutes, or until the plantain pieces are soft and caramelized.
5. Use kitchen tongs to transfer the pieces to a serving platter. Sprinkle the pieces with salt and cool for a couple of minutes before serving. Or cool to room temperature before serving, about 1 hour.

Cheese Arancini

Servings: 8

Cooking Time: 12 Minutes

Ingredients:

- 1 cup Water
- ½ cup Raw white Arborio rice
- 1½ teaspoons Butter
- ¼ teaspoon Table salt
- 8 ¾-inch semi-firm mozzarella cubes (not fresh mozzarella)
- 2 Large egg(s), well beaten
- 1 cup Seasoned Italian-style dried bread crumbs (gluten-free, if a concern)

- Olive oil spray

Directions:

1. Combine the water, rice, butter, and salt in a small saucepan. Bring to a boil over medium-high heat, stirring occasionally. Cover, reduce the heat to very low, and simmer very slowly for 20 minutes.
2. Take the saucepan off the heat and let it stand, covered, for 10 minutes. Uncover it and fluff the rice. Cool for 20 minutes. (The rice can be made up to 1 hour in advance; keep it covered in its saucepan.)
3. Preheat the air fryer to 375°F .
4. Set up and fill two shallow soup plates or small bowls on your counter: one with the beaten egg(s) and one with the bread crumbs.
5. With clean but wet hands, scoop up about 2 tablespoons of the cooked rice and form it into a ball. Push a cube of mozzarella into the middle of the ball and seal the cheese inside. Dip the ball in the egg(s) to coat completely, letting any excess egg slip back into the rest. Roll the ball in the bread crumbs to coat evenly but lightly. Set aside and continue making more rice balls.
6. Generously spray the balls with olive oil spray, then set them in the basket in one layer. They must not touch. Air-fry undisturbed for 10 minutes, or until crunchy and golden brown. If the machine is at 360°F, you may need to add 2 minutes to the cooking time.
7. Use a nonstick-safe spatula, and maybe a flatware spoon for balance, to gently transfer the balls to a wire rack. Cool for at least 5 minutes or up to 20 minutes before serving.

Sweet Apple Fries

Servings: 3

Cooking Time: 8 Minutes

Ingredients:

- 2 Medium-size sweet apple(s), such as Gala or Fuji
- 1 Large egg white(s)
- 2 tablespoons Water
- 1½ cups Finely ground gingersnap crumbs (gluten-free, if a concern)
- Vegetable oil spray

Directions:

1. Preheat the air fryer to 375°F .
2. Peel and core an apple, then cut it into 12 slices (see the headnote for more information). Repeat with more apples as necessary.
3. Whisk the egg white(s) and water in a medium bowl until foamy. Add the apple slices and toss well to coat.
4. Spread the gingersnap crumbs across a dinner plate. Using clean hands, pick up an apple slice, let any excess egg white mixture slip back into the rest, and dredge the slice in the crumbs, coating it lightly but evenly on all sides. Set it aside and continue coating the remaining apple slices.
5. Lightly coat the slices on all sides with vegetable oil spray, then set them curved side down in the basket in one layer. Air-fry undisturbed for 6 minutes, or until browned and crisp. You may need to air-fry the slices for 2 minutes longer if the temperature is at 360°F.
6. Use kitchen tongs to transfer the slices to a wire rack. Cool for 2 to 3 minutes before serving.

Buffalo Cauliflower

Servings: 6

Cooking Time: 12 Minutes

Ingredients:

- 1 large head of cauliflower, washed and cut into medium-size florets
- ½ cup all-purpose flour
- ¼ cup melted butter
- 3 tablespoons hot sauce
- ½ teaspoon garlic powder
- ½ cup blue cheese dip or ranch dressing (optional)

Directions:

1. Preheat the air fryer to 350°F.
2. Make sure the cauliflower florets are dry, and then coat them in flour.
3. Liberally spray the air fryer basket with an olive oil mist. Place the cauliflower into the basket, making sure not to stack them on top of each other. Depending on the size of your air fryer, you may need to do this in two batches.
4. Cook for 6 minutes, then shake the basket, and cook another 6 minutes.

5. While cooking, mix the melted butter, hot sauce, and garlic powder in a large bowl.
6. Carefully remove the cauliflower from the air fryer. Toss the cauliflower into the butter mixture to coat. Repeat Steps 2–4 for any leftover cauliflower. Serve warm with the dip of your choice.

Crispy Wontons

Servings: 8
Cooking Time: 10 Minutes

Ingredients:

- ½ cup refried beans
- 3 tablespoons salsa
- ¼ cup canned artichoke hearts, drained and patted dry
- ¼ cup frozen spinach, defrosted and squeezed dry
- 2 ounces cream cheese
- 1½ teaspoons dried oregano, divided
- ¼ teaspoon garlic powder
- ¼ teaspoon onion powder
- ½ teaspoon salt
- ¼ cup chopped pepperoni
- ¼ cup grated mozzarella cheese
- 1 tablespoon grated Parmesan
- 2 ounces cream cheese
- ½ teaspoon dried oregano
- 32 wontons
- 1 cup water

Directions:

1. Preheat the air fryer to 370°F.
2. In a medium bowl, mix together the refried beans and salsa.
3. In a second medium bowl, mix together the artichoke hearts, spinach, cream cheese, oregano, garlic powder, onion powder, and salt.
4. In a third medium bowl, mix together the pepperoni, mozzarella cheese, Parmesan cheese, cream cheese, and the remaining ½ teaspoon of oregano.
5. Get a towel lightly damp with water and ring it out. While working with the wontons, leave the unfilled wontons under the damp towel so they don't dry out.
6. Working with 8 wontons at a time, place 2 teaspoons of one of the fillings into the center of the wonton, rotating among the different fillings (one filling per wonton). Working one at a time, use a pastry brush, dip the pastry brush into the water, and brush the edges of the dough with the water. Fold the dough in half to form a triangle and set aside. Continue until 8 wontons are formed. Spray the wontons with cooking spray and cover with a dry towel. Repeat until all 32 wontons have been filled.
7. Place the wontons into the air fryer basket, leaving space between the wontons, and cook for 5 minutes. Turn over and check for brownness, and then cook for another 5 minutes.

Stuffed Baby Bella Caps

Servings: 16
Cooking Time: 12 Minutes

Ingredients:

- 16 fresh, small Baby Bella mushrooms
- 2 green onions
- 4 ounces mozzarella cheese
- ½ cup diced ham
- 2 tablespoons breadcrumbs
- ½ teaspoon garlic powder
- ¼ teaspoon ground oregano
- ¼ teaspoon ground black pepper
- 1 to 2 teaspoons olive oil

Directions:

1. Remove stems and wash mushroom caps.
2. Cut green onions and cheese in small pieces and place in food processor.
3. Add ham, breadcrumbs, garlic powder, oregano, and pepper and mince ingredients.
4. With food processor running, dribble in just enough olive oil to make a thick paste.
5. Divide stuffing among mushroom caps and pack down lightly.
6. Place stuffed mushrooms in air fryer basket in single layer and cook at 390°F for 12minutes or until tops are golden brown and mushrooms are tender.
7. Repeat step 6 to cook remaining mushrooms.

Savory Sausage Balls

Servings: 10

Cooking Time: 8 Minutes

Ingredients:

- 2 cups all-purpose flour
- 1 tablespoon baking powder
- ½ teaspoon garlic powder
- ¼ teaspoon onion powder
- ½ teaspoon salt
- 3 tablespoons milk
- 2½ cups grated pepper jack cheese
- 1 pound fresh sausage, casing removed

Directions:

1. Preheat the air fryer to 370°F.
2. In a large bowl, whisk together the flour, baking powder, garlic powder, onion powder, and salt. Add in the milk, grated cheese, and sausage.
3. Using a tablespoon, scoop out the sausage and roll it between your hands to form a rounded ball. You should end up with approximately 32 balls. Place them in the air fryer basket in a single layer and working in batches as necessary.
4. Cook for 8 minutes, or until the outer coating turns light brown.
5. Carefully remove, repeating with the remaining sausage balls.

Pita Chips

Servings: 4

Cooking Time: 10 Minutes

Ingredients:

- 2 rounds Pocketless pita bread
- Olive oil spray or any flavor spray you prefer, even coconut oil spray
- Up to 1 teaspoon Fine sea salt, garlic salt, onion salt, or other flavored salt

Directions:

1. Preheat the air fryer to 400°F.
2. Lightly coat the pita round(s) on both sides with olive oil spray, then lightly sprinkle each side with salt.
3. Cut each coated pita round into 8 even wedges. Lay these in the basket in as close to a single even layer as possible. Many will overlap or even be on top of each other, depending on the exact size of your machine.
4. Air-fry for 6 minutes, shaking the basket and rearranging the wedges at the 4-minute marks, until the wedges are crisp and brown. Turn them out onto a wire rack to cool a few minutes or to room temperature before digging in.

Vegetable Spring Rolls

Servings: 6

Cooking Time: 8 Minutes

Ingredients:

- ¾ cup (a little more than 2½ ounces) Fresh bean sprouts
- 6 tablespoons Shredded carrots
- 6 tablespoons Slivered, drained, sliced canned bamboo shoots
- 1½ tablespoons Regular or low-sodium soy sauce or gluten-free tamari sauce
- 1½ teaspoons Granulated white sugar
- 1½ teaspoons Toasted sesame oil
- 6 Spring roll wrappers (gluten-free, if a concern)
- 1 Large egg, well beaten
- Vegetable oil spray

Directions:

1. Gently stir the bean sprouts, carrots, bamboo shoots, soy or tamari sauce, sugar, and oil in a large bowl until the vegetables are evenly coated. Set aside at room temperature for 10 to 15 minutes.
2. Preheat the air fryer to 400°F.
3. Set a spring roll wrapper on a clean, dry work surface. Pick up about ¼ cup of the vegetable mixture and gently squeeze it in your clean hand to release most of the liquid. Set this bundle of vegetables along one edge of the wrapper.
4. Fold two opposing sides (at right angles to the filling) up and over the filling, concealing part of it and making a folded-over border down two sides of the wrapper. Brush the top half of the wrapper (including the folded parts) with beaten egg so it will seal when you roll it closed.

5. Starting with the side nearest the filling, roll the wrapper closed, working to make a tight fit, eliminating as much air as possible from inside the wrapper. Set it aside seam side down and continue making more filled rolls using the same techniques.
6. Lightly coat all the sealed rolls with vegetable oil spray on all sides. Set them seam side down in the basket and air-fry undisturbed for 8 minutes, or until golden brown and very crisp.
7. Use a nonstick-safe spatula and a flatware fork for balance to transfer the rolls to a wire rack. Cool for at least 5 minutes or up to 15 minutes before serving.

Turkey Burger Sliders

Servings: 8
Cooking Time: 7 Minutes

Ingredients:

- 1 pound ground turkey
- ¼ teaspoon curry powder
- 1 teaspoon Hoisin sauce
- ½ teaspoon salt
- 8 slider buns
- ½ cup slivered red onions
- ½ cup slivered green or red bell pepper
- ½ cup fresh chopped pineapple (or pineapple tidbits from kids' fruit cups, drained)
- light cream cheese, softened

Directions:

1. Combine turkey, curry powder, Hoisin sauce, and salt and mix together well.
2. Shape turkey mixture into 8 small patties.
3. Place patties in air fryer basket and cook at 360°F for 7minutes, until patties are well done and juices run clear.
4. Place each patty on the bottom half of a slider bun and top with onions, peppers, and pineapple. Spread the remaining bun halves with cream cheese to taste, place on top, and serve.

Granola Three Ways

Servings: 4
Cooking Time: 10 Minutes

Ingredients:

- Nantucket Granola
- ¼ cup maple syrup
- ¼ cup dark brown sugar
- 1 tablespoon butter
- 1 teaspoon vanilla extract
- 1 cup rolled oats
- ½ cup dried cranberries
- ½ cup walnuts, chopped
- ¼ cup pumpkin seeds
- ¼ cup shredded coconut
- Blueberry Delight
- ¼ cup honey
- ¼ cup light brown sugar
- 1 tablespoon butter
- 1 teaspoon lemon extract
- 1 cup rolled oats
- ½ cup sliced almonds
- ½ cup dried blueberries
- ¼ cup pumpkin seeds
- ¼ cup sunflower seeds
- Cherry Black Forest Mix
- ¼ cup honey
- ¼ cup light brown sugar
- 1 tablespoon butter
- 1 teaspoon almond extract
- 1 cup rolled oats
- ½ cup sliced almonds
- ½ cup dried cherries
- ¼ cup shredded coconut
- ¼ cup dark chocolate chips
- oil for misting or cooking spray

Directions:

1. Combine the syrup or honey, brown sugar, and butter in a small saucepan or microwave-safe bowl. Heat and stir just until butter melts and sugar dissolves. Stir in the extract.
2. Place all other dry ingredients in a large bowl. (For the Cherry Black Forest Mix, don't add the chocolate chips yet.)
3. Pour melted butter mixture over dry ingredients and stir until oat mixture is well coated.
4. Lightly spray a baking pan with oil or cooking spray.

5. Pour granola into pan and cook at 390°F for 5minutes. Stir. Continue cooking for 5minutes, stirring every minute or two, until golden brown. Watch closely. Once the mixture begins to brown, it will cook quickly.
6. Remove granola from pan and spread on wax paper. It will become crispier as it cools.
7. For the Cherry Black Forest Mix, stir in chocolate chips after granola has cooled completely.
8. Store in an airtight container.

Corn Dog Bites

Servings: 3
Cooking Time: 12 Minutes

Ingredients:

- 3 cups Purchased cornbread stuffing mix
- ⅓ cup All-purpose flour
- 2 Large egg(s), well beaten
- 3 Hot dogs, cut into 2-inch pieces (vegetarian hot dogs, if preferred)
- Vegetable oil spray

Directions:

1. Preheat the air fryer to 375°F .
2. Put the cornbread stuffing mix in a food processor. Cover and pulse to grind into a mixture like fine bread crumbs.
3. Set up and fill three shallow soup plates or small pie plates on your counter: one for the flour, one for the egg(s), and one for the stuffing mix crumbs.
4. Dip a hot dog piece in the flour to coat it completely, then gently shake off any excess. Dip the hot dog piece into the egg(s) and gently roll it around to coat all surfaces, then pick it up and allow any excess egg to slip back into the rest. Set the hot dog piece in the stuffing mix crumbs and roll it gently to coat it evenly and well on all sides, even the ends. Set it aside on a cutting board and continue dipping and coating the remaining hot dog pieces.
5. Give the coated hot dog pieces a generous coating of vegetable oil spray on all sides, then set them in the basket in one layer with some space between them. Air-fry undisturbed for 10 minutes, or until golden brown and crunchy. (You'll need to add 2 minutes in the air fryer if the temperature is at 360°F.)
6. Use a nonstick-safe spatula, and perhaps a flatware fork for balance, to transfer the corn dog bites to a wire rack. Cool for 5 minutes before serving.

Mozzarella En Carrozza With Puttanesca Sauce

Servings: 6
Cooking Time: 8 Minutes

Ingredients:

- Puttanesca Sauce
- 2 teaspoons olive oil
- 1 anchovy, chopped (optional)
- 2 cloves garlic, minced
- 1 (14-ounce) can petite diced tomatoes
- ½ cup chicken stock or water
- ⅓ cup Kalamata olives, chopped
- 2 tablespoons capers
- ½ teaspoon dried oregano
- ¼ teaspoon crushed red pepper flakes
- salt and freshly ground black pepper
- 1 tablespoon fresh parsley, chopped
- 8 slices of thinly sliced white bread (Pepperidge Farm®)
- 8 ounces mozzarella cheese, cut into ¼-inch slices
- ½ cup all-purpose flour
- 3 eggs, beaten
- 1½ cups seasoned panko breadcrumbs
- ½ teaspoon garlic powder
- ½ teaspoon salt
- freshly ground black pepper
- olive oil, in a spray bottle

Directions:

1. Start by making the puttanesca sauce. Heat the olive oil in a medium saucepan on the stovetop. Add the anchovies (if using, and I really think you should!) and garlic and sauté for 3 minutes, or until the anchovies have "melted" into the oil. Add the tomatoes, chicken stock, olives, capers, oregano and crushed red pepper flakes and simmer the sauce for 20 minutes. Season with

salt and freshly ground black pepper and stir in the fresh parsley.

2. Cut the crusts off the slices of bread. Place four slices of the bread on a cutting board. Divide the cheese between the four slices of bread. Top the cheese with the remaining four slices of bread to make little sandwiches and cut each sandwich into 4 triangles.

3. Set up a dredging station using three shallow dishes. Place the flour in the first shallow dish, the eggs in the second dish and in the third dish, combine the panko breadcrumbs, garlic powder, salt and black pepper. Dredge each little triangle in the flour first (you might think this is redundant, but it helps to get the coating to adhere to the edges of the sandwiches) and then dip them into the egg, making sure both the sides and the edges are coated. Let the excess egg drip off and then press the triangles into the breadcrumb mixture, pressing the crumbs on with your hands so they adhere. Place the coated triangles in the freezer for 2 hours, until the cheese is frozen.

4. Preheat the air fryer to 390°F. Spray all sides of the mozzarella triangles with oil and transfer a single layer of triangles to the air fryer basket. Air-fry in batches at 390°F for 5 minutes. Turn the triangles over and air-fry for an additional 3 minutes.

5. Serve mozzarella triangles immediately with the warm puttanesca sauce.

Country Wings

Servings: 4

Cooking Time: 19 Minutes

Ingredients:

- 2 pounds chicken wings
- Marinade
- 1 cup buttermilk
- ½ teaspoon black pepper
- ½ teaspoon salt
- Coating
- 1 cup flour
- 1 cup panko breadcrumbs
- 2 teaspoons salt
- 2 tablespoons poultry seasoning
- oil for misting or cooking spray

Directions:

1. Cut the tips off the wings. Discard or freeze for stock. Cut remaining wing sections apart at the joint to make 2 pieces per wing. Place wings in a large bowl or plastic bag.

2. Mix together all marinade ingredients and pour over wings. Refrigerate for at least 1 hour but for no more than 8 hours.

3. Preheat air fryer to 360°F.

4. Mix all coating ingredients together in a shallow dish or on wax paper.

5. Remove wings from marinade, shaking off excess, and roll in coating mixture.

6. Spray both sides of each wing with oil or cooking spray.

7. Place wings in air fryer basket in single layer, close but not too crowded. Cook for 19minutes or until chicken is done and juices run clear.

8. Repeat step 7 to cook remaining wings.

Classic Potato Chips

Servings: 4

Cooking Time: 8 Minutes

Ingredients:

- 2 medium russet potatoes, washed
- 2 cups filtered water
- 1 tablespoon avocado oil
- ½ teaspoon salt

Directions:

1. Using a mandolin, slice the potatoes into ⅛-inch-thick pieces.

2. Pour the water into a large bowl. Place the potatoes in the bowl and soak for at least 30 minutes.

3. Preheat the air fryer to 350°F.

4. Drain the water and pat the potatoes dry with a paper towel or kitchen cloth. Toss with avocado oil and salt. Liberally spray the air fryer basket with olive oil mist.

5. Set the potatoes inside the air fryer basket, separating them so they're not on top of each other. Cook for 5 minutes, shake the basket, and cook another 5 minutes, or until browned.

6. Remove and let cool a few minutes prior to serving. Repeat until all the chips are cooked.

Spinach Cups

Servings: 30
Cooking Time: 5 Minutes

Ingredients:

- 1 6-ounce can crabmeat, drained to yield ⅓ cup meat
- ¼ cup frozen spinach, thawed, drained, and chopped
- 1 clove garlic, minced
- ½ cup grated Parmesan cheese
- 3 tablespoons plain yogurt
- ¼ teaspoon lemon juice
- ½ teaspoon Worcestershire sauce
- 30 mini phyllo shells (2 boxes of 15 each), thawed
- cooking spray

Directions:

1. Remove any bits of shell that might remain in the crabmeat.
2. Mix crabmeat, spinach, garlic, and cheese together.
3. Stir in the yogurt, lemon juice, and Worcestershire sauce and mix well.
4. Spoon a teaspoon of filling into each phyllo shell.
5. Spray air fryer basket and arrange half the shells in the basket.
6. Cook at 390°F for 5minutes.
7. Repeat with remaining shells.

Asian Five-spice Wings

Servings: 4
Cooking Time: 15 Minutes

Ingredients:

- 2 pounds chicken wings
- ½ cup Asian-style salad dressing
- 2 tablespoons Chinese five-spice powder

Directions:

1. Cut off wing tips and discard or freeze for stock. Cut remaining wing pieces in two at the joint.
2. Place wing pieces in a large sealable plastic bag. Pour in the Asian dressing, seal bag, and massage the marinade into the wings until well coated. Refrigerate for at least an hour.
3. Remove wings from bag, drain off excess marinade, and place wings in air fryer basket.
4. Cook at 360°F for 15minutes or until juices run clear. About halfway through cooking time, shake the basket or stir wings for more even cooking.
5. Transfer cooked wings to plate in a single layer. Sprinkle half of the Chinese five-spice powder on the wings, turn, and sprinkle other side with remaining seasoning.

Cauliflower "tater" Tots

Servings: 6
Cooking Time: 10 Minutes

Ingredients:

- 1 head of cauliflower
- 2 eggs
- ¼ cup all-purpose flour*
- ½ cup grated Parmesan cheese
- 1 teaspoon salt
- freshly ground black pepper
- vegetable or olive oil, in a spray bottle

Directions:

1. Grate the head of cauliflower with a box grater or finely chop it in a food processor. You should have about 3½ cups. Place the chopped cauliflower in the center of a clean kitchen towel and twist the towel tightly to squeeze all the water out of the cauliflower. (This can be done in two batches to make it easier to drain all the water from the cauliflower.)
2. Place the squeezed cauliflower in a large bowl. Add the eggs, flour, Parmesan cheese, salt and freshly ground black pepper. Shape the cauliflower into small cylinders or "tater tot" shapes, rolling roughly one tablespoon of the mixture at a time. Place the tots on a cookie sheet lined with paper towel to absorb any residual moisture. Spray the cauliflower tots all over with oil.
3. Preheat the air fryer to 400°F.
4. Air-fry the tots at 400°F, one layer at a time for 10 minutes, turning them over for the last few minutes of the cooking process for even browning. Season with salt and black pepper. Serve hot with your favorite dipping sauce.

Fried Green Tomatoes

Servings: 4
Cooking Time: 15 Minutes

Ingredients:

- 2 eggs
- ¼ cup buttermilk
- ½ cup cornmeal
- ½ cup breadcrumbs
- ¼ teaspoon salt
- 1½ pounds firm green tomatoes, cut in ¼-inch slices
- oil for misting or cooking spray
- Horseradish Drizzle
- ¼ cup mayonnaise
- ¼ cup sour cream
- 2 teaspoons prepared horseradish
- ½ teaspoon Worcestershire sauce
- ½ teaspoon lemon juice
- ⅛ teaspoon black pepper

Directions:

1. Mix all ingredients for Horseradish Drizzle together and chill while you prepare the green tomatoes.
2. Preheat air fryer to 390°F.
3. Beat the eggs and buttermilk together in a shallow bowl.
4. Mix cornmeal, breadcrumbs, and salt together in a plate or shallow dish.
5. Dip 4 tomato slices in the egg mixture, then roll in the breadcrumb mixture.
6. Mist one side with oil and place in air fryer basket, oil-side down, in a single layer.
7. Mist the top with oil.
8. Cook for 15minutes, turning once, until brown and crispy.
9. Repeat steps 5 through 8 to cook remaining tomatoes.
10. Drizzle horseradish sauce over tomatoes just before serving.

Garlic Breadsticks

Servings: 12
Cooking Time: 7 Minutes

Ingredients:

- 1½ tablespoons Olive oil
- 1½ teaspoons Minced garlic
- ¼ teaspoon Table salt
- ¼ teaspoon Ground black pepper
- 6 ounces Purchased pizza dough (vegan dough, if that's a concern)

Directions:

1. Preheat the air fryer to 400°F. Mix the oil, garlic, salt, and pepper in a small bowl.
2. Divide the pizza dough into 4 balls for a small air fryer, 6 for a medium machine, or 8 for a large, each ball about the size of a walnut in its shell. (Each should weigh 1 ounce, if you want to drag out a scale and get obsessive.) Roll each ball into a 5-inch-long stick under your clean palms on a clean, dry work surface. Brush the sticks with the oil mixture.
3. When the machine is at temperature, place the prepared dough sticks in the basket, leaving a 1-inch space between them. Air-fry undisturbed for 7 minutes, or until puffed, golden, and set to the touch.
4. Use kitchen tongs to gently transfer the breadsticks to a wire rack and repeat step 3 with the remaining dough sticks.

Sweet-and-salty Pretzels

Servings: 4
Cooking Time: 5 Minutes

Ingredients:

- 2 cups Plain pretzel nuggets
- 1 tablespoon Worcestershire sauce
- 2 teaspoons Granulated white sugar
- 1 teaspoon Mild smoked paprika
- ½ teaspoon Garlic or onion powder

Directions:

1. Preheat the air fryer to 350°F .
2. Put the pretzel nuggets, Worcestershire sauce, sugar, smoked paprika, and garlic or onion powder in a large bowl. Toss gently until the nuggets are well coated.
3. When the machine is at temperature, pour the nuggets into the basket, spreading them into as close to a single layer as possible. Air-fry, shaking the basket three or four times to rearrange the nuggets, for 5 minutes, or

until the nuggets are toasted and aromatic. Although the coating will darken, don't let it burn, especially if the machine's temperature is 360°F.

4. Pour the nuggets onto a wire rack and gently spread them into one layer. (A rubber spatula does a good job.) Cool for 5 minutes before serving.

Fried Wontons

Servings: 24

Cooking Time: 6 Minutes

Ingredients:

- 6 ounces Lean ground beef, pork, or turkey
- 1 tablespoon Regular or reduced-sodium soy sauce or tamari sauce
- 1½ teaspoons Minced garlic
- ¾ teaspoon Ground dried ginger
- ½ teaspoon Ground white pepper
- 24 Wonton wrappers (thawed, if necessary)
- Vegetable oil spray

Directions:

1. Preheat the air fryer to 350°F .
2. Stir the ground meat, soy or tamari sauce, garlic, ginger, and white pepper in a bowl until the spices are uniformly distributed in the mixture.
3. Set a small bowl of water on a clean, dry surface or next to a clean, dry cutting board. Set one wonton wrapper on the surface. Dip your clean finger in the water, then run it along the edges of the wrapper. Set 1 teaspoon of the ground meat mixture in the center of the wrapper. Fold it over, corner to corner, to create a filled triangle. Press to seal the edges, then pull the corners on the longest side up and together over the filling to create the classic wonton shape. Press the corners together to seal. Set aside and continue filling and making more filled wontons.
4. Generously coat the filled wontons on all sides with vegetable oil spray. Arrange them in the basket in one layer and air-fry for 6 minutes, shaking the basket gently at the 2- and 4-minute marks to rearrange the wontons (but always making sure they're still in one layer), until golden brown and crisp.
5. Pour the wontons in the basket onto a wire rack or even into a serving bowl. Cool for 2 or 3 minutes (but not much longer) and serve hot.

"fried" Pickles With Homemade Ranch

Servings: 8

Cooking Time: 8 Minutes

Ingredients:

- 1 cup all-purpose flour
- 2 teaspoons dried dill
- ½ teaspoon paprika
- ¾ cup buttermilk
- 1 egg
- 4 large kosher dill pickles, sliced ¼-inch thick
- 2 cups panko breadcrumbs

Directions:

1. Preheat the air fryer to 380°F.
2. In a medium bowl, whisk together the flour, dill, paprika, buttermilk, and egg.
3. Dip and coat thick slices of dill pickles into the batter. Next, dredge into the panko breadcrumbs.
4. Place a single layer of breaded pickles into the air fryer basket. Spray the pickles with cooking spray. Cook for 4 minutes, turn over, and cook another 4 minutes. Repeat until all the pickle chips have been cooked.

Smoked Salmon Puffs

Servings: 2

Cooking Time: 8 Minutes

Ingredients:

- Two quarters of one thawed sheet (that is, a half of the sheet; wrap and refreeze the remainder) A 17.25-ounce box frozen puff pastry
- 4 ½-ounce smoked salmon slices
- 2 tablespoons Softened regular or low-fat cream cheese (not fat-free)
- Up to 2 teaspoons Drained and rinsed capers, minced
- Up to 2 teaspoons Minced red onion
- 1 Large egg white

- 1 tablespoon Water

Directions:

1. Preheat the air fryer to 400°F.
2. For a small air fryer, roll the piece of puff pastry into a 6 x 6-inch square on a clean, dry work surface.
3. For a medium or larger air fryer, roll each piece of puff pastry into a 6 x 6-inch square.
4. Set 2 salmon slices on the diagonal, corner to corner, on each rolled-out sheet. Smear the salmon with cream cheese, then sprinkle with capers and red onion. Fold the sheet closed by picking up one corner that does not have an edge of salmon near it and folding the dough across the salmon to its opposite corner. Seal the edges closed by pressing the tines of a flatware fork into them.
5. Whisk the egg white and water in a small bowl until uniform. Brush this mixture over the top(s) of the packet(s).
6. Set the packet(s) in the basket (if you're working with more than one, they cannot touch). Air-fry undisturbed for 8 minutes, or until golden brown and flaky.
7. Use a nonstick-safe spatula to transfer the packet(s) to a wire rack. Cool for 5 minutes before serving.

Potato Samosas

Servings: 12

Cooking Time: 10 Minutes

Ingredients:

- ¾ cup Instant mashed potato flakes
- ¾ cup Boiling water
- ⅓ cup Plain full-fat or low-fat yogurt (not Greek yogurt or fat-free yogurt)
- 1 teaspoon Yellow curry powder, purchased or homemade (see here)
- ½ teaspoon Table salt
- 1½ Purchased refrigerated pie crust(s), from a minimum 14.1-ounce box
- All-purpose flour
- Vegetable oil spray

Directions:

1. Put the potato flakes in a medium bowl and pour the boiling water over them. Stir well to form a mixture like thick mashed potatoes. Cool for 15 minutes.
2. Preheat the air fryer to 400°F.
3. Stir the yogurt, curry powder, and salt into the potato mixture until smooth and uniform.
4. Unwrap and unroll the sheet(s) of pie crust dough onto a clean, dry work surface. Cut out as many 4-inch circles as you can with a big cookie cutter or a giant sturdy water glass, or even by tracing the circle with the rim of a 4-inch plate. Gather up the scraps of dough. Lightly flour your work surface and set the scraps on top. Roll them together into a sheet that matches the thickness of the original crusts and cut more circles until you have the number you need—8 circles for the small batch, 12 for the medium batch, or 16 for the large.
5. Pick up one of the circles and create something like an ice cream cone by folding and sealing the circle together so that it is closed at the bottom and flared open at the top, in a conical shape. Put 1 tablespoon of the potato filling into the open cone, then push the filling into the cone toward the point. Fold the top over the filling and press to seal the dough into a triangular shape with corners, taking care to seal those corners all around. Set aside and continue forming and filling the remainder of the dough circles as directed.
6. Lightly coat the filled dough pockets with vegetable oil spray on all sides. Set them in the basket in one layer and air-fry undisturbed for 10 minutes, or until lightly browned and crisp.
7. Gently turn the contents of the basket out onto a wire rack. Use kitchen tongs to gently set all the samosas seam side up. Cool for 10 minutes before serving.

Avocado Toast With Lemony Shrimp

Servings: 4
Cooking Time: 6 Minutes

Ingredients:

- 6 ounces Raw medium shrimp (30 to 35 per pound), peeled and deveined
- 1½ teaspoons Finely grated lemon zest
- 2 teaspoons Lemon juice
- 1½ teaspoons Minced garlic
- 1½ teaspoons Ground black pepper
- 4 Rye or whole-wheat bread slices (gluten-free, if a concern)
- 2 Ripe Hass avocado(s), halved, pitted, peeled and roughly chopped
- For garnishing Coarse sea salt or kosher salt

Directions:

1. Preheat the air fryer to 400°F.
2. Toss the shrimp, lemon zest, lemon juice, garlic, and pepper in a bowl until the shrimp are evenly coated.
3. When the machine is at temperature, use kitchen tongs to place the shrimp in a single layer in the basket. Air-fry undisturbed for 4 minutes, or until the shrimp are pink and barely firm. Use kitchen tongs to transfer the shrimp to a cutting board.
4. Working in batches, set as many slices of bread as will fit in the basket in one layer. Air-fry undisturbed for 2 minutes, just until warmed through and crisp. The bread will not brown much.
5. Arrange the bread slices on a clean, dry work surface. Divide the avocado bits among them and gently smash the avocado into a coarse paste with the tines of a flatware fork. Top the toasts with the shrimp and sprinkle with salt as a garnish.

Zucchini Chips

Servings: 3
Cooking Time: 17 Minutes

Ingredients:

- 1½ small (about 1½ cups) Zucchini, washed but not peeled, and cut into ¼-inch-thick rounds
- Olive oil spray
- ¼ teaspoon Table salt

Directions:

1. Preheat the air fryer to 375°F .
2. Lay some paper towels on your work surface. Set the zucchini rounds on top, then set more paper towels over the rounds. Press gently to remove some of the moisture. Remove the top layer of paper towels and lightly coat the rounds with olive oil spray on both sides.
3. When the machine is at temperature, set the rounds in the basket, overlapping them a bit as needed. (They'll shrink as they cook.) Air-fry for 15 minutes, tossing and rearranging the rounds at the 5- and 10-minute marks, until browned, soft, yet crisp at the edges. (You'll need to air-fry the rounds 2 minutes more if the temperature is set at 360°F.)
4. Gently pour the contents of the basket onto a wire rack. Cool for at least 10 minutes or up to 2 hours before serving.

Prosciutto Mozzarella Bites

Servings: 8
Cooking Time: 6 Minutes

Ingredients:

- 8 pieces full-fat mozzarella string cheese
- 8 thin slices prosciutto
- 16 basil leaves

Directions:

1. Preheat the air fryer to 360°F.
2. Cut the string cheese in half across the center, not lengthwise. Do the same with the prosciutto.
3. Place a piece of prosciutto onto a clean workspace. Top the prosciutto with a basil leaf and then a piece of string cheese. Roll up the string cheese inside the prosciutto and secure with a wooden toothpick. Repeat with the remaining cheese sticks.
4. Place the prosciutto mozzarella bites into the air fryer basket and cook for 6 minutes, checking for doneness at 4 minutes.

Halloumi Fries

Servings: 3

Cooking Time: 12 Minutes

Ingredients:

- 1½ tablespoons Olive oil
- 1½ teaspoons Minced garlic
- ⅛ teaspoon Dried oregano
- ⅛ teaspoon Dried thyme
- ⅛ teaspoon Table salt
- ⅛ teaspoon Ground black pepper
- ¾ pound Halloumi

Directions:

1. Preheat the air fryer to 400°F.
2. Whisk the oil, garlic, oregano, thyme, salt, and pepper in a medium bowl.
3. Lay the piece of halloumi flat on a cutting board. Slice it widthwise into ½-inch-thick sticks. Cut each stick lengthwise into ½-inch-thick batons.
4. Put these batons into the olive oil mixture. Toss gently but well to coat.
5. Place the batons in the basket in a single layer. Air-fry undisturbed for 12 minutes, or until lightly browned, particularly at the edges.
6. Dump the fries out onto a wire rack. They may need a little coaxing with a nonstick-safe spatula to come free. Cool for a couple of minutes before serving hot.

Asian Rice Logs

Servings: 8

Cooking Time: 5 Minutes

Ingredients:

- 1½ cups cooked jasmine or sushi rice
- ¼ teaspoon salt
- 2 teaspoons five-spice powder
- 2 teaspoons diced shallots
- 1 tablespoon tamari sauce
- 1 egg, beaten
- 1 teaspoon sesame oil
- 2 teaspoons water
- ⅓ cup plain breadcrumbs
- ¾ cup panko breadcrumbs
- 2 tablespoons sesame seeds
- Orange Marmalade Dipping Sauce
- ½ cup all-natural orange marmalade
- 1 tablespoon soy sauce

Directions:

1. Make the rice according to package instructions. While the rice is cooking, make the dipping sauce by combining the marmalade and soy sauce and set aside.
2. Stir together the cooked rice, salt, five-spice powder, shallots, and tamari sauce.
3. Divide rice into 8 equal pieces. With slightly damp hands, mold each piece into a log shape. Chill in freezer for 10 to 15minutes.
4. Mix the egg, sesame oil, and water together in a shallow bowl.
5. Place the plain breadcrumbs on a sheet of wax paper.
6. Mix the panko breadcrumbs with the sesame seeds and place on another sheet of wax paper.
7. Roll the rice logs in plain breadcrumbs, then dip in egg wash, and then dip in the panko and sesame seeds.
8. Cook the logs at 390°F for approximately 5minutes, until golden brown.
9. Cool slightly before serving with Orange Marmalade Dipping Sauce.

Blistered Shishito Peppers

Servings: 3

Cooking Time: 5 Minutes

Ingredients:

- 6 ounces (about 18) Shishito peppers
- Vegetable oil spray
- For garnishing Coarse sea or kosher salt and lemon wedges

Directions:

1. Preheat the air fryer to 400°F.
2. Put the peppers in a bowl and lightly coat them with vegetable oil spray. Toss gently, spray again, and toss until the peppers are glistening but not drenched.
3. Pour the peppers into the basket, spread them into as close to one layer as you can, and air-fry for 5 minutes, tossing and rearranging the peppers at the 2- and 4-minute marks, until the peppers are blistered and even blackened in spots.

4. Pour the peppers into a bowl, add salt to taste, and toss gently. Serve the peppers with lemon wedges to squeeze over them.

Crispy Tofu Bites

Servings: 4
Cooking Time: 20 Minutes

Ingredients:

- 1 pound Extra firm unflavored tofu
- Vegetable oil spray

Directions:

1. Wrap the piece of tofu in a triple layer of paper towels. Place it on a wooden cutting board and set a large pot on top of it to press out excess moisture. Set aside for 10 minutes.
2. Preheat the air fryer to 400°F.
3. Remove the pot and unwrap the tofu. Cut it into 1-inch cubes. Place these in a bowl and coat them generously with vegetable oil spray. Toss gently, then spray generously again before tossing, until all are glistening.
4. Gently pour the tofu pieces into the basket, spread them into as close to one layer as possible, and air-fry for 20 minutes, using kitchen tongs to gently rearrange the pieces at the 7- and 14-minute marks, until light brown and crisp.
5. Gently pour the tofu pieces onto a wire rack. Cool for 5 minutes before serving warm.

Rumaki

Servings: 24
Cooking Time: 12 Minutes

Ingredients:

- 10 ounces raw chicken livers
- 1 can sliced water chestnuts, drained
- ¼ cup low-sodium teriyaki sauce
- 12 slices turkey bacon
- toothpicks

Directions:

1. Cut livers into 1½-inch pieces, trimming out tough veins as you slice.
2. Place livers, water chestnuts, and teriyaki sauce in small container with lid. If needed, add another tablespoon of teriyaki sauce to make sure livers are covered. Refrigerate for 1 hour.
3. When ready to cook, cut bacon slices in half crosswise.
4. Wrap 1 piece of liver and 1 slice of water chestnut in each bacon strip. Secure with toothpick.
5. When you have wrapped half of the livers, place them in the air fryer basket in a single layer.
6. Cook at 390°F for 12 minutes, until liver is done and bacon is crispy.
7. While first batch cooks, wrap the remaining livers. Repeat step 6 to cook your second batch.

Fried Goat Cheese

Servings: 3
Cooking Time: 4 Minutes

Ingredients:

- 7 ounces 1- to 1½-inch-diameter goat cheese log
- 2 Large egg(s)
- 1¾ cups Plain dried bread crumbs (gluten-free, if a concern)
- Vegetable oil spray

Directions:

1. Slice the goat cheese log into ½-inch-thick rounds. Set these flat on a small cutting board, a small baking sheet, or a large plate. Freeze uncovered for 30 minutes.
2. Preheat the air fryer to 400°F.
3. Set up and fill two shallow soup plates or small pie plates on your counter: one in which you whisk the egg(s) until uniform and the other for the bread crumbs.
4. Take the goat cheese rounds out of the freezer. With clean, dry hands, dip one round in the egg(s) to coat it on all sides. Let the excess egg slip back into the rest, then dredge the round in the bread crumbs, turning it to coat all sides, even the edges. Repeat this process—egg, then bread crumbs—for a second coating. Coat both sides of the round and its edges with vegetable oil spray, then set it aside. Continue double-dipping, double-dredging, and spraying the remaining rounds.

5. Place the rounds in one layer in the basket. Air-fry undisturbed for 4 minutes, or until lightly browned and crunchy. Do not overcook. Some of the goat cheese may break through the crust. A few little breaks are fine but stop the cooking before the coating reaches structural failure.

6. Remove the basket from the machine and set aside for 3 minutes. Use a nonstick-safe spatula, and maybe a flatware fork for balance, to transfer the rounds to a wire rack. Cool for 5 minutes more before serving.

Garlic Wings

Servings: 4

Cooking Time: 15 Minutes

Ingredients:

- 2 pounds chicken wings
- oil for misting
- cooking spray
- Marinade
- 1 cup buttermilk
- 2 cloves garlic, mashed flat
- 1 teaspoon Worcestershire sauce
- 1 bay leaf
- Coating
- 1½ cups grated Parmesan cheese
- ¾ cup breadcrumbs
- 1½ tablespoons garlic powder
- ½ teaspoon salt

Directions:

1. Mix all marinade ingredients together.
2. Remove wing tips (the third joint) and discard or freeze for stock. Cut the remaining wings at the joint and toss them into the marinade, stirring to coat well. Refrigerate for at least an hour but no more than 8 hours.
3. When ready to cook, combine all coating ingredients in a shallow dish.
4. Remove wings from marinade, shaking off excess, and roll in coating mixture. Press coating into wings so that it sticks well. Spray wings with oil.
5. Spray air fryer basket with cooking spray. Place wings in basket in single layer, close but not touching.
6. Cook at 360°F for 15minutes or until chicken is done and juices run clear.
7. Repeat previous step to cook remaining wings.

Cheeseburger Slider Pockets

Servings: 4

Cooking Time: 13 Minutes

Ingredients:

- 1 pound extra lean ground beef
- 2 teaspoons steak seasoning
- 2 tablespoons Worcestershire sauce
- 8 ounces Cheddar cheese
- ⅓ cup ketchup
- ¼ cup light mayonnaise
- 1 tablespoon pickle relish
- 1 pound frozen bread dough, defrosted
- 1 egg, beaten
- sesame seeds
- vegetable or olive oil, in a spray bottle

Directions:

1. Combine the ground beef, steak seasoning and Worcestershire sauce in a large bowl. Divide the meat mixture into 12 equal portions. Cut the Cheddar cheese into twelve 2-inch squares, about ¼-inch thick. Stuff a square of cheese into the center of each portion of meat and shape into a 3-inch patty.
2. Make the slider sauce by combining the ketchup, mayonnaise, and relish in a small bowl. Set aside.
3. Cut the bread dough into twelve pieces. Shape each piece of dough into a ball and use a rolling pin to roll them out into 4-inch circles. Dollop ½ teaspoon of the slider sauce into the center of each dough circle. Place a beef patty on top of the sauce and wrap the dough around the patty, pinching the dough together to seal the pocket shut. Try not to stretch the dough too much when bringing the edges together. Brush both sides of the slider pocket with the beaten egg. Sprinkle sesame seeds on top of each pocket.
4. Preheat the air fryer to 350°F.
5. Spray or brush the bottom of the air fryer basket with oil. Air-fry the slider pockets four at a time. Transfer the slider pockets to the air fryer basket, seam

side down and air-fry at 350°F for 10 minutes, until the dough is golden brown. Flip the slider pockets over and air-fry for another 3 minutes. When all the batches are done, pop all the sliders into the air fryer for a few minutes to re-heat and serve them hot out of the fryer.

Carrot Chips

Servings: 4

Cooking Time: 10 Minutes

Ingredients:

- 1 pound carrots, thinly sliced
- 2 tablespoons extra-virgin olive oil
- ¼ teaspoon garlic powder
- ¼ teaspoon black pepper
- ½ teaspoon salt

Directions:

1. Preheat the air fryer to 390°F.
2. In a medium bowl, toss the carrot slices with the olive oil, garlic powder, pepper, and salt.
3. Liberally spray the air fryer basket with olive oil mist.
4. Place the carrot slices in the air fryer basket. To allow for even cooking, don't overlap the carrots; cook in batches if necessary.
5. Cook for 5 minutes, shake the basket, and cook another 5 minutes.
6. Remove from the basket and serve warm. Repeat with the remaining carrot slices until they're all cooked.

Onion Ring Nachos

Servings: 3

Cooking Time: 8 Minutes

Ingredients:

- ¾ pound Frozen breaded (not battered) onion rings (do not thaw)
- 1½ cups (about 6 ounces) Shredded Cheddar, Monterey Jack, or Swiss cheese, or a purchased Tex-Mex blend
- Up to 12 Pickled jalapeño rings

Directions:

1. Preheat the air fryer to 400°F.
2. When the machine is at temperature, spread the onion rings in the basket in a fairly even layer. Air-fry undisturbed for 6 minutes, or until crisp. Remove the basket from the machine.
3. Cut a circle of parchment paper to line a 6-inch round cake pan for a small air fryer, a 7-inch round cake pan for a medium air fryer, or an 8-inch round cake pan for a large machine.
4. Pour the onion rings into a fairly even layer in the cake pan, then sprinkle the cheese evenly over them. Dot with the jalapeño rings.
5. Set the pan in the basket and air-fry undisturbed for 2 minutes, until the cheese has melted and is bubbling.
6. Remove the pan from the basket. Cool for 5 minutes before serving.

Indian Cauliflower Tikka Bites

Servings: 6

Cooking Time: 20 Minutes

Ingredients:

- 1 cup plain Greek yogurt
- 1 teaspoon fresh ginger
- 1 teaspoon minced garlic
- 1 teaspoon vindaloo
- ½ teaspoon cardamom
- ½ teaspoon paprika
- ½ teaspoon turmeric powder
- ½ teaspoon cumin powder
- 1 large head of cauliflower, washed and cut into medium-size florets
- ½ cup panko breadcrumbs
- 1 lemon, quartered

Directions:

1. Preheat the air fryer to 350°F.
2. In a large bowl, mix the yogurt, ginger, garlic, vindaloo, cardamom, paprika, turmeric, and cumin. Add the cauliflower florets to the bowl, and coat them with the yogurt.
3. Remove the cauliflower florets from the bowl and place them on a baking sheet. Sprinkle the panko breadcrumbs over the top. Place the cauliflower bites into the air fryer basket, leaving space between the florets. Depending on the size of your air fryer, you may need to make more than one batch.

4. Cook the cauliflower for 10 minutes, shake the basket, and continue cooking another 10 minutes (or until the florets are lightly browned).
5. Remove from the air fryer and keep warm. Continue to cook until all the florets are done.
6. Before serving, lightly squeeze lemon over the top. Serve warm.

Meatball Arancini

Servings: 6
Cooking Time: 10 Minutes

Ingredients:

- 1⅓ cups Water
- ⅔ cup Raw white Arborio rice
- 2 teaspoons Butter
- ¼ teaspoon Table salt
- 2 Large egg(s), well beaten
- ¾ cup Seasoned Italian-style dried bread crumbs (gluten-free, if a concern)
- ⅓ cup (about 1 ounce) Finely grated Parmesan cheese
- 6 ½-ounce "bite-size" frozen meatballs (any variety, even vegan and/or gluten-free, if a concern), thawed
- Olive oil spray

Directions:

1. Combine the water, rice, butter, and salt in a small saucepan. Bring to a boil over medium-high heat, stirring occasionally. Cover, reduce the heat to very low, and simmer very slowly for 20 minutes.
2. Take the saucepan off the heat and let it stand, covered, for 10 minutes. Uncover it and fluff the rice. Cool for 20 minutes. (The rice can be made up to 1 hour in advance; keep it covered in its saucepan.)
3. Preheat the air fryer to 375°F .
4. Set up and fill two shallow soup plates or small bowls on your counter: one with the beaten egg(s) and one with the bread crumbs mixed with the grated cheese.
5. With clean but wet hands, scoop up about 3 tablespoons of the cooked rice and form it into a ball around a mini meatball, forming a sealed casing. Dip the ball in the egg(s) to coat completely, letting any excess egg slip back into the rest. Set the ball in the bread-crumb mixture and roll it gently to coat evenly but lightly all over. Set aside and continue making more rice balls.
6. Generously spray the balls with olive oil spray, then set them in the basket in one layer. They must not touch. Air-fry undisturbed for 10 minutes, or until crunchy and golden brown. Use kitchen tongs to gently transfer the balls to a wire rack. Cool for at least 5 minutes before serving.

Warm And Salty Edamame

Servings: 4
Cooking Time: 10 Minutes

Ingredients:

- 1 pound Unshelled edamame
- Vegetable oil spray
- ¾ teaspoon Coarse sea salt or kosher salt

Directions:

1. Preheat the air fryer to 400°F.
2. Place the edamame in a large bowl and lightly coat them with vegetable oil spray. Toss well, spray again, and toss until they are evenly coated.
3. When the machine is at temperature, pour the edamame into the basket and air-fry, tossing the basket quite often to rearrange the edamame, for 7 minutes, or until warm and aromatic. (Air-fry for 10 minutes if the edamame were frozen and not thawed.)
4. Pour the edamame into a bowl and sprinkle the salt on top. Toss well, then set aside for a couple of minutes before serving with an empty bowl on the side for the pods.

Spiced Nuts

Servings: 3
Cooking Time: 25 Minutes

Ingredients:

- 1 egg white, lightly beaten
- ¼ cup sugar
- 1 teaspoon salt
- ½ teaspoon ground cinnamon
- ¼ teaspoon ground cloves
- ¼ teaspoon ground allspice
- pinch ground cayenne pepper

- 1 cup pecan halves
- 1 cup cashews
- 1 cup almonds

Directions:

1. Combine the egg white with the sugar and spices in a bowl.
2. Preheat the air fryer to 300°F.
3. Spray or brush the air fryer basket with vegetable oil. Toss the nuts together in the spiced egg white and transfer the nuts to the air fryer basket.
4. Air-fry for 25 minutes, stirring the nuts in the basket a few times during the cooking process. Taste the nuts to see if they are crunchy and nicely toasted. Air-fry for a few more minutes if necessary.
5. Serve warm or cool to room temperature and store in an airtight container for up to two weeks.

Classic Chicken Wings

Servings: 8

Cooking Time: 20 Minutes

Ingredients:

- 16 chicken wings
- ¼ cup all-purpose flour
- ¼ teaspoon garlic powder
- ¼ teaspoon paprika
- ½ teaspoon salt
- ½ teaspoon black pepper
- ¼ cup butter
- ½ cup hot sauce
- ½ teaspoon Worcestershire sauce
- 2 ounces crumbled blue cheese, for garnish

Directions:

1. Preheat the air fryer to 380°F.
2. Pat the chicken wings dry with paper towels.
3. In a medium bowl, mix together the flour, garlic powder, paprika, salt, and pepper. Toss the chicken wings with the flour mixture, dusting off any excess.
4. Place the chicken wings in the air fryer basket, making sure that the chicken wings aren't touching. Cook the chicken wings for 10 minutes, turn over, and cook another 5 minutes. Raise the temperature to 400°F and continue crisping the chicken wings for an additional 3 to 5 minutes.
5. Meanwhile, in a microwave-safe bowl, melt the butter and hot sauce for 1 to 2 minutes in the microwave. Remove from the microwave and stir in the Worcestershire sauce.
6. When the chicken wings have cooked, immediately transfer the chicken wings into the hot sauce mixture. Serve the coated chicken wings on a plate, and top with crumbled blue cheese.

Buffalo Wings

Servings: 2

Cooking Time: 12 Minutes Per Batch

Ingredients:

- 2 pounds chicken wings
- 3 tablespoons butter, melted
- ¼ cup hot sauce (like Crystal® or Frank's®)
- Finishing Sauce:
- 3 tablespoons butter, melted
- ¼ cup hot sauce (like Crystal® or Frank's®)
- 1 teaspoon Worcestershire sauce

Directions:

1. Prepare the chicken wings by cutting off the wing tips and discarding (or freezing for chicken stock). Divide the drumettes from the wingettes by cutting through the joint. Place the chicken wing pieces in a large bowl.
2. Combine the melted butter and the hot sauce and stir to blend well. Pour the marinade over the chicken wings, cover and let the wings marinate for 2 hours or up to overnight in the refrigerator.
3. Preheat the air fryer to 400°F.
4. Air-fry the wings in two batches for 10 minutes per batch, shaking the basket halfway through the cooking process. When both batches are done, toss all the wings back into the basket for another 2 minutes to heat through and finish cooking.
5. While the wings are air-frying, combine the remaining 3 tablespoons of butter, ¼ cup of hot sauce and the Worcestershire sauce. Remove the wings from the air fryer, toss them in the finishing sauce and serve with some cooling blue cheese dip and celery sticks.

Albóndigas

Servings: 4
Cooking Time: 15 Minutes

Ingredients:

- 1 pound Lean ground pork
- 3 tablespoons Very finely chopped trimmed scallions
- 3 tablespoons Finely chopped fresh cilantro leaves
- 3 tablespoons Plain panko bread crumbs (gluten-free, if a concern)
- 3 tablespoons Dry white wine, dry sherry, or unsweetened apple juice
- 1½ teaspoons Minced garlic
- 1¼ teaspoons Mild smoked paprika
- ¾ teaspoon Dried oregano
- ¾ teaspoon Table salt
- ¼ teaspoon Ground black pepper
- Olive oil spray

Directions:

1. Preheat the air fryer to 400°F.
2. Mix the ground pork, scallions, cilantro, bread crumbs, wine or its substitute, garlic, smoked paprika, oregano, salt, and pepper in a bowl until the herbs and spices are evenly distributed in the mixture.
3. Lightly coat your clean hands with olive oil spray, then form the ground pork mixture into balls, using 2 tablespoons for each one. Spray your hands frequently so that the meat mixture doesn't stick.
4. Set the balls in the basket so that they're not touching, even if they're close together. Air-fry undisturbed for 15 minutes, or until well browned and an instant-read meat thermometer inserted into one or two balls registers 165°F.
5. Use a nonstick-safe spatula and kitchen tongs for balance to gently transfer the fragile balls to a wire rack to cool for 5 minutes before serving.

Teriyaki Country-style Pork Ribs

Servings: 3
Cooking Time: 30 Minutes

Ingredients:

- 3 tablespoons Regular or low-sodium soy sauce or gluten-free tamari sauce
- 3 tablespoons Honey
- ¾ teaspoon Ground dried ginger
- ¾ teaspoon Garlic powder
- 3 8-ounce boneless country-style pork ribs
- Vegetable oil spray

Directions:

1. Preheat the air fryer to 350°F .
2. Mix the soy or tamari sauce, honey, ground ginger, and garlic powder in another bowl until uniform.
3. Smear about half of this teriyaki sauce over all sides of the country-style ribs. Reserve the remainder of the teriyaki sauce. Generously coat the meat with vegetable oil spray.
4. When the machine is at temperature, place the country-style ribs in the basket with as much air space between them as possible. Air-fry undisturbed for 15 minutes. Turn the country-style ribs (but keep the space between them) and brush them all over with the remaining teriyaki sauce. Continue air-frying undisturbed for 15 minutes, or until an instant-read meat thermometer inserted into the center of one rib registers at least 145°F.
5. Use kitchen tongs to transfer the country-style ribs to a wire rack. Cool for 5 minutes before serving.

Italian Sausage & Peppers

Servings: 6
Cooking Time: 25 Minutes

Ingredients:

- 1 6-ounce can tomato paste
- ⅔ cup water
- 1 8-ounce can tomato sauce
- 1 teaspoon dried parsley flakes
- ½ teaspoon garlic powder
- ⅛ teaspoon oregano
- ½ pound mild Italian bulk sausage
- 1 tablespoon extra virgin olive oil
- ½ large onion, cut in 1-inch chunks

- 4 ounces fresh mushrooms, sliced
- 1 large green bell pepper, cut in 1-inch chunks
- 8 ounces spaghetti, cooked
- Parmesan cheese for serving

Directions:

1. In a large saucepan or skillet, stir together the tomato paste, water, tomato sauce, parsley, garlic, and oregano. Heat on stovetop over very low heat while preparing meat and vegetables.
2. Break sausage into small chunks, about ½-inch pieces. Place in air fryer baking pan.
3. Cook at 390°F for 5minutes. Stir. Cook 7 minutes longer or until sausage is well done. Remove from pan, drain on paper towels, and add to the sauce mixture.
4. If any sausage grease remains in baking pan, pour it off or use paper towels to soak it up. (Be careful handling that hot pan!)
5. Place olive oil, onions, and mushrooms in pan and stir. Cook for 5minutes or just until tender. Using a slotted spoon, transfer onions and mushrooms from baking pan into the sauce and sausage mixture.
6. Place bell pepper chunks in air fryer baking pan and cook for 8 minutes or until tender. When done, stir into sauce with sausage and other vegetables.
7. Serve over cooked spaghetti with plenty of Parmesan cheese.

Beef Al Carbon (street Taco Meat)

Servings: 6

Cooking Time: 8 Minutes

Ingredients:

- 1½ pounds sirloin steak, cut into ½-inch cubes
- ¾ cup lime juice
- ½ cup extra-virgin olive oil
- 1 teaspoon ground cumin
- 2 teaspoons garlic powder
- 1 teaspoon salt

Directions:

1. In a large bowl, toss together the steak, lime juice, olive oil, cumin, garlic powder, and salt. Allow the meat to marinate for 30 minutes. Drain off all the marinade and pat the meat dry with paper towels.
2. Preheat the air fryer to 400°F.
3. Place the meat in the air fryer basket and spray with cooking spray. Cook the meat for 5 minutes, toss the meat, and continue cooking another 3 minutes, until slightly crispy.

Mustard-crusted Rib-eye

Servings: 2

Cooking Time: 9 Minutes

Ingredients:

- Two 6-ounce rib-eye steaks, about 1-inch thick
- 1 teaspoon coarse salt
- ½ teaspoon coarse black pepper
- 2 tablespoons Dijon mustard

Directions:

1. Rub the steaks with the salt and pepper. Then spread the mustard on both sides of the steaks. Cover with foil and let the steaks sit at room temperature for 30 minutes.
2. Preheat the air fryer to 390°F.
3. Cook the steaks for 9 minutes. Check for an internal temperature of 140°F and immediately remove the steaks and let them rest for 5 minutes before slicing.

Easy Carnitas

Servings: 3

Cooking Time: 25 Minutes

Ingredients:

- 1½ pounds Boneless country-style pork ribs, cut into 2-inch pieces
- ¼ cup Orange juice
- 2 tablespoons Brine from a jar of pickles, any type, even pickled jalapeño rings (gluten-free, if a concern)
- 2 teaspoons Minced garlic
- 2 teaspoons Minced fresh oregano leaves
- ¾ teaspoon Ground cumin
- ¾ teaspoon Table salt
- ¾ teaspoon Ground black pepper

Directions:

1. Mix the country-style pork rib pieces, orange juice, pickle brine, garlic, oregano, cumin, salt, and pepper in a

large bowl. Cover and refrigerate for at least 2 hours or up to 10 hours, stirring the mixture occasionally.

2. Preheat the air fryer to 400°F. Set the rib pieces in their bowl on the counter as the machine heats.

3. Use kitchen tongs to transfer the rib pieces to the basket, arranging them in one layer. Some may touch. Air-fry for 25 minutes, turning and rearranging the pieces at the 10- and 20-minute marks to make sure all surfaces have been exposed to the air currents, until browned and sizzling.

4. Use clean kitchen tongs to transfer the rib pieces to a wire rack. Cool for a couple of minutes before serving.

Chicken Fried Steak

Servings: 4

Cooking Time: 15 Minutes

Ingredients:

- 2 eggs
- ½ cup buttermilk
- 1½ cups flour
- ¾ teaspoon salt
- ½ teaspoon pepper
- 1 pound beef cube steaks
- salt and pepper
- oil for misting or cooking spray

Directions:

1. Beat together eggs and buttermilk in a shallow dish.
2. In another shallow dish, stir together the flour, ½ teaspoon salt, and ¼ teaspoon pepper.
3. Season cube steaks with remaining salt and pepper to taste. Dip in flour, buttermilk egg wash, and then flour again.
4. Spray both sides of steaks with oil or cooking spray.
5. Cooking in 2 batches, place steaks in air fryer basket in single layer. Cook at 360°F for 10minutes. Spray tops of steaks with oil and cook 5minutes or until meat is well done.
6. Repeat to cook remaining steaks.

Apple Cornbread Stuffed Pork Loin With Apple Gravy

Servings: 4

Cooking Time: 61 Minutes

Ingredients:

- 4 strips of bacon, chopped
- 1 Granny Smith apple, peeled, cored and finely chopped
- 2 teaspoons fresh thyme leaves
- ¼ cup chopped fresh parsley
- 2 cups cubed cornbread
- ½ cup chicken stock
- salt and freshly ground black pepper
- 1 (2-pound) boneless pork loin
- kitchen twine
- Apple Gravy:
- 2 tablespoons butter
- 1 shallot, minced
- 1 Granny Smith apple, peeled, cored and finely chopped
- 3 sprigs fresh thyme
- 2 tablespoons flour
- 1 cup chicken stock
- ½ cup apple cider
- salt and freshly ground black pepper, to taste

Directions:

1. Preheat the air fryer to 400°F.
2. Add the bacon to the air fryer and air-fry for 6 minutes until crispy. While the bacon is cooking, combine the apple, fresh thyme, parsley and cornbread in a bowl and toss well. Moisten the mixture with the chicken stock and season to taste with salt and freshly ground black pepper. Add the cooked bacon to the mixture.
3. Butterfly the pork loin by holding it flat on the cutting board with one hand, while slicing into the pork loin parallel to the cutting board with the other. Slice into the longest side of the pork loin, but stop before you cut all the way through. You should then be able to open the pork loin up like a book, making it twice as wide as it was when you started. Season the inside of the pork with salt and freshly ground black pepper.
4. Spread the cornbread mixture onto the butterflied pork loin, leaving a one-inch border around the edge of the pork. Roll the pork loin up around the stuffing to enclose the stuffing, and tie the rolled pork in several

places with kitchen twine or secure with toothpicks. Try to replace any stuffing that falls out of the roast as you roll it, by stuffing it into the ends of the rolled pork. Season the outside of the pork with salt and freshly ground black pepper.

5. Preheat the air fryer to 360°F.

6. Place the stuffed pork loin into the air fryer, seam side down. Air-fry the pork loin for 15 minutes at 360°F. Turn the pork loin over and air-fry for an additional 15 minutes. Turn the pork loin a quarter turn and air-fry for an additional 15 minutes. Turn the pork loin over again to expose the fourth side, and air-fry for an additional 10 minutes. The pork loin should register 155°F on an instant read thermometer when it is finished.

7. While the pork is cooking, make the apple gravy. Preheat a saucepan over medium heat on the stovetop and melt the butter. Add the shallot, apple and thyme sprigs and sauté until the apple starts to soften and brown a little. Add the flour and stir for a minute or two. Whisk in the stock and apple cider vigorously to prevent the flour from forming lumps. Bring the mixture to a boil to thicken and season to taste with salt and pepper.

8. Transfer the pork loin to a resting plate and loosely tent with foil, letting the pork rest for at least 5 minutes before slicing and serving with the apple gravy poured over the top.

Crunchy Veal Cutlets

Servings: 2

Cooking Time: 5 Minutes

Ingredients:

- ½ cup All-purpose flour or tapioca flour
- 1 Large egg(s), well beaten
- ¾ cup Seasoned Italian-style dried bread crumbs (gluten-free, if a concern)
- 2 tablespoons Yellow cornmeal
- 4 Thinly pounded 2-ounce veal leg cutlets (less than ¼ inch thick)
- Olive oil spray

Directions:

1. Preheat the air fryer to 400°F.

2. Set up and fill three shallow soup plates or small pie plates on your counter: one for the flour; one for the egg(s); and one for the bread crumbs, whisked with the cornmeal until well combined.

3. Dredge a veal cutlet in the flour, coating it on both sides. Gently shake off any excess flour, then gently dip it in the beaten egg(s), coating both sides. Let the excess egg slip back into the rest. Dip the cutlet in the bread-crumb mixture, turning it several times and pressing gently to make an even coating on both sides. Coat it on both sides with olive oil spray, then set it aside and continue dredging and coating more cutlets.

4. When the machine is at temperature, set the cutlets in the basket so that they don't touch each other. Air-fry undisturbed for 5 minutes, or until crisp and brown. (If only some of the veal cutlets will fit in one layer for any selected batch—the sizes of air fryer baskets vary dramatically—work in batches as necessary.)

5. Use kitchen tongs to transfer the cutlets to a wire rack. Cool for only 1 to 2 minutes before serving.

Orange Glazed Pork Tenderloin

Servings: 3

Cooking Time: 23 Minutes

Ingredients:

- 2 tablespoons brown sugar
- 2 teaspoons cornstarch
- 2 teaspoons Dijon mustard
- ½ cup orange juice
- ½ teaspoon soy sauce*
- 2 teaspoons grated fresh ginger
- ¼ cup white wine
- zest of 1 orange
- 1 pound pork tenderloin
- salt and freshly ground black pepper
- oranges, halved (for garnish)
- fresh parsley or other green herb (for garnish)

Directions:

1. Combine the brown sugar, cornstarch, Dijon mustard, orange juice, soy sauce, ginger, white wine and orange zest in a small saucepan and bring the mixture to a boil on the stovetop. Lower the heat and simmer while

you cook the pork tenderloin or until the sauce has thickened.

2. Preheat the air fryer to 370°F.

3. Season all sides of the pork tenderloin with salt and freshly ground black pepper. Transfer the tenderloin to the air fryer basket, bending the pork into a wide "U" shape if necessary to fit in the basket. Air-fry at 370°F for 20 to 23 minutes, or until the internal temperature reaches 145°F. Flip the tenderloin over halfway through the cooking process and baste with the sauce.

4. Transfer the tenderloin to a cutting board and let it rest for 5 minutes. Slice the pork at a slight angle and serve immediately with orange halves and fresh herbs to dress it up. Drizzle any remaining glaze over the top.

Pepper Steak

Servings: 4

Cooking Time: 30 Minutes

Ingredients:

- 2 tablespoons cornstarch
- 1 tablespoon sugar
- ¾ cup beef broth
- ¼ cup hoisin sauce
- 3 tablespoons soy sauce
- 1 teaspoon sesame oil
- ½ teaspoon freshly ground black pepper
- 1½ pounds boneless New York strip steaks, sliced into ½-inch strips
- 1 onion, sliced
- 3 small bell peppers, red, yellow and green, sliced

Directions:

1. Whisk the cornstarch and sugar together in a large bowl to break up any lumps in the cornstarch. Add the beef broth and whisk until combined and smooth. Stir in the hoisin sauce, soy sauce, sesame oil and freshly ground black pepper. Add the beef, onion and peppers, and toss to coat. Marinate the beef and vegetables at room temperature for 30 minutes, stirring a few times to keep meat and vegetables coated.

2. Preheat the air fryer to 350°F.

3. Transfer the beef, onion, and peppers to the air fryer basket with tongs, reserving the marinade. Air-fry the beef and vegetables for 30 minutes, stirring well two or three times during the cooking process.

4. While the beef is air-frying, bring the reserved marinade to a simmer in a small saucepan over medium heat on the stovetop. Simmer for 5 minutes until the sauce thickens.

5. When the steak and vegetables have finished cooking, transfer them to a serving platter. Pour the hot sauce over the pepper steak and serve with white rice.

Bacon, Blue Cheese And Pear Stuffed Pork Chops

Servings: 3

Cooking Time: 24 Minutes

Ingredients:

- 4 slices bacon, chopped
- 1 tablespoon butter
- ½ cup finely diced onion
- ⅓ cup chicken stock
- 1½ cups seasoned stuffing cubes
- 1 egg, beaten
- ½ teaspoon dried thyme
- ½ teaspoon salt
- ⅛ teaspoon black pepper
- 1 pear, finely diced
- ⅓ cup crumbled blue cheese
- 3 boneless center-cut pork chops (2-inch thick)
- olive oil
- salt and freshly ground black pepper

Directions:

1. Preheat the air fryer to 400°F.

2. Place the bacon into the air fryer basket and air-fry for 6 minutes, stirring halfway through the cooking time. Remove the bacon and set it aside on a paper towel. Pour out the grease from the bottom of the air fryer.

3. To make the stuffing, melt the butter in a medium saucepan over medium heat on the stovetop. Add the onion and sauté for a few minutes, until it starts to soften. Add the chicken stock and simmer for 1 minute. Remove the pan from the heat and add the stuffing cubes. Stir until the stock has been absorbed. Add the egg, dried thyme, salt and freshly ground black pepper,

and stir until combined. Fold in the diced pear and crumbled blue cheese.

4. Place the pork chops on a cutting board. Using the palm of your hand to hold the chop flat and steady, slice into the side of the pork chop to make a pocket in the center of the chop. Leave about an inch of chop uncut and make sure you don't cut all the way through the pork chop. Brush both sides of the pork chops with olive oil and season with salt and freshly ground black pepper. Stuff each pork chop with a third of the stuffing, packing the stuffing tightly inside the pocket.

5. Preheat the air fryer to 360°F.

6. Spray or brush the sides of the air fryer basket with oil. Place the pork chops in the air fryer basket with the open stuffed edge of the pork chop facing the outside edges of the basket.

7. Air-fry the pork chops for 18 minutes, turning the pork chops over halfway through the cooking time. When the chops are done, let them rest for 5 minutes and then transfer to a serving platter.

Korean-style Lamb Shoulder Chops

Servings: 3

Cooking Time: 28 Minutes

Ingredients:

- ⅓ cup Regular or low-sodium soy sauce or gluten-free tamari sauce
- 1½ tablespoons Toasted sesame oil
- 1½ tablespoons Granulated white sugar
- 2 teaspoons Minced peeled fresh ginger
- 1 teaspoon Minced garlic
- ¼ teaspoon Red pepper flakes
- 3 6-ounce bone-in lamb shoulder chops, any excess fat trimmed
- ⅔ cup Tapioca flour
- Vegetable oil spray

Directions:

1. Put the soy or tamari sauce, sesame oil, sugar, ginger, garlic, and red pepper flakes in a large, heavy zip-closed plastic bag. Add the chops, seal, and rub the marinade evenly over them through the bag. Refrigerate for at least 2 hours or up to 6 hours, turning the bag at least once so the chops move around in the marinade.

2. Set the bag out on the counter as the air fryer heats. Preheat the air fryer to 375°F .

3. Pour the tapioca flour on a dinner plate or in a small pie plate. Remove a chop from the marinade and dredge it on both sides in the tapioca flour, coating it evenly and well. Coat both sides with vegetable oil spray, set it in the basket, and dredge and spray the remaining chop(s), setting them in the basket in a single layer with space between them. Discard the bag with the marinade.

4. Air-fry, turning once, for 25 minutes, or until the chops are well browned and tender when pierced with the point of a paring knife. If the machine is at 360°F, you may need to add up to 3 minutes to the cooking time.

5. Use kitchen tongs to transfer the chops to a wire rack. Cool for just a couple of minutes before serving.

Carne Asada

Servings: 4

Cooking Time: 15 Minutes

Ingredients:

- 4 cloves garlic, minced
- 3 chipotle peppers in adobo, chopped
- ⅓ cup chopped fresh parsley
- ⅓ cup chopped fresh oregano
- 1 teaspoon ground cumin seed
- juice of 2 limes
- ⅓ cup olive oil
- 1 to 1½ pounds flank steak (depending on your appetites)
- salt
- tortillas and guacamole (optional – for serving)

Directions:

1. Make the marinade: Combine the garlic, chipotle, parsley, oregano, cumin, lime juice and olive oil in a non-reactive bowl. Coat the flank steak with the marinade and let it marinate for 30 minutes to 8 hours. (Don't leave the steak out of refrigeration for longer than 2 hours, however.)

2. Preheat the air fryer to 390°F.

3. Remove the steak from the marinade and place it in the air fryer basket. Season the steak with salt and air-fry for 15 minutes, turning the steak over halfway through the cooking time and seasoning again with salt. This should cook the steak to medium. Add or subtract two minutes for medium-well or medium-rare.
4. Remember to let the steak rest before slicing the meat against the grain. Serve with warm tortillas, guacamole and a fresh salsa like the Tomato-Corn Salsa below.

Air-fried Roast Beef With Rosemary Roasted Potatoes

Servings: 8
Cooking Time: 60 Minutes

Ingredients:

- 1 (5-pound) top sirloin roast
- salt and freshly ground black pepper
- 1 teaspoon dried thyme
- 2 pounds red potatoes, halved or quartered
- 2 teaspoons olive oil
- 1 teaspoon very finely chopped fresh rosemary, plus more for garnish

Directions:

1. Start by making sure your roast will fit into the air fryer basket without touching the top element. Trim it if you have to in order to get it to fit nicely in your air fryer. (You can always save the trimmings for another use, like a beef sandwich.)
2. Preheat the air fryer to 360°F.
3. Season the beef all over with salt, pepper and thyme. Transfer the seasoned roast to the air fryer basket.
4. Air-fry at 360°F for 20 minutes. Turn the roast over and continue to air-fry at 360°F for another 20 minutes.
5. Toss the potatoes with the olive oil, salt, pepper and fresh rosemary. Turn the roast over again in the air fryer basket and toss the potatoes in around the sides of the roast. Air-fry the roast and potatoes at 360°F for another 20 minutes. Check the internal temperature of the roast with an instant-read thermometer, and continue to roast until the beef is 5° lower than your desired degree of doneness. (Rare – 130°F, Medium – 150°F, Well done – 170°F.) Let the roast rest for 5 to 10 minutes before slicing and serving. While the roast is resting, continue to air-fry the potatoes if desired for extra browning and crispiness.
6. Slice the roast and serve with the potatoes, adding a little more fresh rosemary if desired.

Steak Fingers

Servings: 4
Cooking Time: 8 Minutes

Ingredients:

- 4 small beef cube steaks
- salt and pepper
- ½ cup flour
- oil for misting or cooking spray

Directions:

1. Cut cube steaks into 1-inch-wide strips.
2. Sprinkle lightly with salt and pepper to taste.
3. Roll in flour to coat all sides.
4. Spray air fryer basket with cooking spray or oil.
5. Place steak strips in air fryer basket in single layer, very close together but not touching. Spray top of steak strips with oil or cooking spray.
6. Cook at 390°F for 4minutes, turn strips over, and spray with oil or cooking spray.
7. Cook 4 more minutes and test with fork for doneness. Steak fingers should be crispy outside with no red juices inside. If needed, cook an additional 4 minutes or until well done. (Don't eat beef cube steak rare.)
8. Repeat steps 5 through 7 to cook remaining strips.

Kielbasa Sausage With Pierogies And Caramelized Onions

Servings: 3
Cooking Time: 30 Minutes

Ingredients:

- 1 Vidalia or sweet onion, sliced
- olive oil
- salt and freshly ground black pepper
- 2 tablespoons butter, cut into small cubes
- 1 teaspoon sugar

- 1 pound light Polish kielbasa sausage, cut into 2-inch chunks
- 1 (13-ounce) package frozen mini pierogies
- 2 teaspoons vegetable or olive oil
- chopped scallions

Directions:

1. Preheat the air fryer to 400°F.
2. Toss the sliced onions with a little olive oil, salt and pepper and transfer them to the air fryer basket. Dot the onions with pieces of butter and air-fry at 400°F for 2 minutes. Then sprinkle the sugar over the onions and stir. Pour any melted butter from the bottom of the air fryer drawer over the onions (do this over the sink – some of the butter will spill through the basket). Continue to air-fry for another 13 minutes, stirring or shaking the basket every few minutes to cook the onions evenly.
3. Add the kielbasa chunks to the onions and toss. Air-fry for another 5 minutes, shaking the basket halfway through the cooking time. Transfer the kielbasa and onions to a bowl and cover with aluminum foil to keep warm.
4. Toss the frozen pierogies with the vegetable or olive oil and transfer them to the air fryer basket. Air-fry at 400°F for 8 minutes, shaking the basket twice during the cooking time.
5. When the pierogies have finished cooking, return the kielbasa and onions to the air fryer and gently toss with the pierogies. Air-fry for 2 more minutes and then transfer everything to a serving platter. Garnish with the chopped scallions and serve hot with the spicy sour cream sauce below.
6. Kielbasa Sausage with Pierogies and Caramelized Onions

Bacon Wrapped Filets Mignons

Servings: 4

Cooking Time: 18 Minutes

Ingredients:

- 4 slices bacon (not thick cut)
- 4 (8-ounce) filets mignons
- 1 tablespoon fresh thyme leaves
- salt and freshly ground black pepper

Directions:

1. Preheat the air fryer to 400°F.
2. Lay the bacon slices down on a cutting board and sprinkle the thyme leaves on the bacon slices. Remove any string tying the filets and place the steaks down on their sides on top of the bacon slices. Roll the bacon around the side of the filets and secure the bacon to the fillets with a toothpick or two.
3. Season the steaks generously with salt and freshly ground black pepper and transfer the steaks to the air fryer.
4. Air-fry for 18 minutes, turning the steaks over halfway through the cooking process. This should cook your steaks to about medium, depending on how thick they are. If you'd prefer your steaks medium-rare or medium-well, simply add or subtract two minutes from the cooking time. Remove the steaks from the air fryer and let them rest for 5 minutes before removing the toothpicks and serving. (Just enough time to quickly air-fry some vegetables to go with them!)

Sausage-cheese Calzone

Servings: 8

Cooking Time: 8 Minutes

Ingredients:

- Crust
- 2 cups white wheat flour, plus more for kneading and rolling
- 1 package (¼ ounce) RapidRise yeast
- 1 teaspoon salt
- ½ teaspoon dried basil
- 1 cup warm water (115°F to 125°F)
- 2 teaspoons olive oil
- Filling
- ¼ pound Italian sausage
- ½ cup ricotta cheese
- 4 ounces mozzarella cheese, shredded
- ¼ cup grated Parmesan cheese
- oil for misting or cooking spray
- marinara sauce for serving

Directions:

1. Crumble Italian sausage into air fryer baking pan and cook at 390°F for 5minutes. Stir, breaking apart, and cook for 3 to 4minutes, until well done. Remove and set aside on paper towels to drain.
2. To make dough, combine flour, yeast, salt, and basil. Add warm water and oil and stir until a soft dough forms. Turn out onto lightly floured board and knead for 3 or 4minutes. Let dough rest for 10minutes.
3. To make filling, combine the three cheeses in a medium bowl and mix well. Stir in the cooked sausage.
4. Cut dough into 8 pieces.
5. Working with 4 pieces of the dough, press each into a circle about 5 inches in diameter. Top each dough circle with 2 heaping tablespoons of filling. Fold over to create a half-moon shape and press edges firmly together. Be sure that edges are firmly sealed to prevent leakage. Spray both sides with oil or cooking spray.
6. Place 4 calzones in air fryer basket and cook at 360°F for 5minutes. Mist with oil and cook for 3 minutes, until crust is done and nicely browned.
7. While the first batch is cooking, press out the remaining dough, fill, and shape into calzones.
8. Spray both sides with oil and cook for 5minutes. If needed, mist with oil and continue cooking for 3 minutes longer. This second batch will cook a little faster than the first because your air fryer is already hot.
9. Serve with marinara sauce on the side for dipping.

Cinnamon-stick Kofta Skewers

Servings: 8
Cooking Time: 15 Minutes

Ingredients:

- 1 pound Lean ground beef
- ½ teaspoon Ground cumin
- ½ teaspoon Onion powder
- ½ teaspoon Ground dried turmeric
- ½ teaspoon Ground cinnamon
- ½ teaspoon Table salt
- Up to a ⅛ teaspoon Cayenne
- 8 3½- to 4-inch-long cinnamon sticks (see the headnote)
- Vegetable oil spray

Directions:

1. Preheat the air fryer to 375°F .
2. Gently mix the ground beef, cumin, onion powder, turmeric, cinnamon, salt, and cayenne in a bowl until the meat is evenly mixed with the spices. (Clean, dry hands work best!) Divide this mixture into 2-ounce portions, each about the size of a golf ball.
3. Wrap one portion of the meat mixture around a cinnamon stick, using about three-quarters of the length of the stick, covering one end but leaving a little "handle" of cinnamon stick protruding from the other end. Set aside and continue making more kofta skewers.
4. Generously coat the formed kofta skewers on all sides with vegetable oil spray. Set them in the basket with as much air space between them as possible. Air-fry undisturbed for 13 minutes, or until browned and cooked through. If the machine is at 360°F, you may need to add 2 minutes to the cooking time.
5. Use a nonstick-safe spatula, and perhaps kitchen tongs for balance, to gently transfer the kofta skewers to a wire rack. Cool for at least 5 minutes or up to 20 minutes before serving.

Calf's Liver

Servings: 4
Cooking Time: 5 Minutes

Ingredients:

- 1 pound sliced calf's liver
- salt and pepper
- 2 eggs
- 2 tablespoons milk
- ½ cup whole wheat flour
- 1½ cups panko breadcrumbs
- ½ cup plain breadcrumbs
- ½ teaspoon salt
- ¼ teaspoon pepper
- oil for misting or cooking spray

Directions:

1. Cut liver slices crosswise into strips about ½-inch wide. Sprinkle with salt and pepper to taste.
2. Beat together egg and milk in a shallow dish.
3. Place wheat flour in a second shallow dish.

4. In a third shallow dish, mix together panko, plain breadcrumbs, ½ teaspoon salt, and ¼ teaspoon pepper.
5. Preheat air fryer to 390°F.
6. Dip liver strips in flour, egg wash, and then breadcrumbs, pressing in coating slightly to make crumbs stick.
7. Cooking half the liver at a time, place strips in air fryer basket in a single layer, close but not touching. Cook at 390°F for 5 minutes or until done to your preference.
8. Repeat step 7 to cook remaining liver.

Vietnamese Beef Lettuce Wraps

Servings: 4
Cooking Time: 12 Minutes

Ingredients:

- ⅓ cup low-sodium soy sauce*
- 2 teaspoons fish sauce*
- 2 teaspoons brown sugar
- 1 tablespoon chili paste
- juice of 1 lime
- 2 cloves garlic, minced
- 2 teaspoons fresh ginger, minced
- 1 pound beef sirloin
- Sauce
- ⅓ cup low-sodium soy sauce*
- juice of 2 limes
- 1 tablespoon mirin wine
- 2 teaspoons chili paste
- Serving
- 1 head butter lettuce
- ½ cup julienned carrots
- ½ cup julienned cucumber
- ½ cup sliced radishes, sliced into half moons
- 2 cups cooked rice noodles
- ⅓ cup chopped peanuts

Directions:

1. Combine the soy sauce, fish sauce, brown sugar, chili paste, lime juice, garlic and ginger in a bowl. Slice the beef into thin slices, then cut those slices in half. Add the beef to the marinade and marinate for 1 to 3 hours in the refrigerator. When you are ready to cook, remove the steak from the refrigerator and let it sit at room temperature for 30 minutes.
2. Preheat the air fryer to 400°F.
3. Transfer the beef and marinade to the air fryer basket. Air-fry at 400°F for 12 minutes, shaking the basket a few times during the cooking process.
4. While the beef is cooking, prepare a wrap-building station. Combine the soy sauce, lime juice, mirin wine and chili paste in a bowl and transfer to a little pouring vessel. Separate the lettuce leaves from the head of lettuce and put them in a serving bowl. Place the carrots, cucumber, radish, rice noodles and chopped peanuts all in separate serving bowls.
5. When the beef has finished cooking, transfer it to another serving bowl and invite your guests to build their wraps. To build the wraps, place some beef in a lettuce leaf and top with carrots, cucumbers, some rice noodles and chopped peanuts. Drizzle a little sauce over top, fold the lettuce around the ingredients and enjoy!

Wasabi-coated Pork Loin Chops

Servings: 3
Cooking Time: 14 Minutes

Ingredients:

- 1½ cups Wasabi peas
- ¼ cup Plain panko bread crumbs
- 1 Large egg white(s)
- 2 tablespoons Water
- 3 5- to 6-ounce boneless center-cut pork loin chops (about ½ inch thick)

Directions:

1. Preheat the air fryer to 375°F .
2. Put the wasabi peas in a food processor. Cover and process until finely ground, about like panko bread crumbs. Add the bread crumbs and pulse a few times to blend.
3. Set up and fill two shallow soup plates or small pie plates on your counter: one for the egg white(s), whisked with the water until uniform; and one for the wasabi pea mixture.
4. Dip a pork chop in the egg white mixture, coating the chop on both sides as well as around the edge. Allow

any excess egg white mixture to slip back into the rest, then set the chop in the wasabi pea mixture. Press gently and turn it several times to coat evenly on both sides and around the edge. Set aside, then dip and coat the remaining chop(s).

5. Set the chops in the basket with as much air space between them as possible. Air-fry, turning once at the 6-minute mark, for 12 minutes, or until the chops are crisp and browned and an instant-read meat thermometer inserted into the center of a chop registers 145°F. If the machine is at 360°F, you may need to add 2 minutes to the cooking time.

6. Use kitchen tongs to transfer the chops to a wire rack. Cool for a couple of minutes before serving.

Meatball Subs

Servings: 4

Cooking Time: 11 Minutes

Ingredients:

- Marinara Sauce
- 1 15-ounce can diced tomatoes
- 1 teaspoon garlic powder
- 1 teaspoon dried basil
- ½ teaspoon oregano
- ⅛ teaspoon salt
- 1 tablespoon robust olive oil
- Meatballs
- ¼ pound ground turkey
- ¾ pound very lean ground beef
- 1 tablespoon milk
- ½ cup torn bread pieces
- 1 egg
- ¼ teaspoon salt
- ½ teaspoon dried onion
- 1 teaspoon garlic powder
- ¼ teaspoon smoked paprika
- ¼ teaspoon crushed red pepper
- 1½ teaspoons dried parsley
- ¼ teaspoon oregano
- 2 teaspoons Worcestershire sauce
- Sandwiches
- 4 large whole-grain sub or hoagie rolls, split
- toppings, sliced or chopped:
- mushrooms
- jalapeño or banana peppers
- red or green bell pepper
- red onions
- grated cheese

Directions:

1. Place all marinara ingredients in saucepan and bring to a boil. Lower heat and simmer 10minutes, uncovered.
2. Combine all meatball ingredients in large bowl and stir. Mixture should be well blended but don't overwork it. Excessive mixing will toughen the meatballs.
3. Divide meat into 16 equal portions and shape into balls.
4. Cook the balls at 360°F until meat is done and juices run clear, about 11 minutes.
5. While meatballs are cooking, taste marinara. If you prefer stronger flavors, add more seasoning and simmer another 5minutes.
6. When meatballs finish cooking, drain them on paper towels.
7. To assemble subs, place 4 meatballs on each sub roll, spoon sauce over meat, and add preferred toppings. Serve with additional marinara for dipping.

Extra Crispy Country-style Pork Riblets

Servings: 3

Cooking Time: 30 Minutes

Ingredients:

- ⅓ cup Tapioca flour
- 2½ tablespoons Chile powder
- ¾ teaspoon Table salt (optional)
- 1¼ pounds Boneless country-style pork ribs, cut into 1½-inch chunks
- Vegetable oil spray

Directions:

1. Preheat the air fryer to 375°F .
2. Mix the tapioca flour, chile powder, and salt (if using) in a large bowl until well combined. Add the country-style rib chunks and toss well to coat thoroughly.

3. When the machine is at temperature, gently shake off any excess tapioca coating from the chunks. Generously coat them on all sides with vegetable oil spray. Arrange the chunks in the basket in one (admittedly fairly tight) layer. The pieces may touch. Air-fry for 30 minutes, rearranging the pieces at the 10- and 20-minute marks to expose any touching bits, until very crisp and well browned.
4. Gently pour the contents of the basket onto a wire rack. Cool for 5 minutes before serving.

Blackberry Bbq Glazed Country-style Ribs

Servings: 2
Cooking Time: 40 Minutes

Ingredients:

- ½ cup + 2 tablespoons sherry or Madeira wine, divided
- 1 pound boneless country-style pork ribs
- salt and freshly ground black pepper
- 1 tablespoon Chinese 5-spice powder
- ¼ cup blackberry preserves
- ¼ cup hoisin sauce*
- 1 clove garlic, minced
- 1 generous tablespoon grated fresh ginger
- 2 scallions, chopped
- 1 tablespoon sesame seeds, toasted

Directions:

1. Preheat the air fryer to 330°F and pour ½ cup of the sherry into the bottom of the air fryer drawer.
2. Season the ribs with salt, pepper and the 5-spice powder.
3. Air-fry the ribs at 330°F for 20 minutes, turning them over halfway through the cooking time.
4. While the ribs are cooking, make the sauce. Combine the remaining sherry, blackberry preserves, hoisin sauce, garlic and ginger in a small saucepan. Bring to a simmer on the stovetop for a few minutes, until the sauce thickens.
5. When the time is up on the air fryer, turn the ribs over, pour a little sauce on the ribs and air-fry for another 10 minutes at 330°F. Turn the ribs over again, pour on more of the sauce and air-fry at 330°F for a final 10 minutes.
6. Let the ribs rest for at least 5 minutes before serving them warm with a little more glaze brushed on and the scallions and sesame seeds sprinkled on top.

Sweet And Sour Pork

Servings: 2
Cooking Time: 11 Minutes

Ingredients:

- ⅓ cup all-purpose flour
- ⅓ cup cornstarch
- 2 teaspoons Chinese 5-spice powder
- 1 teaspoon salt
- freshly ground black pepper
- 1 egg
- 2 tablespoons milk
- ¾ pound boneless pork, cut into 1-inch cubes
- vegetable or canola oil, in a spray bottle
- 1½ cups large chunks of red and green peppers
- ½ cup ketchup
- 2 tablespoons rice wine vinegar or apple cider vinegar
- 2 tablespoons brown sugar
- ¼ cup orange juice
- 1 tablespoon soy sauce
- 1 clove garlic, minced
- 1 cup cubed pineapple
- chopped scallions

Directions:

1. Set up a dredging station with two bowls. Combine the flour, cornstarch, Chinese 5-spice powder, salt and pepper in one large bowl. Whisk the egg and milk together in a second bowl. Dredge the pork cubes in the flour mixture first, then dip them into the egg and then back into the flour to coat on all sides. Spray the coated pork cubes with vegetable or canola oil.
2. Preheat the air fryer to 400°F.
3. Toss the pepper chunks with a little oil and air-fry at 400°F for 5 minutes, shaking the basket halfway through the cooking time.

4. While the peppers are cooking, start making the sauce. Combine the ketchup, rice wine vinegar, brown sugar, orange juice, soy sauce, and garlic in a medium saucepan and bring the mixture to a boil on the stovetop. Reduce the heat and simmer for 5 minutes. When the peppers have finished air-frying, add them to the saucepan along with the pineapple chunks. Simmer the peppers and pineapple in the sauce for an additional 2 minutes. Set aside and keep warm.
5. Add the dredged pork cubes to the air fryer basket and air-fry at 400°F for 6 minutes, shaking the basket to turn the cubes over for the last minute of the cooking process.
6. When ready to serve, toss the cooked pork with the pineapple, peppers and sauce. Serve over white rice and garnish with chopped scallions.

Lemon-butter Veal Cutlets

Servings: 2
Cooking Time: 4 Minutes

Ingredients:

- 3 strips Butter (see step 2)
- 3 Thinly pounded 2-ounce veal leg cutlets (less than ¼ inch thick)
- ¼ teaspoon Lemon-pepper seasoning

Directions:

1. Preheat the air fryer to 400°F.
2. Run a vegetable peeler lengthwise along a hard, cold stick of butter, making 2, 3, or 4 long strips as the recipe requires for the number of cutlets you're making.
3. Lay the veal cutlets on a clean, dry cutting board or work surface. Sprinkle about ⅛ teaspoon lemon-pepper seasoning over each. Set a strip of butter on top of each cutlet.
4. When the machine is at temperature, set the topped cutlets in the basket so that they don't overlap or even touch. Air-fry undisturbed for 4 minutes without turning.
5. Use a nonstick-safe spatula to transfer the cutlets to a serving plate or plates, taking care to keep as much of the butter on top as possible. Remove the basket from the drawer or from over the baking tray. Carefully pour the browned butter over the cutlets.

Corned Beef Hash

Servings: 6
Cooking Time: 15 Minutes

Ingredients:

- 3 cups (about 14 ounces) Frozen unseasoned hash brown cubes (no need to thaw)
- 9 ounces Deli corned beef, cut into ¾-inch-thick slices, then cubed
- ¾ cup Roughly chopped yellow or white onion
- ¾ cup Stemmed, cored, and roughly chopped red bell pepper
- 2½ tablespoons Olive oil
- ¼ teaspoon Dried thyme
- ¼ teaspoon Dried sage leaves
- Up to a ⅛ teaspoon Cayenne

Directions:

1. Preheat the air fryer to 400°F.
2. Mix all the ingredients in a large or very large bowl until the potato cubes and corned beef are coated in the spices.
3. Spread the mixture in the basket in as close to an even layer as you can. Air-fry for 15 minutes, tossing and rearranging the pieces at the 5- and 10-minute marks to expose covered bits, until the potatoes are browned, even crisp, and the mixture is very fragrant.
4. Pour the contents of the basket onto a serving platter or divide between serving plates. Cool for a couple of minutes before serving.

Sweet Potato–crusted Pork Rib Chops

Servings: 2
Cooking Time: 14 Minutes

Ingredients:

- 2 Large egg white(s), well beaten
- 1½ cups (about 6 ounces) Crushed sweet potato chips (certified gluten-free, if a concern)
- 1 teaspoon Ground cinnamon
- 1 teaspoon Ground dried ginger
- 1 teaspoon Table salt (optional)
- 2 10-ounce, 1-inch-thick bone-in pork rib chop(s)

Directions:

1. Preheat the air fryer to 375°F .
2. Set up and fill two shallow soup plates or small pie plates on your counter: one for the beaten egg white(s); and one for the crushed chips, mixed with the cinnamon, ginger, and salt (if using).
3. Dip a chop in the egg white(s), coating it on both sides as well as the edges. Let the excess egg white slip back into the rest, then set it in the crushed chip mixture. Turn it several times, pressing gently, until evenly coated on both sides and the edges. If necessary, set the chop aside and coat the remaining chop(s).
4. Set the chop(s) in the basket with as much air space between them as possible. Air-fry undisturbed for 12 minutes, or until crunchy and browned and an instant-read meat thermometer inserted into the center of a chop (without touching bone) registers 145°F. If the machine is at 360°F, you may need to add 2 minutes to the cooking time.
5. Use kitchen tongs to transfer the chop(s) to a wire rack. Cool for 2 or 3 minutes before serving.

Fried Spam

Servings: 2

Cooking Time: 12 Minutes

Ingredients:

- ½ cup All-purpose flour or gluten-free all-purpose flour
- 1 Large egg(s)
- 1 tablespoon Wasabi paste
- 1⅓ cups Plain panko bread crumbs (gluten-free, if a concern)
- 4 ½-inch-thick Spam slices
- Vegetable oil spray

Directions:

1. Preheat the air fryer to 400°F.
2. Set up and fill three shallow soup plates or small pie plates on your counter: one for the flour; one for the egg(s), whisked with the wasabi paste until uniform; and one for the bread crumbs.
3. Dip a slice of Spam in the flour, coating both sides. Slip it into the egg mixture and turn to coat on both sides, even along the edges. Let any excess egg mixture slip back into the rest, then set the slice in the bread crumbs. Turn it several times, pressing gently to make an even coating on both sides. Generously coat both sides of the slice with vegetable oil spray. Set aside so you can dip, coat, and spray the remaining slice(s).
4. Set the slices in the basket in a single layer so that they don't touch (even if they're close together). Air-fry undisturbed for 12 minutes, or until very brown and quite crunchy.
5. Use kitchen tongs to transfer the slices to a wire rack. Cool for a minute or two before serving.

Pork Cutlets With Aloha Salsa

Servings: 4

Cooking Time: 9 Minutes

Ingredients:

- Aloha Salsa
- 1 cup fresh pineapple, chopped in small pieces
- ¼ cup red onion, finely chopped
- ¼ cup green or red bell pepper, chopped
- ½ teaspoon ground cinnamon
- 1 teaspoon low-sodium soy sauce
- ⅛ teaspoon crushed red pepper
- ⅛ teaspoon ground black pepper
- 2 eggs
- 2 tablespoons milk
- ¼ cup flour
- ¼ cup panko breadcrumbs
- 4 teaspoons sesame seeds
- 1 pound boneless, thin pork cutlets (⅜- to ½-inch thick)
- lemon pepper and salt
- ¼ cup cornstarch
- oil for misting or cooking spray

Directions:

1. In a medium bowl, stir together all ingredients for salsa. Cover and refrigerate while cooking pork.
2. Preheat air fryer to 390°F.
3. Beat together eggs and milk in shallow dish.
4. In another shallow dish, mix together the flour, panko, and sesame seeds.

5. Sprinkle pork cutlets with lemon pepper and salt to taste. Most lemon pepper seasoning contains salt, so go easy adding extra.
6. Dip pork cutlets in cornstarch, egg mixture, and then panko coating. Spray both sides with oil or cooking spray.
7. Cook cutlets for 3minutes. Turn cutlets over, spraying both sides, and continue cooking for 6 minutes or until well done.
8. Serve fried cutlets with salsa on the side.

Beef Short Ribs

Servings: 4
Cooking Time: 20 Minutes

Ingredients:

- 2 tablespoons soy sauce
- 1 tablespoon sesame oil
- 2 tablespoons brown sugar
- 1 teaspoon ground ginger
- 2 garlic cloves, crushed
- 1 pound beef short ribs

Directions:

1. In a small bowl, mix together the soy sauce, sesame oil, brown sugar, and ginger. Transfer the mixture to a large resealable plastic bag, and place the garlic cloves and short ribs into the bag. Secure and place in the refrigerator for an hour (or overnight).
2. When you're ready to prepare the dish, preheat the air fryer to 330°F.
3. Liberally spray the air fryer basket with olive oil mist and set the beef short ribs in the basket.
4. Cook for 10 minutes, flip the short ribs, and then cook another 10 minutes.
5. Remove the short ribs from the air fryer basket, loosely cover with aluminum foil, and let them rest. The short ribs will continue to cook after they're removed from the basket. Check the internal temperature after 5 minutes to make sure it reached 145°F if you prefer a well-done meat. If it didn't reach 145°F and you would like it to be cooked longer, you can put it back into the air fryer basket at 330°F for another 3 minutes.
6. Remove from the basket and let it rest, covered with aluminum foil, for 5 minutes. Serve immediately.

Almond And Sun-dried Tomato Crusted Pork Chops

Servings: 4
Cooking Time: 10 Minutes

Ingredients:

- ½ cup oil-packed sun-dried tomatoes
- ½ cup toasted almonds
- ¼ cup grated Parmesan cheese
- ½ cup olive oil
- 2 tablespoons water
- ½ teaspoon salt
- freshly ground black pepper
- 4 center-cut boneless pork chops (about 1¼ pounds)

Directions:

1. Place the sun-dried tomatoes into a food processor and pulse them until they are coarsely chopped. Add the almonds, Parmesan cheese, olive oil, water, salt and pepper. Process all the ingredients into a smooth paste. Spread most of the paste (leave a little in reserve) onto both sides of the pork chops and then pierce the meat several times with a needle-style meat tenderizer or a fork. Let the pork chops sit and marinate for at least 1 hour (refrigerate if marinating for longer than 1 hour).
2. Preheat the air fryer to 370°F.
3. Brush a little olive oil on the bottom of the air fryer basket. Transfer the pork chops into the air fryer basket, spooning a little more of the sun-dried tomato paste onto the pork chops if there are any gaps where the paste may have been rubbed off. Air-fry the pork chops at 370°F for 10 minutes, turning the chops over halfway through the cooking process.
4. When the pork chops have finished cooking, transfer them to a serving plate and serve with mashed potatoes and vegetables for a hearty meal.

Pizza Tortilla Rolls

Servings: 4
Cooking Time: 8 Minutes

Ingredients:

- 1 teaspoon butter
- ½ medium onion, slivered
- ½ red or green bell pepper, julienned
- 4 ounces fresh white mushrooms, chopped
- 8 flour tortillas (6- or 7-inch size)
- ½ cup pizza sauce
- 8 thin slices deli ham
- 24 pepperoni slices (about 1½ ounces)
- 1 cup shredded mozzarella cheese (about 4 ounces)
- oil for misting or cooking spray

Directions:

1. Place butter, onions, bell pepper, and mushrooms in air fryer baking pan. Cook at 390°F for 3minutes. Stir and cook 4 minutes longer until just crisp and tender. Remove pan and set aside.
2. To assemble rolls, spread about 2 teaspoons of pizza sauce on one half of each tortilla. Top with a slice of ham and 3 slices of pepperoni. Divide sautéed vegetables among tortillas and top with cheese.
3. Roll up tortillas, secure with toothpicks if needed, and spray with oil.
4. Place 4 rolls in air fryer basket and cook for 4minutes. Turn and cook 4 minutes, until heated through and lightly browned.
5. Repeat step 4 to cook remaining pizza rolls.

Pork Taco Gorditas

Servings: 4
Cooking Time: 21 Minutes

Ingredients:

- 1 pound lean ground pork
- 2 tablespoons chili powder
- 2 tablespoons ground cumin
- 1 teaspoon dried oregano
- 2 teaspoons paprika
- 1 teaspoon garlic powder
- ½ cup water
- 1 (15-ounce) can pinto beans, drained and rinsed
- ½ cup taco sauce
- salt and freshly ground black pepper
- 2 cups grated Cheddar cheese
- 5 (12-inch) flour tortillas
- 4 (8-inch) crispy corn tortilla shells
- 4 cups shredded lettuce
- 1 tomato, diced
- ⅓ cup sliced black olives
- sour cream, for serving
- tomato salsa, for serving

Directions:

1. Preheat the air fryer to 400°F.
2. Place the ground pork in the air fryer basket and air-fry at 400°F for 10 minutes, stirring a few times during the cooking process to gently break up the meat. Combine the chili powder, cumin, oregano, paprika, garlic powder and water in a small bowl. Stir the spice mixture into the browned pork. Stir in the beans and taco sauce and air-fry for an additional minute. Transfer the pork mixture to a bowl. Season to taste with salt and freshly ground black pepper.
3. Sprinkle ½ cup of the shredded cheese in the center of four of the flour tortillas, making sure to leave a 2-inch border around the edge free of cheese and filling. Divide the pork mixture among the four tortillas, placing it on top of the cheese. Place a crunchy corn tortilla on top of the pork and top with shredded lettuce, diced tomatoes, and black olives. Cut the remaining flour tortilla into 4 quarters. These quarters of tortilla will serve as the bottom of the gordita. Place one quarter tortilla on top of each gordita and fold the edges of the bottom flour tortilla up over the sides, enclosing the filling. While holding the seams down, brush the bottom of the gordita with olive oil and place the seam side down on the countertop while you finish the remaining three gorditas.
4. Preheat the air fryer to 380°F.
5. Air-fry one gordita at a time. Transfer the gordita carefully to the air fryer basket, seam side down. Brush or spray the top tortilla with oil and air-fry for 5 minutes. Carefully turn the gordita over and air-fry for an additional 5 minutes, until both sides are browned. When finished air frying all four gorditas, layer them back into the air fryer for an additional minute to make sure they are all warm before serving with sour cream and salsa.

Stuffed Bell Peppers

Servings: 4
Cooking Time: 10 Minutes

Ingredients:

- ¼ pound lean ground pork
- ¾ pound lean ground beef
- ¼ cup onion, minced
- 1 15-ounce can Red Gold crushed tomatoes
- 1 teaspoon Worcestershire sauce
- 1 teaspoon barbeque seasoning
- 1 teaspoon honey
- ½ teaspoon dried basil
- ½ cup cooked brown rice
- ½ teaspoon garlic powder
- ½ teaspoon oregano
- ½ teaspoon salt
- 2 small bell peppers

Directions:

1. Place pork, beef, and onion in air fryer baking pan and cook at 360°F for 5minutes.
2. Stir to break apart chunks and cook 3 more minutes. Continue cooking and stirring in 2-minute intervals until meat is well done. Remove from pan and drain.
3. In a small saucepan, combine the tomatoes, Worcestershire, barbeque seasoning, honey, and basil. Stir well to mix in honey and seasonings.
4. In a large bowl, combine the cooked meat mixture, rice, garlic powder, oregano, and salt. Add ¼ cup of the seasoned crushed tomatoes. Stir until well mixed.
5. Cut peppers in half and remove stems and seeds.
6. Stuff each pepper half with one fourth of the meat mixture.
7. Place the peppers in air fryer basket and cook for 10 minutes, until peppers are crisp tender.
8. Heat remaining tomato sauce. Serve peppers with warm sauce spooned over top.

Pork Cutlets With Almond-lemon Crust

Servings: 3

Cooking Time: 14 Minutes

Ingredients:

- ¾ cup Almond flour
- ¾ cup Plain dried bread crumbs (gluten-free, if a concern)
- 1½ teaspoons Finely grated lemon zest
- 1¼ teaspoons Table salt
- ¾ teaspoon Garlic powder
- ¾ teaspoon Dried oregano
- 1 Large egg white(s)
- 2 tablespoons Water
- 3 6-ounce center-cut boneless pork loin chops (about ¾ inch thick)
- Olive oil spray

Directions:

1. Preheat the air fryer to 375°F .
2. Mix the almond flour, bread crumbs, lemon zest, salt, garlic powder, and dried oregano in a large bowl until well combined.
3. Whisk the egg white(s) and water in a shallow soup plate or small pie plate until uniform.
4. Dip a chop in the egg white mixture, turning it to coat all sides, even the ends. Let any excess egg white mixture slip back into the rest, then set it in the almond flour mixture. Turn it several times, pressing gently to coat it evenly. Generously coat the chop with olive oil spray, then set aside to dip and coat the remaining chop(s).
5. Set the chops in the basket with as much air space between them as possible. Air-fry undisturbed for 12 minutes, or until browned and crunchy. You may need to add 2 minutes to the cooking time if the machine is at 360°F.
6. Use kitchen tongs to transfer the chops to a wire rack. Cool for a few minutes before serving.

Better-than-chinese-take-out Sesame Beef

Servings: 4
Cooking Time: 14 Minutes

Ingredients:

- 1¼ pounds Beef flank steak
- 2½ tablespoons Regular or low-sodium soy sauce or gluten-free tamari sauce
- 2 tablespoons Toasted sesame oil
- 2½ teaspoons Cornstarch
- 1 pound 2 ounces (about 4½ cups) Frozen mixed vegetables for stir-fry, thawed, seasoning packet discarded
- 3 tablespoons Unseasoned rice vinegar (see here)
- 3 tablespoons Thai sweet chili sauce
- 2 tablespoons Light brown sugar
- 2 tablespoons White sesame seeds
- 2 teaspoons Water
- Vegetable oil spray
- 1½ tablespoons Minced peeled fresh ginger
- 1 tablespoon Minced garlic

Directions:

1. Set the flank steak on a cutting board and run your clean fingers across it to figure out which way the meat's fibers are running. (Usually, they run the long way from end to end, or perhaps slightly at an angle lengthwise along the cut.) Cut the flank steak into three pieces parallel to the meat's grain. Then cut each of these pieces into ½-inch-wide strips against the grain.
2. Put the meat strips in a large bowl. For a small batch, add 2 teaspoons of the soy or tamari sauce, 2 teaspoons of the sesame oil, and ½ teaspoon of the cornstarch; for a medium batch, add 1 tablespoon of the soy or tamari sauce, 1 tablespoon of the sesame oil, and 1 teaspoon of the cornstarch; and for a large batch, add 1½ tablespoons of the soy or tamari sauce, 1½ tablespoons of the sesame oil, and 1½ teaspoons of the cornstarch. Toss well until the meat is thoroughly coated in the marinade. Set aside at room temperature.
3. Preheat the air fryer to 400°F.
4. When the machine is at temperature, place the beef strips in the basket in as close to one layer as possible. The strips will overlap or even cover each other. Air-fry for 10 minutes, tossing and rearranging the strips three times so that the covered parts get exposed, until browned and even a little crisp. Pour the strips into a clean bowl.
5. Spread the vegetables in the basket and air-fry undisturbed for 4 minutes, just until they are heated through and somewhat softened. Pour these into the bowl with the meat strips. Turn off the air fryer.
6. Whisk the rice vinegar, sweet chili sauce, brown sugar, sesame seeds, the remaining soy sauce, and the remaining sesame oil in a small bowl until well combined. For a small batch, whisk the remaining 1 teaspoon cornstarch with the water in a second small bowl to make a smooth slurry; for medium batch, whisk the remaining 1½ teaspoons cornstarch with the water in a second small bowl to make a smooth slurry; and for a large batch, whisk the remaining 2 teaspoons cornstarch with the water in a second small bowl to make a smooth slurry.
7. Generously coat the inside of a large wok with vegetable oil spray, then set the wok over high heat for a few minutes. Add the ginger and garlic; stir-fry for 10 seconds or so, just until fragrant. Add the meat and vegetables; stir-fry for 1 minute to heat through.
8. Add the rice vinegar mixture and continue stir-frying until the sauce is bubbling, less than 1 minute. Add the cornstarch slurry and stir-fry until the sauce has thickened, just a few seconds. Remove the wok from the heat and serve hot.

Beef And Spinach Braciole

Servings: 4
Cooking Time: 92 Minutes

Ingredients:

- 7-inch oven-safe baking pan or casserole
- ½ onion, finely chopped
- 1 teaspoon olive oil
- ⅓ cup red wine
- 2 cups crushed tomatoes
- 1 teaspoon Italian seasoning
- ½ teaspoon garlic powder

- ¼ teaspoon crushed red pepper flakes
- 2 tablespoons chopped fresh parsley
- 2 top round steaks (about 1½ pounds)
- salt and freshly ground black pepper
- 2 cups fresh spinach, chopped
- 1 clove minced garlic
- ½ cup roasted red peppers, julienned
- ½ cup grated pecorino cheese
- ¼ cup pine nuts, toasted and rough chopped
- 2 tablespoons olive oil

Directions:

1. Preheat the air fryer to 400°F.
2. Toss the onions and olive oil together in a 7-inch metal baking pan or casserole dish. Air-fry at 400°F for 5 minutes, stirring a couple times during the cooking process. Add the red wine, crushed tomatoes, Italian seasoning, garlic powder, red pepper flakes and parsley and stir. Cover the pan tightly with aluminum foil, lower the air fryer temperature to 350°F and continue to air-fry for 15 minutes.
3. While the sauce is simmering, prepare the beef. Using a meat mallet, pound the beef until it is ¼-inch thick. Season both sides of the beef with salt and pepper. Combine the spinach, garlic, red peppers, pecorino cheese, pine nuts and olive oil in a medium bowl. Season with salt and freshly ground black pepper. Spread the mixture evenly over the steaks. Starting at one of the short ends, roll the beef around the filling, tucking in the sides as you roll to ensure the filling is completely enclosed. Secure the beef rolls with toothpicks.
4. Remove the baking pan with the sauce from the air fryer and set it aside. Preheat the air fryer to 400°F.
5. Brush or spray the beef rolls with a little olive oil and air-fry at 400°F for 12 minutes, rotating the beef during the cooking process for even browning. When the beef is browned, submerge the rolls into the sauce in the baking pan, cover the pan with foil and return it to the air fryer. Air-fry at 250°F for 60 minutes.
6. Remove the beef rolls from the sauce. Cut each roll into slices and serve with pasta, ladling some of the sauce overtop.

Lamb Burger With Feta And Olives

Servings: 3

Cooking Time: 16 Minutes

Ingredients:

- 2 teaspoons olive oil
- ⅓ onion, finely chopped
- 1 clove garlic, minced
- 1 pound ground lamb
- 2 tablespoons fresh parsley, finely chopped
- 1½ teaspoons fresh oregano, finely chopped
- ½ cup black olives, finely chopped
- ⅓ cup crumbled feta cheese
- ½ teaspoon salt
- freshly ground black pepper
- 4 thick pita breads
- toppings and condiments

Directions:

1. Preheat a medium skillet over medium-high heat on the stovetop. Add the olive oil and cook the onion until tender, but not browned – about 4 to 5 minutes. Add the garlic and cook for another minute. Transfer the onion and garlic to a mixing bowl and add the ground lamb, parsley, oregano, olives, feta cheese, salt and pepper. Gently mix the ingredients together.
2. Divide the mixture into 3 or 4 equal portions and then form the hamburgers, being careful not to over-handle the meat. One good way to do this is to throw the meat back and forth between your hands like a baseball, packing the meat each time you catch it. Flatten the balls into patties, making an indentation in the center of each patty. Flatten the sides of the patties as well to make it easier to fit them into the air fryer basket.
3. Preheat the air fryer to 370°F.
4. If you don't have room for all four burgers, air-fry two or three burgers at a time for 8 minutes at 370°F. Flip the burgers over and air-fry for another 8 minutes. If you cooked your burgers in batches, return the first batch of burgers to the air fryer for the last two minutes of cooking to re-heat. This should give you a medium-well burger. If you'd prefer a medium-rare burger, shorten the cooking time to about 13 minutes. Remove

the burgers to a resting plate and let the burgers rest for a few minutes before dressing and serving.

5. While the burgers are resting, toast the pita breads in the air fryer for 2 minutes. Tuck the burgers into the toasted pita breads, or wrap the pitas around the burgers and serve with a tzatziki sauce or some mayonnaise.

T-bone Steak With Roasted Tomato, Corn And Asparagus Salsa

Servings: 2

Cooking Time: 15-20 Minutes

Ingredients:

- 1 (20-ounce) T-bone steak
- salt and freshly ground black pepper
- Salsa
- 1½ cups cherry tomatoes
- ¾ cup corn kernels (fresh, or frozen and thawed)
- 1½ cups sliced asparagus (1-inch slices) (about ½ bunch)
- 1 tablespoon + 1 teaspoon olive oil, divided
- salt and freshly ground black pepper
- 1½ teaspoons red wine vinegar
- 3 tablespoons chopped fresh basil
- 1 tablespoon chopped fresh chives

Directions:

1. Preheat the air fryer to 400°F.
2. Season the steak with salt and pepper and air-fry at 400°F for 10 minutes (medium-rare), 12 minutes (medium), or 15 minutes (well-done), flipping the steak once halfway through the cooking time.
3. In the meantime, toss the tomatoes, corn and asparagus in a bowl with a teaspoon or so of olive oil, salt and freshly ground black pepper.
4. When the steak has finished cooking, remove it to a cutting board, tent loosely with foil and let it rest. Transfer the vegetables to the air fryer and air-fry at 400°F for 5 minutes, shaking the basket once or twice during the cooking process. Transfer the cooked vegetables back into the bowl and toss with the red wine vinegar, remaining olive oil and fresh herbs.
5. To serve, slice the steak on the bias and serve with some of the salsa on top.

Flank Steak With Roasted Peppers And Chimichurri

Servings: 4

Cooking Time: 22 Minutes

Ingredients:

- 2 cups flat-leaf parsley leaves
- ¼ cup fresh oregano leaves
- 3 cloves garlic
- ½ cup olive oil
- ¼ cup red wine vinegar
- ½ teaspoon salt
- freshly ground black pepper
- ¼ teaspoon crushed red pepper flakes
- ½ teaspoon ground cumin
- 1 pound flank steak
- 1 red bell pepper, cut into strips
- 1 yellow bell pepper, cut into strips

Directions:

1. Make the chimichurri sauce by chopping the parsley, oregano and garlic in a food processor. Add the olive oil, vinegar and seasonings and process again. Pour half of the sauce into a shallow dish with the flank steak and set the remaining sauce aside. Pierce the flank steak with a needle-style meat tenderizer or a paring knife and marinate the steak for 2 to 24 hours in the refrigerator. When you are ready to cook, remove the steak from the refrigerator and let it sit at room temperature for 30 minutes.
2. Preheat the air fryer to 400°F.
3. Cut the flank steak in half so that it fits more easily into the air fryer and transfer both pieces to the air fryer basket. Air-fry for 14 minutes, depending on how you like your steak cooked (10 minutes will give you medium for a 1-inch thick flank steak). Flip the steak over halfway through the cooking time.
4. When the flank steak is cooked to your liking, transfer it to a cutting board, loosely tent with foil and let it rest while you cook the peppers.
5. Toss the peppers in a little olive oil, salt and freshly ground black pepper and transfer them to the air fryer basket. Air-fry at 400°F for 8 minutes, shaking the basket once or twice throughout the cooking process. To

serve, slice the flank steak against the grain of the meat and top with the roasted peppers. Drizzle the reserved chimichurri sauce on top, thinning the sauce with another tablespoon of olive oil if desired.

Lamb Chops

Servings: 2
Cooking Time: 20 Minutes

Ingredients:

- 2 teaspoons oil
- ½ teaspoon ground rosemary
- ½ teaspoon lemon juice
- 1 pound lamb chops, approximately 1-inch thick
- salt and pepper
- cooking spray

Directions:

1. Mix the oil, rosemary, and lemon juice together and rub into all sides of the lamb chops. Season to taste with salt and pepper.
2. For best flavor, cover lamb chops and allow them to rest in the fridge for 20 minutes.
3. Spray air fryer basket with nonstick spray and place lamb chops in it.
4. Cook at 360°F for approximately 20minutes. This will cook chops to medium. The meat will be juicy but have no remaining pink. Cook for a minute or two longer for well done chops. For rare chops, stop cooking after about 12minutes and check for doneness.

Better-than-chinese-take-out Pork Ribs

Servings: 3
Cooking Time: 35 Minutes

Ingredients:

- 1½ tablespoons Hoisin sauce (see here; gluten-free, if a concern)
- 1½ tablespoons Regular or low-sodium soy sauce or gluten-free tamari sauce
- 1½ tablespoons Shaoxing (Chinese cooking rice wine), dry sherry, or white grape juice
- 1½ teaspoons Minced garlic
- ¾ teaspoon Ground dried ginger
- ¾ teaspoon Ground white pepper
- 1½ pounds Pork baby back rib rack(s), cut into 2-bone pieces

Directions:

1. Mix the hoisin sauce, soy or tamari sauce, Shaoxing or its substitute, garlic, ginger, and white pepper in a large bowl. Add the rib sections and stir well to coat. Cover and refrigerate for at least 2 hours or up to 24 hours, stirring the rib sections in the marinade occasionally.
2. Preheat the air fryer to 350°F . Set the ribs in their bowl on the counter as the machine heats.
3. When the machine is at temperature, set the rib pieces on their sides in a single layer in the basket with as much air space between them as possible. Air-fry for 35 minutes, turning and rearranging the pieces once, until deeply browned and sizzling.
4. Use kitchen tongs to transfer the rib pieces to a large serving bowl or platter. Wait a minute or two before serving them so the meat can reabsorb some of its own juices.

Rosemary Lamb Chops

Servings: 4
Cooking Time: 6 Minutes

Ingredients:

- 8 lamb chops
- 1 tablespoon extra-virgin olive oil
- 1 teaspoon dried rosemary, crushed
- 2 cloves garlic, minced
- 1 teaspoon sea salt
- ¼ teaspoon black pepper

Directions:

1. In a large bowl, mix together the lamb chops, olive oil, rosemary, garlic, salt, and pepper. Let sit at room temperature for 10 minutes.
2. Meanwhile, preheat the air fryer to 380°F.
3. Cook the lamb chops for 3 minutes, flip them over, and cook for another 3 minutes.

Crispy Ham And Eggs

Servings: 3
Cooking Time: 9 Minutes

Ingredients:

- 2 cups Rice-puff cereal, such as Rice Krispies

- ¼ cup Maple syrup
- ½ pound ¼- to ½-inch-thick ham steak (gluten-free, if a concern)
- 1 tablespoon Unsalted butter
- 3 Large eggs
- ⅛ teaspoon Table salt
- ⅛ teaspoon Ground black pepper

Directions:

1. Preheat the air fryer to 400°F.
2. Pour the cereal into a food processor, cover, and process until finely ground. Pour the ground cereal into a shallow soup plate or a small pie plate.
3. Smear the maple syrup on both sides of the ham, then set the ham into the ground cereal. Turn a few times, pressing gently, until evenly coated.
4. Set the ham steak in the basket and air-fry undisturbed for 5 minutes, or until browned.
5. Meanwhile, melt the butter in a medium or large nonstick skillet set over medium heat. Crack the eggs into the skillet and cook until the whites are set and the yolks are hot, about 3 minutes (or 4 minutes for a more set yolk.) Season with the salt and pepper.
6. When the ham is ready, transfer it to a serving platter, then slip the eggs from the skillet on top of it. Divide into portions to serve.

Lamb Meatballs With Quick Tomato Sauce

Servings: 4

Cooking Time: 8 Minutes

Ingredients:

- ½ small onion, finely diced
- 1 clove garlic, minced
- 1 pound ground lamb
- 2 tablespoons fresh parsley, finely chopped (plus more for garnish)
- 2 teaspoons fresh oregano, finely chopped
- 2 tablespoons milk
- 1 egg yolk
- salt and freshly ground black pepper
- ½ cup crumbled feta cheese, for garnish
- Tomato Sauce:
- 2 tablespoons butter
- 1 clove garlic, smashed
- pinch crushed red pepper flakes
- ¼ teaspoon ground cinnamon
- 1 (28-ounce) can crushed tomatoes
- salt, to taste

Directions:

1. Combine all ingredients for the meatballs in a large bowl and mix just until everything is combined. Shape the mixture into 1½-inch balls or shape the meat between two spoons to make quenelles (little three-sided footballs).
2. Preheat the air fryer to 400°F.
3. While the air fryer is Preheating, start the quick tomato sauce. Place the butter, garlic and red pepper flakes in a sauté pan and heat over medium heat on the stovetop. Let the garlic sizzle a little, but before the butter starts to brown, add the cinnamon and tomatoes. Bring to a simmer and simmer for 15 minutes. Season to taste with salt (but not too much as the feta that you will be sprinkling on at the end will be salty).
4. Brush the bottom of the air fryer basket with a little oil and transfer the meatballs to the air fryer basket in one layer, air-frying in batches if necessary.
5. Air-fry at 400°F for 8 minutes, giving the basket a shake once during the cooking process to turn the meatballs over.
6. To serve, spoon a pool of the tomato sauce onto plates and add the meatballs in a decorative manner. Sprinkle the feta cheese on top and garnish with more fresh parsley. Serve immediately.

Honey Mesquite Pork Chops

Servings: 2

Cooking Time: 10 Minutes

Ingredients:

- 2 tablespoons mesquite seasoning
- ¼ cup honey
- 1 tablespoon olive oil
- 1 tablespoon water
- freshly ground black pepper
- 2 bone-in center cut pork chops (about 1 pound)

Directions:

1. Whisk the mesquite seasoning, honey, olive oil, water and freshly ground black pepper together in a shallow glass dish. Pierce the chops all over and on both sides with a fork or meat tenderizer. Add the pork chops to the marinade and massage the marinade into the chops. Cover and marinate for 30 minutes.
2. Preheat the air fryer to 330°F.
3. Transfer the pork chops to the air fryer basket and pour half of the marinade over the chops, reserving the remaining marinade. Air-fry the pork chops for 6 minutes. Flip the pork chops over and pour the remaining marinade on top. Air-fry for an additional 3 minutes at 330°F. Then, increase the air fryer temperature to 400°F and air-fry the pork chops for an additional minute.
4. Transfer the pork chops to a serving plate, and let them rest for 5 minutes before serving. If you'd like a sauce for these chops, pour the cooked marinade from the bottom of the air fryer over the top.

Stuffed Pork Chops

Servings: 4

Cooking Time: 12 Minutes

Ingredients:

- 4 boneless pork chops
- ½ teaspoon salt
- ½ teaspoon black pepper
- ¼ teaspoon paprika
- 1 cup frozen spinach, defrosted and squeezed dry
- 2 cloves garlic, minced
- 2 ounces cream cheese
- ¼ cup grated Parmesan cheese
- 1 tablespoon extra-virgin olive oil

Directions:

1. Pat the pork chops with a paper towel. Make a slit in the side of each pork chop to create a pouch.
2. Season the pork chops with the salt, pepper, and paprika.
3. In a small bowl, mix together the spinach, garlic, cream cheese, and Parmesan cheese.
4. Divide the mixture into fourths and stuff the pork chop pouches. Secure the pouches with toothpicks.
5. Preheat the air fryer to 400°F.
6. Place the stuffed pork chops in the air fryer basket and spray liberally with cooking spray. Cook for 6 minutes, flip and coat with more cooking spray, and cook another 6 minutes. Check to make sure the meat is cooked to an internal temperature of 145°F. Cook the pork chops in batches, as needed.

Rack Of Lamb With Pistachio Crust

Servings: 2

Cooking Time: 19 Minutes

Ingredients:

- ½ cup finely chopped pistachios
- 3 tablespoons panko breadcrumbs
- 1 teaspoon chopped fresh rosemary
- 2 teaspoons chopped fresh oregano
- salt and freshly ground black pepper
- 1 tablespoon olive oil
- 1 rack of lamb, bones trimmed of fat and frenched
- 1 tablespoon Dijon mustard

Directions:

1. Preheat the air fryer to 380°F.
2. Combine the pistachios, breadcrumbs, rosemary, oregano, salt and pepper in a small bowl. Drizzle in the olive oil and stir to combine.
3. Season the rack of lamb with salt and pepper on all sides and transfer it to the air fryer basket with the fat side facing up. Air-fry the lamb for 12 minutes. Remove the lamb from the air fryer and brush the fat side of the lamb rack with the Dijon mustard. Coat the rack with the pistachio mixture, pressing the breadcrumbs onto the

lamb with your hands and rolling the bottom of the rack in any of the crumbs that fall off.

4. Return the rack of lamb to the air fryer and air-fry for another 3 to 7 minutes or until an instant read thermometer reads 140°F for medium. Add or subtract a couple of minutes for lamb that is more or less well cooked. (Your time will vary depending on how big the rack of lamb is.)

5. Let the lamb rest for at least 5 minutes. Then, slice into chops and serve.

Baby Back Ribs

Servings: 4

Cooking Time: 36 Minutes

Ingredients:

- 2¼ pounds Pork baby back rib rack(s)
- 1 tablespoon Dried barbecue seasoning blend or rub (gluten-free, if a concern)
- 1 cup Water
- 3 tablespoons Purchased smooth barbecue sauce (gluten-free, if a concern)

Directions:

1. Preheat the air fryer to 350°F .
2. Cut the racks into 4- to 5-bone sections, about two sections for the small batch, three for the medium, and four for the large. Sprinkle both sides of these sections with the seasoning blend.
3. Pour the water into the bottom of the air-fryer drawer or into a tray placed under the rack. (The rack cannot then sit in water—adjust the amount of water for your machine.) Set the rib sections in the basket so that they're not touching. Air-fry for 30 minutes, turning once.
4. If using a tray with water, check it a couple of times to make sure it still has water in it or hasn't overflowed from the rendered fat.
5. Brush half the barbecue sauce on the exposed side of the ribs. Air-fry undisturbed for 3 minutes. Turn the racks over (but make sure they're still not touching), brush with the remaining sauce, and air-fry undisturbed for 3 minutes more, or until sizzling and brown.
6. Use kitchen tongs to transfer the racks to a cutting board. Let stand for 5 minutes, then slice between the bones to serve.

Brie And Cranberry Burgers

Servings: 3

Cooking Time: 9 Minutes

Ingredients:

- 1 pound ground beef (80% lean)
- 1 tablespoon chopped fresh thyme
- 1 tablespoon Worcestershire sauce
- ½ teaspoon salt
- freshly ground black pepper
- 1 (4-ounce) wheel of Brie cheese, sliced
- handful of arugula
- 3 or 4 brioche hamburger buns (or potato hamburger buns), toasted
- ¼ to ½ cup whole berry cranberry sauce

Directions:

1. Combine the beef, thyme, Worcestershire sauce, salt and pepper together in a large bowl and mix well. Divide the meat into 4 (¼-pound) portions or 3 larger portions and then form them into burger patties, being careful not to over-handle the meat.
2. Preheat the air fryer to 390°F and pour a little water into the bottom of the air fryer drawer. (This will help prevent the grease that drips into the bottom drawer from burning and smoking.)
3. Transfer the burgers to the air fryer basket. Air-fry the burgers at 390°F for 5 minutes. Flip the burgers over and air-fry for another 2 minutes. Top each burger with a couple slices of brie and air-fry for another minute or two, just to soften the cheese.
4. Build the burgers by placing a few leaves of arugula on the bottom bun, adding the burger and a spoonful of cranberry sauce on top. Top with the other half of the hamburger bun and enjoy.

Boneless Ribeyes

Servings: 2

Cooking Time: 10-15 Minutes

Ingredients:

- 2 8-ounce boneless ribeye steaks
- 4 teaspoons Worcestershire sauce
- ½ teaspoon garlic powder
- pepper
- 4 teaspoons extra virgin olive oil
- salt

Directions:

1. Season steaks on both sides with Worcestershire sauce. Use the back of a spoon to spread evenly.
2. Sprinkle both sides of steaks with garlic powder and coarsely ground black pepper to taste.
3. Drizzle both sides of steaks with olive oil, again using the back of a spoon to spread evenly over surfaces.
4. Allow steaks to marinate for 30minutes.
5. Place both steaks in air fryer basket and cook at 390°F for 5minutes.
6. Turn steaks over and cook until done:
7. Medium rare: additional 5 minutes
8. Medium: additional 7 minutes
9. Well done: additional 10 minutes
10. Remove steaks from air fryer basket and let sit 5minutes. Salt to taste and serve.

Zesty London Broil

Servings: 4

Cooking Time: 28 Minutes

Ingredients:

- ⅔ cup ketchup
- ¼ cup honey
- ¼ cup olive oil
- 2 tablespoons apple cider vinegar
- 2 tablespoons Worcestershire sauce
- 2 tablespoons minced onion
- ½ teaspoon paprika
- 1 teaspoon salt
- 1 teaspoon freshly ground black pepper
- 2 pounds London broil, top round or flank steak (about 1-inch thick)

Directions:

1. Combine the ketchup, honey, olive oil, apple cider vinegar, Worcestershire sauce, minced onion, paprika, salt and pepper in a small bowl and whisk together.
2. Generously pierce both sides of the meat with a fork or meat tenderizer and place it in a shallow dish. Pour the marinade mixture over the steak, making sure all sides of the meat get coated with the marinade. Cover and refrigerate overnight.
3. Preheat the air fryer to 400°F.
4. Transfer the London broil to the air fryer basket and air-fry for 28 minutes, depending on how rare or well done you like your steak. Flip the steak over halfway through the cooking time.
5. Remove the London broil from the air fryer and let it rest for five minutes on a cutting board. To serve, thinly slice the meat against the grain and transfer to a serving platter.

Pork Chops

Servings: 2

Cooking Time: 16 Minutes

Ingredients:

- 2 bone-in, centercut pork chops, 1-inch thick (10 ounces each)
- 2 teaspoons Worcestershire sauce
- salt and pepper
- cooking spray

Directions:

1. Rub the Worcestershire sauce into both sides of pork chops.
2. Season with salt and pepper to taste.
3. Spray air fryer basket with cooking spray and place the chops in basket side by side.
4. Cook at 360°F for 16 minutes or until well done. Let rest for 5minutes before serving.

Crispy Pork Medallions With Radicchio And Endive Salad

Servings: 4
Cooking Time: 7 Minutes

Ingredients:

- 1 (8-ounce) pork tenderloin
- salt and freshly ground black pepper
- ¼ cup flour
- 2 eggs, lightly beaten
- ¾ cup cracker meal
- 1 teaspoon paprika
- 1 teaspoon dry mustard
- 1 teaspoon garlic powder
- 1 teaspoon dried thyme
- 1 teaspoon salt
- vegetable or canola oil, in spray bottle
- Vinaigrette
- ¼ cup white balsamic vinegar
- 2 tablespoons agave syrup (or honey or maple syrup)
- 1 tablespoon Dijon mustard
- juice of ½ lemon
- 2 tablespoons chopped chervil or flat-leaf parsley
- salt and freshly ground black pepper
- ½ cup extra-virgin olive oil
- Radicchio and Endive Salad
- 1 heart romaine lettuce, torn into large pieces
- ½ head radicchio, coarsely chopped
- 2 heads endive, sliced
- ½ cup cherry tomatoes, halved
- 3 ounces fresh mozzarella, diced
- salt and freshly ground black pepper

Directions:

1. Slice the pork tenderloin into 1-inch slices. Using a meat pounder, pound the pork slices into thin ½-inch medallions. Generously season the pork with salt and freshly ground black pepper on both sides.
2. Set up a dredging station using three shallow dishes. Place the flour in one dish and the beaten eggs in a second dish. Combine the cracker meal, paprika, dry mustard, garlic powder, thyme and salt in a third dish.
3. Preheat the air fryer to 400°F.
4. Dredge the pork medallions in flour first and then into the beaten egg. Let the excess egg drip off and coat both sides of the medallions with the cracker meal crumb mixture. Spray both sides of the coated medallions with vegetable or canola oil.
5. Air-fry the medallions in two batches at 400°F for 5 minutes. Once you have air-fried all the medallions, flip them all over and return the first batch of medallions back into the air fryer on top of the second batch. Air-fry at 400°F for an additional 2 minutes.
6. While the medallions are cooking, make the salad and dressing. Whisk the white balsamic vinegar, agave syrup, Dijon mustard, lemon juice, chervil, salt and pepper together in a small bowl. Whisk in the olive oil slowly until combined and thickened.
7. Combine the romaine lettuce, radicchio, endive, cherry tomatoes, and mozzarella cheese in a large salad bowl. Drizzle the dressing over the vegetables and toss to combine. Season with salt and freshly ground black pepper.
8. Serve the pork medallions warm on or beside the salad.

Pork Schnitzel

Servings: 4
Cooking Time: 14 Minutes

Ingredients:

- 4 boneless pork chops, pounded to ¼-inch thickness
- 1 teaspoon salt, divided
- 1 teaspoon black pepper, divided
- ½ cup all-purpose flour
- 2 eggs
- 1 cup breadcrumbs
- ¼ teaspoon paprika
- 1 lemon, cut into wedges

Directions:

1. Season both sides of the pork chops with ½ teaspoon of the salt and ½ teaspoon of the pepper.
2. On a plate, place the flour.
3. In a large bowl, whisk the eggs.
4. In another large bowl, place the breadcrumbs.

5. Season the flour with the paprika and season the breadcrumbs with the remaining ½ teaspoon of salt and ½ teaspoon of pepper.

6. To bread the pork, place a pork chop in the flour, then into the whisked eggs, and then into the breadcrumbs. Place the breaded pork onto a plate and finish breading the remaining pork chops.

7. Preheat the air fryer to 390°F.

8. Place the pork chops into the air fryer, not overlapping and working in batches as needed. Spray the pork chops with cooking spray and cook for 8 minutes; flip the pork and cook for another 4 to 6 minutes or until cooked to an internal temperature of 145°F.

9. Serve with lemon wedges.

Red Curry Flank Steak

Servings: 4

Cooking Time: 18 Minutes

Ingredients:

- 3 tablespoons red curry paste
- ¼ cup olive oil
- 2 teaspoons grated fresh ginger
- 2 tablespoons soy sauce
- 2 tablespoons rice wine vinegar
- 3 scallions, minced
- 1½ pounds flank steak
- fresh cilantro (or parsley) leaves

Directions:

1. Mix the red curry paste, olive oil, ginger, soy sauce, rice vinegar and scallions together in a bowl. Place the flank steak in a shallow glass dish and pour half the marinade over the steak. Pierce the steak several times with a fork or meat tenderizer to let the marinade penetrate the meat. Turn the steak over, pour the remaining marinade over the top and pierce the steak several times again. Cover and marinate the steak in the refrigerator for 6 to 8 hours.

2. When you are ready to cook, remove the steak from the refrigerator and let it sit at room temperature for 30 minutes.

3. Preheat the air fryer to 400°F.

4. Cut the flank steak in half so that it fits more easily into the air fryer and transfer both pieces to the air fryer basket. Pour the marinade over the steak. Air-fry for 18 minutes, depending on your preferred degree of doneness of the steak (12 minutes = medium rare). Flip the steak over halfway through the cooking time.

5. When your desired degree of doneness has been reached, remove the steak to a cutting board and let it rest for 5 minutes before slicing. Thinly slice the flank steak against the grain of the meat. Transfer the slices to a serving platter, pour any juice from the bottom of the air fryer over the sliced flank steak and sprinkle the fresh cilantro on top.

Balsamic Marinated Rib Eye Steak With Balsamic Fried Cipollini Onions

Servings: 2

Cooking Time: 22-26 Minutes

Ingredients:

- 3 tablespoons balsamic vinegar
- 2 cloves garlic, sliced
- 1 tablespoon Dijon mustard
- 1 teaspoon fresh thyme leaves
- 1 (16-ounce) boneless rib eye steak
- coarsely ground black pepper
- salt
- 1 (8-ounce) bag cipollini onions, peeled
- 1 teaspoon balsamic vinegar

Directions:

1. Combine the 3 tablespoons of balsamic vinegar, garlic, Dijon mustard and thyme in a small bowl. Pour this marinade over the steak. Pierce the steak several times with a paring knife or

2. a needle-style meat tenderizer and season it generously with coarsely ground black pepper. Flip the steak over and pierce the other side in a similar fashion, seasoning again with the coarsely ground black pepper. Marinate the steak for 2 to 24 hours in the refrigerator. When you are ready to cook, remove the steak from the

refrigerator and let it sit at room temperature for 30 minutes.

3. Preheat the air fryer to 400°F.
4. Season the steak with salt and air-fry at 400°F for 12 minutes (medium-rare), 14 minutes (medium), or 16 minutes (well-done), flipping the steak once half way through the cooking time.
5. While the steak is air-frying, toss the onions with 1 teaspoon of balsamic vinegar and season with salt.
6. Remove the steak from the air fryer and let it rest while you fry the onions. Transfer the onions to the air fryer basket and air-fry for 10 minutes, adding a few more minutes if your onions are very large. Then, slice the steak on the bias and serve with the fried onions on top.

Crispy Lamb Shoulder Chops

Servings: 3

Cooking Time: 28 Minutes

Ingredients:

- ¾ cup All-purpose flour or gluten-free all-purpose flour
- 2 teaspoons Mild paprika
- 2 teaspoons Table salt
- 1½ teaspoons Garlic powder
- 1½ teaspoons Dried sage leaves
- 3 6-ounce bone-in lamb shoulder chops, any excess fat trimmed
- Olive oil spray

Directions:

1. Whisk the flour, paprika, salt, garlic powder, and sage in a large bowl until the mixture is of a uniform color. Add the chops and toss well to coat. Transfer them to a cutting board.
2. Preheat the air fryer to 375°F .
3. When the machine is at temperature, again dredge the chops one by one in the flour mixture. Lightly coat both sides of each chop with olive oil spray before putting it in the basket. Continue on with the remaining chop(s), leaving air space between them in the basket.
4. Air-fry, turning once, for 25 minutes, or until the chops are well browned and tender when pierced with the point of a paring knife. If the machine is at 360°F, you may need to add up to 3 minutes to the cooking time.
5. Use kitchen tongs to transfer the chops to a wire rack. Cool for 5 minutes before serving.

Steakhouse Burgers With Red Onion Compote

Servings: 4

Cooking Time: 22 Minutes

Ingredients:

- 1½ pounds lean ground beef
- 2 cloves garlic, minced and divided
- 1 teaspoon Worcestershire sauce
- 1 teaspoon sea salt, divided
- ½ teaspoon black pepper
- 1 tablespoon extra-virgin olive oil
- 1 red onion, thinly sliced
- ¼ cup balsamic vinegar
- 1 teaspoon sugar
- 1 tablespoon tomato paste
- 2 tablespoons mayonnaise
- 2 tablespoons sour cream
- 4 brioche hamburger buns
- 1 cup arugula

Directions:

1. In a large bowl, mix together the ground beef, 1 of the minced garlic cloves, the Worcestershire sauce, ½ teaspoon of the salt, and the black pepper. Form the meat into 1-inch-thick patties. Make a dent in the center (this helps the center cook evenly). Let the meat sit for 15 minutes.
2. Meanwhile, in a small saucepan over medium heat, cook the olive oil and red onion for 4 minutes, stirring frequently to avoid burning. Add in the balsamic vinegar, sugar, and tomato paste, and cook for an additional 3 minutes, stirring frequently. Transfer the onion compote to a small bowl.
3. Preheat the air fryer to 350°F.
4. In another small bowl, mix together the remaining minced garlic, the mayonnaise, and the sour cream.

Spread the mayo mixture on the insides of the brioche buns.

5. Cook the hamburgers for 6 minutes, flip the burgers, and cook an additional 2 to 6 minutes. Check the internal temperature to avoid under- or overcooking. Hamburgers should be cooked to at least 160°F. After cooking, cover with foil and let the meat rest for 5 minutes.

6. Meanwhile, place the buns inside the air fryer and toast them for 3 minutes.

7. To assemble the burgers, place the hamburger on one side of the bun, top with onion compote and ¼ cup arugula, and then place the other half of the bun on top.

Marinated Rib-eye Steak With Herb Roasted Mushrooms

Servings: 2

Cooking Time: 10-15 Minutes

Ingredients:

- 2 tablespoons Worcestershire sauce
- ¼ cup red wine
- 2 (8-ounce) boneless rib-eye steaks
- coarsely ground black pepper
- 8 ounces baby bella (cremini) mushrooms, stems trimmed and caps halved
- 2 tablespoons olive oil
- 1 teaspoon dried parsley
- 1 teaspoon fresh thyme leaves
- salt and freshly ground black pepper
- chopped fresh chives or parsley

Directions:

1. Combine the Worcestershire sauce and red wine in a shallow baking dish. Add the steaks to the marinade, pierce them several times with the tines of a fork or a meat tenderizer and season them generously with the coarsely ground black pepper. Flip the steaks over and pierce the other side in a similar fashion, seasoning again with the coarsely ground black pepper. Marinate the steaks for 2 hours.

2. Preheat the air fryer to 400°F.

3. Toss the mushrooms in a bowl with the olive oil, dried parsley, thyme, salt and freshly ground black pepper. Transfer the steaks from the marinade to the air fryer basket, season with salt and scatter the mushrooms on top.

4. Air-fry the steaks for 10 minutes for medium-rare, 12 minutes for medium, or 15 minutes for well-done, flipping the steaks once halfway through the cooking time.

5. Serve the steaks and mushrooms together with the chives or parsley sprinkled on top. A good steak sauce or some horseradish would be a nice accompaniment.

Pretzel-coated Pork Tenderloin

Servings: 4

Cooking Time: 10 Minutes

Ingredients:

- 1 Large egg white(s)
- 2 teaspoons Dijon mustard (gluten-free, if a concern)
- 1½ cups (about 6 ounces) Crushed pretzel crumbs (see the headnote; gluten-free, if a concern)
- 1 pound (4 sections) Pork tenderloin, cut into ¼-pound (4-ounce) sections
- Vegetable oil spray

Directions:

1. Preheat the air fryer to 350°F .

2. Set up and fill two shallow soup plates or small pie plates on your counter: one for the egg white(s), whisked with the mustard until foamy; and one for the pretzel crumbs.

3. Dip a section of pork tenderloin in the egg white mixture and turn it to coat well, even on the ends. Let any excess egg white mixture slip back into the rest, then set the pork in the pretzel crumbs. Roll it several times, pressing gently, until the pork is evenly coated, even on the ends. Generously coat the pork section with vegetable oil spray, set it aside, and continue coating and spraying the remaining sections.

4. Set the pork sections in the basket with at least ¼ inch between them. Air-fry undisturbed for 10 minutes, or until an instant-read meat thermometer inserted into the center of one section registers 145°F.

5. Use kitchen tongs to transfer the pieces to a wire rack. Cool for 3 to 5 minutes before serving.

Meat Loaves

Servings: 4

Cooking Time: 19 Minutes

Ingredients:

- Sauce
- ¼ cup white vinegar
- ¼ cup brown sugar
- 2 tablespoons Worcestershire sauce
- ½ cup ketchup
- Meat Loaves
- 1 pound very lean ground beef
- ⅔ cup dry bread (approx. 1 slice torn into small pieces)
- 1 egg
- ⅓ cup minced onion
- 1 teaspoon salt
- 2 tablespoons ketchup

Directions:

1. In a small saucepan, combine all sauce ingredients and bring to a boil. Remove from heat and stir to ensure that brown sugar dissolves completely.
2. In a large bowl, combine the beef, bread, egg, onion, salt, and ketchup. Mix well.
3. Divide meat mixture into 4 portions and shape each into a thick, round patty. Patties will be about 3 to 3½ inches in diameter, and all four should fit easily into the air fryer basket at once.
4. Cook at 360°F for 18 minutes, until meat is well done. Baste tops of mini loaves with a small amount of sauce, and cook 1 minute.
5. Serve hot with additional sauce on the side.

Vegetable Side Dishes Recipes

Crispy Noodle Salad

Servings: 3
Cooking Time: 22 Minutes

Ingredients:

- 6 ounces Fresh Chinese-style stir-fry or lo mein wheat noodles
- 1½ tablespoons Cornstarch
- ¾ cup Chopped stemmed and cored red bell pepper
- 2 Medium scallion(s), trimmed and thinly sliced
- 2 teaspoons Sambal oelek or other pulpy hot red pepper sauce (see here)
- 2 teaspoons Thai sweet chili sauce or red ketchup-like chili sauce, such as Heinz
- 2 teaspoons Regular or low-sodium soy sauce or tamari sauce
- 2 teaspoons Unseasoned rice vinegar (see here)
- 1 tablespoon White or black sesame seeds

Directions:

1. Bring a large saucepan of water to a boil over high heat. Add the noodles and boil for 2 minutes. Drain in a colander set in the sink. Rinse several times with cold water, shaking the colander to drain the noodles very well. Spread the noodles out on a large cutting board and air-dry for 10 minutes.
2. Preheat the air fryer to 400°F.
3. Toss the noodles in a bowl with the cornstarch until well coated. Spread them out across the entire basket (although they will be touching and overlapping a bit). Air-fry for 6 minutes, then turn the solid mass of noodles over as one piece. If it cracks in half or smaller pieces, just fit these back together after turning. Continue air-frying for 6 minutes, or until golden brown and crisp.
4. As the noodles cook, stir the bell pepper, scallion(s), sambal oelek, red chili sauce, soy sauce, vinegar, and sesame seeds in a serving bowl until well combined.
5. Turn the basket of noodles out onto a cutting board and cool for a minute or two. Break the mass of noodles into individual noodles and/or small chunks and add to the dressing in the serving bowl. Toss well to serve.

Chicken Salad With Sunny Citrus Dressing

Servings: 4
Cooking Time: 8 Minutes

Ingredients:

- Sunny Citrus Dressing
- 1 cup first cold-pressed extra virgin olive oil
- ⅓ cup red wine vinegar
- 2 tablespoons all natural orange marmalade
- 1 teaspoon dry mustard
- 1 teaspoon ground black pepper
- California Chicken
- 4 large chicken tenders
- 1 teaspoon olive oil
- juice of 1 small orange or clementine
- salt and pepper
- ½ teaspoon rosemary
- Salad
- 8 cups romaine or leaf lettuce, chopped or torn into bite-size pieces
- 2 clementines or small oranges, peeled and sectioned
- ½ cup dried cranberries
- 4 tablespoons sliced almonds

Directions:

1. In a 2-cup jar or container with lid, combine all dressing ingredients and shake until well blended. Refrigerate for at least 30minutes for flavors to blend.
2. Brush chicken tenders lightly with oil.
3. Drizzle orange juice over chicken.
4. Sprinkle with salt and pepper to taste.
5. Crush the rosemary and sprinkle over chicken.
6. Cook at 390°F for 3minutes, turn over, and cook for an additional 5 minutes or until chicken is tender and juices run clear.
7. When ready to serve, toss lettuce with 2 tablespoons of dressing to coat.
8. Divide lettuce among 4 plates or bowls. Arrange chicken and clementines on top and sprinkle cranberries and almonds. Pass extra dressing at the table.

Grits Casserole

Servings: 4

Cooking Time: 30 Minutes

Ingredients:

- 10 fresh asparagus spears, cut into 1-inch pieces
- 2 cups cooked grits, cooled to room temperature
- 1 egg, beaten
- 2 teaspoons Worcestershire sauce
- ½ teaspoon garlic powder
- ¼ teaspoon salt
- 2 slices provolone cheese (about 1½ ounces)
- oil for misting or cooking spray

Directions:

1. Mist asparagus spears with oil and cook at 390°F for 5minutes, until crisp-tender.
2. In a medium bowl, mix together the grits, egg, Worcestershire, garlic powder, and salt.
3. Spoon half of grits mixture into air fryer baking pan and top with asparagus.
4. Tear cheese slices into pieces and layer evenly on top of asparagus.
5. Top with remaining grits.
6. Bake at 360°F for 25 minutes. The casserole will rise a little as it cooks. When done, the top will have browned lightly with just a hint of crispiness.

Roasted Eggplant Halves With Herbed Ricotta

Servings: 3

Cooking Time: 20 Minutes

Ingredients:

- 3 5- to 6-ounce small eggplants, stemmed
- Olive oil spray
- ¼ teaspoon Table salt
- ¼ teaspoon Ground black pepper
- ½ cup Regular or low-fat ricotta
- 1½ tablespoons Minced fresh basil leaves
- 1¼ teaspoons Minced fresh oregano leaves
- Honey

Directions:

1. Preheat the air fryer to 325°F (or 330°F, if that's the closest setting).
2. Cut the eggplants in half lengthwise. Set them cut side up on your work surface. Using the tip of a paring knife, make a series of slits about three-quarters down into the flesh of each eggplant half; work at a 45-degree angle to the (former) stem across the vegetable and make the slits about ½ inch apart. Make a second set of equidistant slits at a 90-degree angle to the first slits, thus creating a crosshatch pattern in the vegetable.
3. Generously coat the cut sides of the eggplants with olive oil spray. Sprinkle the salt and pepper over the cut surfaces.
4. Set the eggplant halves cut side up in the basket with as much air space between them as possible. Air-fry undisturbed for 20 minutes, or until soft and golden.
5. Use kitchen tongs to gently transfer the eggplant halves to serving plates or a platter. Cool for 5 minutes.
6. Whisk the ricotta, basil, and oregano in a small bowl until well combined. Top the eggplant halves with this mixture. Drizzle the halves with honey to taste before serving warm.

Jerk Rubbed Corn On The Cob

Servings: 4

Cooking Time: 6 Minutes

Ingredients:

- 1 teaspoon ground allspice
- 1 teaspoon dried thyme
- ½ teaspoon ground ginger
- ½ teaspoon ground cinnamon
- ¼ teaspoon ground nutmeg
- ⅛ teaspoon ground cayenne pepper
- 1 teaspoon salt
- 2 tablespoons butter, melted
- 4 ears of corn, husked

Directions:

1. Preheat the air fryer to 380°F.
2. Combine all the spices in a bowl. Brush the corn with the melted butter and then sprinkle the spices generously on all sides of each ear of corn.

3. Transfer the ears of corn to the air fryer basket. It's ok if they are crisscrossed on top of each other. Air-fry at 380°F for 6 minutes, rotating the ears as they cook.
4. Brush more butter on at the end and sprinkle with any remaining spice mixture.

Latkes

Servings: 12
Cooking Time: 13 Minutes

Ingredients:

- 1 russet potato
- ¼ onion
- 2 eggs, lightly beaten
- ⅓ cup flour*
- ½ teaspoon baking powder
- 1 teaspoon salt
- freshly ground black pepper
- canola or vegetable oil, in a spray bottle
- chopped chives, for garnish
- apple sauce
- sour cream

Directions:

1. Shred the potato and onion with a coarse box grater or a food processor with the shredding blade. Place the shredded vegetables into a colander or mesh strainer and squeeze or press down firmly to remove the excess water.
2. Transfer the onion and potato to a large bowl and add the eggs, flour, baking powder, salt and black pepper. Mix to combine and then shape the mixture into patties, about ¼-cup of mixture each. Brush or spray both sides of the latkes with oil.
3. Preheat the air fryer to 400°F.
4. Air-fry the latkes in batches. Transfer one layer of the latkes to the air fryer basket and air-fry at 400°F for 12 to 13 minutes, flipping them over halfway through the cooking time. Transfer the finished latkes to a platter and cover with aluminum foil, or place them in a warm oven to keep warm.
5. Garnish the latkes with chopped chives and serve with sour cream and applesauce.

Air-fried Potato Salad

Servings: 4
Cooking Time: 15 Minutes

Ingredients:

- 1⅓ pounds Yellow potatoes, such as Yukon Golds, cut into ½-inch chunks
- 1 large Sweet white onion(s), such as Vidalia, chopped into ½-inch pieces
- 1 tablespoon plus 2 teaspoons Olive oil
- ¾ cup Thinly sliced celery
- 6 tablespoons Regular or low-fat mayonnaise (gluten-free, if a concern)
- 2½ tablespoons Apple cider vinegar
- 1½ teaspoons Dijon mustard (gluten-free, if a concern)
- ¾ teaspoon Table salt
- ¼ teaspoon Ground black pepper

Directions:

1. Preheat the air fryer to 400°F.
2. Toss the potatoes, onion(s), and oil in a large bowl until the vegetables are glistening with oil.
3. When the machine is at temperature, transfer the vegetables to the basket, spreading them out into as even a layer as you can. Air-fry for 15 minutes, tossing and rearranging the vegetables every 3 minutes so that all surfaces get exposed to the air currents, until the vegetables are tender and even browned at the edges.
4. Pour the contents of the basket into a serving bowl. Cool for at least 5 minutes or up to 30 minutes. Add the celery, mayonnaise, vinegar, mustard, salt, and pepper. Stir well to coat. The potato salad can be made in advance; cover and refrigerate for up to 4 days.

Salmon Salad With Steamboat Dressing

Servings: 4
Cooking Time: 18 Minutes

Ingredients:

- ¼ teaspoon salt
- 1½ teaspoons dried dill weed
- 1 tablespoon fresh lemon juice

- 8 ounces fresh or frozen salmon fillet (skin on)
- 8 cups shredded romaine, Boston, or other leaf lettuce
- 8 spears cooked asparagus, cut in 1-inch pieces
- 8 cherry tomatoes, halved or quartered

Directions:

1. Mix the salt and dill weed together. Rub the lemon juice over the salmon on both sides and sprinkle the dill and salt all over. Refrigerate for 15 to 20minutes.
2. Make Steamboat Dressing and refrigerate while cooking salmon and preparing salad.
3. Cook salmon in air fryer basket at 330°F for 18 minutes. Cooking time will vary depending on thickness of fillets. When done, salmon should flake with fork but still be moist and tender.
4. Remove salmon from air fryer and cool slightly. At this point, the skin should slide off easily. Cut salmon into 4 pieces and discard skin.
5. Divide the lettuce among 4 plates. Scatter asparagus spears and tomato pieces evenly over the lettuce, allowing roughly 2 whole spears and 2 whole cherry tomatoes per plate.
6. Top each salad with one portion of the salmon and drizzle with a tablespoon of dressing. Serve with additional dressing to pass at the table.

Roasted Corn Salad

Servings: 3

Cooking Time: 15 Minutes

Ingredients:

- 3 4-inch lengths husked and de-silked corn on the cob
- Olive oil spray
- 1 cup Packed baby arugula leaves
- 12 Cherry tomatoes, halved
- Up to 3 Medium scallion(s), trimmed and thinly sliced
- 2 tablespoons Lemon juice
- 1 tablespoon Olive oil
- 1½ teaspoons Honey
- ¼ teaspoon Mild paprika
- ¼ teaspoon Dried oregano
- ¼ teaspoon, plus more to taste Table salt
- ¼ teaspoon Ground black pepper

Directions:

1. Preheat the air fryer to 400°F.
2. When the machine is at temperature, lightly coat the pieces of corn on the cob with olive oil spray. Set the pieces of corn in the basket with as much air space between them as possible. Air-fry undisturbed for 15 minutes, or until the corn is charred in a few spots.
3. Use kitchen tongs to transfer the corn to a wire rack. Cool for 15 minutes.
4. Cut the kernels off the ears by cutting the fat end off each piece so it will stand up straight on a cutting board, then running a knife down the corn. (Or you can save your fingers and buy a fancy tool to remove kernels from corn cobs. Check it out at online kitchenware stores.) Scoop the kernels into a serving bowl.
5. Chop the arugula into bite-size bits and add these to the kernels. Add the tomatoes and scallions, too. Whisk the lemon juice, olive oil, honey, paprika, oregano, salt, and pepper in a small bowl until the honey dissolves. Pour over the salad and toss well to coat, tasting for extra salt before serving.

Acorn Squash Halves With Maple Butter Glaze

Servings: 2

Cooking Time: 33 Minutes

Ingredients:

- 1 medium (1 to 1¼ pounds) Acorn squash
- Vegetable oil spray
- ¼ teaspoon Table salt
- 1½ tablespoons Butter, melted
- 1½ tablespoons Maple syrup

Directions:

1. Preheat the air fryer to 325°F (or 330°F, if that's the closest setting).
2. Cut a squash in half through the stem end. Use a flatware spoon (preferably, a serrated grapefruit spoon) to scrape out and discard the seeds and membranes in each half. Use a paring knife to make a crisscross pattern of cuts about ½ inch apart and ¼ inch deep across the

"meat" of the squash. If working with a second squash, repeat this step for that one.

3. Generously coat the cut side of the squash halves with vegetable oil spray. Sprinkle the halves with the salt. Set them in the basket cut side up with at least ¼ inch between them. Air-fry undisturbed for 30 minutes.

4. Increase the machine's temperature to 400°F. Mix the melted butter and syrup in a small bowl until uniform. Brush this mixture over the cut sides of the squash(es), letting it pool in the center. Air-fry undisturbed for 3 minutes, or until the glaze is bubbling.

5. Use a nonstick-safe spatula and kitchen tongs to transfer the squash halves cut side up to a wire rack. Cool for 5 to 10 minutes before serving.

Stuffed Onions

Servings: 6

Cooking Time: 27 Minutes

Ingredients:

- 6 Small 3½- to 4-ounce yellow or white onions
- Olive oil spray
- 6 ounces Bulk sweet Italian sausage meat (gluten-free, if a concern)
- 9 Cherry tomatoes, chopped
- 3 tablespoons Seasoned Italian-style dried bread crumbs (gluten-free, if a concern)
- 3 tablespoons (about ½ ounce) Finely grated Parmesan cheese

Directions:

1. Preheat the air fryer to 325°F (or 330°F, if that's the closest setting).
2. Cut just enough off the root ends of the onions so they will stand up on a cutting board when this end is turned down. Carefully peel off just the brown, papery skin. Now cut the top quarter off each and place the onion back on the cutting board with this end facing up. Use a flatware spoon (preferably a serrated grapefruit spoon) or a melon baller to scoop out the "insides" (interior layers) of the onion, leaving enough of the bottom and side walls so that the onion does not collapse. Depending on the thickness of the layers in the onion, this may be one or two of those layers—or even three, if they're very thin.
3. Coat the insides and outsides of the onions with olive oil spray. Set the onion "shells" in the basket and air-fry for 15 minutes.
4. Meanwhile, make the filling. Set a medium skillet over medium heat for a couple of minutes, then crumble in the sausage meat. Cook, stirring often, until browned, about 4 minutes. Transfer the contents of the skillet to a medium bowl (leave the fat behind in the skillet or add it to the bowl, depending on your cross-trainer regimen). Stir in the tomatoes, bread crumbs, and cheese until well combined.
5. When the onions are ready, use a nonstick-safe spatula to gently transfer them to a cutting board. Increase the air fryer's temperature to 350°F .
6. Pack the sausage mixture into the onion shells, gently compacting the filling and mounding it up at the top.
7. When the machine is at temperature, set the onions stuffing side up in the basket with at least ¼ inch between them. Air-fry for 12 minutes, or until lightly browned and sizzling hot.
8. Use a nonstick-safe spatula, and perhaps a flatware fork for balance, to transfer the onions to a cutting board or serving platter. Cool for 5 minutes before serving.

Brussels Sprouts

Servings: 3

Cooking Time: 5 Minutes

Ingredients:

- 1 10-ounce package frozen brussels sprouts, thawed and halved
- 2 teaspoons olive oil
- salt and pepper

Directions:

1. Toss the brussels sprouts and olive oil together.
2. Place them in the air fryer basket and season to taste with salt and pepper.
3. Cook at 360°F for approximately 5minutes, until the edges begin to brown.

Buttery Rolls

Servings: 6
Cooking Time: 14 Minutes

Ingredients:

- 6½ tablespoons Room-temperature whole or low-fat milk
- 3 tablespoons plus 1 teaspoon Butter, melted and cooled
- 3 tablespoons plus 1 teaspoon (or 1 medium egg, well beaten) Pasteurized egg substitute, such as Egg Beaters
- 1½ tablespoons Granulated white sugar
- 1¼ teaspoons Instant yeast
- ¼ teaspoon Table salt
- 2 cups, plus more for dusting All-purpose flour
- Vegetable oil
- Additional melted butter, for brushing

Directions:

1. Stir the milk, melted butter, pasteurized egg substitute (or whole egg), sugar, yeast, and salt in a medium bowl to combine. Stir in the flour just until the mixture makes a soft dough.
2. Lightly flour a clean, dry work surface. Turn the dough out onto the work surface. Knead the dough for 5 minutes to develop the gluten.
3. Lightly oil the inside of a clean medium bowl. Gather the dough into a compact ball and set it in the bowl. Turn the dough over so that its surface has oil on it all over. Cover the bowl tightly with plastic wrap and set aside in a warm, draft-free place until the dough has doubled in bulk, about 1½ hours.
4. Punch down the dough, then turn it out onto a clean, dry work surface. Divide it into 5 even balls for a small batch, 6 balls for a medium batch, or 8 balls for a large one.
5. For a small batch, lightly oil the inside of a 6-inch round cake pan and set the balls around its perimeter, separating them as much as possible.
6. For a medium batch, lightly oil the inside of a 7-inch round cake pan and set the balls in it with one ball at its center, separating them as much as possible.
7. For a large batch, lightly oil the inside of an 8-inch round cake pan and set the balls in it with one at the center, separating them as much as possible.
8. Cover with plastic wrap and set aside to rise for 30 minutes.
9. Preheat the air fryer to 350°F .
10. Uncover the pan and brush the rolls with a little melted butter, perhaps ½ teaspoon per roll. When the machine is at temperature, set the cake pan in the basket. Air-fry undisturbed for 14 minutes, or until the rolls have risen and browned.
11. Using kitchen tongs and a nonstick-safe spatula, two hot pads, or silicone baking mitts, transfer the cake pan from the basket to a wire rack. Cool the rolls in the pan for a minute or two. Turn the rolls out onto a wire rack, set them top side up again, and cool for at least another couple of minutes before serving warm.

Panko-crusted Zucchini Fries

Servings: 6
Cooking Time: 8 Minutes

Ingredients:

- 3 medium zucchinis
- ½ cup flour
- 1 teaspoon salt, divided
- ½ teaspoon black pepper, divided
- ¾ teaspoon dried thyme, divided
- 2 large eggs
- 1 ½ cups whole-wheat or plain panko breadcrumbs
- ½ cup grated Parmesan cheese

Directions:

1. Preheat the air fryer to 380°F.
2. Slice the zucchinis in half lengthwise, then into long strips about ½-inch thick, like thick fries.
3. In a medium bowl, mix the flour, ½ teaspoon of the salt, ¼ teaspoon of the black pepper, and ½ teaspoon of thyme.
4. In a separate bowl, whisk together the eggs, ½ teaspoon of the salt, and ¼ teaspoon of the black pepper.
5. In a third bowl, combine the breadcrumbs, cheese, and the remaining ¼ teaspoon of dried thyme.

6. Working with one zucchini fry at a time, dip the zucchini fry first into the flour mixture, then into the whisked eggs, and finally into the breading. Repeat until all the fries are breaded.
7. Place the zucchini fries into the air fryer basket, spray with cooking spray, and cook for 4 minutes; shake the basket and cook another 4 to 6 minutes or until golden brown and crispy.
8. Remove and serve warm.

Curried Cauliflower With Cashews And Yogurt

Servings: 2
Cooking Time: 12 Minutes

Ingredients:

- 4 cups cauliflower florets (about half a large head)
- 1 tablespoon olive oil
- salt
- 1 teaspoon curry powder
- ½ cup toasted, chopped cashews
- Cool Yogurt Drizzle
- ¼ cup plain yogurt
- 2 tablespoons sour cream
- 1 teaspoon lemon juice
- pinch cayenne pepper
- salt
- 1 teaspoon honey
- 1 tablespoon chopped fresh cilantro, plus leaves for garnish

Directions:

1. Preheat the air fryer to 400°F.
2. Toss the cauliflower florets with the olive oil, salt and curry powder, coating evenly.
3. Transfer the cauliflower to the air fryer basket and air-fry at 400°F for 12 minutes, shaking the basket a couple of times during the cooking process.
4. While the cauliflower is cooking, make the cool yogurt drizzle by combining all ingredients in a bowl.
5. When the cauliflower is cooked to your liking, serve it warm with the cool yogurt either underneath or drizzled over the top. Scatter the cashews and cilantro leaves around.

Homemade Potato Puffs

Servings: 4
Cooking Time: 15 Minutes

Ingredients:

- 1¾ cups Water
- 4 tablespoons (¼ cup/½ stick) Butter
- 2 cups plus 2 tablespoons Instant mashed potato flakes
- 1½ teaspoons Table salt
- ¾ teaspoon Ground black pepper
- ¼ teaspoon Mild paprika
- ¼ teaspoon Dried thyme
- 1¼ cups Seasoned Italian-style dried bread crumbs (gluten-free, if a concern)
- Olive oil spray

Directions:

1. Heat the water with the butter in a medium saucepan set over medium-low heat just until the butter melts. Do not bring to a boil.
2. Remove the saucepan from the heat and stir in the potato flakes, salt, pepper, paprika, and thyme until smooth. Set aside to cool for 5 minutes.
3. Preheat the air fryer to 400°F. Spread the bread crumbs on a dinner plate.
4. Scrape up 2 tablespoons of the potato flake mixture and form it into a small, oblong puff, like a little cylinder about 1½ inches long. Gently roll the puff in the bread crumbs until coated on all sides. Set it aside and continue making more, about 12 for the small batch, 18 for the medium batch, or 24 for the large.
5. Coat the potato cylinders with olive oil spray on all sides, then arrange them in the basket in one layer with some air space between them. Air-fry undisturbed for 15 minutes, or until crisp and brown.
6. Gently dump the contents of the basket onto a wire rack. Cool for 5 minutes before serving.

Brown Rice And Goat Cheese Croquettes

Servings: 3
Cooking Time: 8 Minutes

Ingredients:

- ¾ cup Water
- 6 tablespoons Raw medium-grain brown rice, such as brown Arborio
- ½ cup Shredded carrot
- ¼ cup Walnut pieces
- 3 tablespoons (about 1½ ounces) Soft goat cheese
- 1 tablespoon Pasteurized egg substitute, such as Egg Beaters (gluten-free, if a concern)
- ¼ teaspoon Dried thyme
- ¼ teaspoon Table salt
- ¼ teaspoon Ground black pepper
- Olive oil spray

Directions:

1. Combine the water, rice, and carrots in a small saucepan set over medium-high heat. Bring to a boil, stirring occasionally. Cover, reduce the heat to very low, and simmer very slowly for 45 minutes, or until the water has been absorbed and the rice is tender. Set aside, covered, for 10 minutes.
2. Scrape the contents of the saucepan into a food processor. Cool for 10 minutes.
3. Preheat the air fryer to 400°F.
4. Put the nuts, cheese, egg substitute, thyme, salt, and pepper into the food processor. Cover and pulse to a coarse paste, stopping the machine at least once to scrape down the inside of the canister.
5. Uncover the food processor; scrape down and remove the blade. Using wet, clean hands, form the mixture into two 4-inch-diameter patties for a small batch, three 4-inch-diameter patties for a medium batch, or four 4-inch-diameter patties for a large one. Generously coat both sides of the patties with olive oil spray.
6. Set the patties in the basket with as much air space between them as possible. Air-fry undisturbed for 8 minutes, or until brown and crisp.
7. Use a nonstick-safe spatula to transfer the croquettes to a wire rack. Cool for 5 minutes before serving.

Perfect Broccolini

Servings: 4
Cooking Time: 15 Minutes

Ingredients:

- 1 pound Broccolini
- Olive oil spray
- Coarse sea salt or kosher salt

Directions:

1. Preheat the air fryer to 375°F .
2. Place the broccolini on a cutting board. Generously coat it with olive oil spray, turning the vegetables and rearranging them before spraying a couple of times more, to make sure everything's well coated, even the flowery bits in their heads.
3. When the machine is at temperature, pile the broccolini in the basket, spreading it into as close to one layer as you can. Air-fry for 5 minutes, tossing once to get any covered or touching parts exposed to the air currents, until the leaves begin to get brown and even crisp. Watch carefully and use this visual cue to know the moment to stop the cooking.
4. Transfer the broccolini to a platter. Spread out the pieces and sprinkle them with salt to taste.

Fried Pearl Onions With Balsamic Vinegar And Basil

Servings: 2
Cooking Time: 10 Minutes

Ingredients:

- 1 pound fresh pearl onions
- 1 tablespoon olive oil
- salt and freshly ground black pepper
- 1 teaspoon high quality aged balsamic vinegar
- 1 tablespoon chopped fresh basil leaves (or mint)

Directions:

1. Preheat the air fryer to 400°F.
2. Decide whether you want to peel the onions before or after they cook. Peeling them ahead of time is a little

more laborious. Peeling after they cook is easier, but a little messier since the onions are hot and you may discard more of the onion than you'd like to. If you opt to peel them first, trim the tiny root of the onions off and pinch off any loose papery skins. (It's ok if there are some skins left on the onions.) Toss the pearl onions with the olive oil, salt and freshly ground black pepper.
3. Air-fry for 10 minutes, shaking the basket a couple of times during the cooking process. (If your pearl onions are very large, you may need to add a couple of minutes to this cooking time.)
4. Let the onions cool slightly and then slip off any remaining skins.
5. Toss the onions with the balsamic vinegar and basil and serve.

Cheesy Potato Pot

Servings: 4
Cooking Time: 13 Minutes

Ingredients:

- 3 cups cubed red potatoes (unpeeled, cut into ½-inch cubes)
- ½ teaspoon garlic powder
- salt and pepper
- 1 tablespoon oil
- chopped chives for garnish (optional)
- Sauce
- 2 tablespoons milk
- 1 tablespoon butter
- 2 ounces sharp Cheddar cheese, grated
- 1 tablespoon sour cream

Directions:

1. Place potato cubes in large bowl and sprinkle with garlic, salt, and pepper. Add oil and stir to coat well.
2. Cook at 390°F for 13 minutes or until potatoes are tender. Stir every 4 or 5minutes during cooking time.
3. While potatoes are cooking, combine milk and butter in a small saucepan. Warm over medium-low heat to melt butter. Add cheese and stir until it melts. The melted cheese will remain separated from the milk mixture. Remove from heat until potatoes are done.
4. When ready to serve, add sour cream to cheese mixture and stir over medium-low heat just until warmed. Place cooked potatoes in serving bowl. Pour sauce over potatoes and stir to combine.
5. Garnish with chives if desired.

Fried Okra

Servings: 4
Cooking Time: 8 Minutes

Ingredients:

- 1 pound okra
- 1 large egg
- 1 tablespoon milk
- 1 teaspoon salt, divided
- ½ teaspoon black pepper, divided
- ¼ teaspoon paprika
- ¼ teaspoon thyme
- ½ cup cornmeal
- ½ cup all-purpose flour

Directions:

1. Preheat the air fryer to 400°F.
2. Cut the okra into ½-inch rounds.
3. In a medium bowl, whisk together the egg, milk, ½ teaspoon of the salt, and ¼ teaspoon of black pepper. Place the okra into the egg mixture and toss until well coated.
4. In a separate bowl, mix together the remaining ½ teaspoon of salt, the remaining ¼ teaspoon of black pepper, the paprika, the thyme, the cornmeal, and the flour. Working in small batches, dredge the egg-coated okra in the cornmeal mixture until all the okra has been breaded.
5. Place a single layer of okra in the air fryer basket and spray with cooking spray. Cook for 4 minutes, toss to check for crispness, and cook another 4 minutes. Repeat in batches, as needed.

Cheesy Texas Toast

Servings: 2

Cooking Time: 4 Minutes

Ingredients:

- 2 1-inch-thick slice(s) Italian bread (each about 4 inches across)
- 4 teaspoons Softened butter
- 2 teaspoons Minced garlic
- ¼ cup (about ¾ ounce) Finely grated Parmesan cheese

Directions:

1. Preheat the air fryer to 400°F.
2. Spread one side of a slice of bread with 2 teaspoons butter. Sprinkle with 1 teaspoon minced garlic, followed by 2 tablespoons grated cheese. Repeat this process if you're making one or more additional toasts.
3. When the machine is at temperature, put the bread slice(s) cheese side up in the basket (with as much air space between them as possible if you're making more than one). Air-fry undisturbed for 4 minutes, or until browned and crunchy.
4. Use a nonstick-safe spatula to transfer the toasts cheese side up to a wire rack. Cool for 5 minutes before serving.

Blistered Tomatoes

Servings: 20

Cooking Time: 15 Minutes

Ingredients:

- 1½ pounds Cherry or grape tomatoes
- Olive oil spray
- 1½ teaspoons Balsamic vinegar
- ¼ teaspoon Table salt
- ¼ teaspoon Ground black pepper

Directions:

1. Put the basket in a drawer-style air fryer, or a baking tray in the lower third of a toaster oven–style air fryer. Place a 6-inch round cake pan in the basket or on the tray for a small batch, a 7-inch round cake pan for a medium batch, or an 8-inch round cake pan for a large one. Heat the air fryer to 400°F with the pan in the basket. When the machine is at temperature, keep heating the pan for 5 minutes more.
2. Place the tomatoes in a large bowl, coat them with the olive oil spray, toss gently, then spritz a couple of times more, tossing after each spritz, until the tomatoes are glistening.
3. Pour the tomatoes into the cake pan and air-fry undisturbed for 10 minutes, or until they split and begin to brown.
4. Use kitchen tongs and a nonstick-safe spatula, or silicone baking mitts, to remove the cake pan from the basket. Toss the hot tomatoes with the vinegar, salt, and pepper. Cool in the pan for a few minutes before serving.

Fingerling Potatoes

Servings: 4

Cooking Time: 15 Minutes

Ingredients:

- 1 pound fingerling potatoes
- 1 tablespoon light olive oil
- ½ teaspoon dried parsley
- ½ teaspoon lemon juice
- coarsely ground sea salt

Directions:

1. Cut potatoes in half lengthwise.
2. In a large bowl, combine potatoes, oil, parsley, and lemon juice. Stir well to coat potatoes.
3. Place potatoes in air fryer basket and cook at 360°F for 15 minutes or until lightly browned and tender inside.
4. Sprinkle with sea salt before serving.

Asparagus

Servings: 4

Cooking Time: 9 Minutes

Ingredients:

- 1 bunch asparagus (approx. 1 pound), washed and trimmed
- ⅛ teaspoon dried tarragon, crushed
- salt and pepper
- 1 to 2 teaspoons extra-light olive oil

Directions:

1. Spread asparagus spears on cookie sheet or cutting board.
2. Sprinkle with tarragon, salt, and pepper.
3. Drizzle with 1 teaspoon of oil and roll the spears or mix by hand. If needed, add up to 1 more teaspoon of oil and mix again until all spears are lightly coated.
4. Place spears in air fryer basket. If necessary, bend the longer spears to make them fit. It doesn't matter if they don't lie flat.
5. Cook at 390°F for 5minutes. Shake basket or stir spears with a spoon.
6. Cook for an additional 4 minutes or just until crisp-tender.

Steamboat Shrimp Salad

Servings: 4
Cooking Time: 4 Minutes

Ingredients:

- Steamboat Dressing
- ½ cup mayonnaise
- ½ cup plain yogurt
- 2 teaspoons freshly squeezed lemon juice (no substitutes)
- 2 teaspoons grated lemon rind
- 1 teaspoon dill weed, slightly crushed
- ½ teaspoon hot sauce
- Steamed Shrimp
- 24 small, raw shrimp, peeled and deveined
- 1 teaspoon lemon juice
- ¼ teaspoon Old Bay Seasoning
- Salad
- 8 cups romaine or Bibb lettuce, chopped or torn
- ¼ cup red onion, cut in thin slivers
- 12 black olives, sliced
- 12 cherry or grape tomatoes, halved
- 1 medium avocado, sliced or cut into large chunks

Directions:

1. Combine all dressing ingredients and mix well. Refrigerate while preparing shrimp and salad.
2. Sprinkle raw shrimp with lemon juice and Old Bay Seasoning. Use more Old Bay if you like your shrimp bold and spicy.
3. Pour 4 tablespoons of water in bottom of air fryer.
4. Place shrimp in air fryer basket in single layer.
5. Cook at 390°F for 4 minutes. Remove shrimp from basket and place in refrigerator to cool.
6. Combine all salad ingredients and mix gently. Divide among 4 salad plates or bowls.
7. Top each salad with 6 shrimp and serve with dressing.

Florentine Stuffed Tomatoes

Servings: 2
Cooking Time: 12 Minutes

Ingredients:

- 1 cup frozen spinach, thawed and squeezed dry
- ¼ cup toasted pine nuts
- ¼ cup grated mozzarella cheese
- ½ cup crumbled feta cheese
- ½ cup coarse fresh breadcrumbs
- 1 tablespoon olive oil
- salt and freshly ground black pepper
- 2 to 3 beefsteak tomatoes, halved horizontally and insides scooped out

Directions:

1. Combine the spinach, pine nuts, mozzarella and feta cheeses, breadcrumbs, olive oil, salt and freshly ground black pepper in a bowl. Spoon the mixture into the tomato halves. You should have enough filling for 2 to 3 tomatoes, depending on how big they are.
2. Preheat the air fryer to 350°F.
3. Place three or four tomato halves (depending on whether you're using 2 or 3 tomatoes and how big they are) into the air fryer and air-fry for 12 minutes. The tomatoes should be soft but still manageable and the tops should be lightly browned. Repeat with second batch if necessary.
4. Let the tomatoes cool for just a minute or two before serving.

Buttermilk Biscuits

Servings: 5

Cooking Time: 14 Minutes

Ingredients:

- 1⅔ cups, plus more for dusting All-purpose flour
- 1½ teaspoons Baking powder
- ¼ teaspoon Table salt
- 3 tablespoons plus 1 teaspoon Butter, cold and cut into small pieces
- ½ cup plus ½ tablespoon Cold buttermilk, regular or low-fat
- 2½ tablespoons Butter, melted and cooled

Directions:

1. Preheat the air fryer to 400°F.
2. Mix the flour, baking powder, and salt in a large bowl. Use a pastry cutter or a sturdy flatware fork to cut the cold butter pieces into the flour mixture, working the fat through the tines again and again until the mixture resembles coarse dry sand. Stir in the buttermilk to make a dough.
3. Very lightly dust a clean, dry work surface with flour. Turn the dough out onto it, dip your clean hands into flour, and press the dough into a ¾-inch-thick circle. Use a 3-inch round cookie cutter or sturdy drinking glass to cut the dough into rounds. Gather the dough scraps together, lightly shape again into a ¾-inch-thick circle, and cut out a few more rounds. You'll end up with 4 raw biscuits for a small air fryer, 5 for a medium, or 6 for a large.
4. For a small air fryer, brush the inside of a 6-inch round cake pan with a little more than half of the melted butter, then set the 4 raw biscuits in it, letting them touch but without squishing them.
5. For a medium air fryer, do the same with half of the melted butter in a 7-inch round cake pan and 5 raw biscuits.
6. And for a large air fryer, use a little more than half the melted butter to brush the inside of an 8-inch round cake pan, and set the 6 raw biscuits in it in the same way.
7. Brush the tops of the raw biscuits with the remaining melted butter.
8. Air-fry undisturbed for 14 minutes, or until the biscuits are golden brown and dry to the touch.
9. Using kitchen tongs and a nonstick-safe spatula, two hot pads, or silicone baking mitts, remove the cake pan from the basket and set it on a wire rack. Cool undisturbed for a couple of minutes. Turn the biscuits out onto the wire rack to cool for a couple of minutes more before serving.

Crispy Herbed Potatoes

Servings: 6

Cooking Time: 20 Minutes

Ingredients:

- 3 medium baking potatoes, washed and cubed
- ½ teaspoon dried thyme
- 1 teaspoon minced dried rosemary
- ½ teaspoon garlic powder
- 1 teaspoon sea salt
- ½ teaspoon black pepper
- 2 tablespoons extra-virgin olive oil
- ¼ cup chopped parsley

Directions:

1. Preheat the air fryer to 390°F.
2. Pat the potatoes dry. In a large bowl, mix together the cubed potatoes, thyme, rosemary, garlic powder, sea salt, and pepper. Drizzle and toss with olive oil.
3. Pour the herbed potatoes into the air fryer basket. Cook for 20 minutes, stirring every 5 minutes.
4. Toss the cooked potatoes with chopped parsley and serve immediately.
5. VARY IT! Potatoes are versatile — add any spice or seasoning mixture you prefer and create your own favorite side dish.

Sesame Carrots And Sugar Snap Peas

Servings: 4

Cooking Time: 16 Minutes

Ingredients:

- 1 pound carrots, peeled sliced on the bias (½-inch slices)

- 1 teaspoon olive oil
- salt and freshly ground black pepper
- ⅓ cup honey
- 1 tablespoon sesame oil
- 1 tablespoon soy sauce
- ½ teaspoon minced fresh ginger
- 4 ounces sugar snap peas (about 1 cup)
- 1½ teaspoons sesame seeds

Directions:

1. Preheat the air fryer to 360°F.
2. Toss the carrots with the olive oil, season with salt and pepper and air-fry for 10 minutes, shaking the basket once or twice during the cooking process.
3. Combine the honey, sesame oil, soy sauce and minced ginger in a large bowl. Add the sugar snap peas and the air-fried carrots to the honey mixture, toss to coat and return everything to the air fryer basket.
4. Turn up the temperature to 400°F and air-fry for an additional 6 minutes, shaking the basket once during the cooking process.
5. Transfer the carrots and sugar snap peas to a serving bowl. Pour the sauce from the bottom of the cooker over the vegetables and sprinkle sesame seeds over top. Serve immediately.

Green Peas With Mint

Servings: 4

Cooking Time: 5 Minutes

Ingredients:

- 1 cup shredded lettuce
- 1 10-ounce package frozen green peas, thawed
- 1 tablespoon fresh mint, shredded
- 1 teaspoon melted butter

Directions:

1. Lay the shredded lettuce in the air fryer basket.
2. Toss together the peas, mint, and melted butter and spoon over the lettuce.
3. Cook at 360°F for 5minutes, until peas are warm and lettuce wilts.

Panzanella Salad With Crispy Croutons

Servings: 4

Cooking Time: 3 Minutes

Ingredients:

- ½ French baguette, sliced in half lengthwise
- 2 large cloves garlic
- 2 large ripe tomatoes, divided
- 2 small Persian cucumbers, quartered and diced
- ¼ cup Kalamata olives
- 1 tablespoon chopped, fresh oregano or 1 teaspoon dried oregano
- ¼ cup chopped fresh basil
- ¼ cup chopped fresh parsley
- ½ cup sliced red onion
- 2 tablespoons red wine vinegar
- ¼ cup extra-virgin olive oil
- Salt and pepper, to taste

Directions:

1. Preheat the air fryer to 380°F.
2. Place the baguette into the air fryer and toast for 3 to 5 minutes or until lightly golden brown.
3. Remove the bread from air fryer and immediately rub 1 raw garlic clove firmly onto the inside portion of each piece of bread, scraping the garlic onto the bread.
4. Slice 1 of the tomatoes in half and rub the cut edge of one half of the tomato onto the toasted bread. Season the rubbed bread with sea salt to taste.
5. Cut the bread into cubes and place in a large bowl. Cube the remaining 1½ tomatoes and add to the bowl. Add the cucumbers, olives, oregano, basil, parsley, and onion; stir to mix. Drizzle the red wine vinegar into the bowl, and stir. Drizzle the olive oil over the top, stir, and adjust the seasonings with salt and pepper.
6. Serve immediately or allow to sit at room temperature up to 1 hour before serving.

Roasted Garlic

Servings: 20
Cooking Time: 40 Minutes

Ingredients:

- 20 Peeled medium garlic cloves
- 2 tablespoons, plus more Olive oil

Directions:

1. Preheat the air fryer to 400°F.
2. Set a 10-inch sheet of aluminum foil on your work surface for a small batch, a 14-inch sheet for a medium batch, or a 16-inch sheet for a large batch. Put the garlic cloves in its center in one layer without bunching the cloves together. (Spread them out a little for even cooking.) Drizzle the small batch with 1 tablespoon oil, the medium batch with 2 tablespoons, or the large one with 3 tablespoons. Fold up the sides and seal the foil into a packet.
3. When the machine is at temperature, put the packet in the basket. Air-fry for 40 minutes, or until very fragrant. The cloves inside should be golden and soft.
4. Transfer the packet to a cutting board. Cool for 5 minutes, then open and use the cloves hot. Or cool them to room temperature, set them in a small container or jar, pour in enough olive oil to cover them, seal or cover the container, and refrigerate for up to 2 weeks.

Steak Fries

Servings: 4
Cooking Time: 20 Minutes

Ingredients:

- 2 russet potatoes, scrubbed and cut into wedges lengthwise
- 1 tablespoon olive oil
- 2 teaspoons seasoning salt (recipe below)

Directions:

1. Preheat the air fryer to 400°F.
2. Toss the potatoes with the olive oil and the seasoning salt.
3. Air-fry for 20 minutes (depending on the size of the wedges), turning the potatoes over gently a few times throughout the cooking process to brown and cook them evenly.

Hasselbacks

Servings: 4
Cooking Time: 41 Minutes

Ingredients:

- 2 large potatoes (approx. 1 pound each)
- oil for misting or cooking spray
- salt, pepper, and garlic powder
- 1½ ounces sharp Cheddar cheese, sliced very thin
- ¼ cup chopped green onions
- 2 strips turkey bacon, cooked and crumbled
- light sour cream for serving (optional)

Directions:

1. Preheat air fryer to 390°F.
2. Scrub potatoes. Cut thin vertical slices ¼-inch thick crosswise about three-quarters of the way down so that bottom of potato remains intact.
3. Fan potatoes slightly to separate slices. Mist with oil and sprinkle with salt, pepper, and garlic powder to taste. Potatoes will be very stiff, but try to get some of the oil and seasoning between the slices.
4. Place potatoes in air fryer basket and cook for 40 minutes or until centers test done when pierced with a fork.
5. Top potatoes with cheese slices and cook for 30 seconds to 1 minute to melt cheese.
6. Cut each potato in half crosswise, and sprinkle with green onions and crumbled bacon. If you like, add a dollop of sour cream before serving.

Fried Eggplant Slices

Servings: 3
Cooking Time: 12 Minutes

Ingredients:

- 1½ sleeves (about 60 saltines) Saltine crackers
- ¾ cup Cornstarch
- 2 Large egg(s), well beaten
- 1 medium (about ¾ pound) Eggplant, stemmed, peeled, and cut into ¼-inch-thick rounds
- Olive oil spray

Directions:

1. Preheat the air fryer to 400°F. Also, position the rack in the center of the oven and heat the oven to 175°F.

2. Grind the saltines, in batches if necessary, in a food processor, pulsing the machine and rearranging the saltine pieces every few pulses. Or pulverize the saltines in a large, heavy zip-closed plastic bag with the bottom of a heavy saucepan. In either case, you want small bits of saltines, not just crumbs.
3. Set up and fill three shallow soup plates or small pie plates on your counter: one for the cornstarch, one for the beaten egg(s), and one for the pulverized saltines.
4. Set an eggplant slice in the cornstarch and turn it to coat on both sides. Use a brush to lightly remove any excess. Dip it into the beaten egg(s) and turn to coat both sides. Let any excess egg slip back into the rest, then set the slice in the saltines. Turn several times, pressing gently to coat both sides evenly but not heavily. Coat both sides of the slice with olive oil spray and set it aside. Continue dipping and coating the remaining slices.
5. Set one, two, or maybe three slices in the basket. There should be at least ½ inch between them for proper air flow. Air-fry undisturbed for 12 minutes, or until crisp and browned.
6. Use a nonstick-safe spatula to transfer the slice(s) to a large baking sheet. Slip it into the oven to keep the slices warm as you air-fry more batches, as needed, always transferring the slices to the baking sheet to stay warm.

Yellow Squash

Servings: 4

Cooking Time: 10 Minutes

Ingredients:

- 1 large yellow squash (about 1½ cups)
- 2 eggs
- ¼ cup buttermilk
- 1 cup panko breadcrumbs
- ¼ cup white cornmeal
- ½ teaspoon salt
- oil for misting or cooking spray

Directions:

1. Preheat air fryer to 390°F.
2. Cut the squash into ¼-inch slices.
3. In a shallow dish, beat together eggs and buttermilk.
4. In sealable plastic bag or container with lid, combine ¼ cup panko crumbs, white cornmeal, and salt. Shake to mix well.
5. Place the remaining ¾ cup panko crumbs in a separate shallow dish.
6. Dump all the squash slices into the egg/buttermilk mixture. Stir to coat.
7. Remove squash from buttermilk mixture with a slotted spoon, letting excess drip off, and transfer to the panko/cornmeal mixture. Close bag or container and shake well to coat.
8. Remove squash from crumb mixture, letting excess fall off. Return squash to egg/buttermilk mixture, stirring gently to coat. If you need more liquid to coat all the squash, add a little more buttermilk.
9. Remove each squash slice from egg wash and dip in a dish of ¾ cup panko crumbs.
10. Mist squash slices with oil or cooking spray and place in air fryer basket. Squash should be in a single layer, but it's okay if the slices crowd together and overlap a little.
11. Cook at 390°F for 5minutes. Shake basket to break up any that have stuck together. Mist again with oil or spray.
12. Cook 5minutes longer and check. If necessary, mist again with oil and cook an additional two minutes, until squash slices are golden brown and crisp.

Fried Eggplant Balls

Servings: 4

Cooking Time: 40 Minutes

Ingredients:

- 1 medium eggplant (about 1 pound)
- olive oil
- salt and freshly ground black pepper
- 1 cup grated Parmesan cheese
- 2 cups fresh breadcrumbs
- 2 tablespoons chopped fresh parsley
- 2 tablespoons chopped fresh basil
- 1 clove garlic, minced
- 1 egg, lightly beaten
- ½ cup fine dried breadcrumbs

Directions:

1. Preheat the air fryer to 400°F.
2. Quarter the eggplant by cutting it in half both lengthwise and horizontally. Make a few slashes in the flesh of the eggplant but not through the skin. Brush the cut surface of the eggplant generously with olive oil and transfer to the air fryer basket, cut side up. Air-fry for 10 minutes. Turn the eggplant quarters cut side down and air-fry for another 15 minutes or until the eggplant is soft all the way through. You may need to rotate the pieces in the air fryer so that they cook evenly. Transfer the eggplant to a cutting board to cool.
3. Place the Parmesan cheese, the fresh breadcrumbs, fresh herbs, garlic and egg in a food processor. Scoop the flesh out of the eggplant, discarding the skin and any pieces that are tough. You should have about 1 to 1½ cups of eggplant. Add the eggplant to the food processor and process everything together until smooth. Season with salt and pepper. Refrigerate the mixture for at least 30 minutes.
4. Place the dried breadcrumbs into a shallow dish or onto a plate. Scoop heaping tablespoons of the eggplant mixture into the dried breadcrumbs. Roll the dollops of eggplant in the breadcrumbs and then shape into small balls. You should have 16 to 18 eggplant balls at the end. Refrigerate until you are ready to air-fry.
5. Preheat the air fryer to 350°F.
6. Spray the eggplant balls and the air fryer basket with olive oil. Air-fry the eggplant balls for 15 minutes, rotating the balls during the cooking process to brown evenly.

Hasselback Garlic-and-butter Potatoes

Servings: 3

Cooking Time: 48 Minutes

Ingredients:

- 3 8-ounce russet potatoes
- 6. Brown button or Baby Bella mushrooms, very thinly sliced
- Olive oil spray
- 3 tablespoons Butter, melted and cooled
- 1 tablespoon Minced garlic
- ¾ teaspoon Table salt
- 3 tablespoons (about ½ ounce) Finely grated Parmesan cheese

Directions:

1. Preheat the air fryer to 350°F .
2. Cut slits down the length of each potato, about three-quarters down into the potato and spaced about ¼ inch apart. Wedge a thin mushroom slice in each slit. Generously coat the potatoes on all sides with olive oil spray.
3. When the machine is at temperature, set the potatoes mushroom side up in the basket with as much air space between them as possible. Air-fry undisturbed for 45 minutes, or tender when pricked with a fork.
4. Increase the machine's temperature to 400°F. Use kitchen tongs, and perhaps a flatware fork for balance, to gently transfer the potatoes to a cutting board. Brush each evenly with butter, then sprinkle the minced garlic and salt over them. Sprinkle the cheese evenly over the potatoes.
5. Use those same tongs to gently transfer the potatoes cheese side up to the basket in one layer with some space for air flow between them. Air-fry undisturbed for 3 minutes, or until the cheese has melted and begun to brown.
6. Use those same tongs to gently transfer the potatoes back to the wire rack. Cool for 5 minutes before serving.

Pork Tenderloin Salad

Servings: 4

Cooking Time: 25 Minutes

Ingredients:

- Pork Tenderloin
- ½ teaspoon smoked paprika
- ¼ teaspoon salt
- ¼ teaspoon garlic powder
- ½ teaspoon onion powder
- ⅛ teaspoon ginger
- 1 teaspoon extra-light olive oil
- ¾ pound pork tenderloin
- Dressing

- 3 tablespoons extra-light olive oil
- 2 tablespoons red wine vinegar
- 2 tablespoons Dijon mustard
- 1 tablespoon honey
- Salad
- ¼ sweet red bell pepper
- 1 large Granny Smith apple
- 8 cups shredded Napa cabbage

Directions:

1. Mix the tenderloin seasonings together with oil and rub all over surface of meat.
2. Place pork tenderloin in the air fryer basket and cook at 390°F for 25minutes, until meat registers 130°F on a meat thermometer.
3. Allow meat to rest while preparing salad and dressing.
4. In a jar, shake all dressing ingredients together until well mixed.
5. Cut the bell pepper into slivers, then core, quarter, and slice the apple crosswise.
6. In a large bowl, toss together the cabbage, bell pepper, apple, and dressing.
7. Divide salad mixture among 4 plates.
8. Slice pork tenderloin into ½-inch slices and divide among the 4 salads.
9. Serve with sweet potato or other vegetable chips.

Perfect Asparagus

Servings: 3

Cooking Time: 10 Minutes

Ingredients:

- 1 pound Very thin asparagus spears
- 2 tablespoons Olive oil
- 1 teaspoon Coarse sea salt or kosher salt
- ¾ teaspoon Finely grated lemon zest

Directions:

1. Preheat the air fryer to 400°F.
2. Trim just enough off the bottom of the asparagus spears so they'll fit in the basket. Put the spears on a large plate and drizzle them with some of the olive oil. Turn them over and drizzle more olive oil, working to get all the spears coated.
3. When the machine is at temperature, place the spears in one direction in the basket. They may be touching. Air-fry for 10 minutes, tossing and rearranging the spears twice, until tender.
4. Dump the contents of the basket on a serving platter. Spread out the spears. Sprinkle them with the salt and lemon zest while still warm. Serve at once.

Stuffed Avocados

Servings: 4

Cooking Time: 8 Minutes

Ingredients:

- 1 cup frozen shoepeg corn, thawed
- 1 cup cooked black beans
- ¼ cup diced onion
- ½ teaspoon cumin
- 2 teaspoons lime juice, plus extra for serving
- salt and pepper
- 2 large avocados, split in half, pit removed

Directions:

1. Mix together the corn, beans, onion, cumin, and lime juice. Season to taste with salt and pepper.
2. Scoop out some of the flesh from center of each avocado and set aside. Divide corn mixture evenly between the cavities.
3. Set avocado halves in air fryer basket and cook at 360°F for 8 minutes, until corn mixture is hot.
4. Season the avocado flesh that you scooped out with a squirt of lime juice, salt, and pepper. Spoon it over the cooked halves.

Rosemary Roasted Potatoes With Lemon

Servings: 4

Cooking Time: 12 Minutes

Ingredients:

- 1 pound small red-skinned potatoes, halved or cut into bite-sized chunks
- 1 tablespoon olive oil
- 1 teaspoon finely chopped fresh rosemary
- ¼ teaspoon salt
- freshly ground black pepper
- 1 tablespoon lemon zest

Directions:

1. Preheat the air fryer to 400°F.
2. Toss the potatoes with the olive oil, rosemary, salt and freshly ground black pepper.
3. Air-fry for 12 minutes (depending on the size of the chunks), tossing the potatoes a few times throughout the cooking process.
4. As soon as the potatoes are tender to a knifepoint, toss them with the lemon zest and more salt if desired.

Asparagus Fries

Servings: 4

Cooking Time: 5 Minutes Per Batch

Ingredients:

- 12 ounces fresh asparagus spears with tough ends trimmed off
- 2 egg whites
- ¼ cup water
- ¾ cup panko breadcrumbs
- ¼ cup grated Parmesan cheese, plus 2 tablespoons
- ¼ teaspoon salt
- oil for misting or cooking spray

Directions:

1. Preheat air fryer to 390°F.
2. In a shallow dish, beat egg whites and water until slightly foamy.
3. In another shallow dish, combine panko, Parmesan, and salt.
4. Dip asparagus spears in egg, then roll in crumbs. Spray with oil or cooking spray.
5. Place a layer of asparagus in air fryer basket, leaving just a little space in between each spear. Stack another layer on top, crosswise. Cook at 390°F for 5 minutes, until crispy and golden brown.
6. Repeat to cook remaining asparagus.

Charred Radicchio Salad

Servings: 4

Cooking Time: 5 Minutes

Ingredients:

- 2 Small 5- to 6-ounce radicchio head(s)
- 3 tablespoons Olive oil
- ½ teaspoon Table salt
- 2 tablespoons Balsamic vinegar
- Up to ¼ teaspoon Red pepper flakes

Directions:

1. Preheat the air fryer to 375°F .
2. Cut the radicchio head(s) into quarters through the stem end. Brush the oil over the heads, particularly getting it between the leaves along the cut sides. Sprinkle the radicchio quarters with the salt.
3. When the machine is at temperature, set the quarters cut sides up in the basket with as much air space between them as possible. They should not touch. Air-fry undisturbed for 5 minutes, watching carefully because they burn quickly, until blackened in bits and soft.
4. Use a nonstick-safe spatula to transfer the quarters to a cutting board. Cool for a minute or two, then cut out the thick stems inside the heads. Discard these tough bits and chop the remaining heads into bite-size bits. Scrape them into a bowl. Add the vinegar and red pepper flakes. Toss well and serve warm.

Mashed Potato Tots

Servings: 18
Cooking Time: 10 Minutes

Ingredients:

- 1 medium potato or 1 cup cooked mashed potatoes
- 1 tablespoon real bacon bits
- 2 tablespoons chopped green onions, tops only
- ¼ teaspoon onion powder
- 1 teaspoon dried chopped chives
- salt
- 2 tablespoons flour
- 1 egg white, beaten
- ½ cup panko breadcrumbs
- oil for misting or cooking spray

Directions:

1. If using cooked mashed potatoes, jump to step 4.
2. Peel potato and cut into ½-inch cubes. (Small pieces cook more quickly.) Place in saucepan, add water to cover, and heat to boil. Lower heat slightly and continue cooking just until tender, about 10minutes.
3. Drain potatoes and place in ice cold water. Allow to cool for a minute or two, then drain well and mash.
4. Preheat air fryer to 390°F.
5. In a large bowl, mix together the potatoes, bacon bits, onions, onion powder, chives, salt to taste, and flour. Add egg white and stir well.
6. Place panko crumbs on a sheet of wax paper.
7. For each tot, use about 2 teaspoons of potato mixture. To shape, drop the measure of potato mixture onto panko crumbs and push crumbs up and around potatoes to coat edges. Then turn tot over to coat other side with crumbs.
8. Mist tots with oil or cooking spray and place in air fryer basket, crowded but not stacked.
9. Cook at 390°F for 10 minutes, until browned and crispy.
10. Repeat steps 8 and 9 to cook remaining tots.

Crispy, Cheesy Leeks

Servings: 4
Cooking Time: 15 Minutes

Ingredients:

- 2 Medium leek(s), about 9 ounces each
- Olive oil spray
- ¼ cup Seasoned Italian-style dried bread crumbs (gluten-free, if a concern)
- ¼ cup (about ¾ ounce) Finely grated Parmesan cheese
- 2 tablespoons Olive oil

Directions:

1. Preheat the air fryer to 350°F .
2. Trim off the root end of the leek(s) as well as the dark green top(s), leaving about a 5-inch usable section. Split the leek section(s) in half lengthwise. Set the leek halves cut side up on your work surface. Pull out and remove in one piece the semicircles that make up the inner structure of the leek, about halfway down. Set the removed "inside" next to the outer leek "shells" on your cutting board. Generously coat them all on all sides (particularly the "bottoms") with olive oil spray.
3. Set the leeks and their insides cut side up in the basket with as much air space between them as possible. Air-fry undisturbed for 12 minutes.
4. Meanwhile, mix the bread crumbs, cheese, and olive oil in a small bowl until well combined.
5. After 12 minutes in the air fryer, sprinkle this mixture inside the leek shells and on top of the leek insides. Increase the machine's temperature to 375°F (or 380°F or 390°F, if one of these is the closest setting). Air-fry undisturbed for 3 minutes, or until the topping is lightly browned.
6. Use a nonstick-safe spatula to transfer the leeks to a serving platter. Cool for a few minutes before serving warm.

Mushrooms

Servings: 4
Cooking Time: 12 Minutes

Ingredients:

- 8 ounces whole white button mushrooms
- ½ teaspoon salt
- ⅛ teaspoon pepper
- ¼ teaspoon garlic powder
- ¼ teaspoon onion powder

- 5 tablespoons potato starch
- 1 egg, beaten
- ¾ cup panko breadcrumbs
- oil for misting or cooking spray

Directions:

1. Place mushrooms in a large bowl. Add the salt, pepper, garlic and onion powders, and stir well to distribute seasonings.
2. Add potato starch to mushrooms and toss in bowl until well coated.
3. Dip mushrooms in beaten egg, roll in panko crumbs, and mist with oil or cooking spray.
4. Place mushrooms in air fryer basket. You can cook them all at once, and it's okay if a few are stacked.
5. Cook at 390°F for 5minutes. Shake basket, then continue cooking for 7 more minutes, until golden brown and crispy.

Roasted Belgian Endive With Pistachios And Lemon

Servings: 2

Cooking Time: 7 Minutes

Ingredients:

- 2 Medium 3-ounce Belgian endive head(s)
- 2 tablespoons Olive oil
- ½ teaspoon Table salt
- ¼ cup Finely chopped unsalted shelled pistachios
- Up to 2 teaspoons Lemon juice

Directions:

1. Preheat the air fryer to 325°F (or 330°F, if that's the closest setting).
2. Trim the Belgian endive head(s), removing the little bit of dried-out stem end but keeping the leaves intact. Quarter the head(s) through the stem (which will hold the leaves intact). Brush the endive quarters with oil, getting it down between the leaves. Sprinkle the quarters with salt.
3. When the machine is at temperature, set the endive quarters cut sides up in the basket with as much air space between them as possible. They should not touch. Air-fry undisturbed for 7 minutes, or until lightly browned along the edges.
4. Use kitchen tongs to transfer the endive quarters to serving plates or a platter. Sprinkle with the pistachios and lemon juice. Serve warm or at room temperature.

Mushrooms, Sautéed

Servings: 4

Cooking Time: 4 Minutes

Ingredients:

- 8 ounces sliced white mushrooms, rinsed and well drained
- ¼ teaspoon garlic powder
- 1 tablespoon Worcestershire sauce

Directions:

1. Place mushrooms in a large bowl and sprinkle with garlic powder and Worcestershire. Stir well to distribute seasonings evenly.
2. Place in air fryer basket and cook at 390°F for 4 minutes, until tender.

Roasted Brussels Sprouts With Bacon

Servings: 4

Cooking Time: 20 Minutes

Ingredients:

- 4 slices thick-cut bacon, chopped (about ¼ pound)
- 1 pound Brussels sprouts, halved (or quartered if large)
- freshly ground black pepper

Directions:

1. Preheat the air fryer to 380°F.
2. Air-fry the bacon for 5 minutes, shaking the basket once or twice during the cooking time.
3. Add the Brussels sprouts to the basket and drizzle a little bacon fat from the bottom of the air fryer drawer into the basket. Toss the sprouts to coat with the bacon fat. Air-fry for an additional 15 minutes, or until the Brussels sprouts are tender to a knifepoint.
4. Season with freshly ground black pepper.

Perfect French Fries

Servings: 3
Cooking Time: 37 Minutes

Ingredients:

- 1 pound Large russet potato(es)
- Vegetable oil or olive oil spray
- ½ teaspoon Table salt

Directions:

1. Cut each potato lengthwise into ¼-inch-thick slices. Cut each of these lengthwise into ¼-inch-thick matchsticks.
2. Set the potato matchsticks in a big bowl of cool water and soak for 5 minutes. Drain in a colander set in the sink, then spread the matchsticks out on paper towels and dry them very well.
3. Preheat the air fryer to 225°F (or 230°F, if that's the closest setting).
4. When the machine is at temperature, arrange the matchsticks in an even layer (if overlapping but not compact) in the basket. Air-fry for 20 minutes, tossing and rearranging the fries twice.
5. Pour the contents of the basket into a big bowl. Increase the air fryer's temperature to 325°F (or 330°F, if that's the closest setting).
6. Generously coat the fries with vegetable or olive oil spray. Toss well, then coat them again to make sure they're covered on all sides, tossing (and maybe spraying) a couple of times to make sure.
7. When the machine is at temperature, pour the fries into the basket and air-fry for 12 minutes, tossing and rearranging the fries at least twice.
8. Increase the machine's temperature to 375°F (or 380°F or 390°F, if one of these is the closest setting). Air-fry for 5 minutes more (from the moment you raise the temperature), tossing and rearranging the fries at least twice to keep them from burning and to make sure they all get an even measure of the heat, until brown and crisp.
9. Pour the contents of the basket into a serving bowl. Toss the fries with the salt and serve hot.

Onions

Servings: 4
Cooking Time: 18 Minutes

Ingredients:

- 2 yellow onions (Vidalia or 1015 recommended)
- salt and pepper
- ¼ teaspoon ground thyme
- ¼ teaspoon smoked paprika
- 2 teaspoons olive oil
- 1 ounce Gruyère cheese, grated

Directions:

1. Peel onions and halve lengthwise (vertically).
2. Sprinkle cut sides of onions with salt, pepper, thyme, and paprika.
3. Place each onion half, cut-surface up, on a large square of aluminum foil. Pull sides of foil up to cup around onion. Drizzle cut surface of onions with oil.
4. Crimp foil at top to seal closed.
5. Place wrapped onions in air fryer basket and cook at 390°F for 18 minutes. When done, onions should be soft enough to pierce with fork but still slightly firm.
6. Open foil just enough to sprinkle each onion with grated cheese.
7. Cook for 30 seconds to 1 minute to melt cheese.

Roasted Garlic And Thyme Tomatoes

Servings: 2
Cooking Time: 15 Minutes

Ingredients:

- 4 Roma tomatoes
- 1 tablespoon olive oil
- salt and freshly ground black pepper
- 1 clove garlic, minced
- ½ teaspoon dried thyme

Directions:

1. Preheat the air fryer to 390°F.
2. Cut the tomatoes in half and scoop out the seeds and any pithy parts with your fingers. Place the tomatoes in a bowl and toss with the olive oil, salt, pepper, garlic and thyme.

3. Transfer the tomatoes to the air fryer, cut side up. Air-fry for 15 minutes. The edges should just start to brown. Let the tomatoes cool to an edible temperature for a few minutes and then use in pastas, on top of crostini, or as an accompaniment to any poultry, meat or fish.

Glazed Carrots

Servings: 4

Cooking Time: 10 Minutes

Ingredients:

- 2 teaspoons honey
- 1 teaspoon orange juice
- ½ teaspoon grated orange rind
- ⅛ teaspoon ginger
- 1 pound baby carrots
- 2 teaspoons olive oil
- ¼ teaspoon salt

Directions:

1. Combine honey, orange juice, grated rind, and ginger in a small bowl and set aside.
2. Toss the carrots, oil, and salt together to coat well and pour them into the air fryer basket.
3. Cook at 390°F for 5minutes. Shake basket to stir a little and cook for 4 minutes more, until carrots are barely tender.
4. Pour carrots into air fryer baking pan.
5. Stir the honey mixture to combine well, pour glaze over carrots, and stir to coat.
6. Cook at 360°F for 1 minute or just until heated through.

Roasted Ratatouille Vegetables

Servings: 2

Cooking Time: 15 Minutes

Ingredients:

- 1 baby or Japanese eggplant, cut into 1½-inch cubes
- 1 red pepper, cut into 1-inch chunks
- 1 yellow pepper, cut into 1-inch chunks
- 1 zucchini, cut into 1-inch chunks
- 1 clove garlic, minced
- ½ teaspoon dried basil
- 1 tablespoon olive oil
- salt and freshly ground black pepper
- ¼ cup sliced sun-dried tomatoes in oil
- 2 tablespoons chopped fresh basil

Directions:

1. Preheat the air fryer to 400°F.
2. Toss the eggplant, peppers and zucchini with the garlic, dried basil, olive oil, salt and freshly ground black pepper.
3. Air-fry the vegetables at 400°F for 15 minutes, shaking the basket a few times during the cooking process to redistribute the ingredients.
4. As soon as the vegetables are tender, toss them with the sliced sun-dried tomatoes and fresh basil and serve.

Roasted Fennel Salad

Servings: 3

Cooking Time: 20 Minutes

Ingredients:

- 3 cups (about ¾ pound) Trimmed fennel (see the headnote), roughly chopped
- 1½ tablespoons Olive oil
- ¼ teaspoon Table salt
- ¼ teaspoon Ground black pepper
- 1½ tablespoons White balsamic vinegar (see here)

Directions:

1. Preheat the air fryer to 400°F.
2. Toss the fennel, olive oil, salt, and pepper in a large bowl until the fennel is well coated in the oil.
3. When the machine is at temperature, pour the fennel into the basket, spreading it out into as close to one layer as possible. Air-fry for 20 minutes, tossing and rearranging the fennel pieces twice so that any covered or touching parts get exposed to the air currents, until golden at the edges and softened.
4. Pour the fennel into a serving bowl. Add the vinegar while hot. Toss well, then cool a couple of minutes before serving. Or serve at room temperature.

Buttery Stuffed Tomatoes

Servings: 6
Cooking Time: 15 Minutes

Ingredients:

- 3 8-ounce round tomatoes
- ½ cup plus 1 tablespoon Plain panko bread crumbs (gluten-free, if a concern)
- 3 tablespoons (about ½ ounce) Finely grated Parmesan cheese
- 3 tablespoons Butter, melted and cooled
- 4 teaspoons Stemmed and chopped fresh parsley leaves
- 1 teaspoon Minced garlic
- ¼ teaspoon Table salt
- Up to ¼ teaspoon Red pepper flakes
- Olive oil spray

Directions:

1. Preheat the air fryer to 375°F .
2. Cut the tomatoes in half through their "equators" (that is, not through the stem ends). One at a time, gently squeeze the tomato halves over a trash can, using a clean finger to gently force out the seeds and most of the juice inside, working carefully so that the tomato doesn't lose its round shape or get crushed.
3. Stir the bread crumbs, cheese, butter, parsley, garlic, salt, and red pepper flakes in a bowl until the bread crumbs are moistened and the parsley is uniform throughout the mixture. Pile this mixture into the spaces left in the tomato halves. Press gently to compact the filling. Coat the tops of the tomatoes with olive oil spray.
4. Place the tomatoes cut side up in the basket. They may touch each other. Air-fry for 15 minutes, or until the filling is lightly browned and crunchy.
5. Use nonstick-safe spatula and kitchen tongs for balance to gently transfer the stuffed tomatoes to a platter or a cutting board. Cool for a couple of minutes before serving.

Summer Vegetables With Balsamic Drizzle, Goat Cheese And Basil

Servings: 2
Cooking Time: 17 Minutes

Ingredients:

- 1 cup balsamic vinegar
- 1 zucchini, sliced
- 1 yellow squash, sliced
- 2 tablespoons olive oil
- 1 clove garlic, minced
- ½ teaspoon Italian seasoning
- salt and freshly ground black pepper
- ½ cup cherry tomatoes, halved
- 2 ounces crumbled goat cheese
- 2 tablespoons chopped fresh basil, plus more leaves for garnish

Directions:

1. Place the balsamic vinegar in a small saucepot on the stovetop. Bring the vinegar to a boil, lower the heat and simmer uncovered for 20 minutes, until the mixture reduces and thickens. Set aside to cool.
2. Preheat the air fryer to 390°F.
3. Combine the zucchini and yellow squash in a large bowl. Add the olive oil, minced garlic, Italian seasoning, salt and pepper and toss to coat.
4. Air-fry the vegetables at 390°F for 10 minutes, shaking the basket several times during the cooking process. Add the cherry tomatoes and continue to air-fry for another 5 minutes. Sprinkle the goat cheese over the vegetables and air-fry for 2 more minutes.
5. Transfer the vegetables to a serving dish, drizzle with the balsamic reduction and season with freshly ground black pepper. Garnish with the fresh basil leaves.

Hawaiian Brown Rice

Servings: 4
Cooking Time: 12 Minutes

Ingredients:

- ¼ pound ground sausage
- 1 teaspoon butter
- ¼ cup minced onion
- ¼ cup minced bell pepper
- 2 cups cooked brown rice
- 1 8-ounce can crushed pineapple, drained

Directions:

1. Shape sausage into 3 or 4 thin patties. Cook at 390°F for 6 to 8minutes or until well done. Remove from air fryer, drain, and crumble. Set aside.
2. Place butter, onion, and bell pepper in baking pan. Cook at 390°F for 1 minute and stir. Cook 4 minutes longer or just until vegetables are tender.
3. Add sausage, rice, and pineapple to vegetables and stir together.
4. Cook at 390°F for 2 minutes, until heated through.

Wilted Brussels Sprout Slaw

Servings: 4

Cooking Time: 18 Minutes

Ingredients:

- 2 Thick-cut bacon strip(s), halved widthwise (gluten-free, if a concern)
- 4½ cups (about 1 pound 2 ounces) Bagged shredded Brussels sprouts
- ¼ teaspoon Table salt
- 2 tablespoons White balsamic vinegar (see here)
- 2 teaspoons Worcestershire sauce (gluten-free, if a concern)
- 1 teaspoon Dijon mustard (gluten-free, if a concern)
- ¼ teaspoon Ground black pepper

Directions:

1. Preheat the air fryer to 375°F .
2. When the machine is at temperature, lay the bacon strip halves in the basket in one layer and air-fry for 10 minutes, or until crisp.
3. Use kitchen tongs to transfer the bacon pieces to a wire rack. Put the shredded Brussels sprouts in a large bowl. Drain any fat from the basket or the tray under the basket onto the Brussels sprouts. Add the salt and toss well to coat.
4. Put the Brussels sprout shreds in the basket, spreading them out into as close to an even layer as you can. Air-fry for 8 minutes, tossing the basket's contents at least three times, until wilted and lightly browned.
5. Pour the contents of the basket into a serving bowl. Chop the bacon and add it to the Brussels sprouts. Add the vinegar, Worcestershire sauce, mustard, and pepper. Toss well to blend the dressing and coat the Brussels sprout shreds. Serve warm.

Mashed Sweet Potato Tots

Servings: 18

Cooking Time: 12 Minutes

Ingredients:

- 1 cup cooked mashed sweet potatoes
- 1 egg white, beaten
- ⅛ teaspoon ground cinnamon
- 1 dash nutmeg
- 2 tablespoons chopped pecans
- 1½ teaspoons honey
- salt
- ½ cup panko breadcrumbs
- oil for misting or cooking spray

Directions:

1. Preheat air fryer to 390°F.
2. In a large bowl, mix together the potatoes, egg white, cinnamon, nutmeg, pecans, honey, and salt to taste.
3. Place panko crumbs on a sheet of wax paper.
4. For each tot, use about 2 teaspoons of sweet potato mixture. To shape, drop the measure of potato mixture onto panko crumbs and push crumbs up and around potatoes to coat edges. Then turn tot over to coat other side with crumbs.
5. Mist tots with oil or cooking spray and place in air fryer basket in single layer.
6. Cook at 390°F for 12 minutes, until browned and crispy.
7. Repeat steps 5 and 6 to cook remaining tots.

Five-spice Roasted Sweet Potatoes

Servings: 4

Cooking Time: 12 Minutes

Ingredients:

- ½ teaspoon ground cinnamon
- ¼ teaspoon ground cumin
- ¼ teaspoon paprika
- 1 teaspoon chile powder
- ⅛ teaspoon turmeric
- ½ teaspoon salt (optional)

- freshly ground black pepper
- 2 large sweet potatoes, peeled and cut into ¾-inch cubes (about 3 cups)
- 1 tablespoon olive oil

Directions:

1. In a large bowl, mix together cinnamon, cumin, paprika, chile powder, turmeric, salt, and pepper to taste.
2. Add potatoes and stir well.
3. Drizzle the seasoned potatoes with the olive oil and stir until evenly coated.
4. Place seasoned potatoes in the air fryer baking pan or an ovenproof dish that fits inside your air fryer basket.
5. Cook for 6minutes at 390°F, stop, and stir well.
6. Cook for an additional 6minutes.

Parsnip Fries With Romesco Sauce

Servings: 2

Cooking Time: 24 Minutes

Ingredients:

- Romesco Sauce:
- 1 red bell pepper, halved and seeded
- 1 (1-inch) thick slice of Italian bread, torn into pieces (about 1 to 1½ cups)
- 1 cup almonds, toasted
- olive oil
- ½ Jalapeño pepper, seeded
- 1 tablespoon fresh parsley leaves
- 1 clove garlic
- 2 Roma tomatoes, peeled and seeded (or ⅓ cup canned crushed tomatoes)
- 1 tablespoon red wine vinegar
- ¼ teaspoon smoked paprika
- ½ teaspoon salt
- ¾ cup olive oil
- 3 parsnips, peeled and cut into long strips
- 2 teaspoons olive oil
- salt and freshly ground black pepper

Directions:

1. Preheat the air fryer to 400°F.
2. Place the red pepper halves, cut side down, in the air fryer basket and air-fry for 10 minutes, or until the skin turns black all over. Remove the pepper from the air fryer and let it cool. When it is cool enough to handle, peel the pepper.
3. Toss the torn bread and almonds with a little olive oil and air-fry for 4 minutes, shaking the basket a couple times throughout the cooking time. When the bread and almonds are nicely toasted, remove them from the air fryer and let them cool for just a minute or two.
4. Combine the toasted bread, almonds, roasted red pepper, Jalapeño pepper, parsley, garlic, tomatoes, vinegar, smoked paprika and salt in a food processor or blender. Process until smooth. With the processor running, add the olive oil through the feed tube until the sauce comes together in a smooth paste that is barely pourable.
5. Toss the parsnip strips with the olive oil, salt and freshly ground black pepper and air-fry at 400°F for 10 minutes, shaking the basket a couple times during the cooking process so they brown and cook evenly. Serve the parsnip fries warm with the Romesco sauce to dip into.

Okra

Servings: 4

Cooking Time: 12 Minutes

Ingredients:

- 7–8 ounces fresh okra
- 1 egg
- 1 cup milk
- 1 cup breadcrumbs
- ½ teaspoon salt
- oil for misting or cooking spray

Directions:

1. Remove stem ends from okra and cut in ½-inch slices.

2. In a medium bowl, beat together egg and milk. Add okra slices and stir to coat.
3. In a sealable plastic bag or container with lid, mix together the breadcrumbs and salt.
4. Remove okra from egg mixture, letting excess drip off, and transfer into bag with breadcrumbs.
5. Shake okra in crumbs to coat well.
6. Place all of the coated okra into the air fryer basket and mist with oil or cooking spray. Okra doesn't need to cook in a single layer, nor is it necessary to spray all sides at this point. A good spritz on top will do.
7. Cook at 390°F for 5minutes. Shake basket to redistribute and give it another spritz as you shake.
8. Cook 5 more minutes. Shake and spray again. Cook for 2 minutes longer or until golden brown and crispy.

Hole In One

Servings: 1

Cooking Time: 7 Minutes

Ingredients:

- 1 slice bread
- 1 teaspoon soft butter
- 1 egg
- salt and pepper
- 1 tablespoon shredded Cheddar cheese
- 2 teaspoons diced ham

Directions:

1. Place a 6 x 6-inch baking dish inside air fryer basket and preheat fryer to 330°F.
2. Using a 2½-inch-diameter biscuit cutter, cut a hole in center of bread slice.
3. Spread softened butter on both sides of bread.
4. Lay bread slice in baking dish and crack egg into the hole. Sprinkle egg with salt and pepper to taste.
5. Cook for 5minutes.
6. Turn toast over and top it with shredded cheese and diced ham.
7. Cook for 2 more minutes or until yolk is done to your liking.

Garlic Parmesan Bread Ring

Servings: 6

Cooking Time: 30 Minutes

Ingredients:

- ½ cup unsalted butter, melted
- ¼ teaspoon salt (omit if using salted butter)
- ¾ cup grated Parmesan cheese
- 3 to 4 cloves garlic, minced
- 1 tablespoon chopped fresh parsley
- 1 pound frozen bread dough, defrosted
- olive oil
- 1 egg, beaten

Directions:

1. Combine the melted butter, salt, Parmesan cheese, garlic and chopped parsley in a small bowl.
2. Roll the dough out into a rectangle that measures 8 inches by 17 inches. Spread the butter mixture over the dough, leaving a half-inch border un-buttered along one of the long edges. Roll the dough from one long edge to the other, ending with the un-buttered border. Pinch the seam shut tightly. Shape the log into a circle sealing the ends together by pushing one end into the other and stretching the dough around it.
3. Cut out a circle of aluminum foil that is the same size as the air fryer basket. Brush the foil circle with oil and place an oven safe ramekin or glass in the center. Transfer the dough ring to the aluminum foil circle, around the ramekin. This will help you make sure the dough will fit in the basket and maintain its ring shape. Use kitchen shears to cut 8 slits around the outer edge of the dough ring halfway to the center. Brush the dough ring with egg wash.
4. Preheat the air fryer to 400°F for 4 minutes. When it has Preheated, brush the sides of the basket with oil and transfer the dough ring, foil circle and ramekin into the basket. Slide the drawer back into the air fryer, but do not turn the air fryer on. Let the dough rise inside the warm air fryer for 30 minutes.
5. After the bread has proofed in the air fryer for 30 minutes, set the temperature to 340°F and air-fry the bread ring for 15 minutes. Flip the bread over by inverting it onto a plate or cutting board and sliding it back into the air fryer basket. Air-fry for another 15 minutes. Let the bread cool for a few minutes before slicing the bread ring in between the slits and serving warm.

Chocolate Almond Crescent Rolls

Servings: 4

Cooking Time: 8 Minutes

Ingredients:

- 1 (8-ounce) tube of crescent roll dough
- ⅔ cup semi-sweet or bittersweet chocolate chunks
- 1 egg white, lightly beaten
- ¼ cup sliced almonds
- powdered sugar, for dusting

- butter or oil

Directions:

1. Preheat the air fryer to 350°F.
2. Unwrap the crescent roll dough and separate it into triangles with the points facing away from you. Place a row of chocolate chunks along the bottom edge of the dough. (If you are using chips, make it a double row.) Roll the dough up around the chocolate and then place another row of chunks on the dough. Roll again and finish with one or two chocolate chunks. Be sure to leave the end free of chocolate so that it can adhere to the rest of the roll.
3. Brush the tops of the crescent rolls with the lightly beaten egg white and sprinkle the almonds on top, pressing them into the crescent dough so they adhere.
4. Brush the bottom of the air fryer basket with butter or oil and transfer the crescent rolls to the basket. Air-fry at 350°F for 8 minutes. Remove and let the crescent rolls cool before dusting with powdered sugar and serving.

Cinnamon Sugar Donut Holes

Servings: 12

Cooking Time: 6 Minutes

Ingredients:

- 1 cup all-purpose flour
- 6 tablespoons cane sugar, divided
- 1 teaspoon baking powder
- 3 teaspoons ground cinnamon, divided
- ¼ teaspoon salt
- 1 large egg
- 1 teaspoon vanilla extract
- 2 tablespoons melted butter

Directions:

1. Preheat the air fryer to 370°F.
2. In a small bowl, combine the flour, 2 tablespoons of the sugar, the baking powder, 1 teaspoon of the cinnamon, and the salt. Mix well.
3. In a larger bowl, whisk together the egg, vanilla extract, and butter.
4. Slowly add the dry ingredients into the wet until all the ingredients are uniformly combined. Set the bowl inside the refrigerator for at least 30 minutes.
5. Before you're ready to cook, in a small bowl, mix together the remaining 4 tablespoons of sugar and 2 teaspoons of cinnamon.
6. Liberally spray the air fryer basket with olive oil mist so the donut holes don't stick to the bottom. Note: You do not want to use parchment paper in this recipe; it may burn if your air fryer is hotter than others.
7. Remove the dough from the refrigerator and divide it into 12 equal donut holes. You can use a 1-ounce serving scoop if you have one.
8. Roll each donut hole in the sugar and cinnamon mixture; then place in the air fryer basket. Repeat until all the donut holes are covered in the sugar and cinnamon mixture.
9. When the basket is full, cook for 6 minutes. Remove the donut holes from the basket using oven-safe tongs and let cool 5 minutes. Repeat until all 12 are cooked.

Spinach-bacon Rollups

Servings: 4

Cooking Time: 9 Minutes

Ingredients:

- 4 flour tortillas (6- or 7-inch size)
- 4 slices Swiss cheese
- 1 cup baby spinach leaves
- 4 slices turkey bacon

Directions:

1. Preheat air fryer to 390°F.
2. On each tortilla, place one slice of cheese and ¼ cup of spinach.
3. Roll up tortillas and wrap each with a strip of bacon. Secure each end with a toothpick.
4. Place rollups in air fryer basket, leaving a little space in between them.
5. Cook for 4minutes. Turn and rearrange rollups (for more even cooking) and cook for 5minutes longer, until bacon is crisp.

Baked Eggs

Servings: 4
Cooking Time: 6 Minutes

Ingredients:

- 4 large eggs
- ⅛ teaspoon black pepper
- ⅛ teaspoon salt

Directions:

1. Preheat the air fryer to 330°F. Place 4 silicone muffin liners into the air fryer basket.
2. Crack 1 egg at a time into each silicone muffin liner. Sprinkle with black pepper and salt.
3. Bake for 6 minutes. Remove and let cool 2 minutes prior to serving.

Goat Cheese, Beet, And Kale Frittata

Servings: 6
Cooking Time: 20 Minutes

Ingredients:

- 6 large eggs
- ½ teaspoon garlic powder
- ¼ teaspoon black pepper
- ¼ teaspoon salt
- 1 cup chopped kale
- 1 cup cooked and chopped red beets
- ⅓ cup crumbled goat cheese

Directions:

1. Preheat the air fryer to 320°F.
2. In a medium bowl, whisk the eggs with the garlic powder, pepper, and salt. Mix in the kale, beets, and goat cheese.
3. Spray an oven-safe 7-inch springform pan with cooking spray. Pour the egg mixture into the pan and place it in the air fryer basket.
4. Cook for 20 minutes, or until the internal temperature reaches 145°F.
5. When the frittata is cooked, let it set for 5 minutes before removing from the pan.
6. Slice and serve immediately.

Strawberry Bread

Servings: 6
Cooking Time: 28 Minutes

Ingredients:

- ½ cup frozen strawberries in juice, completely thawed (do not drain)
- 1 cup flour
- ½ cup sugar
- 1 teaspoon cinnamon
- ½ teaspoon baking soda
- ⅛ teaspoon salt
- 1 egg, beaten
- ⅓ cup oil
- cooking spray

Directions:

1. Cut any large berries into smaller pieces no larger than ½ inch.
2. Preheat air fryer to 330°F.
3. In a large bowl, stir together the flour, sugar, cinnamon, soda, and salt.
4. In a small bowl, mix together the egg, oil, and strawberries. Add to dry ingredients and stir together gently.
5. Spray 6 x 6-inch baking pan with cooking spray.
6. Pour batter into prepared pan and cook at 330°F for 28 minutes.
7. When bread is done, let cool for 10minutes before removing from pan.

Cheddar Cheese Biscuits

Servings: 8
Cooking Time: 22 Minutes

Ingredients:

- 2⅓ cups self-rising flour
- 2 tablespoons sugar
- ½ cup butter (1 stick), frozen for 15 minutes
- ½ cup grated Cheddar cheese, plus more to melt on top
- 1⅓ cups buttermilk
- 1 cup all-purpose flour, for shaping
- 1 tablespoon butter, melted

Directions:

1. Line a buttered 7-inch metal cake pan with parchment paper or a silicone liner.
2. Combine the flour and sugar in a large mixing bowl. Grate the butter into the flour. Add the grated cheese and stir to coat the cheese and butter with flour. Then add the buttermilk and stir just until you can no longer see streaks of flour. The dough should be quite wet.
3. Spread the all-purpose (not self-rising) flour out on a small cookie sheet. With a spoon, scoop 8 evenly sized balls of dough into the flour, making sure they don't touch each other. With floured hands, coat each dough ball with flour and toss them gently from hand to hand to shake off any excess flour. Place each floured dough ball into the prepared pan, right up next to the other. This will help the biscuits rise up, rather than spreading out.
4. Preheat the air fryer to 380°F.
5. Transfer the cake pan to the basket of the air fryer, lowering it into the basket using a sling made of aluminum foil (fold a piece of aluminum foil into a strip about 2-inches wide by 24-inches long). Let the ends of the aluminum foil sling hang across the cake pan before returning the basket to the air fryer.
6. Air-fry for 20 minutes. Check the biscuits a couple of times to make sure they are not getting too brown on top. If they are, re-arrange the aluminum foil strips to cover any brown parts. After 20 minutes, check the biscuits by inserting a toothpick into the center of the biscuits. It should come out clean. If it needs a little more time, continue to air-fry for a couple of extra minutes. Brush the tops of the biscuits with some melted butter and sprinkle a little more grated cheese on top if desired. Pop the basket back into the air fryer for another 2 minutes. Remove the cake pan from the air fryer using the aluminum sling. Let the biscuits cool for just a minute or two and then turn them out onto a plate and pull apart. Serve immediately.

Cheddar-ham-corn Muffins

Servings: 8

Cooking Time: 8 Minutes

Ingredients:

- ¾ cup yellow cornmeal
- ¼ cup flour
- 1½ teaspoons baking powder
- ¼ teaspoon salt
- 1 egg, beaten
- 2 tablespoons canola oil
- ½ cup milk
- ½ cup shredded sharp Cheddar cheese
- ½ cup diced ham
- 8 foil muffin cups, liners removed and sprayed with cooking spray

Directions:

1. Preheat air fryer to 390°F.
2. In a medium bowl, stir together the cornmeal, flour, baking powder, and salt.
3. Add egg, oil, and milk to dry ingredients and mix well.
4. Stir in shredded cheese and diced ham.
5. Divide batter among the muffin cups.
6. Place 4 filled muffin cups in air fryer basket and bake for 5minutes.
7. Reduce temperature to 330°F and bake for 1 to 2minutes or until toothpick inserted in center of muffin comes out clean.
8. Repeat steps 6 and 7 to cook remaining muffins.

English Scones

Servings: 8

Cooking Time: 8 Minutes

Ingredients:

- 2 cups all-purpose flour
- 1 tablespoon baking powder
- ½ teaspoon salt
- 2 tablespoons sugar
- ¼ cup unsalted butter
- ⅔ cup plus 1 tablespoon whole milk, divided

Directions:

1. Preheat the air fryer to 380°F.
2. In a large bowl, whisk together the flour, baking powder, salt, and sugar. Using a pastry blender or your fingers, cut in the butter until pea-size crumbles appear. Make a well in the center and pour in ⅔ cup of the milk.

Quickly mix the batter until a ball forms. Knead the dough 3 times.

3. Place the dough onto a floured surface and, using your hands or a rolling pin, flatten the dough until it's ¾ inch thick. Using a biscuit cutter or drinking glass, cut out 10 circles, reforming the dough and flattening as needed to use up the batter.

4. Brush the tops lightly with the remaining 1 tablespoon of milk.

5. Place the scones into the air fryer basket. Cook for 8 minutes or until golden brown and cooked in the center.

Tuscan Toast

Servings: 4

Cooking Time: 5 Minutes

Ingredients:

- ¼ cup butter
- ½ teaspoon lemon juice
- ½ clove garlic
- ½ teaspoon dried parsley flakes
- 4 slices Italian bread, 1-inch thick

Directions:

1. Place butter, lemon juice, garlic, and parsley in a food processor. Process about 1 minute, or until garlic is pulverized and ingredients are well blended.
2. Spread garlic butter on both sides of bread slices.
3. Place bread slices upright in air fryer basket. (They can lie flat but cook better standing on end.)
4. Cook at 390°F for 5minutes or until toasty brown.

Cinnamon Biscuit Rolls

Servings: 12

Cooking Time: 5 Minutes

Ingredients:

- Dough
- ¼ cup warm water (105–115°F)
- 1 teaspoon active dry yeast
- 1 tablespoon sugar
- ½ cup buttermilk, lukewarm
- 2 cups flour, plus more for dusting
- 1 teaspoon baking powder
- ½ teaspoon salt
- 3 tablespoons cold butter
- Filling
- 1 tablespoon butter, melted
- 1 teaspoon cinnamon
- 2 tablespoons sugar
- Icing
- ⅔ cup powdered sugar
- ¼ teaspoon vanilla
- 2–3 teaspoons milk

Directions:

1. Dissolve yeast and sugar in warm water. Add buttermilk, stir, and set aside.
2. In a large bowl, sift together flour, baking powder, and salt. Using knives or a pastry blender, cut in butter until mixture is well combined and crumbly.
3. Pour in buttermilk mixture and stir with fork until a ball of dough forms.
4. Knead dough on a lightly floured surface for 5minutes. Roll into an 8 x 11-inch rectangle.
5. For the filling, spread the melted butter over the dough.
6. In a small bowl, stir together the cinnamon and sugar, then sprinkle over dough.
7. Starting on a long side, roll up dough so that you have a roll about 11 inches long. Cut into 12 slices with a serrated knife and sawing motion so slices remain round.
8. Place rolls on a plate or cookie sheet about an inch apart and let rise for 30minutes.
9. For icing, mix the powdered sugar, vanilla, and milk. Stir and add additional milk until icing reaches a good spreading consistency.
10. Preheat air fryer to 360°F.
11. Place 6 cinnamon rolls in basket and cook 5 minutes or until top springs back when lightly touched. Repeat to cook remaining 6 rolls.
12. Spread icing over warm rolls and serve.

All-in-one Breakfast Toast

Servings: 1

Cooking Time: 10 Minutes

Ingredients:

- 1 strip of bacon, diced
- 1 slice of 1-inch thick bread (such as Texas Toast or hand-sliced bread)
- 1 tablespoon softened butter (optional)
- 1 egg
- salt and freshly ground black pepper
- ¼ cup grated Colby or Jack cheese

Directions:

1. Preheat the air fryer to 400°F.
2. Air-fry the bacon for 3 minutes, shaking the basket once or twice while it cooks. Remove the bacon to a paper towel lined plate and set aside.
3. Use a sharp paring knife to score a large circle in the middle of the slice of bread, cutting halfway through, but not all the way through to the cutting board. Press down on the circle in the center of the bread slice to create an indentation. If using, spread the softened butter on the edges and in the hole of the bread.
4. Transfer the slice of bread, hole side up, to the air fryer basket. Crack the egg into the center of the bread, and season with salt and pepper.
5. Air-fry at 380°F for 5 minutes. Sprinkle the grated cheese around the edges of the bread leaving the center of the yolk uncovered, and top with the cooked bacon. Press the cheese and bacon into the bread lightly to help anchor it to the bread and prevent it from blowing around in the air fryer.
6. Air-fry for one or two more minutes (depending on how you like your egg cooked), just to melt the cheese and finish cooking the egg. Serve immediately.

Cajun Breakfast Potatoes

Servings: 4

Cooking Time: 20 Minutes

Ingredients:

- 1 pound roasting potatoes (like russet), scrubbed clean
- 1 tablespoon vegetable oil
- 2 teaspoons paprika
- ½ teaspoon garlic powder
- ¼ teaspoon onion powder
- ¼ teaspoon ground cumin
- 1 teaspoon thyme
- 1 teaspoon sea salt
- ½ teaspoon black pepper

Directions:

1. Cut the potatoes into 1-inch cubes.
2. In a large bowl, toss the cut potatoes with vegetable oil.
3. Sprinkle paprika, garlic powder, onion powder, cumin, thyme, salt, and pepper onto the potatoes, and toss to coat well.
4. Preheat the air fryer to 400°F for 4 minutes.
5. Add the potatoes to the air fryer basket and bake for 10 minutes. Stir or toss the potatoes and continue baking for an additional 5 minutes. Stir or toss again and continue baking for an additional 5 minutes or until the desired crispness is achieved.

Sweet-hot Pepperoni Pizza

Servings: 2

Cooking Time: 18 Minutes

Ingredients:

- 1 (6- to 8-ounce) pizza dough ball*
- olive oil
- ½ cup pizza sauce
- ¾ cup grated mozzarella cheese
- ½ cup thick sliced pepperoni
- ⅓ cup sliced pickled hot banana peppers
- ¼ teaspoon dried oregano
- 2 teaspoons honey

Directions:

1. Preheat the air fryer to 390°F.
2. Cut out a piece of aluminum foil the same size as the bottom of the air fryer basket. Brush the foil circle with olive oil. Shape the dough into a circle and place it on top of the foil. Dock the dough by piercing it several times with a fork. Brush the dough lightly with olive oil and transfer it into the air fryer basket with the foil on the bottom.

3. Air-fry the plain pizza dough for 6 minutes. Turn the dough over, remove the aluminum foil and brush again with olive oil. Air-fry for an additional 4 minutes.
4. Spread the pizza sauce on top of the dough and sprinkle the mozzarella cheese over the sauce. Top with the pepperoni, pepper slices and dried oregano. Lower the temperature of the air fryer to 350°F and cook for 8 minutes, until the cheese has melted and lightly browned. Transfer the pizza to a cutting board and drizzle with the honey. Slice and serve.

Green Onion Pancakes

Servings: 4
Cooking Time: 8 Minutes

Ingredients:

- 2 cup all-purpose flour
- ½ teaspoon salt
- ¾ cup hot water
- 1 tablespoon vegetable oil
- 1 tablespoon butter, melted
- 2 cups finely chopped green onions
- 1 tablespoon black sesame seeds, for garnish

Directions:

1. In a large bowl, whisk together the flour and salt. Make a well in the center and pour in the hot water. Quickly stir the flour mixture together until a dough forms. Knead the dough for 5 minutes; then cover with a warm, wet towel and set aside for 30 minutes to rest.
2. In a small bowl, mix together the vegetable oil and melted butter.
3. On a floured surface, place the dough and cut it into 8 pieces. Working with 1 piece of dough at a time, use a rolling pin to roll out the dough until it's ¼ inch thick; then brush the surface with the oil and butter mixture and sprinkle with green onions. Next, fold the dough in half and then in half again. Roll out the dough again until it's ¼ inch thick and brush with the oil and butter mixture and green onions. Fold the dough in half and then in half again and roll out one last time until it's ¼ inch thick. Repeat this technique with all 8 pieces.
4. Meanwhile, preheat the air fryer to 400°F.
5. Place 1 or 2 pancakes into the air fryer basket (or as many as will fit in your fryer), and cook for 2 minutes or until crispy and golden brown. Repeat until all the pancakes are cooked. Top with black sesame seeds for garnish, if desired.

Baked Eggs With Bacon-tomato Sauce

Servings: 1
Cooking Time: 12 Minutes

Ingredients:

- 1 teaspoon olive oil
- 2 tablespoons finely chopped onion
- 1 teaspoon chopped fresh oregano
- pinch crushed red pepper flakes
- 1 (14-ounce) can crushed or diced tomatoes
- salt and freshly ground black pepper
- 2 slices of bacon, chopped
- 2 large eggs
- ¼ cup grated Cheddar cheese
- fresh parsley, chopped

Directions:

1. Start by making the tomato sauce. Preheat a medium saucepan over medium heat on the stovetop. Add the olive oil and sauté the onion, oregano and pepper flakes for 5 minutes. Add the tomatoes and bring to a simmer. Season with salt and freshly ground black pepper and simmer for 10 minutes.
2. Meanwhile, Preheat the air fryer to 400°F and pour a little water into the bottom of the air fryer drawer. (This will help prevent the grease that drips into the bottom drawer from burning and smoking.) Place the bacon in the air fryer basket and air-fry at 400°F for 5 minutes, shaking the basket every once in a while.
3. When the bacon is almost crispy, remove it to a paper-towel lined plate and rinse out the air fryer drawer, draining away the bacon grease.
4. Transfer the tomato sauce to a shallow 7-inch pie dish. Crack the eggs on top of the sauce and scatter the cooked bacon back on top. Season with salt and freshly ground black pepper and transfer the pie dish into the air fryer basket. You can use an aluminum foil sling to help

with this by taking a long piece of aluminum foil, folding it in half lengthwise twice until it is roughly 26-inches by 3-inches. Place this under the pie dish and hold the ends of the foil to move the pie dish in and out of the air fryer basket. Tuck the ends of the foil beside the pie dish while it cooks in the air fryer.

5. Air-fry at 400°F for 5 minutes, or until the eggs are almost cooked to your liking. Sprinkle cheese on top and air-fry for an additional 2 minutes. When the cheese has melted, remove the pie dish from the air fryer, sprinkle with a little chopped parsley and let the eggs cool for a few minutes – just enough time to toast some buttered bread in your air fryer!

Zucchini Walnut Bread

Servings: 6
Cooking Time: 30 Minutes

Ingredients:

- ¾ cup all-purpose flour
- ½ teaspoon baking soda
- 1 teaspoon ground cinnamon
- ⅛ teaspoon salt
- 1 large egg
- ⅓ cup packed brown sugar
- ¼ cup canola oil
- 1 teaspoon vanilla extract
- ⅓ cup milk
- 1 medium zucchini, shredded (about 1⅓ cups)
- ⅓ cup chopped walnuts

Directions:

1. Preheat the air fryer to 320°F.
2. In a medium bowl, mix together the flour, baking soda, cinnamon, and salt.
3. In a large bowl, whisk together the egg, brown sugar, oil, vanilla, and milk. Stir in the zucchini.
4. Slowly fold the dry ingredients into the wet ingredients. Stir in the chopped walnuts. Then pour the batter into two 4-inch oven-safe loaf pans.
5. Bake for 30 minutes or until a toothpick inserted into the center comes out clean. Let cool before slicing.
6. NOTE: Store tightly wrapped on the counter for up to 5 days, in the refrigerator for up to 10 days, or in the freezer for 3 months.

Breakfast Pot Pies

Servings: 4
Cooking Time: 20 Minutes

Ingredients:

- 1 refrigerated pie crust
- ½ pound pork breakfast sausage
- ¼ cup diced onion
- 1 garlic clove, minced
- ½ teaspoon ground black pepper
- ¼ teaspoon salt
- 1 cup chopped bell peppers
- 1 cup roasted potatoes
- 2 cups milk
- 2 to 3 tablespoons all-purpose flour

Directions:

1. Flatten the store-bought pie crust out on an even surface. Cut 4 equal circles that are slightly larger than the circumference of ramekins (by about ¼ inch). Set aside.
2. In a medium pot, sauté the breakfast sausage with the onion, garlic, black pepper, and salt. When browned, add in the bell peppers and potatoes and cook an additional 3 to 4 minutes to soften the bell peppers. Remove from the heat and portion equally into the ramekins.
3. To the same pot (without washing it), add the milk. Heat over medium-high heat until boiling. Slowly reduce to a simmer and stir in the flour, 1 tablespoon at a time, until the gravy thickens and coats the back of a wooden spoon (about 5 minutes).
4. Remove from the heat and equally portion ½ cup of gravy into each ramekin on top of the sausage and potato mixture.
5. Place the circle pie crusts on top of the ramekins, lightly pressing them down on the perimeter of each ramekin with the prongs of a fork. Gently poke the prongs into the center top of the pie crust a few times to create holes for the steam to escape as the pie cooks.
6. Bake in the air fryer for 6 minutes (or until the tops are golden brown).
7. Remove and let cool 5 minutes before serving.

Breakfast Chimichangas

Servings: 4
Cooking Time: 8 Minutes

Ingredients:

- Four 8-inch flour tortillas
- ½ cup canned refried beans
- 1 cup scrambled eggs
- ½ cup grated cheddar or Monterey jack cheese
- 1 tablespoon vegetable oil
- 1 cup salsa

Directions:

1. Lay the flour tortillas out flat on a cutting board. In the center of each tortilla, spread 2 tablespoons refried beans. Next, add ¼ cup eggs and 2 tablespoons cheese to each tortilla.
2. To fold the tortillas, begin on the left side and fold to the center. Then fold the right side into the center. Next fold the bottom and top down and roll over to completely seal the chimichanga. Using a pastry brush or oil mister, brush the tops of the tortilla packages with oil.
3. Preheat the air fryer to 400°F for 4 minutes. Place the chimichangas into the air fryer basket, seam side down, and air fry for 4 minutes. Using tongs, turn over the chimichangas and cook for an additional 2 to 3 minutes or until light golden brown.

Strawberry Streusel Muffins

Servings: 12
Cooking Time: 14 Minutes

Ingredients:

- 1¾ cups all-purpose flour
- ½ cup granulated sugar
- 2 teaspoons baking powder
- ¼ teaspoon baking soda
- ½ teaspoon salt
- ½ cup plain yogurt
- ½ cup milk
- ¼ cup vegetable oil
- 2 large eggs
- 1 teaspoon vanilla extract
- ½ cup freeze-dried strawberries
- 2 tablespoons brown sugar
- ¼ cup oats
- 2 tablespoons butter

Directions:

1. Preheat the air fryer to 330°F.
2. In a large bowl, whisk together the flour, sugar, baking powder, baking soda, and salt; set aside.
3. In a separate bowl, whisk together the yogurt, milk, vegetable oil, eggs, and vanilla extract.
4. Make a well in the dry ingredients; then pour the wet ingredients into the well of the dry ingredients. Using a rubber spatula, mix the ingredients for 1 minute or until slightly lumpy. Fold in the strawberries.
5. In a small bowl, use your fingers to mix together the brown sugar, oats, and butter until coarse crumbles appear. Divide the mixture in half.
6. Using silicone muffin liners, fill 6 muffin liners two-thirds full.
7. Crumble half of the streusel topping onto the first batch of muffins.
8. Carefully place the muffin liners in the air fryer basket and bake for 14 minutes (or until the tops are browned and a toothpick inserted in the center comes out clean). Carefully remove the muffins from the basket and repeat with the remaining batter and topping.
9. Serve warm.

Hashbrown Potatoes Lyonnaise

Servings: 4
Cooking Time: 33 Minutes

Ingredients:

- 1 Vidalia (or other sweet) onion, sliced
- 1 teaspoon butter, melted
- 1 teaspoon brown sugar
- 2 large russet potatoes (about 1 pound), sliced ½-inch thick
- 1 tablespoon vegetable oil
- salt and freshly ground black pepper

Directions:

1. Preheat the air fryer to 370°F.
2. Toss the sliced onions, melted butter and brown sugar together in the air fryer basket. Air-fry for 8

minutes, shaking the basket occasionally to help the onions cook evenly.

3. While the onions are cooking, bring a 3-quart saucepan of salted water to a boil on the stovetop. Par-cook the potatoes in boiling water for 3 minutes. Drain the potatoes and pat them dry with a clean kitchen towel.

4. Add the potatoes to the onions in the air fryer basket and drizzle with vegetable oil. Toss to coat the potatoes with the oil and season with salt and freshly ground black pepper.

5. Increase the air fryer temperature to 400°F and air-fry for 22 minutes tossing the vegetables a few times during the cooking time to help the potatoes brown evenly. Season to taste again with salt and freshly ground black pepper and serve warm.

Sweet And Spicy Pumpkin Scones

Servings: 8

Cooking Time: 8 Minutes

Ingredients:

- 2 cups all-purpose flour
- 3 tablespoons packed brown sugar
- ½ teaspoon baking powder
- ¼ teaspoon baking soda
- ½ teaspoon kosher salt
- ½ teaspoon ground cinnamon
- ¼ teaspoon ground ginger
- ¼ teaspoon ground cardamom
- 4 tablespoons cold unsalted butter
- ½ cup plus 2 tablespoons pumpkin puree, divided
- 4 tablespoons milk, divided
- 1 large egg
- 1 cup powdered sugar

Directions:

1. In a large bowl, mix together the flour, brown sugar, baking powder, baking soda, salt, cinnamon, ginger, and cardamom. Using a pastry blender or two knives, cut in the butter until coarse crumbles appear.

2. In a small bowl, whisk together ½ cup of the pumpkin puree, 2 tablespoons of the milk, and the egg until combined. Pour the wet ingredients into the dry ingredients; stir to combine.

3. Form the dough into a ball and place onto a floured service. Press the dough out or use a rolling pin to roll out the dough until ½ inch thick and in a circle. Cut the dough into 8 wedges.

4. Bake at 360°F for 8 to 10 minutes or until completely cooked through. Cook in batches as needed.

5. In a medium bowl, whisk together the powdered sugar, the remaining 2 tablespoons of pumpkin puree, and the remaining 2 tablespoons of milk. When the pumpkin scones have cooled, drizzle the pumpkin glaze over the top before serving.

Nutty Whole Wheat Muffins

Servings: 8

Cooking Time: 11 Minutes

Ingredients:

- ½ cup whole-wheat flour, plus 2 tablespoons
- ¼ cup oat bran
- 2 tablespoons flaxseed meal
- ¼ cup brown sugar
- ½ teaspoon baking soda
- ½ teaspoon baking powder
- ¼ teaspoon salt
- ½ teaspoon cinnamon
- ½ cup buttermilk
- 2 tablespoons melted butter
- 1 egg
- ½ teaspoon pure vanilla extract
- ½ cup grated carrots
- ¼ cup chopped pecans
- ¼ cup chopped walnuts
- 1 tablespoon pumpkin seeds
- 1 tablespoon sunflower seeds
- 16 foil muffin cups, paper liners removed
- cooking spray

Directions:

1. Preheat air fryer to 330°F.

2. In a large bowl, stir together the flour, bran, flaxseed meal, sugar, baking soda, baking powder, salt, and cinnamon.

3. In a medium bowl, beat together the buttermilk, butter, egg, and vanilla. Pour into flour mixture and stir just until dry ingredients moisten. Do not beat.
4. Gently stir in carrots, nuts, and seeds.
5. Double up the foil cups so you have 8 total and spray with cooking spray.
6. Place 4 foil cups in air fryer basket and divide half the batter among them.
7. Cook at 330°F for 11minutes or until toothpick inserted in center comes out clean.
8. Repeat step 7 to cook remaining 4 muffins.

Garlic Bread Knots

Servings: 8
Cooking Time: 5 Minutes

Ingredients:

- ¼ cup melted butter
- 2 teaspoons garlic powder
- 1 teaspoon dried parsley
- 1 (11-ounce) tube of refrigerated French bread dough

Directions:

1. Mix the melted butter, garlic powder and dried parsley in a small bowl and set it aside.
2. To make smaller knots, cut the long tube of bread dough into 16 slices. If you want to make bigger knots, slice the dough into 8 slices. Shape each slice into a long rope about 6 inches long by rolling it on a flat surface with the palm of your hands. Tie each rope into a knot and place them on a plate.
3. Preheat the air fryer to 350°F.
4. Transfer half of the bread knots into the air fryer basket, leaving space in between each knot. Brush each knot with the butter mixture using a pastry brush.
5. Air-fry for 5 minutes. Remove the baked knots and brush a little more of the garlic butter mixture on each. Repeat with the remaining bread knots and serve warm.

Strawberry Toast

Servings: 4
Cooking Time: 8 Minutes

Ingredients:

- 4 slices bread, ½-inch thick
- butter-flavored cooking spray
- 1 cup sliced strawberries
- 1 teaspoon sugar

Directions:

1. Spray one side of each bread slice with butter-flavored cooking spray. Lay slices sprayed side down.
2. Divide the strawberries among the bread slices.
3. Sprinkle evenly with the sugar and place in the air fryer basket in a single layer.
4. Cook at 390°F for 8minutes. The bottom should look brown and crisp and the top should look glazed.

Orange Rolls

Servings: 8
Cooking Time: 10 Minutes

Ingredients:

- parchment paper
- 3 ounces low-fat cream cheese
- 1 tablespoon low-fat sour cream or plain yogurt (not Greek yogurt)
- 2 teaspoons sugar
- ¼ teaspoon pure vanilla extract
- ¼ teaspoon orange extract
- 1 can (8 count) organic crescent roll dough
- ¼ cup chopped walnuts
- ¼ cup dried cranberries
- ¼ cup shredded, sweetened coconut
- butter-flavored cooking spray
- Orange Glaze
- ½ cup powdered sugar
- 1 tablespoon orange juice
- ¼ teaspoon orange extract
- dash of salt

Directions:

1. Cut a circular piece of parchment paper slightly smaller than the bottom of your air fryer basket. Set aside.
2. In a small bowl, combine the cream cheese, sour cream or yogurt, sugar, and vanilla and orange extracts. Stir until smooth.
3. Preheat air fryer to 300°F.

4. Separate crescent roll dough into 8 triangles and divide cream cheese mixture among them. Starting at wide end, spread cheese mixture to within 1 inch of point.
5. Sprinkle nuts and cranberries evenly over cheese mixture.
6. Starting at wide end, roll up triangles, then sprinkle with coconut, pressing in lightly to make it stick. Spray tops of rolls with butter-flavored cooking spray.
7. Place parchment paper in air fryer basket, and place 4 rolls on top, spaced evenly.
8. Cook for 10minutes, until rolls are golden brown and cooked through.
9. Repeat steps 7 and 8 to cook remaining 4 rolls. You should be able to use the same piece of parchment paper twice.
10. In a small bowl, stir together ingredients for glaze and drizzle over warm rolls.

Roasted Vegetable Frittata

Servings: 1
Cooking Time: 19 Minutes

Ingredients:

- ½ red or green bell pepper, cut into ½-inch chunks
- 4 button mushrooms, sliced
- ½ cup diced zucchini
- ½ teaspoon chopped fresh oregano or thyme
- 1 teaspoon olive oil
- 3 eggs, beaten
- ½ cup grated Cheddar cheese
- salt and freshly ground black pepper, to taste
- 1 teaspoon butter
- 1 teaspoon chopped fresh parsley

Directions:

1. Preheat the air fryer to 400°F.
2. Toss the peppers, mushrooms, zucchini and oregano with the olive oil and air-fry for 6 minutes, shaking the basket once or twice during the cooking process to redistribute the ingredients.
3. While the vegetables are cooking, beat the eggs well in a bowl, stir in the Cheddar cheese and season with salt and freshly ground black pepper. Add the air-fried vegetables to this bowl when they have finished cooking.
4. Place a 6- or 7-inch non-stick metal cake pan into the air fryer basket with the butter using an aluminum sling to lower the pan into the basket. (Fold a piece of aluminum foil into a strip about 2-inches wide by 24-inches long.) Air-fry for 1 minute at 380°F to melt the butter. Remove the cake pan and rotate the pan to distribute the butter and grease the pan. Pour the egg mixture into the cake pan and return the pan to the air fryer, using the aluminum sling.
5. Air-fry at 380°F for 12 minutes, or until the frittata has puffed up and is lightly browned. Let the frittata sit in the air fryer for 5 minutes to cool to an edible temperature and set up. Remove the cake pan from the air fryer, sprinkle with parsley and serve immediately.

Pizza Dough

Servings: 3
Cooking Time: 10 Minutes

Ingredients:

- 4 cups bread flour, pizza ("00") flour or all-purpose flour
- 1 teaspoon active dry yeast
- 2 teaspoons sugar
- 2 teaspoons salt
- 1½ cups water
- 1 tablespoon olive oil

Directions:

1. Combine the flour, yeast, sugar and salt in the bowl of a stand mixer. Add the olive oil to the flour mixture and start to mix using the dough hook attachment. As you're mixing, add 1¼ cups of the water, mixing until the dough comes together. Continue to knead the dough with the dough hook for another 10 minutes, adding enough water to the dough to get it to the right consistency.
2. Transfer the dough to a floured counter and divide it into 3 equal portions. Roll each portion into a ball. Lightly coat each dough ball with oil and transfer to the refrigerator, covered with plastic wrap. You can place them all on a baking sheet, or place each dough ball into

its own oiled zipper sealable plastic bag or container. (You can freeze the dough balls at this stage, removing as much air as possible from the oiled bag.) Keep in the refrigerator for at least one day, or as long as five days.

3. When you're ready to use the dough, remove your dough from the refrigerator at least 1 hour prior to baking and let it sit on the counter, covered gently with plastic wrap.

Pepperoni Pizza Bread

Servings: 4

Cooking Time: 15 Minutes

Ingredients:

- 7-inch round bread boule
- 2 cups grated mozzarella cheese
- 1 tablespoon dried oregano
- 1 cup pizza sauce
- 1 cup mini pepperoni or pepperoni slices, cut in quarters
- Pizza sauce for dipping (optional)

Directions:

1. Make 7 to 8 deep slices across the bread boule, leaving 1 inch of bread uncut at the bottom of every slice before you reach the cutting board. The slices should go about three quarters of the way through the boule and be about 2 inches apart from each other. Turn the bread boule 90 degrees and make 7 to 8 similar slices perpendicular to the first slices to form squares in the bread. Again, make sure you don't cut all the way through the bread.
2. Combine the mozzarella cheese and oregano in a small bowl.
3. Fill the slices in the bread with pizza sauce by gently spreading the bread apart and spooning the sauce in between the squares of bread. Top the sauce with the mozzarella cheese mixture and then the pepperoni. Do your very best to get the cheese and pepperoni in between the slices, rather than on top of the bread. Keep spreading the bread apart and stuffing the ingredients in, but be careful not to tear the bottom of the bread.
4. Preheat the air fryer to 320°F.
5. Transfer the bread boule to the air fryer basket and air-fry for 15 minutes, making sure the top doesn't get too dark. (It will just be the cheese on top that gets dark, so if you've done a good job of tucking the cheese in between the slices, this shouldn't be an issue.)
6. Carefully remove the bread from the basket with a spatula. Transfer it to a serving platter with more sauce to dip into if desired. Serve with a lot of napkins so that people can just pull the bread apart with their hands and enjoy!

Banana Bread

Servings: 6

Cooking Time: 20 Minutes

Ingredients:

- cooking spray
- 1 cup white wheat flour
- ½ teaspoon baking powder
- ¼ teaspoon salt
- ¼ teaspoon baking soda
- 1 egg
- ½ cup mashed ripe banana
- ¼ cup plain yogurt
- ¼ cup pure maple syrup
- 2 tablespoons coconut oil
- ½ teaspoon pure vanilla extract

Directions:

1. Preheat air fryer to 330°F.
2. Lightly spray 6 x 6-inch baking dish with cooking spray.
3. In a medium bowl, mix together the flour, baking powder, salt, and soda.
4. In a separate bowl, beat the egg and add the mashed banana, yogurt, syrup, oil, and vanilla. Mix until well combined.
5. Pour liquid mixture into dry ingredients and stir gently to blend. Do not beat. Batter may be slightly lumpy.
6. Pour batter into baking dish and cook at 330°F for 20 minutes or until toothpick inserted in center of loaf comes out clean.

Seasoned Herbed Sourdough Croutons

Servings: 4

Cooking Time: 7 Minutes

Ingredients:

- 4 cups cubed sourdough bread, 1-inch cubes (about 8 ounces)
- 1 tablespoon olive oil
- 1 teaspoon fresh thyme leaves
- ¼ – ½ teaspoon salt
- freshly ground black pepper

Directions:

1. Combine all ingredients in a bowl and taste to make sure it is seasoned to your liking.
2. Preheat the air fryer to 400°F.
3. Toss the bread cubes into the air fryer and air-fry for 7 minutes, shaking the basket once or twice while they cook.
4. Serve warm or store in an airtight container.

Chocolate Chip Banana Muffins

Servings: 12

Cooking Time: 14 Minutes

Ingredients:

- 2 medium bananas, mashed
- ¼ cup brown sugar
- 1½ teaspoons vanilla extract
- ⅔ cup milk
- 2 tablespoons butter
- 1 large egg
- 1 cup white whole-wheat flour
- ½ cup old-fashioned oats
- 1 teaspoon baking soda
- ½ teaspoon baking powder
- ⅛ teaspoon sea salt
- ¼ cup mini chocolate chips

Directions:

1. Preheat the air fryer to 330°F.
2. In a large bowl, combine the bananas, brown sugar, vanilla extract, milk, butter, and egg; set aside.
3. In a separate bowl, combine the flour, oats, baking soda, baking powder, and salt.
4. Slowly add the dry ingredients into the wet ingredients, folding in the flour mixture ⅓ cup at a time.
5. Mix in the chocolate chips and set aside.
6. Using silicone muffin liners, fill 6 muffin liners two-thirds full. Carefully place the muffin liners in the air fryer basket and bake for 20 minutes (or until the tops are browned and a toothpick inserted in the center comes out clean). Carefully remove the muffins from the basket and repeat with the remaining batter.
7. Serve warm.

Mini Pita Breads

Servings: 8

Cooking Time: 6 Minutes

Ingredients:

- 2 teaspoons active dry yeast
- 1 tablespoon sugar
- 1¼ to 1½ cups warm water (90° - 110°F)
- 3¼ cups all-purpose flour
- 2 teaspoons salt
- 1 tablespoon olive oil, plus more for brushing
- kosher salt (optional)

Directions:

1. Dissolve the yeast, sugar and water in the bowl of a stand mixer. Let the mixture sit for 5 minutes to make sure the yeast is active – it should foam a little. (If there's no foaming, discard and start again with new yeast.) Combine the flour and salt in a bowl, and add it to the water, along with the olive oil. Mix with the dough hook until combined. Add a little more flour if needed to get the dough to pull away from the sides of the mixing bowl, or add a little more water if the dough seems too dry.
2. Knead the dough until it is smooth and elastic (about 8 minutes in the mixer or 15 minutes by hand). Transfer the dough to a lightly oiled bowl, cover and let it rise in a warm place until doubled in bulk. Divide the dough into 8 portions and roll each portion into a circle about 4-inches in diameter. Don't roll the balls too thin, or you won't get the pocket inside the pita.
3. Preheat the air fryer to 400°F.

4. Brush both sides of the dough with olive oil, and sprinkle with kosher salt if desired. Air-fry one at a time at 400°F for 6 minutes, flipping it over when there are two minutes left in the cooking time.

Quiche Cups

Servings: 10
Cooking Time: 16 Minutes

Ingredients:

- ¼ pound all-natural ground pork sausage
- 3 eggs
- ¾ cup milk
- 20 foil muffin cups
- cooking spray
- 4 ounces sharp Cheddar cheese, grated

Directions:

1. Divide sausage into 3 portions and shape each into a thin patty.
2. Place patties in air fryer basket and cook 390°F for 6minutes.
3. While sausage is cooking, prepare the egg mixture. A large measuring cup or bowl with a pouring lip works best. Combine the eggs and milk and whisk until well blended. Set aside.
4. When sausage has cooked fully, remove patties from basket, drain well, and use a fork to crumble the meat into small pieces.
5. Double the foil cups into 10 sets. Remove paper liners from the top muffin cups and spray the foil cups lightly with cooking spray.
6. Divide crumbled sausage among the 10 muffin cup sets.
7. Top each with grated cheese, divided evenly among the cups.
8. Place 5 cups in air fryer basket.
9. Pour egg mixture into each cup, filling until each cup is at least ⅔ full.
10. Cook for 8 minutes and test for doneness. A knife inserted into the center shouldn't have any raw egg on it when removed.
11. If needed, cook 2 more minutes, until egg completely sets.
12. Repeat steps 8 through 11 for the remaining quiches.

Farmers Market Quiche

Servings: 4
Cooking Time: 35 Minutes

Ingredients:

- 4 button mushrooms
- ¼ medium red bell pepper
- 1 teaspoon extra-virgin olive oil
- One 9-inch pie crust, at room temperature
- ¼ cup grated carrot
- ¼ cup chopped, fresh baby spinach leaves
- 3 eggs, whisked
- ¼ cup half-and-half
- ½ teaspoon thyme
- ½ teaspoon sea salt
- 2 ounces crumbled goat cheese or feta

Directions:

1. In a medium bowl, toss the mushrooms and bell pepper with extra-virgin olive oil; place into the air fryer basket. Set the temperature to 400°F for 8 minutes, stirring after 4 minutes. Remove from the air fryer, and roughly chop the mushrooms and bell peppers. Wipe the air fryer clean.
2. Prep a 7-inch oven-safe baking dish by spraying the bottom of the pan with cooking spray.
3. Place the pie crust into the baking dish; fold over and crimp the edges or use a fork to press to give the edges some shape.
4. In a medium bowl, mix together the mushrooms, bell peppers, carrots, spinach, and eggs. Stir in the half-and-half, thyme, and salt.
5. Pour the quiche mixture into the base of the pie shell. Top with crumbled cheese.
6. Place the quiche into the air fryer basket. Set the temperature to 325°F for 30 minutes.
7. When complete, turn the quiche halfway and cook an additional 5 minutes. Allow the quiche to rest 20 minutes prior to slicing and serving.

Bacon, Broccoli And Swiss Cheese Bread Pudding

Servings: 2

Cooking Time: 48 Minutes

Ingredients:

- ½ pound thick cut bacon, cut into ¼-inch pieces
- 3 cups brioche bread or rolls, cut into ½-inch cubes
- 3 eggs
- 1 cup milk
- ½ teaspoon salt
- freshly ground black pepper
- 1 cup frozen broccoli florets, thawed and chopped
- 1½ cups grated Swiss cheese

Directions:

1. Preheat the air fryer to 400°F.
2. Air-fry the bacon for 6 minutes until crispy, shaking the basket a few times while it cooks to help it cook evenly. Remove the bacon and set it aside on a paper towel.
3. Air-fry the brioche bread cubes for 2 minutes to dry and toast lightly. (If your brioche is a few days old and slightly stale, you can omit this step.)
4. Butter a 6- or 7-inch cake pan. Combine all the ingredients in a large bowl and toss well. Transfer the mixture to the buttered cake pan, cover with aluminum foil and refrigerate the bread pudding overnight, or for at least 8 hours.
5. Remove the casserole from the refrigerator an hour before you plan to cook, and let it sit on the countertop to come to room temperature.
6. Preheat the air fryer to 330°F. Transfer the covered cake pan, to the basket of the air fryer, lowering the dish into the basket using a sling made of aluminum foil (fold a piece of aluminum foil into a strip about 2-inches wide by 24-inches long). Fold the ends of the aluminum foil over the top of the dish before returning the basket to the air fryer. Air-fry for 20 minutes. Remove the foil and air-fry for an additional 20 minutes. If the top starts to brown a little too much before the custard has set, simply return the foil to the pan. The bread pudding has cooked through when a skewer inserted into the center comes out clean.

Mini Everything Bagels

Servings: 4

Cooking Time: 6 Minutes

Ingredients:

- 1 cup all-purpose flour
- 2 teaspoons baking powder
- ½ teaspoon salt
- 1 cup plain Greek yogurt
- 1 egg, whisked
- 1 teaspoon sesame seeds
- 1 teaspoon dehydrated onions
- ½ teaspoon poppy seeds
- ½ teaspoon garlic powder
- ½ teaspoon sea salt flakes

Directions:

1. In a large bowl, mix together the flour, baking powder, and salt. Make a well in the dough and add in the Greek yogurt. Mix with a spoon until a dough forms.
2. Place the dough onto a heavily floured surface and knead for 3 minutes. You may use up to 1 cup of additional flour as you knead the dough, if necessary.
3. Cut the dough into 8 pieces and roll each piece into a 6-inch, snakelike piece. Touch the ends of each piece together so it closes the circle and forms a bagel shape. Brush the tops of the bagels with the whisked egg.
4. In a small bowl, combine the sesame seeds, dehydrated onions, poppy seeds, garlic powder, and sea salt flakes. Sprinkle the seasoning on top of the bagels.
5. Preheat the air fryer to 360°F. Using a bench scraper or flat-edged spatula, carefully place the bagels into the air fryer basket. Spray the bagel tops with cooking spray. Air-fry the bagels for 6 minutes or until golden brown. Allow the bread to cool at least 10 minutes before slicing for serving.

Ham And Cheddar Gritters

Servings: 6

Cooking Time: 12 Minutes

Ingredients:

- 4 cups water
- 1 cup quick-cooking grits
- ¼ teaspoon salt

- 2 tablespoons butter
- 2 cups grated Cheddar cheese, divided
- 1 cup finely diced ham
- 1 tablespoon chopped chives
- salt and freshly ground black pepper
- 1 egg, beaten
- 2 cups panko breadcrumbs
- vegetable oil

Directions:

1. Bring the water to a boil in a saucepan. Whisk in the grits and ¼ teaspoon of salt, and cook for 7 minutes until the grits are soft. Remove the pan from the heat and stir in the butter and 1 cup of the grated Cheddar cheese. Transfer the grits to a bowl and let them cool for just 10 to 15 minutes.
2. Stir the ham, chives and the rest of the cheese into the grits and season with salt and pepper to taste. Add the beaten egg and refrigerate the mixture for 30 minutes. (Try not to chill the grits much longer than 30 minutes, or the mixture will be too firm to shape into patties.)
3. While the grit mixture is chilling, make the country gravy and set it aside.
4. Place the panko breadcrumbs in a shallow dish. Measure out ¼-cup portions of the grits mixture and shape them into patties. Coat all sides of the patties with the panko breadcrumbs, patting them with your hands so the crumbs adhere to the patties. You should have about 16 patties. Spray both sides of the patties with oil.
5. Preheat the air fryer to 400°F.
6. In batches of 5 or 6, air-fry the fritters for 8 minutes. Using a flat spatula, flip the fritters over and air-fry for another 4 minutes.
7. Serve hot with country gravy.

Southwest Cornbread

Servings: 6

Cooking Time: 18 Minutes

Ingredients:

- cooking spray
- ½ cup yellow cornmeal
- ½ cup flour
- 2 teaspoons baking powder
- ½ teaspoon salt
- ½ cup frozen corn kernels, thawed and drained
- ¼ cup finely chopped onion
- 1 or 2 small jalapeño peppers, seeded and chopped
- 1 egg
- ½ cup milk
- 2 tablespoons melted butter
- 2 ounces sharp Cheddar cheese, grated

Directions:

1. Preheat air fryer to 360°F.
2. Spray air fryer baking pan with nonstick cooking spray.
3. In a medium bowl, stir together the cornmeal, flour, baking powder, and salt.
4. Stir in the corn, onion, and peppers.
5. In a small bowl, beat together the egg, milk, and butter. Stir into dry ingredients until well combined.
6. Spoon half the batter into prepared baking pan, spreading to edges. Top with grated cheese. Spoon remaining batter on top of cheese and gently spread to edges of pan so it completely covers the cheese.
7. Cook at 360°F for 18 minutes, until cornbread is done and top is crispy brown.

Brown Sugar Grapefruit

Servings: 2

Cooking Time: 4 Minutes

Ingredients:

- 1 grapefruit
- 2 to 4 teaspoons brown sugar

Directions:

1. Preheat the air fryer to 400°F.
2. While the air fryer is Preheating, cut the grapefruit in half horizontally (in other words not through the stem or blossom end of the grapefruit). Slice the bottom of the grapefruit to help it sit flat on the counter if necessary. Using a sharp paring knife (serrated is great), cut around the grapefruit between the flesh of the fruit and the peel. Then, cut each segment away from the membrane so that it is sitting freely in the fruit.
3. Sprinkle 1 to 2 teaspoons of brown sugar on each half of the prepared grapefruit. Set up a rack in the air

fryer basket (use an air fryer rack or make your own rack with some crumpled up aluminum foil). You don't have to use a rack, but doing so will get the grapefruit closer to the element so that the brown sugar can caramelize a little better. Transfer the grapefruit half to the rack in the air fryer basket. Depending on how big your grapefruit are and what size air fryer you have, you may need to do each half separately to make sure they sit flat.

4. Air-fry at 400°F for 4 minutes.
5. Remove and let it cool for just a minute before enjoying.

White Wheat Walnut Bread

Servings: 8

Cooking Time: 25 Minutes

Ingredients:

- 1 cup lukewarm water (105–115°F)
- 1 packet RapidRise yeast
- 1 tablespoon light brown sugar
- 2 cups whole-grain white wheat flour
- 1 egg, room temperature, beaten with a fork
- 2 teaspoons olive oil
- ½ teaspoon salt
- ½ cup chopped walnuts
- cooking spray

Directions:

1. In a small bowl, mix the water, yeast, and brown sugar.
2. Pour yeast mixture over flour and mix until smooth.
3. Add the egg, olive oil, and salt and beat with a wooden spoon for 2minutes.
4. Stir in chopped walnuts. You will have very thick batter rather than stiff bread dough.
5. Spray air fryer baking pan with cooking spray and pour in batter, smoothing the top.
6. Let batter rise for 15minutes.
7. Preheat air fryer to 360°F.
8. Cook bread for 25 minutes, until toothpick pushed into center comes out with crumbs clinging. Let bread rest for 10minutes before removing from pan.

Spinach And Artichoke White Pizza

Servings: 2

Cooking Time: 18 Minutes

Ingredients:

- olive oil
- 3 cups fresh spinach
- 2 cloves garlic, minced, divided
- 1 (6- to 8-ounce) pizza dough ball*
- ½ cup grated mozzarella cheese
- ¼ cup grated Fontina cheese
- ¼ cup artichoke hearts, coarsely chopped
- 2 tablespoons grated Parmesan cheese
- ¼ teaspoon dried oregano
- salt and freshly ground black pepper

Directions:

1. Heat the oil in a medium sauté pan on the stovetop. Add the spinach and half the minced garlic to the pan and sauté for a few minutes, until the spinach has wilted. Remove the sautéed spinach from the pan and set it aside.
2. Preheat the air fryer to 390°F.
3. Cut out a piece of aluminum foil the same size as the bottom of the air fryer basket. Brush the foil circle with olive oil. Shape the dough into a circle and place it on top of the foil. Dock the dough by piercing it several times with a fork. Brush the dough lightly with olive oil and transfer it into the air fryer basket with the foil on the bottom.
4. Air-fry the plain pizza dough for 6 minutes. Turn the dough over, remove the aluminum foil and brush again with olive oil. Air-fry for an additional 4 minutes.
5. Sprinkle the mozzarella and Fontina cheeses over the dough. Top with the spinach and artichoke hearts. Sprinkle the Parmesan cheese and dried oregano on top and drizzle with olive oil. Lower the temperature of the air fryer to 350°F and cook for 8 minutes, until the cheese has melted and is lightly browned. Season to taste with salt and freshly ground black pepper.

Pancake Muffins

Servings: 4

Cooking Time: 8 Minutes

Ingredients:

- 1 cup flour
- 2 tablespoons sugar (optional)
- ½ teaspoon baking soda
- 1 teaspoon baking powder
- ¼ teaspoon salt
- 1 egg, beaten
- 1 cup buttermilk
- 2 tablespoons melted butter
- 1 teaspoon pure vanilla extract
- 24 foil muffin cups
- cooking spray
- Suggested Fillings
- 1 teaspoon of jelly or fruit preserves
- 1 tablespoon or less fresh blueberries; chopped fresh strawberries; chopped frozen cherries; dark chocolate chips; chopped walnuts, pecans, or other nuts; cooked, crumbled bacon or sausage

Directions:

1. In a large bowl, stir together flour, optional sugar, baking soda, baking powder, and salt.
2. In a small bowl, combine egg, buttermilk, butter, and vanilla. Mix well.
3. Pour egg mixture into dry ingredients and stir to mix well but don't overbeat.
4. Double up the muffin cups and remove the paper liners from the top cups. Spray the foil cups lightly with cooking spray.
5. Place 6 sets of muffin cups in air fryer basket. Pour just enough batter into each cup to cover the bottom. Sprinkle with desired filling. Pour in more batter to cover the filling and fill the cups about ¾ full.
6. Cook at 330°F for 8minutes.
7. Repeat steps 5 and 6 for the remaining 6 pancake muffins.

Apple Fritters

Servings: 6

Cooking Time: 12 Minutes

Ingredients:

- 1 cup all-purpose flour
- 1½ teaspoons baking powder
- ¼ teaspoon salt
- 2 tablespoon brown sugar
- 1 teaspoon vanilla extract
- ¾ cup plain Greek yogurt
- 1 tablespoon cinnamon
- 1 large Granny Smith apple, cored, peeled, and finely chopped
- ¼ cup chopped walnuts
- ½ cup powdered sugar
- 1 tablespoon milk

Directions:

1. Preheat the air fryer to 320°F.
2. In a medium bowl, combine the flour, baking powder, and salt.
3. In a large bowl, add the brown sugar, vanilla, yogurt, cinnamon, apples, and walnuts. Mix the dry ingredients into the wet, using your hands to combine, until all the ingredients are mixed together. Knead the mixture in the bowl about 4 times.
4. Lightly spray the air fryer basket with olive oil spray.
5. Divide the batter into 6 equally sized balls; then lightly flatten them and place inside the basket. Repeat until all the fritters are formed.
6. Place the basket in the air fryer and cook for 6 minutes, flip, and then cook another 6 minutes.
7. While the fritters are cooking, in a small bowl, mix the powdered sugar with the milk. Set aside.
8. When the cooking completes, remove the air fryer basket and allow the fritters to cool on a wire rack. Drizzle with the homemade glaze and serve.

Fry Bread

Servings: 4

Cooking Time: 5 Minutes

Ingredients:

- 1 cup flour
- 2 teaspoons baking powder
- ¼ teaspoon salt
- ¼ cup lukewarm milk
- 1 teaspoon oil
- 2–3 tablespoons water
- oil for misting or cooking spray

Directions:

1. Stir together flour, baking powder, and salt. Gently mix in the milk and oil. Stir in 1 tablespoon water. If needed, add more water 1 tablespoon at a time until stiff dough forms. Dough shouldn't be sticky, so use only as much as you need.
2. Divide dough into 4 portions and shape into balls. Cover with a towel and let rest for 10minutes.
3. Preheat air fryer to 390°F.
4. Shape dough as desired:
5. a. Pat into 3-inch circles. This will make a thicker bread to eat plain or with a sprinkle of cinnamon or honey butter. You can cook all 4 at once.
6. b. Pat thinner into rectangles about 3 x 6 inches. This will create a thinner bread to serve as a base for dishes such as Indian tacos. The circular shape is more traditional, but rectangles allow you to cook 2 at a time in your air fryer basket.
7. Spray both sides of dough pieces with oil or cooking spray.
8. Place the 4 circles or 2 of the dough rectangles in the air fryer basket and cook at 390°F for 3minutes. Spray tops, turn, spray other side, and cook for 2 more minutes. If necessary, repeat to cook remaining bread.
9. Serve piping hot as is or allow to cool slightly and add toppings to create your own Native American tacos.

Egg And Sausage Crescent Rolls

Servings: 8

Cooking Time: 11 Minutes

Ingredients:

- 5 large eggs
- ¼ teaspoon black pepper
- ¼ teaspoon salt
- 1 tablespoon milk
- ¼ cup shredded cheddar cheese
- One 8-ounce package refrigerated crescent rolls
- 4 tablespoon pesto sauce
- 8 fully cooked breakfast sausage links, defrosted

Directions:

1. Preheat the air fryer to 320°F.
2. In a medium bowl, crack the eggs and whisk with the pepper, salt, and milk. Pour into a frying pan over medium heat and scramble. Just before the eggs are done, turn off the heat and add in the cheese. Continue to cook until the cheese has melted and the eggs are finished (about 5 minutes total). Remove from the heat.
3. Remove the crescent rolls from the package and press them flat onto a clean surface lightly dusted with flour. Add 1½ teaspoons of pesto sauce across the center of each roll. Place equal portions of eggs across all 8 rolls. Then top each roll with a sausage link and roll the dough up tight so it resembles the crescent-roll shape.
4. Lightly spray your air fryer basket with olive oil mist and place the rolls on top. Bake for 6 minutes or until the tops of the rolls are lightly browned.
5. Remove and let cool 3 to 5 minutes before serving.

Western Omelet

Servings: 2

Cooking Time: 22 Minutes

Ingredients:

- ¼ cup chopped onion
- ¼ cup chopped bell pepper, green or red
- ¼ cup diced ham
- 1 teaspoon butter
- 4 large eggs
- 2 tablespoons milk
- ⅛ teaspoon salt
- ¾ cup grated sharp Cheddar cheese

Directions:

1. Place onion, bell pepper, ham, and butter in air fryer baking pan. Cook at 390°F for 1 minute and stir. Continue cooking 5minutes, until vegetables are tender.
2. Beat together eggs, milk, and salt. Pour over vegetables and ham in baking pan. Cook at 360°F for 15minutes or until eggs set and top has browned slightly.
3. Sprinkle grated cheese on top of omelet. Cook 1 minute or just long enough to melt the cheese.

Southern Sweet Cornbread

Servings: 6

Cooking Time: 17 Minutes

Ingredients:

- cooking spray
- ½ cup white cornmeal
- ½ cup flour
- 2 teaspoons baking powder
- ½ teaspoon salt
- 4 teaspoons sugar
- 1 egg
- 2 tablespoons oil
- ½ cup milk

Directions:

1. Preheat air fryer to 360°F.
2. Spray air fryer baking pan with nonstick cooking spray.
3. In a medium bowl, stir together the cornmeal, flour, baking powder, salt, and sugar.
4. In a small bowl, beat together the egg, oil, and milk. Stir into dry ingredients until well combined.
5. Pour batter into prepared baking pan.
6. Cook at 360°F for 17 minutes or until toothpick inserted in center comes out clean or with crumbs clinging.

Crustless Broccoli, Roasted Pepper And Fontina Quiche

Servings: 4

Cooking Time: 60 Minutes

Ingredients:

- 7-inch cake pan
- 1 cup broccoli florets
- ¾ cup chopped roasted red peppers
- 1¼ cups grated Fontina cheese
- 6 eggs
- ¾ cup heavy cream
- ½ teaspoon salt
- freshly ground black pepper

Directions:

1. Preheat the air fryer to 360°F.
2. Grease the inside of a 7-inch cake pan (4 inches deep) or other oven-safe pan that will fit into your air fryer. Place the broccoli florets and roasted red peppers in the cake pan and top with the grated Fontina cheese.
3. Whisk the eggs and heavy cream together in a bowl. Season the eggs with salt and freshly ground black pepper. Pour the egg mixture over the cheese and vegetables and cover the pan with aluminum foil. Transfer the cake pan to the air fryer basket.
4. Air-fry at 360°F for 60 minutes. Remove the aluminum foil for the last two minutes of cooking time.
5. Unmold the quiche onto a platter and cut it into slices to serve with a side salad or perhaps some air-fried potatoes.

Peppered Maple Bacon Knots

Servings: 6

Cooking Time: 8 Minutes

Ingredients:

- 1 pound maple smoked center-cut bacon
- ¼ cup maple syrup
- ¼ cup brown sugar
- coarsely cracked black peppercorns

Directions:

1. Tie each bacon strip in a loose knot and place them on a baking sheet.
2. Combine the maple syrup and brown sugar in a bowl. Brush each knot generously with this mixture and sprinkle with coarsely cracked black pepper.
3. Preheat the air fryer to 390°F.
4. Air-fry the bacon knots in batches. Place one layer of knots in the air fryer basket and air-fry for 5 minutes. Turn the bacon knots over and air-fry for an additional 3 minutes.
5. Serve warm.

Scones

Servings: 9

Cooking Time: 8 Minutes Per Batch

Ingredients:

- 2 cups self-rising flour, plus ¼ cup for kneading
- ⅓ cup granulated sugar
- ¼ cup butter, cold
- 1 cup milk

Directions:

1. Preheat air fryer at 360°F.
2. In large bowl, stir together flour and sugar.
3. Cut cold butter into tiny cubes, and stir into flour mixture with fork.
4. Stir in milk until soft dough forms.
5. Sprinkle ¼ cup of flour onto wax paper and place dough on top. Knead lightly by folding and turning the dough about 6 to 8 times.
6. Pat dough into a 6 x 6-inch square.
7. Cut into 9 equal squares.
8. Place all squares in air fryer basket or as many as will fit in a single layer, close together but not touching.
9. Cook at 360°F for 8minutes. When done, scones will be lightly browned on top and will spring back when pressed gently with a dull knife.
10. Repeat steps 8 and 9 to cook remaining scones.

Roasted Tomato And Cheddar Rolls

Servings: 12

Cooking Time: 55 Minutes

Ingredients:

- 4 Roma tomatoes
- ½ clove garlic, minced
- 1 tablespoon olive oil
- ¼ teaspoon dried thyme
- salt and freshly ground black pepper
- 4 cups all-purpose flour
- 1 teaspoon active dry yeast
- 2 teaspoons sugar
- 2 teaspoons salt
- 1 tablespoon olive oil
- 1 cup grated Cheddar cheese, plus more for sprinkling at the end
- 1½ cups water

Directions:

1. Cut the Roma tomatoes in half, remove the seeds with your fingers and transfer to a bowl. Add the garlic, olive oil, dried thyme, salt and freshly ground black pepper and toss well.
2. Preheat the air fryer to 390°F.
3. Place the tomatoes, cut side up in the air fryer basket and air-fry for 10 minutes. The tomatoes should just start to brown. Shake the basket to redistribute the tomatoes, and air-fry for another 5 to 10 minutes at 330°F until the tomatoes are no longer juicy. Let the tomatoes cool and then rough chop them.
4. Combine the flour, yeast, sugar and salt in the bowl of a stand mixer. Add the olive oil, chopped roasted tomatoes and Cheddar cheese to the flour mixture and start to mix using the dough hook attachment. As you're mixing, add 1¼ cups of the water, mixing until the dough comes together. Continue to knead the dough with the dough hook for another 10 minutes, adding enough water to the dough to get it to the right consistency.
5. Transfer the dough to an oiled bowl, cover with a clean kitchen towel and let it rest and rise until it has doubled in volume – about 1 to 2 hours. Then, divide the dough into 12 equal portions. Roll each portion of dough into a ball. Lightly coat each dough ball with oil and let the dough balls rest and rise a second time, covered lightly with plastic wrap for 45 minutes. (Alternately, you can place the rolls in the refrigerator overnight and take them out 2 hours before you bake them.)
6. Preheat the air fryer to 360°F.
7. Spray the dough balls and the air fryer basket with a little olive oil. Place three rolls at a time in the basket and bake for 10 minutes. Add a little grated Cheddar cheese on top of the rolls for the last 2 minutes of air frying for an attractive finish.

Classic Cinnamon Rolls

Servings: 4
Cooking Time: 6 Minutes

Ingredients:

- 1½ cups all-purpose flour
- 1 tablespoon granulated sugar
- 2 teaspoons baking powder
- ½ teaspoon salt
- 4 tablespoons butter, divided
- ½ cup buttermilk
- 2 tablespoons brown sugar
- 1 teaspoon cinnamon
- 1 cup powdered sugar
- 2 tablespoons milk

Directions:

1. Preheat the air fryer to 360°F.
2. In a large bowl, stir together the flour, sugar, baking powder, and salt. Cut in 3 tablespoons of the butter with a pastry blender or two knives until coarse crumbs remain. Stir in the buttermilk until a dough forms.
3. Place the dough onto a floured surface and roll out into a square shape about ½ inch thick.
4. Melt the remaining 1 tablespoon of butter in the microwave for 20 seconds. Using a pastry brush or your fingers, spread the melted butter onto the dough.
5. In a small bowl, mix together the brown sugar and cinnamon. Sprinkle the mixture across the surface of the dough. Roll the dough up, forming a long log. Using a pastry cutter or sharp knife, cut 10 cinnamon rolls.
6. Carefully place the cinnamon rolls into the air fryer basket. Then bake at 360°F for 6 minutes or until golden brown.
7. Meanwhile, in a small bowl, whisk together the powdered sugar and milk.
8. Plate the cinnamon rolls and drizzle the glaze over the surface before serving.

Broccoli Cornbread

Servings: 6
Cooking Time: 18 Minutes

Ingredients:

- 1 cup frozen chopped broccoli, thawed and drained
- ¼ cup cottage cheese
- 1 egg, beaten
- 2 tablespoons minced onion
- 2 tablespoons melted butter
- ½ cup flour
- ½ cup yellow cornmeal
- 1 teaspoon baking powder
- ½ teaspoon salt
- ¼ cup milk, plus 2 tablespoons
- cooking spray

Directions:

1. Place thawed broccoli in colander and press with a spoon to squeeze out excess moisture.
2. Stir together all ingredients in a large bowl.
3. Spray 6 x 6-inch baking pan with cooking spray.
4. Spread batter in pan and cook at 330°F for 18 minutes or until cornbread is lightly browned and loaf starts to pull away from sides of pan.

Cinnamon Rolls With Cream Cheese Glaze

Servings: 8
Cooking Time: 9 Minutes

Ingredients:

- 1 pound frozen bread dough, thawed
- ¼ cup butter, melted and cooled
- ¾ cup brown sugar
- 1½ tablespoons ground cinnamon
- Cream Cheese Glaze:
- 4 ounces cream cheese, softened
- 2 tablespoons butter, softened
- 1¼ cups powdered sugar
- ½ teaspoon vanilla

Directions:

1. Let the bread dough come to room temperature on the counter. On a lightly floured surface roll the dough into a 13-inch by 11-inch rectangle. Position the rectangle so the 13-inch side is facing you. Brush the melted butter all over the dough, leaving a 1-inch border uncovered along the edge farthest away from you.
2. Combine the brown sugar and cinnamon in a small bowl. Sprinkle the mixture evenly over the buttered

dough, keeping the 1-inch border uncovered. Roll the dough into a log starting with the edge closest to you. Roll the dough tightly, making sure to roll evenly and push out any air pockets. When you get to the uncovered edge of the dough, press the dough onto the roll to seal it together.

3. Cut the log into 8 pieces slicing slowly with a sawing motion so you don't flatten the dough. Turn the slices on their sides and cover with a clean kitchen towel. Let the rolls sit in the warmest part of your kitchen for 1½ to 2 hours to rise.
4. To make the glaze, place the cream cheese and butter in a microwave-safe bowl. Soften the mixture in the microwave for 30 seconds at a time until it is easy to stir. Gradually add the powdered sugar and stir to combine. Add the vanilla extract and whisk until smooth. Set aside.
5. When the rolls have risen, Preheat the air fryer to 350°F.
6. Transfer 4 of the rolls to the air fryer basket. Air-fry for 5 minutes. Turn the rolls over and air-fry for another 4 minutes. Repeat with the remaining 4 rolls.
7. Let the rolls cool for a couple of minutes before glazing. Spread large dollops of cream cheese glaze on top of the warm cinnamon rolls, allowing some of the glaze to drip down the side of the rolls. Serve warm and enjoy!

Apple-cinnamon-walnut Muffins

Servings: 8

Cooking Time: 11 Minutes

Ingredients:

- 1 cup flour
- ⅓ cup sugar
- 1 teaspoon baking powder
- ¼ teaspoon baking soda
- ¼ teaspoon salt
- 1 teaspoon cinnamon
- ¼ teaspoon ginger
- ¼ teaspoon nutmeg
- 1 egg
- 2 tablespoons pancake syrup, plus 2 teaspoons
- 2 tablespoons melted butter, plus 2 teaspoons
- ¾ cup unsweetened applesauce
- ½ teaspoon vanilla extract
- ¼ cup chopped walnuts
- ¼ cup diced apple
- 8 foil muffin cups, liners removed and sprayed with cooking spray

Directions:

1. Preheat air fryer to 330°F.
2. In a large bowl, stir together flour, sugar, baking powder, baking soda, salt, cinnamon, ginger, and nutmeg.
3. In a small bowl, beat egg until frothy. Add syrup, butter, applesauce, and vanilla and mix well.
4. Pour egg mixture into dry ingredients and stir just until moistened.
5. Gently stir in nuts and diced apple.
6. Divide batter among the 8 muffin cups.
7. Place 4 muffin cups in air fryer basket and cook at 330°F for 11minutes.
8. Repeat with remaining 4 muffins or until toothpick inserted in center comes out clean.

Western Frittata

Servings: 1

Cooking Time: 19 Minutes

Ingredients:

- ½ red or green bell pepper, cut into ½-inch chunks
- 1 teaspoon olive oil
- 3 eggs, beaten
- ¼ cup grated Cheddar cheese
- ¼ cup diced cooked ham
- salt and freshly ground black pepper, to taste
- 1 teaspoon butter
- 1 teaspoon chopped fresh parsley

Directions:

1. Preheat the air fryer to 400°F.
2. Toss the peppers with the olive oil and air-fry for 6 minutes, shaking the basket once or twice during the cooking process to redistribute the ingredients.
3. While the vegetables are cooking, beat the eggs well in a bowl, stir in the Cheddar cheese and ham, and

season with salt and freshly ground black pepper. Add the air-fried peppers to this bowl when they have finished cooking.

4. Place a 6- or 7-inch non-stick metal cake pan into the air fryer basket with the butter using an aluminum sling to lower the pan into the basket. (Fold a piece of aluminum foil into a strip about 2-inches wide by 24-inches long.) Air-fry for 1 minute at 380°F to melt the butter. Remove the cake pan and rotate the pan to distribute the butter and grease the pan. Pour the egg mixture into the cake pan and return the pan to the air fryer, using the aluminum sling.

5. Air-fry at 380°F for 12 minutes, or until the frittata has puffed up and is lightly browned. Let the frittata sit in the air fryer for 5 minutes to cool to an edible temperature and set up. Remove the cake pan from the air fryer, sprinkle with parsley and serve immediately.

Crunchy French Toast Sticks

Servings: 2

Cooking Time: 9 Minutes

Ingredients:

- 2 eggs, beaten
- ¾ cup milk
- ½ teaspoon vanilla extract
- ½ teaspoon ground cinnamon
- 1½ cups crushed crunchy cinnamon cereal, or any cereal flakes
- 4 slices Texas Toast (or other bread that you can slice into 1-inch thick slices)
- maple syrup, for serving
- vegetable oil or melted butter

Directions:

1. Combine the eggs, milk, vanilla and cinnamon in a shallow bowl. Place the crushed cereal in a second shallow bowl.
2. Trim the crusts off the slices of bread and cut each slice into 3 sticks. Dip the sticks of bread into the egg mixture, turning them over to coat all sides. Let the bread sticks absorb the egg mixture for ten seconds or so, but don't let them get too wet. Roll the bread sticks in the cereal crumbs, pressing the cereal gently onto all sides so that it adheres to the bread.
3. Preheat the air fryer to 400°F.
4. Spray or brush the air fryer basket with oil or melted butter. Place the coated sticks in the basket. It's ok to stack a few on top of the others in the opposite direction.
5. Air-fry for 9 minutes. Turn the sticks over a couple of times during the cooking process so that the sticks crisp evenly. Serve warm with the maple syrup or some berries.

Carrot Orange Muffins

Servings: 12

Cooking Time: 12 Minutes

Ingredients:

- 1½ cups all-purpose flour
- ½ cup granulated sugar
- ½ teaspoon ground cinnamon
- 2 teaspoons baking powder
- ¼ teaspoon baking soda
- ½ teaspoon salt
- 2 large eggs
- ¼ cup vegetable oil
- ⅓ cup orange marmalade
- 2 cups grated carrots

Directions:

1. Preheat the air fryer to 320°F.
2. In a large bowl, whisk together the flour, sugar, cinnamon, baking powder, baking soda, and salt; set aside.
3. In a separate bowl, whisk together the eggs, vegetable oil, orange marmalade, and grated carrots.
4. Make a well in the dry ingredients; then pour the wet ingredients into the well of the dry ingredients. Using a rubber spatula, mix the ingredients for 1 minute or until slightly lumpy.
5. Using silicone muffin liners, fill 6 muffin liners two-thirds full.
6. Carefully place the muffin liners in the air fryer basket and bake for 12 minutes (or until the tops are browned and a toothpick inserted in the center comes out clean). Carefully remove the muffins from the basket and repeat with remaining batter.
7. Serve warm.

Parmesan Garlic Naan

Servings: 6

Cooking Time: 4 Minutes

Ingredients:

- 1 cup bread flour
- 1 teaspoon baking powder
- ⅛ teaspoon salt
- 1 teaspoon garlic powder
- 2 tablespoon shredded parmesan cheese
- 1 cup plain 2% fat Greek yogurt
- 1 tablespoon extra-virgin olive oil

Directions:

1. Preheat the air fryer to 400°F.
2. In a medium bowl, mix the flour, baking powder, salt, garlic powder, and cheese. Mix the yogurt into the flour, using your hands to combine if necessary.
3. On a flat surface covered with flour, divide the dough into 6 equal balls and roll each out into a 4-inch-diameter circle.
4. Lightly brush both sides of each naan with olive oil and place one naan at a time into the basket. Cook for 3 to 4 minutes (or until the bread begins to rise and brown on the outside). Remove and repeat for the remaining breads.
5. Serve warm.

Quesadillas

Servings: 4

Cooking Time: 12 Minutes

Ingredients:

- 4 eggs
- 2 tablespoons skim milk
- salt and pepper
- oil for misting or cooking spray
- 4 flour tortillas
- 4 tablespoons salsa
- 2 ounces Cheddar cheese, grated
- ½ small avocado, peeled and thinly sliced

Directions:

1. Preheat air fryer to 270°F.
2. Beat together eggs, milk, salt, and pepper.
3. Spray a 6 x 6-inch air fryer baking pan lightly with cooking spray and add egg mixture.
4. Cook 9minutes, stirring every 1 to 2minutes, until eggs are scrambled to your liking. Remove and set aside.
5. Spray one side of each tortilla with oil or cooking spray. Flip over.
6. Divide eggs, salsa, cheese, and avocado among the tortillas, covering only half of each tortilla.
7. Fold each tortilla in half and press down lightly.
8. Place 2 tortillas in air fryer basket and cook at 390°F for 3minutes or until cheese melts and outside feels slightly crispy. Repeat with remaining two tortillas.
9. Cut each cooked tortilla into halves or thirds.

Pumpkin Loaf

Servings: 6

Cooking Time: 22 Minutes

Ingredients:

- cooking spray
- 1 large egg
- ½ cup granulated sugar
- ⅓ cup oil
- ½ cup canned pumpkin (not pie filling)
- ½ teaspoon vanilla
- ⅔ cup flour plus 1 tablespoon
- ½ teaspoon baking powder
- ½ teaspoon baking soda
- ½ teaspoon salt
- 1 teaspoon pumpkin pie spice
- ¼ teaspoon cinnamon

Directions:

1. Spray 6 x 6-inch baking dish lightly with cooking spray.
2. Place baking dish in air fryer basket and preheat air fryer to 330°F.
3. In a large bowl, beat eggs and sugar together with a hand mixer.
4. Add oil, pumpkin, and vanilla and mix well.
5. Sift together all dry ingredients. Add to pumpkin mixture and beat well, about 1 minute.
6. Pour batter in baking dish and cook at 330°F for 22 minutes or until toothpick inserted in center of loaf comes out clean.

French Toast Sticks

Servings: 4

Cooking Time: 7 Minutes

Ingredients:

- 2 eggs
- ½ cup milk
- ⅛ teaspoon salt
- ½ teaspoon pure vanilla extract
- ¾ cup crushed cornflakes
- 6 slices sandwich bread, each slice cut into 4 strips
- oil for misting or cooking spray
- maple syrup or honey

Directions:

1. In a small bowl, beat together eggs, milk, salt, and vanilla.
2. Place crushed cornflakes on a plate or in a shallow dish.
3. Dip bread strips in egg mixture, shake off excess, and roll in cornflake crumbs.
4. Spray both sides of bread strips with oil.
5. Place bread strips in air fryer basket in single layer.
6. Cook at 390°F for 7minutes or until they're dark golden brown.
7. Repeat steps 5 and 6 to cook remaining French toast sticks.
8. Serve with maple syrup or honey for dipping.

Vanilla Butter Cake

Servings: 6

Cooking Time: 20-24 Minutes

Ingredients:

- ¾ cup plus 1 tablespoon All-purpose flour
- 1 teaspoon Baking powder
- ¼ teaspoon Table salt
- 8 tablespoons (½ cup/1 stick) Butter, at room temperature
- ½ cup Granulated white sugar
- 2 Large egg(s)
- 2 tablespoons Whole or low-fat milk (not fat-free)
- ¾ teaspoon Vanilla extract
- Baking spray (see here)

Directions:

1. Preheat the air fryer to 325°F (or 330°F, if that's the closest setting).
2. Mix the flour, baking powder, and salt in a small bowl until well combined.
3. Using an electric hand mixer at medium speed, beat the butter and sugar in a medium bowl until creamy and smooth, about 3 minutes, occasionally scraping down the inside of the bowl.
4. Beat in the egg or eggs, as well as the white or a yolk as necessary. Beat in the milk and vanilla until smooth. Turn off the beaters and add the flour mixture. Beat at low speed until thick and smooth.
5. Use the baking spray to generously coat the inside of a 6-inch round cake pan for a small batch, a 7-inch round cake pan for a medium batch, or an 8-inch round cake pan for a large batch. Scrape and spread the batter into the pan, smoothing the batter out to an even layer.
6. Set the pan in the basket and air-fry undisturbed for 20 minutes for a 6-inch layer, 22 minutes for a 7-inch layer, or 24 minutes for an 8-inch layer, or until a toothpick or cake tester inserted into the center of the cake comes out clean. Start checking it at the 15-minute mark to know where you are.
7. Use hot pads or silicone baking mitts to transfer the cake pan to a wire rack. Cool for 5 minutes. To unmold, set a cutting board over the baking pan and invert both the board and the pan. Lift the still-warm pan off the cake layer. Set the wire rack on top of the cake layer and invert all of it with the cutting board so that the cake layer is now right side up on the wire rack. Remove the cutting board and continue cooling the cake for at least 10 minutes or to room temperature, about 30 minutes, before slicing into wedges.

Giant Buttery Oatmeal Cookie

Servings: 4

Cooking Time: 16 Minutes

Ingredients:

- 1 cup Rolled oats (not quick-cooking or steel-cut oats)
- ½ cup All-purpose flour
- ½ teaspoon Baking soda
- ½ teaspoon Ground cinnamon
- ½ teaspoon Table salt
- 3½ tablespoons Butter, at room temperature
- ⅓ cup Packed dark brown sugar
- 1½ tablespoons Granulated white sugar
- 3 tablespoons (or 1 medium egg, well beaten) Pasteurized egg substitute, such as Egg Beaters
- ¾ teaspoon Vanilla extract
- ⅓ cup Chopped pecans
- Baking spray

Directions:

1. Preheat the air fryer to 350°F .
2. Stir the oats, flour, baking soda, cinnamon, and salt in a bowl until well combined.
3. Using an electric hand mixer at medium speed , beat the butter, brown sugar, and granulated white sugar until creamy and thick, about 3 minutes, scraping down the inside of the bowl occasionally. Beat in the egg substitute or egg (as applicable) and vanilla until uniform.
4. Scrape down and remove the beaters. Fold in the flour mixture and pecans with a rubber spatula just until all the flour is moistened and the nuts are even throughout the dough.

5. For a small air fryer, coat the inside of a 6-inch round cake pan with baking spray. For a medium air fryer, coat the inside of a 7-inch round cake pan with baking spray. And for a large air fryer, coat the inside of an 8-inch round cake pan with baking spray. Scrape and gently press the dough into the prepared pan, spreading it into an even layer to the perimeter.
6. Set the pan in the basket and air-fry undisturbed for 16 minutes, or until puffed and browned.
7. Transfer the pan to a wire rack and cool for 10 minutes. Loosen the cookie from the perimeter with a spatula, then invert the pan onto a cutting board and let the cookie come free. Remove the pan and reinvert the cookie onto the wire rack. Cool for 5 minutes more before slicing into wedges to serve.

Baked Apple

Servings: 6

Cooking Time: 20 Minutes

Ingredients:

- 3 small Honey Crisp or other baking apples
- 3 tablespoons maple syrup
- 3 tablespoons chopped pecans
- 1 tablespoon firm butter, cut into 6 pieces

Directions:

1. Put ½ cup water in the drawer of the air fryer.
2. Wash apples well and dry them.
3. Split apples in half. Remove core and a little of the flesh to make a cavity for the pecans.
4. Place apple halves in air fryer basket, cut side up.
5. Spoon 1½ teaspoons pecans into each cavity.
6. Spoon ½ tablespoon maple syrup over pecans in each apple.
7. Top each apple with ½ teaspoon butter.
8. Cook at 360°F for 20 minutes, until apples are tender.

Cheesecake Wontons

Servings:16

Cooking Time: 6 Minutes

Ingredients:

- ¼ cup Regular or low-fat cream cheese (not fat-free)
- 2 tablespoons Granulated white sugar
- 1½ tablespoons Egg yolk
- ¼ teaspoon Vanilla extract
- ⅛ teaspoon Table salt
- 1½ tablespoons All-purpose flour
- 16 Wonton wrappers (vegetarian, if a concern)
- Vegetable oil spray

Directions:

1. Preheat the air fryer to 400°F.
2. Using a flatware fork, mash the cream cheese, sugar, egg yolk, and vanilla in a small bowl until smooth. Add the salt and flour and continue mashing until evenly combined.
3. Set a wonton wrapper on a clean, dry work surface so that one corner faces you (so that it looks like a diamond on your work surface). Set 1 teaspoon of the cream cheese mixture in the middle of the wrapper but just above a horizontal line that would divide the wrapper in half. Dip your clean finger in water and run it along the edges of the wrapper. Fold the corner closest to you up and over the filling, lining it up with the corner farthest from you, thereby making a stuffed triangle. Press gently to seal. Wet the two triangle tips nearest you, then fold them up and together over the filling. Gently press together to seal and fuse. Set aside and continue making more stuffed wontons, 11 more for the small batch, 15 more for the medium batch, or 23 more for the large one.
4. Lightly coat the stuffed wrappers on all sides with vegetable oil spray. Set them with the fused corners up in the basket with as much air space between them as possible. Air-fry undisturbed for 6 minutes, or until golden brown and crisp.
5. Gently dump the contents of the basket onto a wire rack. Cool for at least 5 minutes before serving.

Glazed Cherry Turnovers

Servings: 8

Cooking Time: 14 Minutes

Ingredients:

- 2 sheets frozen puff pastry, thawed
- 1 (21-ounce) can premium cherry pie filling

- 2 teaspoons ground cinnamon
- 1 egg, beaten
- 1 cup sliced almonds
- 1 cup powdered sugar
- 2 tablespoons milk

Directions:

1. Roll a sheet of puff pastry out into a square that is approximately 10-inches by 10-inches. Cut this large square into quarters.
2. Mix the cherry pie filling and cinnamon together in a bowl. Spoon ¼ cup of the cherry filling into the center of each puff pastry square. Brush the perimeter of the pastry square with the egg wash. Fold one corner of the puff pastry over the cherry pie filling towards the opposite corner, forming a triangle. Seal the two edges of the pastry together with the tip of a fork, making a design with the tines. Brush the top of the turnovers with the egg wash and sprinkle sliced almonds over each one. Repeat these steps with the second sheet of puff pastry. You should have eight turnovers at the end.
3. Preheat the air fryer to 370°F.
4. Air-fry two turnovers at a time for 14 minutes, carefully turning them over halfway through the cooking time.
5. While the turnovers are cooking, make the glaze by whisking the powdered sugar and milk together in a small bowl until smooth. Let the glaze sit for a minute so the sugar can absorb the milk. If the consistency is still too thick to drizzle, add a little more milk, a drop at a time, and stir until smooth.
6. Let the cooked cherry turnovers sit for at least 10 minutes. Then drizzle the glaze over each turnover in a zigzag motion. Serve warm or at room temperature.

Cherry Hand Pies

Servings: 8

Cooking Time: 8 Minutes

Ingredients:

- 4 cups frozen or canned pitted tart cherries (if using canned, drain and pat dry)
- 2 teaspoons lemon juice
- ½ cup sugar
- ¼ cup cornstarch
- 1 teaspoon vanilla extract
- 1 Basic Pie Dough (see the preceding recipe) or store-bought pie dough

Directions:

1. In a medium saucepan, place the cherries and lemon juice and cook over medium heat for 10 minutes, or until the cherries begin to break down.
2. In a small bowl, stir together the sugar and cornstarch. Pour the sugar mixture into the cherries, stirring constantly. Cook the cherry mixture over low heat for 2 to 3 minutes, or until thickened. Remove from the heat and stir in the vanilla extract. Allow the cherry mixture to cool to room temperature, about 30 minutes.
3. Meanwhile, bring the pie dough to room temperature. Divide the dough into 8 equal pieces. Roll out the dough to ¼-inch thickness in circles. Place ¼ cup filling in the center of each rolled dough. Fold the dough to create a half-circle. Using a fork, press around the edges to seal the hand pies. Pierce the top of the pie with a fork for steam release while cooking. Continue until 8 hand pies are formed.
4. Preheat the air fryer to 350°F.
5. Place a single layer of hand pies in the air fryer basket and spray with cooking spray. Cook for 8 to 10 minutes or until golden brown and cooked through.

Grilled Pineapple Dessert

Servings: 4

Cooking Time: 12 Minutes

Ingredients:

- oil for misting or cooking spray
- 4 ½-inch-thick slices fresh pineapple, core removed
- 1 tablespoon honey
- ¼ teaspoon brandy
- 2 tablespoons slivered almonds, toasted
- vanilla frozen yogurt or coconut sorbet

Directions:

1. Spray both sides of pineapple slices with oil or cooking spray. Place on grill plate or directly into air fryer basket.

2. Cook at 390°F for 6minutes. Turn slices over and cook for an additional 6minutes.
3. Mix together the honey and brandy.
4. Remove cooked pineapple slices from air fryer, sprinkle with toasted almonds, and drizzle with honey mixture.
5. Serve with a scoop of frozen yogurt or sorbet on the side.

Cinnamon Sugar Banana Rolls

Servings: 6
Cooking Time: 8 Minutes

Ingredients:

- ¼ cup Granulated white sugar
- 2 teaspoons Ground cinnamon
- 2 tablespoons Peach or apricot jam or orange marmalade
- 6 Spring roll wrappers, thawed if necessary
- 2 Ripe banana(s), peeled and cut into 3-inch-long sections
- 1 Large egg, well beaten
- Vegetable oil spray

Directions:

1. Preheat the air fryer to 400°F.
2. Stir the sugar and cinnamon in a small bowl until well combined. Stir the jam or marmalade with a fork to loosen it up.
3. Set a spring roll wrapper on a clean, dry work surface. Roll a banana section in the sugar mixture until evenly and well coated. Set the coated banana along one edge of the wrapper. Top it with about 1 teaspoon of the jam or marmalade. Fold the sides of the wrapper perpendicular to the banana up and over the banana, partially covering it. Brush beaten egg over the side of the wrapper farthest from the banana. Starting with the banana, roll the wrapper closed, ending at the part with the beaten egg. Press gently to seal. Set the roll aside seam side down and continue filling and rolling the remaining wrappers in the same way.
4. Lightly coat the wrappers with vegetable oil spray. Set them seam side down in the basket with as much air space between them as possible. Air-fry undisturbed for 8 minutes, or until crisp and golden brown.
5. Use kitchen tongs to gently transfer the rolls to a wire rack. Cool for at least 5 minutes or up to 30 minutes before serving.

Fried Pineapple Chunks

Servings: 3
Cooking Time: 10 Minutes

Ingredients:

- 3 tablespoons Cornstarch
- 1 Large egg white, beaten until foamy
- 1 cup (4 ounces) Ground vanilla wafer cookies (not low-fat cookies)
- ¼ teaspoon Ground dried ginger
- 18 (about 2¼ cups) Fresh 1-inch chunks peeled and cored pineapple

Directions:

1. Preheat the air fryer to 400°F.
2. Put the cornstarch in a medium or large bowl. Put the beaten egg white in a small bowl. Pour the cookie crumbs and ground dried ginger into a large zip-closed plastic bag, shaking it a bit to combine them.
3. Dump the pineapple chunks into the bowl with the cornstarch. Toss and stir until well coated. Use your cleaned fingers or a large fork like a shovel to pick up a few pineapple chunks, shake off any excess cornstarch, and put them in the bowl with the egg white. Stir gently, then pick them up and let any excess egg white slip back into the rest. Put them in the bag with the crumb mixture. Repeat the cornstarch-then-egg process until all the pineapple chunks are in the bag. Seal the bag and shake gently, turning the bag this way and that, to coat the pieces well.
4. Set the coated pineapple chunks in the basket with as much air space between them as possible. Even a fraction of an inch will work, but they should not touch. Air-fry undisturbed for 10 minutes, or until golden brown and crisp.
5. Gently dump the contents of the basket onto a wire rack. Cool for at least 5 minutes or up to 15 minutes before serving.

Blueberry Crisp

Servings: 6

Cooking Time: 13 Minutes

Ingredients:

- 3 cups Fresh or thawed frozen blueberries
- ⅓ cup Granulated white sugar
- 1 tablespoon Instant tapioca
- ⅓ cup All-purpose flour
- ⅓ cup Rolled oats (not quick-cooking or steel-cut)
- ⅓ cup Chopped walnuts or pecans
- ⅓ cup Packed light brown sugar
- 5 tablespoons plus 1 teaspoon (⅔ stick) Butter, melted and cooled
- ¾ teaspoon Ground cinnamon
- ¼ teaspoon Table salt

Directions:

1. Preheat the air fryer to 400°F.
2. Mix the blueberries, granulated white sugar, and instant tapioca in a 6-inch round cake pan for a small batch, a 7-inch round cake pan for a medium batch, or an 8-inch round cake pan for a large batch.
3. When the machine is at temperature, set the cake pan in the basket and air-fry undisturbed for 5 minutes, or just until the blueberries begin to bubble.
4. Meanwhile, mix the flour, oats, nuts, brown sugar, butter, cinnamon, and salt in a medium bowl until well combined.
5. When the blueberries have begun to bubble, crumble this flour mixture evenly on top. Continue air-frying undisturbed for 8 minutes, or until the topping has browned a bit and the filling is bubbling.
6. Use two hot pads or silicone baking mitts to transfer the cake pan to a wire rack. Cool for at least 10 minutes or to room temperature before serving.

Air-fried Beignets

Servings: 24

Cooking Time: 5 Minutes

Ingredients:

- ¾ cup lukewarm water (about 90°F)
- ¼ cup sugar
- 1 generous teaspoon active dry yeast (½ envelope)
- 3½ to 4 cups all-purpose flour
- ½ teaspoon salt
- 2 tablespoons unsalted butter, room temperature and cut into small pieces
- 1 egg, lightly beaten
- ½ cup evaporated milk
- ¼ cup melted butter
- 1 cup confectioners' sugar
- chocolate sauce or raspberry sauce, to dip

Directions:

1. Combine the lukewarm water, a pinch of the sugar and the yeast in a bowl and let it proof for 5 minutes. It should froth a little. If it doesn't froth, your yeast is not active and you should start again with new yeast.
2. Combine 3½ cups of the flour, salt, 2 tablespoons of butter and the remaining sugar in a large bowl, or in the bowl of a stand mixer. Add the egg, evaporated milk and yeast mixture to the bowl and mix with a wooden spoon (or the paddle attachment of the stand mixer) until the dough comes together in a sticky ball. Add a little more flour if necessary to get the dough to form. Transfer the dough to an oiled bowl, cover with plastic wrap or a clean kitchen towel and let it rise in a warm place for at least 2 hours or until it has doubled in size. Longer is better for flavor development and you can even let the dough rest in the refrigerator overnight (just remember to bring it to room temperature before proceeding with the recipe).
3. Roll the dough out to ½-inch thickness. Cut the dough into rectangular or diamond-shaped pieces. You can make the beignets any size you like, but this recipe will give you 24 (2-inch x 3-inch) rectangles.
4. Preheat the air fryer to 350°F.
5. Brush the beignets on both sides with some of the melted butter and air-fry in batches at 350°F for 5 minutes, turning them over halfway through if desired. (They will brown on all sides without being flipped, but flipping them will brown them more evenly.)
6. As soon as the beignets are finished, transfer them to a plate or baking sheet and dust with the confectioners' sugar. Serve warm with a chocolate or raspberry sauce.

Apple Dumplings

Servings: 4
Cooking Time: 25 Minutes

Ingredients:

- 1 Basic Pie Dough (see the following recipe)
- 4 medium Granny Smith or Pink Lady apples, peeled and cored
- 4 tablespoons sugar
- 4 teaspoons cinnamon
- ½ teaspoon ground nutmeg
- 4 tablespoons unsalted butter, melted
- 4 scoops ice cream, for serving

Directions:

1. Preheat the air fryer to 330°F.
2. Bring the pie crust recipe to room temperature.
3. Place the pie crust on a floured surface. Divide the dough into 4 equal pieces. Roll out each piece to ¼-inch-thick rounds. Place an apple onto each dough round. Sprinkle 1 tablespoon of sugar in the core part of each apple; sprinkle 1 teaspoon cinnamon and ⅛ teaspoon nutmeg over each. Place 1 tablespoon of butter into the center of each. Fold up the sides and fully cover the cored apples.
4. Place the dumplings into the air fryer basket and spray with cooking spray. Cook for 25 minutes. Check after 14 minutes cooking; if they're getting too brown, reduce the heat to 320°F and complete the cooking.
5. Serve hot apple dumplings with a scoop of ice cream.

Coconut-custard Pie

Servings: 4
Cooking Time: 20 Minutes

Ingredients:

- 1 cup milk
- ¼ cup plus 2 tablespoons sugar
- ¼ cup biscuit baking mix
- 1 teaspoon vanilla
- 2 eggs
- 2 tablespoons melted butter
- cooking spray
- ½ cup shredded, sweetened coconut

Directions:

1. Place all ingredients except coconut in a medium bowl.
2. Using a hand mixer, beat on high speed for 3minutes.
3. Let sit for 5minutes.
4. Preheat air fryer to 330°F.
5. Spray a 6-inch round or 6 x 6-inch square baking pan with cooking spray and place pan in air fryer basket.
6. Pour filling into pan and sprinkle coconut over top.
7. Cook pie at 330°F for 20 minutes or until center sets.

S'mores Pockets

Servings: 6
Cooking Time: 5 Minutes

Ingredients:

- 12 sheets phyllo dough, thawed
- 1½ cups butter, melted
- ¾ cup graham cracker crumbs
- 1 (7-ounce) Giant Hershey's® milk chocolate bar
- 12 marshmallows, cut in half

Directions:

1. Place one sheet of the phyllo on a large cutting board. Keep the rest of the phyllo sheets covered with a slightly damp, clean kitchen towel. Brush the phyllo sheet generously with some melted butter. Place a second phyllo sheet on top of the first and brush it with more butter. Repeat with one more phyllo sheet until you have a stack of 3 phyllo sheets with butter brushed between the layers. Cover the phyllo sheets with one quarter of the graham cracker crumbs leaving a 1-inch border on one of the short ends of the rectangle. Cut the phyllo sheets lengthwise into 3 strips.
2. Take 2 of the strips and crisscross them to form a cross with the empty borders at the top and to the left. Place 2 of the chocolate rectangles in the center of the cross. Place 4 of the marshmallow halves on top of the chocolate. Now fold the pocket together by folding the bottom phyllo strip up over the chocolate and marshmallows. Then fold the right side over, then the top strip down and finally the left side over. Brush all the edges generously with melted butter to seal shut. Repeat with the next three sheets of phyllo, until all the sheets

have been used. You will be able to make 2 pockets with every second batch because you will have an extra graham cracker crumb strip from the previous set of sheets.

3. Preheat the air fryer to 350°F.
4. Transfer 3 pockets at a time to the air fryer basket. Air-fry at 350°F for 4 to 5 minutes, until the phyllo dough is light brown in color. Flip the pockets over halfway through the cooking process. Repeat with the remaining 3 pockets.
5. Serve warm.

Molten Chocolate Almond Cakes

Servings: 3
Cooking Time: 13 Minutes

Ingredients:

- butter and flour for the ramekins
- 4 ounces bittersweet chocolate, chopped
- ½ cup (1 stick) unsalted butter
- 2 eggs
- 2 egg yolks
- ¼ cup sugar
- ½ teaspoon pure vanilla extract, or almond extract
- 1 tablespoon all-purpose flour
- 3 tablespoons ground almonds
- 8 to 12 semisweet chocolate discs (or 4 chunks of chocolate)
- cocoa powder or powdered sugar, for dusting
- toasted almonds, coarsely chopped

Directions:

1. Butter and flour three (6-ounce) ramekins. (Butter the ramekins and then coat the butter with flour by shaking it around in the ramekin and dumping out any excess.)
2. Melt the chocolate and butter together, either in the microwave or in a double boiler. In a separate bowl, beat the eggs, egg yolks and sugar together until light and smooth. Add the vanilla extract. Whisk the chocolate mixture into the egg mixture. Stir in the flour and ground almonds.
3. Preheat the air fryer to 330°F.
4. Transfer the batter carefully to the buttered ramekins, filling halfway. Place two or three chocolate discs in the center of the batter and then fill the ramekins to ½-inch below the top with the remaining batter. Place the ramekins into the air fryer basket and air-fry at 330°F for 13 minutes. The sides of the cake should be set, but the centers should be slightly soft. Remove the ramekins from the air fryer and let the cakes sit for 5 minutes. (If you'd like the cake a little less molten, air-fry for 14 minutes and let the cakes sit for 4 minutes.)
5. Run a butter knife around the edge of the ramekins and invert the cakes onto a plate. Lift the ramekin off the plate slowly and carefully so that the cake doesn't break. Dust with cocoa powder or powdered sugar and serve with a scoop of ice cream and some coarsely chopped toasted almonds.

Sweet Potato Donut Holes

Servings: 18
Cooking Time: 4 Minutes Per Batch

Ingredients:

- 1 cup flour
- ⅓ cup sugar
- ¼ teaspoon baking soda
- 1 teaspoon baking powder
- ⅛ teaspoon salt
- ½ cup cooked mashed purple sweet potatoes
- 1 egg, beaten
- 2 tablespoons butter, melted
- 1 teaspoon pure vanilla extract
- oil for misting or cooking spray

Directions:

1. Preheat air fryer to 390°F.
2. In a large bowl, stir together the flour, sugar, baking soda, baking powder, and salt.
3. In a separate bowl, combine the potatoes, egg, butter, and vanilla and mix well.
4. Add potato mixture to dry ingredients and stir into a soft dough.
5. Shape dough into 1½-inch balls. Mist lightly with oil or cooking spray.

6. Place 9 donut holes in air fryer basket, leaving a little space in between. Cook for 4 minutes, until done in center and lightly browned outside.
7. Repeat step 6 to cook remaining donut holes.

Pear And Almond Biscotti Crumble

Servings: 6

Cooking Time: 65 Minutes

Ingredients:

- 7-inch cake pan or ceramic dish
- 3 pears, peeled, cored and sliced
- ½ cup brown sugar
- ¼ teaspoon ground ginger
- 1 teaspoon ground cinnamon
- ⅛ teaspoon ground nutmeg
- 2 tablespoons cornstarch
- 1¼ cups (4 to 5) almond biscotti, coarsely crushed
- ¼ cup all-purpose flour
- ¼ cup sliced almonds
- ¼ cup butter, melted

Directions:

1. Combine the pears, brown sugar, ginger, cinnamon, nutmeg and cornstarch in a bowl. Toss to combine and then pour the pear mixture into a greased 7-inch cake pan or ceramic dish.
2. Combine the crushed biscotti, flour, almonds and melted butter in a medium bowl. Toss with a fork until the mixture resembles large crumbles. Sprinkle the biscotti crumble over the pears and cover the pan with aluminum foil.
3. Preheat the air fryer to 350°F.
4. Air-fry at 350°F for 60 minutes. Remove the aluminum foil and air-fry for an additional 5 minutes to brown the crumble layer.
5. Serve warm.

Maple Cinnamon Cheesecake

Servings: 4

Cooking Time: 12 Minutes

Ingredients:

- 6 sheets of cinnamon graham crackers
- 2 tablespoons butter
- 8 ounces Neufchâtel cream cheese
- 3 tablespoons pure maple syrup
- 1 large egg
- ½ teaspoon ground cinnamon
- ¼ teaspoon salt

Directions:

1. Preheat the air fryer to 350°F.
2. Place the graham crackers in a food processor and process until crushed into a flour. Mix with the butter and press into a mini air-fryer-safe pan lined at the bottom with parchment paper. Place in the air fryer and cook for 4 minutes.
3. In a large bowl, place the cream cheese and maple syrup. Use a hand mixer or stand mixer and beat together until smooth. Add in the egg, cinnamon, and salt and mix on medium speed until combined.
4. Remove the graham cracker crust from the air fryer and pour the batter into the pan.
5. Place the pan back in the air fryer, adjusting the temperature to 315°F. Cook for 18 minutes. Carefully remove when cooking completes. The top should be lightly browned and firm.
6. Keep the cheesecake in the pan and place in the refrigerator for 3 or more hours to firm up before serving.

Coconut Rice Cake

Servings: 8

Cooking Time: 30 Minutes

Ingredients:

- 1 cup all-natural coconut water
- 1 cup unsweetened coconut milk
- 1 teaspoon almond extract
- ¼ teaspoon salt
- 4 tablespoons honey
- cooking spray
- ¾ cup raw jasmine rice
- 2 cups sliced or cubed fruit

Directions:

1. In a medium bowl, mix together the coconut water, coconut milk, almond extract, salt, and honey.
2. Spray air fryer baking pan with cooking spray and add the rice.

3. Pour liquid mixture over rice.
4. Cook at 360°F for 15minutes. Stir and cook for 15 minutes longer or until rice grains are tender.
5. Allow cake to cool slightly. Run a dull knife around edge of cake, inside the pan. Turn the cake out onto a platter and garnish with fruit.

Custard

Servings: 4
Cooking Time: 45 Minutes

Ingredients:

- 2 cups whole milk
- 2 eggs
- ¼ cup sugar
- ⅛ teaspoon salt
- ¼ teaspoon vanilla
- cooking spray
- ⅛ teaspoon nutmeg

Directions:

1. In a blender, process milk, egg, sugar, salt, and vanilla until smooth.
2. Spray a 6 x 6-inch baking pan with nonstick spray and pour the custard into it.
3. Cook at 300°F for 45 minutes. Custard is done when the center sets.
4. Sprinkle top with the nutmeg.
5. Allow custard to cool slightly.
6. Serve it warm, at room temperature, or chilled.

Fried Cannoli Wontons

Servings: 10
Cooking Time: 8 Minutes

Ingredients:

- 8 ounces Neufchâtel cream cheese
- ¼ cup powdered sugar
- 1 teaspoon vanilla extract
- ¼ teaspoon salt
- ¼ cup mini chocolate chips
- 2 tablespoons chopped pecans (optional)
- 20 wonton wrappers
- ¼ cup filtered water

Directions:

1. Preheat the air fryer to 370°F.
2. In a large bowl, use a hand mixer to combine the cream cheese with the powdered sugar, vanilla, and salt. Fold in the chocolate chips and pecans. Set aside.
3. Lay the wonton wrappers out on a flat, smooth surface and place a bowl with the filtered water next to them.
4. Use a teaspoon to evenly divide the cream cheese mixture among the 20 wonton wrappers, placing the batter in the center of the wontons.
5. Wet the tip of your index finger, and gently moisten the outer edges of the wrapper. Then fold each wrapper until it creates a secure pocket.
6. Liberally spray the air fryer basket with olive oil mist.
7. Place the wontons into the basket, and cook for 5 to 8 minutes. When the outer edges begin to brown, remove the wontons from the air fryer basket. Repeat cooking with remaining wontons.
8. Serve warm.

Fudgy Brownie Cake

Servings: 6
Cooking Time: 25-35 Minutes

Ingredients:

- 6½ tablespoons All-purpose flour
- ¼ cup plus 1 teaspoon Unsweetened cocoa powder
- ½ teaspoon Baking powder
- ¼ teaspoon Table salt
- 6½ tablespoons Butter, at room temperature
- 9½ tablespoons Granulated white sugar
- 1 egg plus 1 large egg white Large egg(s)
- ¾ teaspoon Vanilla extract
- Baking spray (see here)

Directions:

1. Preheat the air fryer to 325°F (or 330°F, if that's the closest setting).
2. Mix the flour, cocoa powder, baking powder, and salt in a small bowl until well combined.
3. Using an electric hand mixer at medium speed, beat the butter and sugar in a medium bowl until creamy and smooth, about 3 minutes, occasionally scraping down the inside of the bowl.

4. Beat in the egg(s) and the white or yolk (as necessary), as well as the vanilla, until smooth. Turn off the beaters and add the flour mixture. Beat at low speed until thick and smooth.
5. Use the baking spray to generously coat the inside of a 6-inch round cake pan for a small batch, a 7-inch round cake pan for a medium batch, or an 8-inch round cake pan for a large batch. Scrape and spread the batter into the pan, smoothing the batter out to an even layer.
6. Set the pan in the basket and air-fry for 25 minutes for a 6-inch layer, 30 minutes for a 7-inch layer, or 35 minutes for an 8-inch layer, or until the cake is set but soft to the touch. Start checking it at the 20-minute mark to know where you are.
7. Use hot pads or silicone baking mitts to transfer the cake pan to a wire rack. Cool for at least 1 hour or up to 4 hours. Using a nonstick-safe knife, slice the cake into wedges right in the pan and lift them out one by one.

Blueberry Cheesecake Tartlets

Servings: 9
Cooking Time: 6 Minutes

Ingredients:

- 8 ounces cream cheese, softened
- ¼ cup sugar
- 1 egg
- ½ teaspoon vanilla extract
- zest of 2 lemons, divided
- 9 mini graham cracker tartlet shells*
- 2 cups blueberries
- ½ teaspoon ground cinnamon
- juice of ½ lemon
- ¼ cup apricot preserves

Directions:

1. Preheat the air fryer to 330°F.
2. Combine the cream cheese, sugar, egg, vanilla and the zest of one lemon in a medium bowl and blend until smooth by hand or with an electric hand mixer. Pour the cream cheese mixture into the tartlet shells.
3. Air-fry 3 tartlets at a time at 330°F for 6 minutes, rotating them in the air fryer basket halfway through the cooking time.
4. Combine the blueberries, cinnamon, zest of one lemon and juice of half a lemon in a bowl. Melt the apricot preserves in the microwave or over low heat in a saucepan. Pour the apricot preserves over the blueberries and gently toss to coat.
5. Allow the cheesecakes to cool completely and then top each one with some of the blueberry mixture. Garnish the tartlets with a little sugared lemon peel and refrigerate until you are ready to serve.

Apple Crisp

Servings: 4
Cooking Time: 16 Minutes

Ingredients:

- Filling
- 3 Granny Smith apples, thinly sliced (about 4 cups)
- ¼ teaspoon ground cinnamon
- ⅛ teaspoon salt
- 1½ teaspoons lemon juice
- 2 tablespoons honey
- 1 tablespoon brown sugar
- cooking spray
- Crumb Topping
- 2 tablespoons oats
- 2 tablespoons oat bran
- 2 tablespoons cooked quinoa
- 2 tablespoons chopped walnuts
- 2 tablespoons brown sugar
- 2 teaspoons coconut oil

Directions:

1. Combine all filling ingredients and stir well so that apples are evenly coated.
2. Spray air fryer baking pan with nonstick cooking spray and spoon in the apple mixture.
3. Cook at 360°F for 5minutes. Stir well, scooping up from the bottom to mix apples and sauce.
4. At this point, the apples should be crisp-tender. Continue cooking in 3-minute intervals until apples are as soft as you like.
5. While apples are cooking, combine all topping ingredients in a small bowl. Stir until coconut oil mixes

in well and distributes evenly. If your coconut oil is cold, it may be easier to mix in by hand.

6. When apples are cooked to your liking, sprinkle crumb mixture on top. Cook at 360°F for 8 minutes or until crumb topping is golden brown and crispy.

Fried Snickers Bars

Servings:8

Cooking Time: 4 Minutes

Ingredients:

- ⅓ cup All-purpose flour
- 1 Large egg white(s), beaten until foamy
- 1½ cups (6 ounces) Vanilla wafer cookie crumbs
- 8 Fun-size (0.6-ounce/17-gram) Snickers bars, frozen
- Vegetable oil spray

Directions:

1. Preheat the air fryer to 400°F.
2. Set up and fill three shallow soup plates or small pie plates on your counter: one for the flour, one for the beaten egg white(s), and one for the cookie crumbs.
3. Unwrap the frozen candy bars. Dip one in the flour, turning it to coat on all sides. Gently shake off any excess, then set it in the beaten egg white(s). Turn it to coat all sides, even the ends, then let any excess egg white slip back into the rest. Set the candy bar in the cookie crumbs. Turn to coat on all sides, even the ends. Dip the candy bar back in the egg white(s) a second time, then into the cookie crumbs a second time, making sure you have an even coating all around. Coat the covered candy bar all over with vegetable oil spray. Set aside so you can dip and coat the remaining candy bars.
4. Set the coated candy bars in the basket with as much air space between them as possible. Air-fry undisturbed for 4 minutes, or until golden brown.
5. Remove the basket from the machine and let the candy bars cool in the basket for 10 minutes. Use a nonstick-safe spatula to transfer them to a wire rack and cool for 5 minutes more before chowing down.

Chocolate Macaroons

Servings: 16

Cooking Time: 8 Minutes

Ingredients:

- 2 Large egg white(s), at room temperature
- ⅛ teaspoon Table salt
- ½ cup Granulated white sugar
- 1½ cups Unsweetened shredded coconut
- 3 tablespoons Unsweetened cocoa powder

Directions:

1. Preheat the air fryer to 375°F .
2. Using an electric mixer at high speed, beat the egg white(s) and salt in a medium or large bowl until stiff peaks can be formed when the turned-off beaters are dipped into the mixture.
3. Still working with the mixer at high speed, beat in the sugar in a slow stream until the meringue is shiny and thick.
4. Scrape down and remove the beaters. Fold in the coconut and cocoa with a rubber spatula until well combined, working carefully to deflate the meringue as little as possible.
5. Scoop up 2 tablespoons of the mixture. Wet your clean hands and roll that little bit of coconut bliss into a ball. Set it aside and continue making more balls: 7 more for a small batch, 15 more for a medium batch, or 23 more for a large one.
6. Line the bottom of the machine's basket or the basket attachment with parchment paper. Set the balls on the parchment with as much air space between them as possible. Air-fry undisturbed for 8 minutes, or until dry, set, and lightly browned.
7. Use a nonstick-safe spatula to transfer the macaroons to a wire rack. Cool for at least 10 minutes before serving. Or cool to room temperature, about 30 minutes, then store in a sealed container at room temperature for up to 3 days.

Cheese Blintzes

Servings: 6

Cooking Time: 10 Minutes

Ingredients:

- 1½ 7½-ounce package(s) farmer cheese

- 3 tablespoons Regular or low-fat cream cheese (not fat-free)
- 3 tablespoons Granulated white sugar
- ¼ teaspoon Vanilla extract
- 6 Egg roll wrappers
- 3 tablespoons Butter, melted and cooled

Directions:

1. Preheat the air fryer to 375°F .
2. Use a flatware fork to mash the farmer cheese, cream cheese, sugar, and vanilla in a small bowl until smooth.
3. Set one egg roll wrapper on a clean, dry work surface. Place ¼ cup of the filling at the edge closest to you, leaving a ½-inch gap before the edge of the wrapper. Dip your clean finger in water and wet the edges of the wrapper. Fold the perpendicular sides over the filling, then roll the wrapper closed with the filling inside. Set it aside seam side down and continue filling the remainder of the wrappers.
4. Brush the wrappers on all sides with the melted butter. Be generous. Set them seam side down in the basket with as much space between them as possible. Air-fry undisturbed for 10 minutes, or until lightly browned.
5. Use a nonstick-safe spatula to transfer the blintzes to a wire rack. Cool for at least 5 minutes or up to 20 minutes before serving.

Orange Gooey Butter Cake

Servings: 6

Cooking Time: 85 Minutes

Ingredients:

- Crust Layer:
- ½ cup flour
- ¼ cup sugar
- ½ teaspoon baking powder
- ⅛ teaspoon salt
- 2 ounces (½ stick) unsalted European style butter, melted
- 1 egg
- 1 teaspoon orange extract
- 2 tablespoons orange zest
- Gooey Butter Layer:
- 8 ounces cream cheese, softened
- 4 ounces (1 stick) unsalted European style butter, melted
- 2 eggs
- 2 teaspoons orange extract
- 2 tablespoons orange zest
- 4 cups powdered sugar
- Garnish:
- powdered sugar
- orange slices

Directions:

1. Preheat the air fryer to 350°F.
2. Grease a 7-inch cake pan and line the bottom with parchment paper. Combine the flour, sugar, baking powder and salt in a bowl. Add the melted butter, egg, orange extract and orange zest. Mix well and press this mixture into the bottom of the greased cake pan. Lower the pan into the basket using an aluminum foil sling (fold a piece of aluminum foil into a strip about 2-inches wide by 24-inches long). Fold the ends of the aluminum foil over the top of the dish before returning the basket to the air fryer. Air-fry uncovered for 8 minutes.
3. To make the gooey butter layer, beat the cream cheese, melted butter, eggs, orange extract and orange zest in a large bowl using an electric hand mixer. Add the powdered sugar in stages, beat until smooth with each addition. Pour this mixture on top of the baked crust in the cake pan. Wrap the pan with a piece of greased aluminum foil, tenting the top of the foil to leave a little room for the cake to rise.
4. Air-fry for 60 minutes at 350°F. Remove the aluminum foil and air-fry for an additional 17 minutes.
5. Let the cake cool inside the pan for at least 10 minutes. Then, run a butter knife around the cake and let the cake cool completely in the pan. When cooled, run the butter knife around the edges of the cake again and invert it onto a plate and then back onto a serving platter. Sprinkle the powdered sugar over the top of the cake and garnish with orange slices.

Tortilla Fried Pies

Servings: 12

Cooking Time: 5 Minutes

Ingredients:

- 12 small flour tortillas (4-inch diameter)
- ½ cup fig preserves

- ¼ cup sliced almonds
- 2 tablespoons shredded, unsweetened coconut
- oil for misting or cooking spray

Directions:

1. Wrap refrigerated tortillas in damp paper towels and heat in microwave 30 seconds to warm.
2. Working with one tortilla at a time, place 2 teaspoons fig preserves, 1 teaspoon sliced almonds, and ½ teaspoon coconut in the center of each.
3. Moisten outer edges of tortilla all around.
4. Fold one side of tortilla over filling to make a half-moon shape and press down lightly on center. Using the tines of a fork, press down firmly on edges of tortilla to seal in filling.
5. Mist both sides with oil or cooking spray.
6. Place hand pies in air fryer basket close but not overlapping. It's fine to lean some against the sides and corners of the basket. You may need to cook in 2 batches.
7. Cook at 390°F for 5minutes or until lightly browned. Serve hot.
8. Refrigerate any leftover pies in a closed container. To serve later, toss them back in the air fryer basket and cook for 2 or 3minutes to reheat.

Wild Blueberry Sweet Empanadas

Servings: 12

Cooking Time: 8 Minutes

Ingredients:

- 2 cups frozen wild blueberries
- 5 tablespoons chia seeds
- ¼ cup honey
- 1 tablespoon lemon or lime juice
- ¼ cup water
- 1½ cups all-purpose flour
- 1 cup whole-wheat flour
- ½ teaspoon salt
- 1 tablespoon sugar
- ½ cup cold unsalted butter
- 1 egg
- ½ cup plus 2 tablespoons milk, divided
- 1 cup powdered sugar
- 1 teaspoon vanilla extract

Directions:

1. To make the wild blueberry chia jam, place the blueberries, chia seeds, honey, lemon or lime juice, and water into a blender and pulse for 2 minutes. Pour the chia jam into a glass jar or bowl and cover. Store in the refrigerator at least 4 to 8 hours or until the jam is thickened.
2. In a food processor, place the all-purpose flour, whole-wheat flour, salt, sugar, and butter and process for 2 minutes, scraping down the sides of the food processor every 30 seconds. Add in the egg and blend for 30 seconds. Using the pulse button, add in ½ cup of the milk 1 tablespoon at a time or until the dough is moist enough to handle and be rolled into a ball. Let the dough rest at room temperature for 30 minutes.
3. On a floured surface, cut the dough in half; then form a ball and cut each ball into 6 equal pieces, totaling 12 equal pieces. Work with one piece at a time, and cover the remaining dough with a towel. Roll out the dough into a 6-inch round, much like a tortilla, with ¼ inch thickness. Place 4 tablespoons of filling in the center of round, fold over to form a half-circle. Using a fork, crimp the edges together and pierce the top with a fork for air holes. Repeat with the remaining dough and filling.
4. Preheat the air fryer to 350°F.
5. Working in batches, place 3 to 4 empanadas in the air fryer basket and spray with cooking spray. Cook for 8 minutes. Repeat in batches, as needed. Allow the sweet empanadas to cool for 15 minutes. Meanwhile, in a small bowl, whisk together the powdered sugar, the remaining 2 tablespoons of milk, and the vanilla extract. Then drizzle the glaze over the surface and serve.

Banana Bread Cake

Servings: 6
Cooking Time: 18-22 Minutes

Ingredients:

- ¾ cup plus 2 tablespoons All-purpose flour
- ½ teaspoon Baking powder
- ¼ teaspoon Baking soda
- ¼ teaspoon Table salt
- 4 tablespoons (¼ cup/½ stick) Butter, at room temperature
- ½ cup Granulated white sugar
- 2 Small ripe bananas, peeled
- 5 tablespoons Pasteurized egg substitute, such as Egg Beaters
- ¼ cup Buttermilk
- ¾ teaspoon Vanilla extract
- Baking spray (see here)

Directions:

1. Preheat the air fryer to 325°F (or 330°F, if that's the closest setting).
2. Mix the flour, baking powder, baking soda, and salt in a small bowl until well combined.
3. Using an electric hand mixer at medium speed, beat the butter and sugar in a medium bowl until creamy and smooth, about 3 minutes, occasionally scraping down the inside of the bowl.
4. Beat in the bananas until smooth. Then beat in egg substitute or egg, buttermilk, and vanilla until uniform. (The batter may look curdled at this stage. The flour mixture will smooth it out.) Add the flour mixture and beat at low speed until smooth and creamy.
5. Use the baking spray to generously coat the inside of a 6-inch round cake pan for a small batch, a 7-inch round cake pan for a medium batch, or an 8-inch round cake pan for a large batch. Scrape and spread the batter into the pan, smoothing the batter out to an even layer.
6. Set the pan in the basket and air-fry for 18 minutes for a 6-inch layer, 20 minutes for a 7-inch layer, or 22 minutes for an 8-inch layer, or until the cake is well browned and set even if there's a little soft give right at the center. Start checking it at the 16-minute mark to know where you are.
7. Use hot pads or silicone baking mitts to transfer the cake pan to a wire rack. To unmold, set a cutting board over the baking pan and invert both the board and the pan. Lift the still-warm pan off the cake layer. Set the wire rack on top of that layer and invert all of it with the cutting board so that the cake layer is now right side up on the wire rack. Remove the cutting board and continue cooling the cake for at least 10 minutes or to room temperature, about 40 minutes, before slicing into wedges.

Annie's Chocolate Chunk Hazelnut Cookies

Servings: 24
Cooking Time: 12 Minutes

Ingredients:

- 1 cup butter, softened
- 1 cup brown sugar
- ½ cup granulated sugar
- 2 eggs, lightly beaten
- 1½ teaspoons vanilla extract
- 1½ cups all-purpose flour
- ½ cup rolled oats
- 1 teaspoon baking soda
- ½ teaspoon salt
- 2 cups chocolate chunks
- ½ cup toasted chopped hazelnuts

Directions:

1. Cream the butter and sugars together until light and fluffy using a stand mixer or electric hand mixer. Add the eggs and vanilla, and beat until well combined.
2. Combine the flour, rolled oats, baking soda and salt in a second bowl. Gradually add the dry ingredients to the wet ingredients with a wooden spoon or spatula. Stir in the chocolate chunks and hazelnuts until distributed throughout the dough.
3. Shape the cookies into small balls about the size of golf balls and place them on a baking sheet. Freeze the cookie balls for at least 30 minutes, or package them in as airtight a package as you can and keep them in your freezer.

4. When you're ready for a delicious snack or dessert, Preheat the air fryer to 350°F. Cut a piece of parchment paper to fit the number of cookies you are baking. Place the parchment down in the air fryer basket and place the frozen cookie ball or balls on top (remember to leave room for them to expand).

5. Air-fry the cookies at 350°F for 12 minutes, or until they are done to your liking. Let them cool for a few minutes before enjoying your freshly baked cookie.

Midnight Nutella® Banana Sandwich

Servings: 2

Cooking Time: 8 Minutes

Ingredients:

- butter, softened
- 4 slices white bread*
- ¼ cup chocolate hazelnut spread (Nutella®)
- 1 banana

Directions:

1. Preheat the air fryer to 370°F.
2. Spread the softened butter on one side of all the slices of bread and place the slices buttered side down on the counter. Spread the chocolate hazelnut spread on the other side of the bread slices. Cut the banana in half and then slice each half into three slices lengthwise. Place the banana slices on two slices of bread and top with the remaining slices of bread (buttered side up) to make two sandwiches. Cut the sandwiches in half (triangles or rectangles) – this will help them all fit in the air fryer at once. Transfer the sandwiches to the air fryer.
3. Air-fry at 370°F for 5 minutes. Flip the sandwiches over and air-fry for another 2 to 3 minutes, or until the top bread slices are nicely browned. Pour yourself a glass of milk or a midnight nightcap while the sandwiches cool slightly and enjoy!

Brownies After Dark

Servings: 4

Cooking Time: 13 Minutes

Ingredients:

- 1 egg
- ½ cup granulated sugar
- ¼ teaspoon salt
- ½ teaspoon vanilla
- ¼ cup butter, melted
- ¼ cup flour, plus 2 tablespoons
- ¼ cup cocoa
- cooking spray
- Optional
- vanilla ice cream
- caramel sauce
- whipped cream

Directions:

1. Beat together egg, sugar, salt, and vanilla until light.
2. Add melted butter and mix well.
3. Stir in flour and cocoa.
4. Spray 6 x 6-inch baking pan lightly with cooking spray.
5. Spread batter in pan and cook at 330°F for 13 minutes. Cool and cut into 4 large squares or 16 small brownie bites.

Chewy Coconut Cake

Servings: 6

Cooking Time: 18-22 Minutes

Ingredients:

- ¾ cup plus 2½ tablespoons All-purpose flour
- ¾ teaspoon Baking powder
- ⅛ teaspoon Table salt
- 7½ tablespoons (1 stick minus ½ tablespoon) Butter, at room temperature
- ⅓ cup plus 1 tablespoon Granulated white sugar
- 5 tablespoons Packed light brown sugar
- 5 tablespoons Pasteurized egg substitute, such as Egg Beaters
- 2 teaspoons Vanilla extract
- ½ cup Unsweetened shredded coconut (see here)
- Baking spray

Directions:

1. Preheat the air fryer to 325°F (or 330°F, if that's the closest setting).

2. Mix the flour, baking powder, and salt in a small bowl until well combined.
3. Using an electric hand mixer at medium speed , beat the butter, granulated white sugar, and brown sugar in a medium bowl until creamy and smooth, about 3 minutes, occasionally scraping down the inside of the bowl. Beat in the egg substitute or egg and vanilla until smooth.
4. Scrape down and remove the beaters. Fold in the flour mixture with a rubber spatula just until all the flour is moistened. Fold in the coconut until the mixture is a uniform color.
5. Use the baking spray to generously coat the inside of a 6-inch round cake pan for a small batch, a 7-inch round cake pan for a medium batch, or an 8-inch round cake pan for a large batch. Scrape and spread the batter into the pan, smoothing the batter out to an even layer.
6. Set the pan in the basket and air-fry for 18 minutes for a 6-inch layer, 20 minutes for a 7-inch layer, or 22 minutes for an 8-inch layer, or until the cake is well browned and set even if there's a little soft give right at the center. Start checking it at the 16-minute mark to know where you are.
7. Use hot pads or silicone baking mitts to transfer the cake pan to a wire rack. Cool for at least 1 hour or up to 4 hours. Use a nonstick-safe knife to slice the cake into wedges right in the pan, lifting them out one by one.

Sea-salted Caramel Cookie Cups

Servings: 12
Cooking Time: 12 Minutes

Ingredients:

- ⅓ cup butter
- ¼ cup brown sugar
- 1 teaspoon vanilla extract
- 1 large egg
- 1 cup all-purpose flour
- ½ cup old-fashioned oats
- ½ teaspoon baking soda
- ¼ teaspoon salt
- ⅓ cup sea-salted caramel chips

Directions:

1. Preheat the air fryer to 300°F.
2. In a large bowl, cream the butter with the brown sugar and vanilla. Whisk in the egg and set aside.
3. In a separate bowl, mix the flour, oats, baking soda, and salt. Then gently mix the dry ingredients into the wet. Fold in the caramel chips.
4. Divide the batter into 12 silicon muffin liners. Place the cookie cups into the air fryer basket and cook for 12 minutes or until a toothpick inserted in the center comes out clean.
5. Remove and let cool 5 minutes before serving.

Baked Apple Crisp

Servings: 4
Cooking Time: 23 Minutes

Ingredients:

- 2 large Granny Smith apples, peeled, cored, and chopped
- ¼ cup granulated sugar
- ¼ cup plus 2 teaspoons flour, divided
- 2 teaspoons milk
- ¼ teaspoon cinnamon
- ¼ cup oats
- ¼ cup brown sugar
- 2 tablespoons unsalted butter
- ⅛ teaspoon baking powder
- ⅛ teaspoon salt

Directions:

1. Preheat the air fryer to 350°F.
2. In a medium bowl, mix the apples, the granulated sugar, 2 teaspoons of the flour, the milk, and the cinnamon.
3. Spray 4 oven-safe ramekins with cooking spray. Divide the filling among the four ramekins.
4. In a small bowl, mix the oats, the brown sugar, the remaining ¼ cup of flour, the butter, the baking powder, and the salt. Use your fingers or a pastry blender to crumble the butter into pea-size pieces. Divide the topping over the top of the apple filling. Cover the apple crisps with foil.
5. Place the covered apple crisps in the air fryer basket and cook for 20 minutes. Uncover and continue cooking for 3 minutes or until the surface is golden and crunchy.

Coconut Crusted Bananas With Pineapple Sauce

Servings: 4

Cooking Time: 5 Minutes

Ingredients:

- Pineapple Sauce
- 1½ cups puréed fresh pineapple
- 2 tablespoons sugar
- juice of 1 lemon
- ¼ teaspoon ground cinnamon
- 3 firm bananas
- ¼ cup sweetened condensed milk
- 1¼ cups shredded coconut
- ⅓ cup crushed graham crackers (crumbs)*
- vegetable or canola oil, in a spray bottle
- vanilla frozen yogurt or ice cream

Directions:

1. Make the pineapple sauce by combining the pineapple, sugar, lemon juice and cinnamon in a saucepan. Simmer the mixture on the stovetop for 20 minutes, and then set it aside.
2. Slice the bananas diagonally into ½-inch thick slices and place them in a bowl. Pour the sweetened condensed milk into the bowl and toss the bananas gently to coat. Combine the coconut and graham cracker crumbs together in a shallow dish. Remove the banana slices from the condensed milk and let any excess milk drip off. Dip the banana slices in the coconut and crumb mixture to coat both sides. Spray the coated slices with oil.
3. Preheat the air fryer to 400°F.
4. Grease the bottom of the air fryer basket with a little oil. Air-fry the bananas in batches at 400°F for 5 minutes, turning them over halfway through the cooking time. Air-fry until the bananas are golden brown on both sides.
5. Serve warm over vanilla frozen yogurt with some of the pineapple sauce spooned over top.

Puff Pastry Apples

Servings: 4

Cooking Time: 10 Minutes

Ingredients:

- 3 Rome or Gala apples, peeled
- 2 tablespoons sugar
- 1 teaspoon all-purpose flour
- 1 teaspoon ground cinnamon
- ⅛ teaspoon ground ginger
- pinch ground nutmeg
- 1 sheet puff pastry
- 1 tablespoon butter, cut into 4 pieces
- 1 egg, beaten
- vegetable oil
- vanilla ice cream (optional)
- caramel sauce (optional)

Directions:

1. Remove the core from the apple by cutting the four sides off the apple around the core. Slice the pieces of apple into thin half-moons, about ¼-inch thick. Combine the sugar, flour, cinnamon, ginger, and nutmeg in a large bowl. Add the apples to the bowl and gently toss until the apples are evenly coated with the spice mixture. Set aside.
2. Cut the puff pastry sheet into a 12-inch by 12-inch square. Then quarter the sheet into four 6-inch squares. Save any remaining pastry for decorating the apples at the end.
3. Divide the spiced apples between the four puff pastry squares, stacking the apples in the center of each square and placing them flat on top of each other in a circle. Top the apples with a piece of the butter.
4. Brush the four edges of the pastry with the egg wash. Bring the four corners of the pastry together, wrapping them around the apple slices and pinching them together at the top in the style of a "beggars purse" appetizer. Fold the ends of the pastry corners down onto the apple making them look like leaves. Brush the entire apple with the egg wash.
5. Using the leftover dough, make leaves to decorate the apples. Cut out 8 leaf shapes, about 1½-inches long, "drawing" the leaf veins on the pastry leaves with a paring knife. Place 2 leaves on the top of each apple, tucking the ends of the leaves under the pastry in the center of the apples. Brush the top of the leaves with additional egg wash. Sprinkle the entire apple with some granulated sugar.
6. Preheat the air fryer to 350°F.
7. Spray or brush the inside of the air fryer basket with oil. Place the apples in the basket and air-fry for 6 minutes. Carefully turn the apples over – it's easiest to

remove one apple, then flip the others over and finally return the last apple to the air fryer. Air-fry for an additional 4 minutes.

8. Serve the puff pastry apples warm with vanilla ice cream and drizzle with some caramel sauce.

Fried Banana S'mores

Servings: 4

Cooking Time: 6 Minutes

Ingredients:

- 4 bananas
- 3 tablespoons mini semi-sweet chocolate chips
- 3 tablespoons mini peanut butter chips
- 3 tablespoons mini marshmallows
- 3 tablespoons graham cracker cereal

Directions:

1. Preheat the air fryer to 400°F.
2. Slice into the un-peeled bananas lengthwise along the inside of the curve, but do not slice through the bottom of the peel. Open the banana slightly to form a pocket.
3. Fill each pocket with chocolate chips, peanut butter chips and marshmallows. Poke the graham cracker cereal into the filling.
4. Place the bananas in the air fryer basket, resting them on the side of the basket and each other to keep them upright with the filling facing up. Air-fry for 6 minutes, or until the bananas are soft to the touch, the peels have blackened and the chocolate and marshmallows have melted and toasted.
5. Let them cool for a couple of minutes and then simply serve with a spoon to scoop out the filling.

Keto Cheesecake Cups

Servings: 6

Cooking Time: 10 Minutes

Ingredients:

- 8 ounces cream cheese
- ¼ cup plain whole-milk Greek yogurt
- 1 large egg
- 1 teaspoon pure vanilla extract
- 3 tablespoons monk fruit sweetener
- ¼ teaspoon salt
- ½ cup walnuts, roughly chopped

Directions:

1. Preheat the air fryer to 315°F.
2. In a large bowl, use a hand mixer to beat the cream cheese together with the yogurt, egg, vanilla, sweetener, and salt. When combined, fold in the chopped walnuts.
3. Set 6 silicone muffin liners inside an air-fryer-safe pan. Note: This is to allow for an easier time getting the cheesecake bites in and out. If you don't have a pan, you can place them directly in the air fryer basket.
4. Evenly fill the cupcake liners with cheesecake batter.
5. Carefully place the pan into the air fryer basket and cook for about 10 minutes, or until the tops are lightly browned and firm.
6. Carefully remove the pan when done and place in the refrigerator for 3 hours to firm up before serving.

Oreo-coated Peanut Butter Cups

Servings:8

Cooking Time: 4 Minutes

Ingredients:

- 8 Standard ¾-ounce peanut butter cups, frozen
- ⅓ cup All-purpose flour
- 2 Large egg white(s), beaten until foamy
- 16 Oreos or other creme-filled chocolate sandwich cookies, ground to crumbs in a food processor
- Vegetable oil spray

Directions:

1. Set up and fill three shallow soup plates or small pie plates on your counter: one for the flour, one for the beaten egg white(s), and one for the cookie crumbs.
2. Dip a frozen peanut butter cup in the flour, turning it to coat all sides. Shake off any excess, then set it in the beaten egg white(s). Turn it to coat all sides, then let any excess egg white slip back into the rest. Set the candy bar in the cookie crumbs. Turn to coat on all parts, even the sides. Dip the peanut butter cup back in the egg white(s) as before, then into the cookie crumbs as before, making sure you have a solid, even coating all around the cup. Set aside while you dip and coat the remaining cups.

3. When all the peanut butter cups are dipped and coated, lightly coat them on all sides with the vegetable oil spray. Set them on a plate and freeze while the air fryer heats.
4. Preheat the air fryer to 400°F.
5. Set the dipped cups wider side up in the basket with as much air space between them as possible. Air-fry undisturbed for 4 minutes, or until they feel soft but the coating is set.
6. Turn off the machine and remove the basket from it. Set aside the basket with the fried cups for 10 minutes. Use a nonstick-safe spatula to transfer the fried cups to a wire rack. Cool for at least another 5 minutes before serving.

Fried Oreos

Servings: 12
Cooking Time: 6 Minutes Per Batch

Ingredients:

- oil for misting or nonstick spray
- 1 cup complete pancake and waffle mix
- 1 teaspoon vanilla extract
- ½ cup water, plus 2 tablespoons
- 12 Oreos or other chocolate sandwich cookies
- 1 tablespoon confectioners' sugar

Directions:

1. Spray baking pan with oil or nonstick spray and place in basket.
2. Preheat air fryer to 390°F.
3. In a medium bowl, mix together the pancake mix, vanilla, and water.
4. Dip 4 cookies in batter and place in baking pan.
5. Cook for 6minutes, until browned.
6. Repeat steps 4 and 5 for the remaining cookies.
7. Sift sugar over warm cookies.

Brown Sugar Baked Apples

Servings: 4
Cooking Time: 15 Minutes

Ingredients:

- 3 Small tart apples, preferably McIntosh
- 4 tablespoons (¼ cup/½ stick) Butter
- 6 tablespoons Light brown sugar
- Ground cinnamon
- Table salt

Directions:

1. Preheat the air fryer to 400°F.
2. Stem the apples, then cut them in half through their "equators" (that is, not the stem ends). Use a melon baller to core the apples, taking care not to break through the flesh and skin at any point but creating a little well in the center of each half.
3. When the machine is at temperature, remove the basket and set it on a heat-safe work surface. Set the apple halves cut side up in the basket with as much air space between them as possible. Even a fraction of an inch will work. Drop 2 teaspoons of butter into the well in the center of each apple half. Sprinkle each half with 1 tablespoon brown sugar and a pinch each ground cinnamon and table salt.
4. Return the basket to the machine. Air-fry undisturbed for 15 minutes, or until the apple halves have softened and the brown sugar has caramelized.
5. Use a nonstick-safe spatula to transfer the apple halves cut side up to a wire rack. Cool for at least 10 minutes before serving, or serve at room temperature.

Giant Buttery Chocolate Chip Cookie

Servings: 4
Cooking Time: 16 Minutes

Ingredients:

- ⅔ cup plus 1 tablespoon All-purpose flour
- ¼ teaspoon Baking soda
- ¼ teaspoon Table salt
- Baking spray (see the headnote)
- 4 tablespoons (¼ cup/½ stick) plus 1 teaspoon Butter, at room temperature
- ¼ cup plus 1 teaspoon Packed dark brown sugar
- 3 tablespoons plus 1 teaspoon Granulated white sugar
- 2½ tablespoons Pasteurized egg substitute, such as Egg Beaters
- ½ teaspoon Vanilla extract

- ¾ cup plus 1 tablespoon Semisweet or bittersweet chocolate chips

Directions:

1. Preheat the air fryer to 350°F .
2. Whisk the flour, baking soda, and salt in a bowl until well combined.
3. For a small air fryer, coat the inside of a 6-inch round cake pan with baking spray. For a medium air fryer, coat the inside of a 7-inch round cake pan with baking spray. And for a large air fryer, coat the inside of an 8-inch round cake pan with baking spray.
4. Using a hand electric mixer at medium speed, beat the butter, brown sugar, and granulated white sugar in a bowl until smooth and thick, about 3 minutes, scraping down the inside of the bowl several times.
5. Beat in the pasteurized egg substitute or egg (as applicable) and vanilla until uniform. Scrape down and remove the beaters. Fold in the flour mixture and chocolate chips with a rubber spatula, just until combined. Scrape and gently press this dough into the prepared pan, getting it even across the pan to the perimeter.
6. Set the pan in the basket and air-fry undisturbed for 16 minutes, or until the cookie is puffed, browned, and feels set to the touch.
7. Transfer the pan to a wire rack and cool for 10 minutes. Loosen the cookie from the perimeter with a spatula, then invert the pan onto a cutting board and let the cookie come free. Remove the pan and reinvert the cookie onto the wire rack. Cool for 5 minutes more before slicing into wedges to serve.

Vegan Brownie Bites

Servings: 10

Cooking Time: 8 Minutes

Ingredients:

- ⅔ cup walnuts
- ⅓ cup all-purpose flour
- ¼ cup dark cocoa powder
- ⅓ cup cane sugar
- ¼ teaspoon salt
- 2 tablespoons vegetable oil
- 1 teaspoon pure vanilla extract
- 1 tablespoon almond milk
- 1 tablespoon powdered sugar

Directions:

1. Preheat the air fryer to 350°F.
2. To a blender or food processor fitted with a metal blade, add the walnuts, flour, cocoa powder, sugar, and salt. Pulse until smooth, about 30 seconds. Add in the oil, vanilla, and milk and pulse until a dough is formed.
3. Remove the dough and place in a bowl. Form into 10 equal-size bites.
4. Liberally spray the metal trivet in the air fryer basket with olive oil mist. Place the brownie bites into the basket and cook for 8 minutes, or until the outer edges begin to slightly crack.
5. Remove the basket from the air fryer and let cool. Sprinkle the brownie bites with powdered sugar and serve.

Gingerbread

Servings: 6

Cooking Time: 20 Minutes

Ingredients:

- cooking spray
- 1 cup flour
- 2 tablespoons sugar
- ¾ teaspoon ground ginger
- ¼ teaspoon cinnamon
- 1 teaspoon baking powder
- ½ teaspoon baking soda
- ⅛ teaspoon salt
- 1 egg
- ¼ cup molasses
- ½ cup buttermilk
- 2 tablespoons oil
- 1 teaspoon pure vanilla extract

Directions:

1. Preheat air fryer to 330°F.
2. Spray 6 x 6-inch baking dish lightly with cooking spray.
3. In a medium bowl, mix together all the dry ingredients.

4. In a separate bowl, beat the egg. Add molasses, buttermilk, oil, and vanilla and stir until well mixed.
5. Pour liquid mixture into dry ingredients and stir until well blended.
6. Pour batter into baking dish and cook at 330°F for 20minutes or until toothpick inserted in center of loaf comes out clean.

Easy Churros

Servings: 12
Cooking Time: 10 Minutes

Ingredients:

- ½ cup Water
- 4 tablespoons (¼ cup/½ stick) Butter
- ¼ teaspoon Table salt
- ½ cup All-purpose flour
- 2 Large egg(s)
- ¼ cup Granulated white sugar
- 2 teaspoons Ground cinnamon

Directions:

1. Bring the water, butter, and salt to a boil in a small saucepan set over high heat, stirring occasionally.
2. When the butter has fully melted, reduce the heat to medium and stir in the flour to form a dough. Continue cooking, stirring constantly, to dry out the dough until it coats the bottom and sides of the pan with a film, even a crust. Remove the pan from the heat, scrape the dough into a bowl, and cool for 15 minutes.
3. Using an electric hand mixer at medium speed, beat in the egg, or eggs one at a time, until the dough is smooth and firm enough to hold its shape.
4. Mix the sugar and cinnamon in a small bowl. Scoop up 1 tablespoon of the dough and roll it in the sugar mixture to form a small, coated tube about ½ inch in diameter and 2 inches long. Set it aside and make 5 more tubes for the small batch or 11 more for the large one.
5. Set the tubes on a plate and freeze for 20 minutes. Meanwhile, Preheat the air fryer to 375°F .
6. Set 3 frozen tubes in the basket for a small batch or 6 for a large one with as much air space between them as possible. Air-fry undisturbed for 10 minutes, or until puffed, brown, and set.
7. Use kitchen tongs to transfer the churros to a wire rack to cool for at least 5 minutes. Meanwhile, air-fry and cool the second batch of churros in the same way.

One-bowl Chocolate Buttermilk Cake

Servings: 6
Cooking Time: 16-20 Minutes

Ingredients:

- ¾ cup All-purpose flour
- ½ cup Granulated white sugar
- 3 tablespoons Unsweetened cocoa powder
- ½ teaspoon Baking soda
- ¼ teaspoon Table salt
- ½ cup Buttermilk
- 2 tablespoons Vegetable oil
- ¾ teaspoon Vanilla extract
- Baking spray (see here)

Directions:

1. Preheat the air fryer to 325°F (or 330°F, if that's the closest setting).
2. Stir the flour, sugar, cocoa powder, baking soda, and salt in a large bowl until well combined. Add the buttermilk, oil, and vanilla. Stir just until a thick, grainy batter forms.
3. Use the baking spray to generously coat the inside of a 6-inch round cake pan for a small batch, a 7-inch round cake pan for a medium batch, or an 8-inch round cake pan for a large batch. Scrape and spread the chocolate batter into this pan, smoothing the batter out to an even layer.
4. Set the pan in the basket and air-fry undisturbed for 16 minutes for a 6-inch layer, 18 minutes for a 7-inch layer, or 20 minutes for an 8-inch layer, or until a toothpick or cake tester inserted into the center of the cake comes out clean. Start checking it at the 14-minute mark to know where you are.
5. Use hot pads or silicone baking mitts to transfer the cake pan to a wire rack. Cool for 5 minutes. To unmold, set a cutting board over the baking pan and invert both the board and the pan. Lift the still-warm pan off the cake layer. Set the wire rack on top of the cake layer and

invert all of it with the cutting board so that the cake layer is now right side up on the wire rack. Remove the cutting board and continue cooling the cake for at least 10 minutes or to room temperature, about 30 minutes, before slicing into wedges.

Chocolate Cake

Servings: 8
Cooking Time: 20 Minutes

Ingredients:

- ½ cup sugar
- ¼ cup flour, plus 3 tablespoons
- 3 tablespoons cocoa
- ½ teaspoon baking powder
- ½ teaspoon baking soda
- ¼ teaspoon salt
- 1 egg
- 2 tablespoons oil
- ½ cup milk
- ½ teaspoon vanilla extract

Directions:

1. Preheat air fryer to 330°F.
2. Grease and flour a 6 x 6-inch baking pan.
3. In a medium bowl, stir together the sugar, flour, cocoa, baking powder, baking soda, and salt.
4. Add all other ingredients and beat with a wire whisk until smooth.
5. Pour batter into prepared pan and bake at 330°F for 20 minutes, until toothpick inserted in center comes out clean or with crumbs clinging to it.

Giant Vegan Chocolate Chip Cookie

Servings: 4
Cooking Time: 16 Minutes

Ingredients:

- ⅔ cup All-purpose flour
- 5 tablespoons Rolled oats (not quick-cooking or steel-cut oats)
- ¼ teaspoon Baking soda
- ¼ teaspoon Table salt
- 5 tablespoons Granulated white sugar
- ¼ cup Vegetable oil
- 2½ tablespoons Tahini (see here)
- 2½ tablespoons Maple syrup
- 2 teaspoons Vanilla extract
- ⅔ cup Vegan semisweet or bittersweet chocolate chips
- Baking spray

Directions:

1. Preheat the air fryer to 325°F (or 330°F, if that's the closest setting).
2. Whisk the flour, oats, baking soda, and salt in a bowl until well combined.
3. Using an electric hand mixer at medium speed, beat the sugar, oil, tahini, maple syrup, and vanilla until rich and creamy, about 3 minutes, scraping down the inside of the bowl occasionally.
4. Scrape down and remove the beaters. Fold in the flour mixture and chocolate chips with a rubber spatula just until all the flour is moistened and the chocolate chips are even throughout the dough.
5. For a small air fryer, coat the inside of a 6-inch round cake pan with baking spray. For a medium air fryer, coat the inside of a 7-inch round cake pan with baking spray. And for a large air fryer, coat the inside of an 8-inch round cake pan with baking spray. Scrape and gently press the dough into the prepared pan, spreading it into an even layer to the perimeter.
6. Set the pan in the basket and air-fry undisturbed for 16 minutes, or until puffed, browned, and firm to the touch.
7. Transfer the pan to a wire rack and cool for 10 minutes. Loosen the cookie from the perimeter with a spatula, then invert the pan onto a cutting board and let the cookie come free. Remove the pan and reinvert the cookie onto the wire rack. Cool for 5 minutes more before slicing into wedges to serve.

White Chocolate Cranberry Blondies

Servings: 6
Cooking Time: 18 Minutes

Ingredients:

- ⅓ cup butter
- ½ cup sugar
- 1 teaspoon vanilla extract
- 1 large egg
- 1 cup all-purpose flour
- ½ teaspoon baking powder
- ⅛ teaspoon salt
- ¼ cup dried cranberries
- ¼ cup white chocolate chips

Directions:

1. Preheat the air fryer to 320°F.
2. In a large bowl, cream the butter with the sugar and vanilla extract. Whisk in the egg and set aside.
3. In a separate bowl, mix the flour with the baking powder and salt. Then gently mix the dry ingredients into the wet. Fold in the cranberries and chocolate chips.
4. Liberally spray an oven-safe 7-inch springform pan with olive oil and pour the batter into the pan.
5. Cook for 17 minutes or until a toothpick inserted in the center comes out clean.
6. Remove and let cool 5 minutes before serving.

Strawberry Pastry Rolls

Servings: 4

Cooking Time: 6 Minutes

Ingredients:

- 3 ounces low-fat cream cheese
- 2 tablespoons plain yogurt
- 2 teaspoons sugar
- ¼ teaspoon pure vanilla extract
- 8 ounces fresh strawberries
- 8 sheets phyllo dough
- butter-flavored cooking spray
- ¼–½ cup dark chocolate chips (optional)

Directions:

1. In a medium bowl, combine the cream cheese, yogurt, sugar, and vanilla. Beat with hand mixer at high speed until smooth, about 1 minute.
2. Wash strawberries and destem. Chop enough of them to measure ½ cup. Stir into cheese mixture.
3. Preheat air fryer to 330°F.
4. Phyllo dough dries out quickly, so cover your stack of phyllo sheets with waxed paper and then place a damp dish towel on top of that. Remove only one sheet at a time as you work.
5. To create one pastry roll, lay out a single sheet of phyllo. Spray lightly with butter-flavored spray, top with a second sheet of phyllo, and spray the second sheet lightly.
6. Place a quarter of the filling (about 3 tablespoons) about ½ inch from the edge of one short side. Fold the end of the phyllo over the filling and keep rolling a turn or two. Fold in both the left and right sides so that the edges meet in the middle of your roll. Then roll up completely. Spray outside of pastry roll with butter spray.
7. When you have 4 rolls, place them in the air fryer basket, seam side down, leaving some space in between each. Cook at 330°F for 6 minutes, until they turn a delicate golden brown.
8. Repeat step 7 for remaining rolls.
9. Allow pastries to cool to room temperature.
10. When ready to serve, slice the remaining strawberries. If desired, melt the chocolate chips in microwave or double boiler. Place 1 pastry on each dessert plate, and top with sliced strawberries. Drizzle melted chocolate over strawberries and onto plate.

Sugared Pizza Dough Dippers With Raspberry Cream Cheese Dip

Servings: 10

Cooking Time: 8 Minutes

Ingredients:

- 1 pound pizza dough*
- ½ cup butter, melted
- ¾ to 1 cup sugar
- Raspberry Cream Cheese Dip
- 4 ounces cream cheese, softened
- 2 tablespoons powdered sugar
- ½ teaspoon almond extract or almond paste
- 1½ tablespoons milk
- ¼ cup raspberry preserves
- fresh raspberries

Directions:

1. Cut the ingredients in half or save half of the dough for another recipe.
2. When you're ready to make your sugared dough dippers, remove your pizza dough from the refrigerator at least 1 hour prior to baking and let it sit on the counter, covered gently with plastic wrap.
3. Roll the dough into two 15-inch logs. Cut each log into 20 slices and roll each slice so that it is 3- to 3½-inches long. Cut each slice in half and twist the dough halves together 3 to 4 times. Place the twisted dough on a cookie sheet, brush with melted butter and sprinkle sugar over the dough twists.
4. Preheat the air fryer to 350°F.
5. Brush the bottom of the air fryer basket with a little melted butter. Air-fry the dough twists in batches. Place 8 to 12 (depending on the size of your air fryer) in the air fryer basket.
6. Air-fry for 6 minutes. Turn the dough strips over and brush the other side with butter. Air-fry for an additional 2 minutes.
7. While the dough twists are cooking, make the cream cheese and raspberry dip. Whip the cream cheese with a hand mixer until fluffy. Add the powdered sugar, almond extract and milk, and beat until smooth. Fold in the raspberry preserves and transfer to a serving dish.
8. As the batches of dough twists are complete, place them into a shallow dish. Brush with more melted butter and generously coat with sugar, shaking the dish to cover both sides. Serve the sugared dough dippers warm with the raspberry cream cheese dip on the side. Garnish with fresh raspberries.

Chocolate Soufflés

Servings: 2

Cooking Time: 14 Minutes

Ingredients:

- butter and sugar for greasing the ramekins
- 3 ounces semi-sweet chocolate, chopped
- ¼ cup unsalted butter
- 2 eggs, yolks and white separated
- 3 tablespoons sugar
- ½ teaspoon pure vanilla extract
- 2 tablespoons all-purpose flour
- powdered sugar, for dusting the finished soufflés
- heavy cream, for serving

Directions:

1. Butter and sugar two 6-ounce ramekins. (Butter the ramekins and then coat the butter with sugar by shaking it around in the ramekin and dumping out any excess.)
2. Melt the chocolate and butter together, either in the microwave or in a double boiler. In a separate bowl, beat the egg yolks vigorously. Add the sugar and the vanilla extract and beat well again. Drizzle in the chocolate and butter, mixing well. Stir in the flour, combining until there are no lumps.
3. Preheat the air fryer to 330°F.
4. In a separate bowl, whisk the egg whites to soft peak stage (the point at which the whites can almost stand up on the end of your whisk). Fold the whipped egg whites into the chocolate mixture gently and in stages.
5. Transfer the batter carefully to the buttered ramekins, leaving about ½-inch at the top. (You may have a little extra batter, depending on how airy the batter is, so you might be able to squeeze out a third soufflé if you want to.) Place the ramekins into the air fryer basket and air-fry for 14 minutes. The soufflés should have risen nicely and be brown on top. (Don't

worry if the top gets a little dark – you'll be covering it with powdered sugar in the next step.)

6. Dust with powdered sugar and serve immediately with heavy cream to pour over the top at the table.

Bananas Foster Bread Pudding

Servings: 4

Cooking Time: 25 Minutes

Ingredients:

- ½ cup brown sugar
- 3 eggs
- ¾ cup half and half
- 1 teaspoon pure vanilla extract
- 6 cups cubed Kings Hawaiian bread (½-inch cubes), ½ pound
- 2 bananas, sliced
- 1 cup caramel sauce, plus more for serving

Directions:

1. Preheat the air fryer to 350°F.
2. Combine the brown sugar, eggs, half and half and vanilla extract in a large bowl, whisking until the sugar has dissolved and the mixture is smooth. Stir in the cubed bread and toss to coat all the cubes evenly. Let the bread sit for 10 minutes to absorb the liquid.
3. Mix the sliced bananas and caramel sauce together in a separate bowl.
4. Fill the bottom of 4 (8-ounce) greased ramekins with half the bread cubes. Divide the caramel and bananas between the ramekins, spooning them on top of the bread cubes. Top with the remaining bread cubes and wrap each ramekin with aluminum foil, tenting the foil at the top to leave some room for the bread to puff up during the cooking process.
5. Air-fry two bread puddings at a time for 25 minutes. Let the puddings cool a little and serve warm with additional caramel sauce drizzled on top. A scoop of vanilla ice cream would be nice too and in keeping with our Bananas Foster theme!

Sweet Potato Pie Rolls

Servings:3

Cooking Time: 8 Minutes

Ingredients:

- 6 Spring roll wrappers
- 1½ cups Canned yams in syrup, drained
- 2 tablespoons Light brown sugar
- ¼ teaspoon Ground cinnamon
- 1 Large egg(s), well beaten
- Vegetable oil spray

Directions:

1. Preheat the air fryer to 400°F.
2. Set a spring roll wrapper on a clean, dry work surface. Scoop up ¼ cup of the pulpy yams and set along one edge of the wrapper, leaving 2 inches on each side of the yams. Top the yams with about 1 teaspoon brown sugar and a pinch of ground cinnamon. Fold the sides of the wrapper perpendicular to the yam filling up and over the filling, partially covering it. Brush beaten egg(s) over the side of the wrapper farthest from the yam. Starting with the yam end, roll the wrapper closed, ending at the part with the beaten egg that you can press gently to seal. Lightly coat the roll on all sides with vegetable oil spray. Set it aside seam side down and continue filling, rolling, and spraying the remaining wrappers in the same way.
3. Set the rolls seam side down in the basket with as much air space between them as possible. Air-fry undisturbed for 8 minutes, or until crisp and golden brown.
4. Use a nonstick-safe spatula and perhaps kitchen tongs for balance to gently transfer the rolls to a wire rack. Cool for at least 5 minutes or up to 30 minutes before serving.

Coconut Macaroons

Servings: 12

Cooking Time: 8 Minutes

Ingredients:

- 1⅓ cups shredded, sweetened coconut
- 4½ teaspoons flour
- 2 tablespoons sugar
- 1 egg white
- ½ teaspoon almond extract

Directions:

1. Preheat air fryer to 330°F.

2. Mix all ingredients together.
3. Shape coconut mixture into 12 balls.
4. Place all 12 macaroons in air fryer basket. They won't expand, so you can place them close together, but they shouldn't touch.
5. Cook at 330°F for 8 minutes, until golden.

Hasselback Apple Crisp

Servings: 4

Cooking Time: 20 Minutes

Ingredients:

- 2 large Gala apples, peeled, cored and cut in half
- ¼ cup butter, melted
- ½ teaspoon ground cinnamon
- 2 tablespoons sugar
- Topping
- 3 tablespoons butter, melted
- 2 tablespoons brown sugar
- ¼ cup chopped pecans
- 2 tablespoons rolled oats*
- 1 tablespoon flour*
- vanilla ice cream
- caramel sauce

Directions:

1. Place the apples cut side down on a cutting board. Slicing from stem end to blossom end, make 8 to 10 slits down the apple halves but only slice three quarters of the way through the apple, not all the way through to the cutting board.
2. Preheat the air fryer to 330°F and pour a little water into the bottom of the air fryer drawer. (This will help prevent the grease that drips into the bottom drawer from burning and smoking.)
3. Transfer the apples to the air fryer basket, flat side down. Combine ¼ cup of melted butter, cinnamon and sugar in a small bowl. Brush this butter mixture onto the apples and air-fry at 330°F for 15 minutes. Baste the apples several times with the butter mixture during the cooking process.
4. While the apples are air-frying, make the filling. Combine 3 tablespoons of melted butter with the brown sugar, pecans, rolled oats and flour in a bowl. Stir with a fork until the mixture resembles small crumbles.
5. When the timer on the air fryer is up, spoon the topping down the center of the apples. Air-fry at 330°F for an additional 5 minutes.
6. Transfer the apples to a serving plate and serve with vanilla ice cream and caramel sauce.

Carrot Cake With Cream Cheese Icing

Servings: 6

Cooking Time: 55 Minutes

Ingredients:

- 1¼ cups all-purpose flour
- 1 teaspoon baking powder
- ½ teaspoon baking soda
- 1 teaspoon ground cinnamon
- ¼ teaspoon ground nutmeg
- ¼ teaspoon salt
- 2 cups grated carrot (about 3 to 4 medium carrots or 2 large)
- ¾ cup granulated sugar
- ¼ cup brown sugar
- 2 eggs
- ¾ cup canola or vegetable oil
- For the icing:
- 8 ounces cream cheese, softened at room , Temperature: 8 tablespoons butter (4 ounces or 1 stick), softened at room , Temperature: 1 cup powdered sugar
- 1 teaspoon pure vanilla extract

Directions:

1. Grease a 7-inch cake pan.
2. Combine the flour, baking powder, baking soda, cinnamon, nutmeg and salt in a bowl. Add the grated carrots and toss well. In a separate bowl, beat the sugars and eggs together until light and frothy. Drizzle in the oil, beating constantly. Fold the egg mixture into the dry ingredients until everything is just combined and you no longer see any traces of flour. Pour the batter into the cake pan and wrap the pan completely in greased aluminum foil.
3. Preheat the air fryer to 350°F.

4. Lower the cake pan into the air fryer basket using a sling made of aluminum foil (fold a piece of aluminum foil into a strip about 2-inches wide by 24-inches long). Fold the ends of the aluminum foil into the air fryer, letting them rest on top of the cake. Air-fry for 40 minutes. Remove the aluminum foil cover and air-fry for an additional 15 minutes or until a skewer inserted into the center of the cake comes out clean and the top is nicely browned.
5. While the cake is cooking, beat the cream cheese, butter, powdered sugar and vanilla extract together using a hand mixer, stand mixer or food processor (or a lot of elbow grease!).
6. Remove the cake pan from the air fryer and let the cake cool in the cake pan for 10 minutes or so. Then remove the cake from the pan and let it continue to cool completely. Frost the cake with the cream cheese icing and serve.

Black And Blue Clafoutis

Servings: 2
Cooking Time: 15minutes

Ingredients:

- 6-inch pie pan
- 3 large eggs
- ½ cup sugar
- 1 teaspoon vanilla extract
- 2 tablespoons butter, melted 1 cup milk
- ½ cup all-purpose flour*
- 1 cup blackberries
- 1 cup blueberries
- 2 tablespoons confectioners' sugar

Directions:

1. Preheat the air fryer to 320°F.
2. Combine the eggs and sugar in a bowl and whisk vigorously until smooth, lighter in color and well combined. Add the vanilla extract, butter and milk and whisk together well. Add the flour and whisk just until no lumps or streaks of white remain.
3. Scatter half the blueberries and blackberries in a greased (6-inch) pie pan or cake pan. Pour half of the batter (about 1¼ cups) on top of the berries and transfer the tart pan to the air fryer basket. You can use an aluminum foil sling to help with this by taking a long piece of aluminum foil, folding it in half lengthwise twice until it is roughly 26-inches by 3-inches. Place this under the pie dish and hold the ends of the foil to move the pie dish in and out of the air fryer basket. Tuck the ends of the foil beside the pie dish while it cooks in the air fryer.
4. Air-fry at 320°F for 15 minutes or until the clafoutis has puffed up and is still a little jiggly in the center. Remove the clafoutis from the air fryer, invert it onto a plate and let it cool while you bake the second batch. Serve the clafoutis warm, dusted with confectioners' sugar on top.

Peach Cobbler

Servings: 4
Cooking Time: 12 Minutes

Ingredients:

- 16 ounces frozen peaches, thawed, with juice (do not drain)
- 6 tablespoons sugar
- 1 tablespoon cornstarch
- 1 tablespoon water
- Crust
- ½ cup flour
- ¼ teaspoon salt
- 3 tablespoons butter
- 1½ tablespoons cold water
- ¼ teaspoon sugar

Directions:

1. Place peaches, including juice, and sugar in air fryer baking pan. Stir to mix well.
2. In a small cup, dissolve cornstarch in the water. Stir into peaches.
3. In a medium bowl, combine the flour and salt. Cut in butter using knives or a pastry blender. Stir in the cold water to make a stiff dough.
4. On a floured board or wax paper, pat dough into a square or circle slightly smaller than your air fryer baking pan. Cut diagonally into 4 pieces.
5. Place dough pieces on top of peaches, leaving a tiny bit of space between the edges. Sprinkle very lightly with sugar, no more than about ¼ teaspoon.

6. Cook at 360°F for 12 minutes, until fruit bubbles and crust browns.

Dark Chocolate Peanut Butter S'mores

Servings: 4
Cooking Time: 6 Minutes

Ingredients:

- 4 graham cracker sheets
- 4 marshmallows
- 4 teaspoons chunky peanut butter
- 4 ounces dark chocolate
- ½ teaspoon ground cinnamon

Directions:

1. Preheat the air fryer to 390°F. Break the graham crackers in half so you have 8 pieces.
2. Place 4 pieces of graham cracker on the bottom of the air fryer. Top each with one of the marshmallows and bake for 6 or 7 minutes, or until the marshmallows have a golden brown center.
3. While cooking, slather each of the remaining graham crackers with 1 teaspoon peanut butter.
4. When baking completes, carefully remove each of the graham crackers, add 1 ounce of dark chocolate on top of the marshmallow, and lightly sprinkle with cinnamon. Top with the remaining peanut butter graham cracker to make the sandwich. Serve immediately.

Thumbprint Sugar Cookies

Servings: 10
Cooking Time: 8 Minutes

Ingredients:

- 2½ tablespoons butter
- ⅓ cup cane sugar
- 1 teaspoon pure vanilla extract
- 1 large egg
- 1 cup all-purpose flour
- ½ teaspoon baking soda
- ¼ teaspoon salt
- 10 chocolate kisses

Directions:

1. Preheat the air fryer to 350°F.
2. In a large bowl, cream the butter with the sugar and vanilla. Whisk in the egg and set aside.
3. In a separate bowl, mix the flour, baking soda, and salt. Then gently mix the dry ingredients into the wet. Portion the dough into 10 balls; then press down on each with the bottom of a cup to create a flat cookie.
4. Liberally spray the metal trivet of an air fryer basket with olive oil mist.
5. Place the cookies in the air fryer basket on the trivet and cook for 8 minutes or until the tops begin to lightly brown.
6. Remove and immediately press the chocolate kisses into the tops of the cookies while still warm.
7. Let cool 5 minutes and then enjoy.

Almond-roasted Pears

Servings: 4
Cooking Time: 15 Minutes

Ingredients:

- Yogurt Topping
- 1 container vanilla Greek yogurt (5–6 ounces)
- ¼ teaspoon almond flavoring
- 2 whole pears
- ¼ cup crushed Biscoff cookies (approx. 4 cookies)
- 1 tablespoon sliced almonds
- 1 tablespoon butter

Directions:

1. Stir almond flavoring into yogurt and set aside while preparing pears.
2. Halve each pear and spoon out the core.
3. Place pear halves in air fryer basket.
4. Stir together the cookie crumbs and almonds. Place a quarter of this mixture into the hollow of each pear half.
5. Cut butter into 4 pieces and place one piece on top of crumb mixture in each pear.
6. Cook at 360°F for 15 minutes or until pears have cooked through but are still slightly firm.
7. Serve pears warm with a dollop of yogurt topping.

Rigatoni With Roasted Onions, Fennel, Spinach And Lemon Pepper Ricotta

Servings: 2

Cooking Time: 13 Minutes

Ingredients:

- 1 red onion, rough chopped into large chunks
- 2 teaspoons olive oil, divided
- 1 bulb fennel, sliced ¼-inch thick
- ¾ cup ricotta cheese
- 1½ teaspoons finely chopped lemon zest, plus more for garnish
- 1 teaspoon lemon juice
- salt and freshly ground black pepper
- 8 ounces (½ pound) dried rigatoni pasta
- 3 cups baby spinach leaves

Directions:

1. Bring a large stockpot of salted water to a boil on the stovetop and Preheat the air fryer to 400°F.
2. While the water is coming to a boil, toss the chopped onion in 1 teaspoon of olive oil and transfer to the air fryer basket. Air-fry at 400°F for 5 minutes. Toss the sliced fennel with 1 teaspoon of olive oil and add this to the air fryer basket with the onions. Continue to air-fry at 400°F for 8 minutes, shaking the basket a few times during the cooking process.
3. Combine the ricotta cheese, lemon zest and juice, ¼ teaspoon of salt and freshly ground black pepper in a bowl and stir until smooth.
4. Add the dried rigatoni to the boiling water and cook according to the package directions. When the pasta is cooked al dente, reserve one cup of the pasta water and drain the pasta into a colander.
5. Place the spinach in a serving bowl and immediately transfer the hot pasta to the bowl, wilting the spinach. Add the roasted onions and fennel and toss together. Add a little pasta water to the dish if it needs moistening. Then, dollop the lemon pepper ricotta cheese on top and nestle it into the hot pasta. Garnish with more lemon zest if desired.

Parmesan Portobello Mushroom Caps

Servings: 2

Cooking Time: 14 Minutes

Ingredients:

- ¼ cup flour*
- 1 egg, lightly beaten
- 1 cup seasoned breadcrumbs*
- 2 large portobello mushroom caps, stems and gills removed
- olive oil, in a spray bottle
- ½ cup tomato sauce
- ¾ cup grated mozzarella cheese
- 1 tablespoon grated Parmesan cheese
- 1 tablespoon chopped fresh basil or parsley

Directions:

1. Set up a dredging station with three shallow dishes. Place the flour in the first shallow dish, egg in the second dish and breadcrumbs in the last dish. Dredge the mushrooms in flour, then dip them into the egg and finally press them into the breadcrumbs to coat on all sides. Spray both sides of the coated mushrooms with olive oil.
2. Preheat the air fryer to 400°F.
3. Air-fry the mushrooms at 400°F for 10 minutes, turning them over halfway through the cooking process.
4. Fill the underside of the mushrooms with the tomato sauce and then top the sauce with the mozzarella and Parmesan cheeses. Reset the air fryer temperature to 350°F and air-fry for an additional 4 minutes, until the cheese has melted and is slightly browned.
5. Serve the mushrooms with pasta tossed with tomato sauce and garnish with some chopped fresh basil or parsley.

Spicy Vegetable And Tofu Shake Fry

Servings: 4
Cooking Time: 17 Minutes

Ingredients:

- 4 teaspoons canola oil, divided
- 2 tablespoons rice wine vinegar
- 1 tablespoon sriracha chili sauce
- ¼ cup soy sauce*
- ½ teaspoon toasted sesame oil
- 1 teaspoon minced garlic
- 1 tablespoon minced fresh ginger
- 8 ounces extra firm tofu
- ½ cup vegetable stock or water
- 1 tablespoon honey
- 1 tablespoon cornstarch
- ½ red onion, chopped
- 1 red or yellow bell pepper, chopped
- 1 cup green beans, cut into 2-inch lengths
- 4 ounces mushrooms, sliced
- 2 scallions, sliced
- 2 tablespoons fresh cilantro leaves
- 2 teaspoons toasted sesame seeds

Directions:

1. Combine 1 tablespoon of the oil, vinegar, sriracha sauce, soy sauce, sesame oil, garlic and ginger in a small bowl. Cut the tofu into bite-sized cubes and toss the tofu in with the marinade while you prepare the other vegetables. When you are ready to start cooking, remove the tofu from the marinade and set it aside. Add the water, honey and cornstarch to the marinade and bring to a simmer on the stovetop, just until the sauce thickens. Set the sauce aside.
2. Preheat the air fryer to 400°F.
3. Toss the onion, pepper, green beans and mushrooms in a bowl with a little canola oil and season with salt. Air-fry at 400°F for 11 minutes, shaking the basket and tossing the vegetables every few minutes. When the vegetables are cooked to your preferred doneness, remove them from the air fryer and set aside.
4. Add the tofu to the air fryer basket and air-fry at 400°F for 6 minutes, shaking the basket a few times during the cooking process. Add the vegetables back to the basket and air-fry for another minute. Transfer the vegetables and tofu to a large bowl, add the scallions and cilantro leaves and toss with the sauce. Serve over rice with sesame seeds sprinkled on top.

Black Bean Empanadas

Servings: 12
Cooking Time: 35 Minutes

Ingredients:

- 1½ cups all-purpose flour
- 1 cup whole-wheat flour
- 1 teaspoon salt
- ½ cup cold unsalted butter
- 1 egg
- ½ cup milk
- One 14.5-ounce can black beans, drained and rinsed
- ¼ cup chopped cilantro
- 1 cup shredded purple cabbage
- 1 cup shredded Monterey jack cheese
- ¼ cup salsa

Directions:

1. In a food processor, place the all-purpose flour, whole-wheat flour, salt, and butter into processor and process for 2 minutes, scraping down the sides of the food processor every 30 seconds. Add in the egg and blend for 30 seconds. Using the pulse button, add in the milk 1 tablespoon at a time, or until dough is moist enough to handle and be rolled into a ball. Let the dough rest at room temperature for 30 minutes.
2. Meanwhile, in a large bowl, mix together the black beans, cilantro, cabbage, Monterey Jack cheese, and salsa.
3. On a floured surface, cut the dough in half; then form a ball and cut each ball into 6 equal pieces, totaling 12 equal pieces. Work with one piece at a time, and cover the remaining dough with a towel.
4. Roll out a piece of dough into a 6-inch round, much like a tortilla, ¼ inch thick. Place 4 tablespoons of filling in the center of the round, and fold over to form a half-circle. Using a fork, crimp the edges together and pierce the top for air holes. Repeat with the remaining dough and filling.

5. Preheat the air fryer to 350°F.

6. Working in batches, place 3 to 4 empanadas in the air fryer basket and spray with cooking spray. Cook for 4 minutes, flip over the empanadas and spray with cooking spray, and cook another 4 minutes.

Spicy Sesame Tempeh Slaw With Peanut Dressing

Servings: 2

Cooking Time: 8 Minutes

Ingredients:

- 2 cups hot water
- 1 teaspoon salt
- 8 ounces tempeh, sliced into 1-inch-long pieces
- 2 tablespoons low-sodium soy sauce
- 2 tablespoons rice vinegar
- 1 tablespoon filtered water
- 2 teaspoons sesame oil
- ½ teaspoon fresh ginger
- 1 clove garlic, minced
- ¼ teaspoon black pepper
- ½ jalapeño, sliced
- 4 cups cabbage slaw
- 4 tablespoons Peanut Dressing (see the following recipe)
- 2 tablespoons fresh chopped cilantro
- 2 tablespoons chopped peanuts

Directions:

1. Mix the hot water with the salt and pour over the tempeh in a glass bowl. Stir and cover with a towel for 10 minutes.
2. Discard the water and leave the tempeh in the bowl.
3. In a medium bowl, mix the soy sauce, rice vinegar, filtered water, sesame oil, ginger, garlic, pepper, and jalapeño. Pour over the tempeh and cover with a towel. Place in the refrigerator to marinate for at least 2 hours.
4. Preheat the air fryer to 370°F. Remove the tempeh from the bowl and discard the remaining marinade.
5. Liberally spray the metal trivet that goes into the air fryer basket and place the tempeh on top of the trivet.
6. Cook for 4 minutes, flip, and cook another 4 minutes.
7. In a large bowl, mix the cabbage slaw with the Peanut Dressing and toss in the cilantro and chopped peanuts.
8. Portion onto 4 plates and place the cooked tempeh on top when cooking completes. Serve immediately.

Cauliflower Steaks Gratin

Servings: 2

Cooking Time: 13 Minutes

Ingredients:

- 1 head cauliflower
- 1 tablespoon olive oil
- salt and freshly ground black pepper
- ½ teaspoon chopped fresh thyme leaves
- 3 tablespoons grated Parmigiano-Reggiano cheese
- 2 tablespoons panko breadcrumbs

Directions:

1. Preheat the air-fryer to 370°F.
2. Cut two steaks out of the center of the cauliflower. To do this, cut the cauliflower in half and then cut one slice about 1-inch thick off each half. The rest of the cauliflower will fall apart into florets, which you can roast on their own or save for another meal.
3. Brush both sides of the cauliflower steaks with olive oil and season with salt, freshly ground black pepper and fresh thyme. Place the cauliflower steaks into the air fryer basket and air-fry for 6 minutes. Turn the steaks over and air-fry for another 4 minutes. Combine the Parmesan cheese and panko breadcrumbs and sprinkle the mixture over the tops of both steaks and air-fry for another 3 minutes until the cheese has melted and the breadcrumbs have browned. Serve this with some sautéed bitter greens and air-fried blistered tomatoes.

Veggie Burgers

Servings: 4
Cooking Time: 15 Minutes

Ingredients:

- 2 cans black beans, rinsed and drained
- ½ cup cooked quinoa
- ½ cup shredded raw sweet potato
- ¼ cup diced red onion
- 2 teaspoons ground cumin
- 1 teaspoon coriander powder
- ½ teaspoon salt
- oil for misting or cooking spray
- 8 slices bread
- suggested toppings: lettuce, tomato, red onion, Pepper Jack cheese, guacamole

Directions:

1. In a medium bowl, mash the beans with a fork.
2. Add the quinoa, sweet potato, onion, cumin, coriander, and salt and mix well with the fork.
3. Shape into 4 patties, each ¾-inch thick.
4. Mist both sides with oil or cooking spray and also mist the basket.
5. Cook at 390°F for 15minutes.
6. Follow the recipe for Toast, Plain & Simple.
7. Pop the veggie burgers back in the air fryer for a minute or two to reheat if necessary.
8. Serve on the toast with your favorite burger toppings.

Quinoa Burgers With Feta Cheese And Dill

Servings: 6
Cooking Time: 10 Minutes

Ingredients:

- 1 cup quinoa (red, white or multi-colored)
- 1½ cups water
- 1 teaspoon salt
- freshly ground black pepper
- 1½ cups rolled oats
- 3 eggs, lightly beaten
- ¼ cup minced white onion
- ½ cup crumbled feta cheese
- ¼ cup chopped fresh dill
- salt and freshly ground black pepper
- vegetable or canola oil, in a spray bottle
- whole-wheat hamburger buns (or gluten-free hamburger buns*)
- arugula
- tomato, sliced
- red onion, sliced
- mayonnaise

Directions:

1. Make the quinoa: Rinse the quinoa in cold water in a saucepan, swirling it with your hand until any dry husks rise to the surface. Drain the quinoa as well as you can and then put the saucepan on the stovetop to dry and toast the quinoa. Turn the heat to medium-high and shake the pan regularly until you see the quinoa moving easily and can hear the seeds moving in the pan, indicating that they are dry. Add the water, salt and pepper. Bring the liquid to a boil and then reduce the heat to low or medium-low. You should see just a few bubbles, not a boil. Cover with a lid, leaving it askew and simmer for 20 minutes. Turn the heat off and fluff the quinoa with a fork. If there's any liquid left in the bottom of the pot, place it back on the burner for another 3 minutes or so. Spread the cooked quinoa out on a sheet pan to cool.
2. Combine the room temperature quinoa in a large bowl with the oats, eggs, onion, cheese and dill. Season with salt and pepper and mix well (remember that feta cheese is salty). Shape the mixture into 6 patties with flat sides (so they fit more easily into the air fryer). Add a little water or a few more rolled oats if necessary to get the mixture to be the right consistency to make patties.
3. Preheat the air-fryer to 400°F.
4. Spray both sides of the patties generously with oil and transfer them to the air fryer basket in one layer (you will probably have to cook these burgers in batches, depending on the size of your air fryer). Air-fry each batch at 400°F for 10 minutes, flipping the burgers over halfway through the cooking time.
5. Build your burger on the whole-wheat hamburger buns with arugula, tomato, red onion and mayonnaise.

Roasted Vegetable Thai Green Curry

Servings: 4
Cooking Time: 16 Minutes

Ingredients:

- 1 (13-ounce) can coconut milk
- 3 tablespoons green curry paste
- 1 tablespoon soy sauce*
- 1 tablespoon rice wine vinegar
- 1 teaspoon sugar
- 1 teaspoon minced fresh ginger
- ½ onion, chopped
- 3 carrots, sliced
- 1 red bell pepper, chopped
- olive oil
- 10 stalks of asparagus, cut into 2-inch pieces
- 3 cups broccoli florets
- basmati rice for serving
- fresh cilantro
- crushed red pepper flakes (optional)

Directions:

1. Combine the coconut milk, green curry paste, soy sauce, rice wine vinegar, sugar and ginger in a medium saucepan and bring to a boil on the stovetop. Reduce the heat and simmer for 20 minutes while you cook the vegetables. Set aside.
2. Preheat the air fryer to 400°F.
3. Toss the onion, carrots, and red pepper together with a little olive oil and transfer the vegetables to the air fryer basket. Air-fry at 400°F for 10 minutes, shaking the basket a few times during the cooking process. Add the asparagus and broccoli florets and air-fry for an additional 6 minutes, again shaking the basket for even cooking.
4. When the vegetables are cooked to your liking, toss them with the green curry sauce and serve in bowls over basmati rice. Garnish with fresh chopped cilantro and crushed red pepper flakes.

Roasted Vegetable Stromboli

Servings: 2
Cooking Time: 29 Minutes

Ingredients:

- ½ onion, thinly sliced
- ½ red pepper, julienned
- ½ yellow pepper, julienned
- olive oil
- 1 small zucchini, thinly sliced
- 1 cup thinly sliced mushrooms
- 1½ cups chopped broccoli
- 1 teaspoon Italian seasoning
- salt and freshly ground black pepper
- ½ recipe of Blue Jean Chef Pizza dough (page 231)

OR 1 (14-ounce) tube refrigerated pizza dough

- 2 cups grated mozzarella cheese
- ¼ cup grated Parmesan cheese
- ½ cup sliced black olives, optional
- dried oregano
- pizza or marinara sauce

Directions:

1. Preheat the air fryer to 400°F.
2. Toss the onions and peppers with a little olive oil and air-fry the vegetables for 7 minutes, shaking the basket once or twice while the vegetables cook. Add the zucchini, mushrooms, broccoli and Italian seasoning to the basket. Add a little more olive oil and season with salt and freshly ground black pepper. Air-fry for an additional 7 minutes, shaking the basket halfway through. Let the vegetables cool slightly while you roll out the pizza dough.
3. On a lightly floured surface, roll or press the pizza dough out into a 13-inch by 11-inch rectangle, with the long side closest to you. Sprinkle half of the mozzarella and Parmesan cheeses over the dough leaving an empty 1-inch border from the edge farthest away from you. Spoon the roasted vegetables over the cheese, sprinkle the olives over everything and top with the remaining cheese.
4. Start rolling the stromboli away from you and toward the empty border. Make sure the filling stays tightly tucked inside the roll. Finally, tuck the ends of the dough in and pinch the seam shut. Place the seam side down and shape the stromboli into a U-shape to fit into the air fryer basket. Cut 4 small slits with the tip of

a sharp knife evenly in the top of the dough, lightly brush the stromboli with a little oil and sprinkle with some dried oregano.

5. Preheat the air fryer to 360°F.

6. Spray or brush the air fryer basket with oil and transfer the U-shaped stromboli to the air fryer basket. Air-fry for 15 minutes, flipping the stromboli over after the first 10 minutes. (Use a plate to invert the Stromboli out of the air fryer basket and then slide it back into the basket off the plate.)

7. To remove, carefully flip the stromboli over onto a cutting board. Let it rest for a couple of minutes before serving. Cut it into 2-inch slices and serve with pizza or marinara sauce.

Roasted Vegetable, Brown Rice And Black Bean Burrito

Servings: 2

Cooking Time: 20 Minutes

Ingredients:

- ½ zucchini, sliced ¼-inch thick
- ½ red onion, sliced
- 1 yellow bell pepper, sliced
- 2 teaspoons olive oil
- salt and freshly ground black pepper
- 2 burrito size flour tortillas
- 1 cup grated pepper jack cheese
- ½ cup cooked brown rice
- ½ cup canned black beans, drained and rinsed
- ¼ teaspoon ground cumin
- 1 tablespoon chopped fresh cilantro
- fresh salsa, guacamole and sour cream, for serving

Directions:

1. Preheat the air fryer to 400°F.

2. Toss the vegetables in a bowl with the olive oil, salt and freshly ground black pepper. Air-fry at 400°F for 12 to 15 minutes, shaking the basket a few times during the cooking process. The vegetables are done when they are cooked to your liking.

3. In the meantime, start building the burritos. Lay the tortillas out on the counter. Sprinkle half of the cheese in the center of the tortillas. Combine the rice, beans, cumin and cilantro in a bowl, season to taste with salt and freshly ground black pepper and then divide the mixture between the two tortillas. When the vegetables have finished cooking, transfer them to the two tortillas, placing the vegetables on top of the rice and beans. Sprinkle the remaining cheese on top and then roll the burritos up, tucking in the sides of the tortillas as you roll. Brush or spray the outside of the burritos with olive oil and transfer them to the air fryer.

4. Air-fry at 360°F for 8 minutes, turning them over when there are about 2 minutes left. The burritos will have slightly brown spots, but will still be pliable.

5. Serve with some fresh salsa, guacamole and sour cream.

Asparagus, Mushroom And Cheese Soufflés

Servings: 3

Cooking Time: 21 Minutes

Ingredients:

- butter
- grated Parmesan cheese
- 3 button mushrooms, thinly sliced
- 8 spears asparagus, sliced ½-inch long
- 1 teaspoon olive oil
- 1 tablespoon butter
- 4½ teaspoons flour
- pinch paprika
- pinch ground nutmeg
- salt and freshly ground black pepper
- ½ cup milk
- ½ cup grated Gruyère cheese or other Swiss cheese (about 2 ounces)
- 2 eggs, separated

Directions:

1. Butter three 6-ounce ramekins and dust with grated Parmesan cheese. (Butter the ramekins and then coat the butter with Parmesan by shaking it around in the ramekin and dumping out any excess.)

2. Preheat the air fryer to 400°F.

3. Toss the mushrooms and asparagus in a bowl with the olive oil. Transfer the vegetables to the air fryer and

air-fry for 7 minutes, shaking the basket once or twice to redistribute the Ingredients while they cook.

4. While the vegetables are cooking, make the soufflé base. Melt the butter in a saucepan on the stovetop over medium heat. Add the flour, stir and cook for a minute or two. Add the paprika, nutmeg, salt and pepper. Whisk in the milk and bring the mixture to a simmer to thicken. Remove the pan from the heat and add the cheese, stirring to melt. Let the mixture cool for just a few minutes and then whisk the egg yolks in, one at a time. Stir in the cooked mushrooms and asparagus. Let this soufflé base cool.

5. In a separate bowl, whisk the egg whites to soft peak stage (the point at which the whites can almost stand up on the end of your whisk). Fold the whipped egg whites into the soufflé base, adding a little at a time.

6. Preheat the air fryer to 330°F.

7. Transfer the batter carefully to the buttered ramekins, leaving about ½-inch at the top. Place the ramekins into the air fryer basket and air-fry for 14 minutes. The soufflés should have risen nicely and be brown on top. Serve immediately.

Broccoli Cheddar Stuffed Potatoes

Servings: 2

Cooking Time: 42 Minutes

Ingredients:

- 2 large russet potatoes, scrubbed
- 1 tablespoon olive oil
- salt and freshly ground black pepper
- 2 tablespoons butter
- ¼ cup sour cream
- 3 tablespoons half-and-half (or milk)
- 1¼ cups grated Cheddar cheese, divided
- ¾ teaspoon salt
- freshly ground black pepper
- 1 cup frozen baby broccoli florets, thawed and drained

Directions:

1. Preheat the air fryer to 400°F.

2. Rub the potatoes all over with olive oil and season generously with salt and freshly ground black pepper. Transfer the potatoes into the air fryer basket and air-fry for 30 minutes, turning the potatoes over halfway through the cooking process.

3. Remove the potatoes from the air fryer and let them rest for 5 minutes. Cut a large oval out of the top of both potatoes. Leaving half an inch of potato flesh around the edge of the potato, scoop the inside of the potato out and into a large bowl to prepare the potato filling. Mash the scooped potato filling with a fork and add the butter, sour cream, half-and-half, 1 cup of the grated Cheddar cheese, salt and pepper to taste. Mix well and then fold in the broccoli florets.

4. Stuff the hollowed out potato shells with the potato and broccoli mixture. Mound the filling high in the potatoes – you will have more filling than room in the potato shells.

5. Transfer the stuffed potatoes back to the air fryer basket and air-fry at 360°F for 10 minutes. Sprinkle the remaining Cheddar cheese on top of each stuffed potato, lower the heat to 330°F and air-fry for an additional minute or two to melt cheese.

Thai Peanut Veggie Burgers

Servings: 6

Cooking Time: 14 Minutes

Ingredients:

- One 15.5-ounce can cannellini beans
- 1 teaspoon minced garlic
- ¼ cup chopped onion
- 1 Thai chili pepper, sliced
- 2 tablespoons natural peanut butter
- ½ teaspoon black pepper
- ½ teaspoon salt
- ⅓ cup all-purpose flour (optional)
- ½ cup cooked quinoa
- 1 large carrot, grated
- 1 cup shredded red cabbage
- ¼ cup peanut dressing
- ¼ cup chopped cilantro
- 6 Hawaiian rolls
- 6 butterleaf lettuce leaves

Directions:

1. Preheat the air fryer to 350°F.
2. To a blender or food processor fitted with a metal blade, add the beans, garlic, onion, chili pepper, peanut butter, pepper, and salt. Pulse for 5 to 10 seconds. Do not over process. The mixture should be coarse, not smooth.
3. Remove from the blender or food processor and spoon into a large bowl. Mix in the cooked quinoa and carrots. At this point, the mixture should begin to hold together to form small patties. If the dough appears to be too sticky (meaning you likely processed a little too long), add the flour to hold the patties together.
4. Using a large spoon, form 8 equal patties out of the batter.
5. Liberally spray a metal trivet with olive oil spray and set in the air fryer basket. Place the patties into the basket, leaving enough space to be able to turn them with a spatula.
6. Cook for 7 minutes, flip, and cook another 7 minutes.
7. Remove from the heat and repeat with additional patties.
8. To serve, place the red cabbage in a bowl and toss with peanut dressing and cilantro. Place the veggie burger on a bun, and top with a slice of lettuce and cabbage slaw.

Mexican Twice Air-fried Sweet Potatoes

Servings: 2
Cooking Time: 42 Minutes

Ingredients:

- 2 large sweet potatoes
- olive oil
- salt and freshly ground black pepper
- ⅓ cup diced red onion
- ⅓ cup diced red bell pepper
- ½ cup canned black beans, drained and rinsed
- ½ cup corn kernels, fresh or frozen
- ½ teaspoon chili powder
- 1½ cups grated pepper jack cheese, divided
- Jalapeño peppers, sliced

Directions:

1. Preheat the air fryer to 400°F.
2. Rub the outside of the sweet potatoes with olive oil and season with salt and freshly ground black pepper. Transfer the potatoes into the air fryer basket and air-fry at 400°F for 30 minutes, rotating the potatoes a few times during the cooking process.
3. While the potatoes are air-frying, start the potato filling. Preheat a large sauté pan over medium heat on the stovetop. Add the onion and pepper and sauté for a few minutes, until the vegetables start to soften. Add the black beans, corn, and chili powder and sauté for another 3 minutes. Set the mixture aside.
4. Remove the sweet potatoes from the air fryer and let them rest for 5 minutes. Slice off one inch of the flattest side of both potatoes. Scrape the potato flesh out of the potatoes, leaving half an inch of potato flesh around the edge of the potato. Place all the potato flesh into a large bowl and mash it with a fork. Add the black bean mixture and 1 cup of the pepper jack cheese to the mashed sweet potatoes. Season with salt and freshly ground black pepper and mix well. Stuff the hollowed out potato shells with the black bean and sweet potato mixture, mounding the filling high in the potatoes.
5. Transfer the stuffed potatoes back into the air fryer basket and air-fry at 370°F for 10 minutes. Sprinkle the remaining cheese on top of each stuffed potato, lower the heat to 340°F and air-fry for an additional 2 minutes to melt the cheese. Top with a couple slices of Jalapeño pepper and serve warm with a green salad.

Falafels

Servings: 12
Cooking Time: 10 Minutes

Ingredients:

- 1 pouch falafel mix
- 2–3 tablespoons plain breadcrumbs
- oil for misting or cooking spray

Directions:

1. Prepare falafel mix according to package directions.
2. Preheat air fryer to 390°F.
3. Place breadcrumbs in shallow dish or on wax paper.

4. Shape falafel mixture into 12 balls and flatten slightly. Roll in breadcrumbs to coat all sides and mist with oil or cooking spray.

5. Place falafels in air fryer basket in single layer and cook for 5minutes. Shake basket, and continue cooking for 5minutes, until they brown and are crispy.

Basic Fried Tofu

Servings: 4

Cooking Time: 17 Minutes

Ingredients:

- 14 ounces extra-firm tofu, drained and pressed
- 1 tablespoon sesame oil
- 2 tablespoons low-sodium soy sauce
- ¼ cup rice vinegar
- 1 tablespoon fresh grated ginger
- 1 clove garlic, minced
- 3 tablespoons cornstarch
- ¼ teaspoon black pepper
- ⅛ teaspoon salt

Directions:

1. Cut the tofu into 16 cubes. Set aside in a glass container with a lid.
2. In a medium bowl, mix the sesame oil, soy sauce, rice vinegar, ginger, and garlic. Pour over the tofu and secure the lid. Place in the refrigerator to marinate for an hour.
3. Preheat the air fryer to 350°F.
4. In a small bowl, mix the cornstarch, black pepper, and salt.
5. Transfer the tofu to a large bowl and discard the leftover marinade. Pour the cornstarch mixture over the tofu and toss until all the pieces are coated.
6. Liberally spray the air fryer basket with olive oil mist and set the tofu pieces inside. Allow space between the tofu so it can cook evenly. Cook in batches if necessary.
7. Cook 15 to 17 minutes, shaking the basket every 5 minutes to allow the tofu to cook evenly on all sides. When it's done cooking, the tofu will be crisped and browned on all sides.
8. Remove the tofu from the air fryer basket and serve warm.

Tacos

Servings: 24

Cooking Time: 8 Minutes Per Batch

Ingredients:

- 1 24-count package 4-inch corn tortillas
- 1½ cups refried beans (about ¾ of a 15-ounce can)
- 4 ounces sharp Cheddar cheese, grated
- ½ cup salsa
- oil for misting or cooking spray

Directions:

1. Preheat air fryer to 390°F.
2. Wrap refrigerated tortillas in damp paper towels and microwave for 30 to 60 seconds to warm. If necessary, rewarm tortillas as you go to keep them soft enough to fold without breaking.
3. Working with one tortilla at a time, top with 1 tablespoon of beans, 1 tablespoon of grated cheese, and 1 teaspoon of salsa. Fold over and press down very gently on the center. Press edges firmly all around to seal. Spray both sides with oil or cooking spray.
4. Cooking in two batches, place half the tacos in the air fryer basket. To cook 12 at a time, you may need to stand them upright and lean some against the sides of basket. It's okay if they're crowded as long as you leave a little room for air to circulate around them.
5. Cook for 8 minutes or until golden brown and crispy.
6. Repeat steps 4 and 5 to cook remaining tacos.

Curried Potato, Cauliflower And Pea Turnovers

Servings: 4

Cooking Time: 40 Minutes

Ingredients:

- Dough:
- 2 cups all-purpose flour
- ½ teaspoon baking powder
- 1 teaspoon salt
- freshly ground black pepper
- ¼ teaspoon dried thyme
- ¼ cup canola oil
- ½ to ⅔ cup water

- Turnover Filling:
- 1 tablespoon canola or vegetable oil
- 1 onion, finely chopped
- 1 clove garlic, minced
- 1 tablespoon grated fresh ginger
- ½ teaspoon cumin seeds
- ½ teaspoon fennel seeds
- 1 teaspoon curry powder
- 2 russet potatoes, diced
- 2 cups cauliflower florets
- ½ cup frozen peas
- 2 tablespoons chopped fresh cilantro
- salt and freshly ground black pepper
- 2 tablespoons butter, melted
- mango chutney, for serving

Directions:

1. Start by making the dough. Combine the flour, baking powder, salt, pepper and dried thyme in a mixing bowl or the bowl of a stand mixer. Drizzle in the canola oil and pinch it together with your fingers to turn the flour into a crumby mixture. Stir in the water (enough to bring the dough together). Knead the dough for 5 minutes or so until it is smooth. Add a little more water or flour as needed. Let the dough rest while you make the turnover filling.
2. Preheat a large skillet on the stovetop over medium-high heat. Add the oil and sauté the onion until it starts to become tender – about 4 minutes. Add the garlic and ginger and continue to cook for another minute. Add the dried spices and toss everything to coat. Add the potatoes and cauliflower to the skillet and pour in 1½ cups of water. Simmer everything together for 20 to 25 minutes, or until the potatoes are soft and most of the water has evaporated. If the water has evaporated and the vegetables still need more time, just add a little water and continue to simmer until everything is tender. Stir well, crushing the potatoes and cauliflower a little as you do so. Stir in the peas and cilantro, season to taste with salt and freshly ground black pepper and set aside to cool.
3. Divide the dough into 4 balls. Roll the dough balls out into ¼-inch thick circles. Divide the cooled potato filling between the dough circles, placing a mound of the filling on one side of each piece of dough, leaving an empty border around the edge of the dough. Brush the edges of the dough with a little water and fold one edge of circle over the filling to meet the other edge of the circle, creating a half moon. Pinch the edges together with your fingers and then press the edge with the tines of a fork to decorate and seal.
4. Preheat the air fryer to 380°F.
5. Spray or brush the air fryer basket with oil. Brush the turnovers with the melted butter and place 2 turnovers into the air fryer basket. Air-fry for 15 minutes. Flip the turnovers over and air-fry for another 5 minutes. Repeat with the remaining 2 turnovers.
6. These will be very hot when they come out of the air fryer. Let them cool for at least 20 minutes before serving warm with mango chutney.

Vegetable Couscous

Servings: 4
Cooking Time: 10 Minutes

Ingredients:

- 4 ounces white mushrooms, sliced
- ½ medium green bell pepper, julienned
- 1 cup cubed zucchini
- ¼ small onion, slivered
- 1 stalk celery, thinly sliced
- ¼ teaspoon ground coriander
- ¼ teaspoon ground cumin
- salt and pepper
- 1 tablespoon olive oil
- Couscous
- ¾ cup uncooked couscous
- 1 cup vegetable broth or water
- ½ teaspoon salt (omit if using salted broth)

Directions:

1. Combine all vegetables in large bowl. Sprinkle with coriander, cumin, and salt and pepper to taste. Stir well, add olive oil, and stir again to coat vegetables evenly.
2. Place vegetables in air fryer basket and cook at 390°F for 5minutes. Stir and cook for 5 more minutes, until tender.

3. While vegetables are cooking, prepare the couscous: Place broth or water and salt in large saucepan. Heat to boiling, stir in couscous, cover, and remove from heat.

4. Let couscous sit for 5minutes, stir in cooked vegetables, and serve hot.

Spinach And Cheese Calzone

Servings: 2

Cooking Time: 10 Minutes

Ingredients:

- ⅔ cup frozen chopped spinach, thawed
- 1 cup grated mozzarella cheese
- 1 cup ricotta cheese
- ½ teaspoon Italian seasoning
- ½ teaspoon salt
- freshly ground black pepper
- 1 store-bought or homemade pizza dough* (about 12 to 16 ounces)
- 2 tablespoons olive oil
- pizza or marinara sauce (optional)

Directions:

1. Drain and squeeze all the water out of the thawed spinach and set it aside. Mix the mozzarella cheese, ricotta cheese, Italian seasoning, salt and freshly ground black pepper together in a bowl. Stir in the chopped spinach.
2. Divide the dough in half. With floured hands or on a floured surface, stretch or roll one half of the dough into a 10-inch circle. Spread half of the cheese and spinach mixture on half of the dough, leaving about one inch of dough empty around the edge.
3. Fold the other half of the dough over the cheese mixture, almost to the edge of the bottom dough to form a half moon. Fold the bottom edge of dough up over the top edge and crimp the dough around the edges in order to make the crust and seal the calzone. Brush the dough with olive oil. Repeat with the second half of dough to make the second calzone.
4. Preheat the air fryer to 360°F.
5. Brush or spray the air fryer basket with olive oil. Air-fry the calzones one at a time for 10 minutes, flipping the calzone over half way through. Serve with warm pizza or marinara sauce if desired.

Cheese Ravioli

Servings: 4

Cooking Time: 9 Minutes

Ingredients:

- 1 egg
- ¼ cup milk
- 1 cup breadcrumbs
- 2 teaspoons Italian seasoning
- ⅛ teaspoon ground rosemary
- ¼ teaspoon basil
- ¼ teaspoon parsley
- 9-ounce package uncooked cheese ravioli
- ¼ cup flour
- oil for misting or cooking spray

Directions:

1. Preheat air fryer to 390°F.
2. In a medium bowl, beat together egg and milk.
3. In a large plastic bag, mix together the breadcrumbs, Italian seasoning, rosemary, basil, and parsley.
4. Place all the ravioli and the flour in a bag or a bowl with a lid and shake to coat.
5. Working with a handful at a time, drop floured ravioli into egg wash. Remove ravioli, letting excess drip off, and place in bag with breadcrumbs.
6. When all ravioli are in the breadcrumbs' bag, shake well to coat all pieces.
7. Dump enough ravioli into air fryer basket to form one layer. Mist with oil or cooking spray. Dump the remaining ravioli on top of the first layer and mist with oil.
8. Cook for 5minutes. Shake well and spray with oil. Break apart any ravioli stuck together and spray any spots you missed the first time.
9. Cook 4 minutes longer, until ravioli puff up and are crispy golden brown.

Lentil Fritters

Servings: 9
Cooking Time: 12 Minutes

Ingredients:

- 1 cup cooked red lentils
- 1 cup riced cauliflower
- ½ medium zucchini, shredded (about 1 cup)
- ¼ cup finely chopped onion
- ¼ teaspoon salt
- ¼ teaspoon black pepper
- ½ teaspoon garlic powder
- ¼ teaspoon paprika
- 1 large egg
- ⅓ cup quinoa flour

Directions:

1. Preheat the air fryer to 370°F.
2. In a large bowl, mix the lentils, cauliflower, zucchini, onion, salt, pepper, garlic powder, and paprika. Mix in the egg and flour until a thick dough forms.
3. Using a large spoon, form the dough into 9 large fritters.
4. Liberally spray the air fryer basket with olive oil. Place the fritters into the basket, leaving space around each fritter so you can flip them.
5. Cook for 6 minutes, flip, and cook another 6 minutes.
6. Remove from the air fryer and repeat with the remaining fritters. Serve warm with desired sauce and sides.

Roasted Vegetable Pita Pizza

Servings: 4
Cooking Time: 20 Minutes

Ingredients:

- 1 medium red bell pepper, seeded and cut into quarters
- 1 teaspoon extra-virgin olive oil
- ⅛ teaspoon black pepper
- ⅛ teaspoon salt
- Two 6-inch whole-grain pita breads
- 6 tablespoons pesto sauce
- ¼ small red onion, thinly sliced
- ½ cup shredded part-skim mozzarella cheese

Directions:

1. Preheat the air fryer to 400°F.
2. In a small bowl, toss the bell peppers with the olive oil, pepper, and salt.
3. Place the bell peppers in the air fryer and cook for 15 minutes, shaking every 5 minutes to prevent burning.
4. Remove the peppers and set aside. Turn the air fryer temperature down to 350°F.
5. Lay the pita bread on a flat surface. Cover each with half the pesto sauce; then top with even portions of the red bell peppers and onions. Sprinkle cheese over the top. Spray the air fryer basket with olive oil mist.
6. Carefully lift the pita bread into the air fryer basket with a spatula.
7. Cook for 5 to 8 minutes, or until the outer edges begin to brown and the cheese is melted.
8. Serve warm with desired sides.

Spaghetti Squash And Kale Fritters With Pomodoro Sauce

Servings: 3
Cooking Time: 45 Minutes

Ingredients:

- 1½-pound spaghetti squash (about half a large or a whole small squash)
- olive oil
- ½ onion, diced
- ½ red bell pepper, diced
- 2 cloves garlic, minced
- 4 cups coarsely chopped kale
- salt and freshly ground black pepper
- 1 egg
- ⅓ cup breadcrumbs, divided*
- ⅓ cup grated Parmesan cheese
- ½ teaspoon dried rubbed sage
- pinch nutmeg
- Pomodoro Sauce:
- 2 tablespoons olive oil
- ½ onion, chopped
- 1 to 2 cloves garlic, minced
- 1 (28-ounce) can peeled tomatoes

- ¼ cup red wine
- 1 teaspoon Italian seasoning
- 2 tablespoons chopped fresh basil, plus more for garnish
- salt and freshly ground black pepper
- ½ teaspoon sugar (optional)

Directions:

1. Preheat the air fryer to 370°F.
2. Cut the spaghetti squash in half lengthwise and remove the seeds. Rub the inside of the squash with olive oil and season with salt and pepper. Place the squash, cut side up, into the air fryer basket and air-fry for 30 minutes, flipping the squash over halfway through the cooking process.
3. While the squash is cooking, Preheat a large sauté pan over medium heat on the stovetop. Add a little olive oil and sauté the onions for 3 minutes, until they start to soften. Add the red pepper and garlic and continue to sauté for an additional 4 minutes. Add the kale and season with salt and pepper. Cook for 2 more minutes, or until the kale is soft. Transfer the mixture to a large bowl and let it cool.
4. While the squash continues to cook, make the Pomodoro sauce. Preheat the large sauté pan again over medium heat on the stovetop. Add the olive oil and sauté the onion and garlic for 2 to 3 minutes, until the onion begins to soften. Crush the canned tomatoes with your hands and add them to the pan along with the red wine and Italian seasoning and simmer for 20 minutes. Add the basil and season to taste with salt, pepper and sugar (if using).
5. When the spaghetti squash has finished cooking, use a fork to scrape the inside flesh of the squash onto a sheet pan. Spread the squash out and let it cool.
6. Once cool, add the spaghetti squash to the kale mixture, along with the egg, breadcrumbs, Parmesan cheese, sage, nutmeg, salt and freshly ground black pepper. Stir to combine well and then divide the mixture into 6 thick portions. You can shape the portions into patties, but I prefer to keep them a little random and unique in shape. Spray or brush the fritters with olive oil.
7. Preheat the air fryer to 370°F.
8. Brush the air fryer basket with a little olive oil and transfer the fritters to the basket. Air-fry the squash and kale fritters at 370°F for 15 minutes, flipping them over halfway through the cooking process.
9. Serve the fritters warm with the Pomodoro sauce spooned over the top or pooled on your plate. Garnish with the fresh basil leaves.

Charred Cauliflower Tacos

Servings: 4

Cooking Time: 10 Minutes

Ingredients:

- 1 head cauliflower, washed and cut into florets
- 2 tablespoons avocado oil
- 2 teaspoons taco seasoning
- 1 medium avocado
- ½ teaspoon garlic powder
- ¼ teaspoon black pepper
- ¼ teaspoon salt
- 2 tablespoons chopped red onion
- 2 teaspoons fresh squeezed lime juice
- ¼ cup chopped cilantro
- Eight 6-inch corn tortillas
- ½ cup cooked corn
- ½ cup shredded purple cabbage

Directions:

1. Preheat the air fryer to 390°F.
2. In a large bowl, toss the cauliflower with the avocado oil and taco seasoning. Set the metal trivet inside the air fryer basket and liberally spray with olive oil.
3. Place the cauliflower onto the trivet and cook for 10 minutes, shaking every 3 minutes to allow for an even char.
4. While the cauliflower is cooking, prepare the avocado sauce. In a medium bowl, mash the avocado; then mix in the garlic powder, pepper, salt, and onion. Stir in the lime juice and cilantro; set aside.
5. Remove the cauliflower from the air fryer basket.
6. Place 1 tablespoon of avocado sauce in the middle of a tortilla, and top with corn, cabbage, and charred cauliflower. Repeat with the remaining tortillas. Serve immediately.

Pizza Portobello Mushrooms

Servings: 2
Cooking Time: 18 Minutes

Ingredients:

- 2 portobello mushroom caps, gills removed (see Figure 13-1)
- 1 teaspoon extra-virgin olive oil
- ¼ cup diced onion
- 1 teaspoon minced garlic
- 1 medium zucchini, shredded
- 1 teaspoon dried oregano
- ½ teaspoon black pepper
- ¼ teaspoon salt
- ⅓ cup marinara sauce
- ¼ cup shredded part-skim mozzarella cheese
- ¼ teaspoon red pepper flakes
- 2 tablespoons Parmesan cheese
- 2 tablespoons chopped basil

Directions:

1. Preheat the air fryer to 370°F.
2. Lightly spray the mushrooms with an olive oil mist and place into the air fryer to cook for 10 minutes, cap side up.
3. Add the olive oil to a pan and sauté the onion and garlic together for about 2 to 4 minutes. Stir in the zucchini, oregano, pepper, and salt, and continue to cook. When the zucchini has cooked down (usually about 4 to 6 minutes), add in the marinara sauce. Remove from the heat and stir in the mozzarella cheese.
4. Remove the mushrooms from the air fryer basket when cooking completes. Reset the temperature to 350°F.
5. Using a spoon, carefully stuff the mushrooms with the zucchini marinara mixture.
6. Return the stuffed mushrooms to the air fryer basket and cook for 5 to 8 minutes, or until the cheese is lightly browned. You should be able to easily insert a fork into the mushrooms when they're cooked.
7. Remove the mushrooms and sprinkle the red pepper flakes, Parmesan cheese, and fresh basil over the top.
8. Serve warm.

Stuffed Zucchini Boats

Servings: 2
Cooking Time: 20 Minutes

Ingredients:

- olive oil
- ½ cup onion, finely chopped
- 1 clove garlic, finely minced
- ½ teaspoon dried oregano
- ¼ teaspoon dried thyme
- ¾ cup couscous
- 1½ cups chicken stock, divided
- 1 tomato, seeds removed and finely chopped
- ½ cup coarsely chopped Kalamata olives
- ½ cup grated Romano cheese
- ¼ cup pine nuts, toasted
- 1 tablespoon chopped fresh parsley
- 1 teaspoon salt
- freshly ground black pepper
- 1 egg, beaten
- 1 cup grated mozzarella cheese, divided
- 2 thick zucchini

Directions:

1. Preheat a sauté pan on the stovetop over medium-high heat. Add the olive oil and sauté the onion until it just starts to soften–about 4 minutes. Stir in the garlic, dried oregano and thyme. Add the couscous and sauté for just a minute. Add 1¼ cups of the chicken stock and simmer over low heat for 3 to 5 minutes, until liquid has been absorbed and the couscous is soft. Remove the pan from heat and set it aside to cool slightly.
2. Fluff the couscous and add the tomato, Kalamata olives, Romano cheese, pine nuts, parsley, salt and pepper. Mix well. Add the remaining chicken stock, the egg and ½ cup of the mozzarella cheese. Stir to ensure everything is combined.
3. Cut each zucchini in half lengthwise. Then, trim each half of the zucchini into four 5-inch lengths. (Save the trimmed ends of the zucchini for another use.) Use a spoon to scoop out the center of the zucchini, leaving some flesh around the sides. Brush both sides of the zucchini with olive oil and season the cut side with salt and pepper.

4. Preheat the air fryer to 380°F.
5. Divide the couscous filling between the four zucchini boats. Use your hands to press the filling together and fill the inside of the zucchini. The filling should be mounded into the boats and rounded on top.
6. Transfer the zucchini boats to the air fryer basket and drizzle the stuffed zucchini boats with olive oil. Air-fry for 19 minutes. Then, sprinkle the remaining mozzarella cheese on top of the zucchini, pressing it down onto the filling lightly to prevent it from blowing around in the air fryer. Air-fry for one more minute to melt the cheese. Transfer the finished zucchini boats to a serving platter and garnish with the chopped parsley.

Roasted Vegetable Lasagna

Servings: 6
Cooking Time: 55 Minutes

Ingredients:

- 1 zucchini, sliced
- 1 yellow squash, sliced
- 8 ounces mushrooms, sliced
- 1 red bell pepper, cut into 2-inch strips
- 1 tablespoon olive oil
- 2 cups ricotta cheese
- 2 cups grated mozzarella cheese, divided
- 1 egg
- 1 teaspoon salt
- freshly ground black pepper
- ¼ cup shredded carrots
- ½ cup chopped fresh spinach
- 8 lasagna noodles, cooked
- Béchamel Sauce:
- 3 tablespoons butter
- 3 tablespoons flour
- 2½ cups milk
- ½ cup grated Parmesan cheese
- ½ teaspoon salt
- freshly ground black pepper
- pinch of ground nutmeg

Directions:

1. Preheat the air fryer to 400°F.
2. Toss the zucchini, yellow squash, mushrooms and red pepper in a large bowl with the olive oil and season with salt and pepper. Air-fry for 10 minutes, shaking the basket once or twice while the vegetables cook.
3. While the vegetables are cooking, make the béchamel sauce and cheese filling. Melt the butter in a medium saucepan over medium-high heat on the stovetop. Add the flour and whisk, cooking for a couple of minutes. Add the milk and whisk vigorously until smooth. Bring the mixture to a boil and simmer until the sauce thickens. Stir in the Parmesan cheese and season with the salt, pepper and nutmeg. Set the sauce aside.
4. Combine the ricotta cheese, 1¼ cups of the mozzarella cheese, egg, salt and pepper in a large bowl and stir until combined. Fold in the carrots and spinach.
5. When the vegetables have finished cooking, build the lasagna. Use a baking dish that is 6 inches in diameter and 4 inches high. Cover the bottom of the baking dish with a little béchamel sauce. Top with two lasagna noodles, cut to fit the dish and overlapping each other a little. Spoon a third of the ricotta cheese mixture and then a third of the roasted veggies on top of the noodles. Pour ½ cup of béchamel sauce on top and then repeat these layers two more times: noodles – cheese mixture – vegetables – béchamel sauce. Sprinkle the remaining mozzarella cheese over the top. Cover the dish with aluminum foil, tenting it loosely so the aluminum doesn't touch the cheese.
6. Lower the dish into the air fryer basket using an aluminum foil sling (fold a piece of aluminum foil into a strip about 2-inches wide by 24-inches long). Fold the ends of the aluminum foil over the top of the dish before returning the basket to the air fryer. Air-fry for 45 minutes, removing the foil for the last 2 minutes, to slightly brown the cheese on top.
7. Let the lasagna rest for at least 20 minutes to set up a little before slicing into it and serving.

Arancini With Marinara

Servings: 6
Cooking Time: 15 Minutes

Ingredients:

- 2 cups cooked rice
- 1 cup grated Parmesan cheese
- 1 egg, whisked
- ¼ teaspoon dried thyme
- ½ teaspoon dried oregano
- ½ teaspoon dried basil
- ½ teaspoon dried parsley
- 1 teaspoon salt
- ¼ teaspoon paprika
- 1 cup breadcrumbs
- 4 ounces mozzarella, cut into 24 cubes
- 2 cups marinara sauce

Directions:

1. In a large bowl, mix together the rice, Parmesan cheese, and egg.
2. In another bowl, mix together the thyme, oregano, basil, parsley, salt, paprika, and breadcrumbs.
3. Form 24 rice balls with the rice mixture. Use your thumb to make an indentation in the center and stuff 1 cube of mozzarella in the center of the rice; close the ball around the cheese.
4. Roll the rice balls in the seasoned breadcrumbs until all are coated.
5. Preheat the air fryer to 400°F.
6. Place the rice balls in the air fryer basket and coat with cooking spray. Cook for 8 minutes, shake the basket, and cook another 7 minutes.
7. Heat the marinara sauce in a saucepan until warm. Serve sauce as a dip for arancini.

Tandoori Paneer Naan Pizza

Servings: 4
Cooking Time: 10 Minutes

Ingredients:

- 6 tablespoons plain Greek yogurt, divided
- 1¼ teaspoons garam marsala, divided
- ½ teaspoon turmeric, divided
- ¼ teaspoon garlic powder
- ½ teaspoon paprika, divided
- ½ teaspoon black pepper, divided
- 3 ounces paneer, cut into small cubes
- 1 tablespoon extra-virgin olive oil
- 2 teaspoons minced garlic
- 4 cups baby spinach
- 2 tablespoons marinara sauce
- ¼ teaspoon salt
- 2 plain naan breads (approximately 6 inches in diameter)
- ½ cup shredded part-skim mozzarella cheese

Directions:

1. Preheat the air fryer to 350°F.
2. In a small bowl, mix 2 tablespoons of the yogurt, ½ teaspoon of the garam marsala, ¼ teaspoon of the turmeric, the garlic powder, ¼ teaspoon of the paprika, and ¼ teaspoon of the black pepper. Toss the paneer cubes in the mixture and let marinate for at least an hour.
3. Meanwhile, in a pan, heat the olive oil over medium heat. Add in the minced garlic and sauté for 1 minute. Stir in the spinach and begin to cook until it wilts. Add in the remaining 4 tablespoons of yogurt and the marinara sauce. Stir in the remaining ¾ teaspoon of garam masala, the remaining ¼ teaspoon of turmeric, the remaining ¼ teaspoon of paprika, the remaining ¼ teaspoon of black pepper, and the salt. Let simmer a minute or two, and then remove from the heat.
4. Equally divide the spinach mixture amongst the two naan breads. Place 1½ ounces of the marinated paneer on each naan.
5. Liberally spray the air fryer basket with olive oil mist.
6. Use a spatula to pick up one naan and place it in the air fryer basket.
7. Cook for 4 minutes, open the basket and sprinkle ¼ cup of mozzarella cheese on top, and cook another 4 minutes.
8. Remove from the air fryer and repeat with the remaining naan.
9. Serve warm.

Egg Rolls

Servings: 4

Cooking Time: 8 Minutes

Ingredients:

- 1 clove garlic, minced
- 1 teaspoon sesame oil
- 1 teaspoon olive oil
- ½ cup chopped celery
- ½ cup grated carrots
- 2 green onions, chopped
- 2 ounces mushrooms, chopped
- 2 cups shredded Napa cabbage
- 1 teaspoon low-sodium soy sauce
- 1 teaspoon cornstarch
- salt
- 1 egg
- 1 tablespoon water
- 4 egg roll wraps
- olive oil for misting or cooking spray

Directions:

1. In a large skillet, sauté garlic in sesame and olive oils over medium heat for 1 minute.
2. Add celery, carrots, onions, and mushrooms to skillet. Cook 1 minute, stirring.
3. Stir in cabbage, cover, and cook for 1 minute or just until cabbage slightly wilts.
4. In a small bowl, mix soy sauce and cornstarch. Stir into vegetables to thicken. Remove from heat. Salt to taste if needed.
5. Beat together egg and water in a small bowl.
6. Divide filling into 4 portions and roll up in egg roll wraps. Brush all over with egg wash to seal.
7. Mist egg rolls very lightly with olive oil or cooking spray and place in air fryer basket.
8. Cook at 390°F for 4minutes. Turn over and cook 4 more minutes, until golden brown and crispy.

Mushroom, Zucchini And Black Bean Burgers

Servings: 4

Cooking Time: 18 Minutes

Ingredients:

- 1 cup diced zucchini, (about ½ medium zucchini)
- 1 tablespoon olive oil
- salt and freshly ground black pepper
- 1 cup chopped brown mushrooms (about 3 ounces)
- 1 small clove garlic
- 1 (15-ounce) can black beans, drained and rinsed
- 1 teaspoon lemon zest
- 1 tablespoon chopped fresh cilantro
- ½ cup plain breadcrumbs
- 1 egg, beaten
- ½ teaspoon salt
- freshly ground black pepper
- whole-wheat pita bread, burger buns or brioche buns
- mayonnaise, tomato, avocado and lettuce, for serving

Directions:

1. Preheat the air fryer to 400°F.
2. Toss the zucchini with the olive oil, season with salt and freshly ground black pepper and air-fry for 6 minutes, shaking the basket once or twice while it cooks.
3. Transfer the zucchini to a food processor with the mushrooms, garlic and black beans and process until still a little chunky but broken down and pasty. Transfer the mixture to a bowl. Add the lemon zest, cilantro, breadcrumbs and egg and mix well. Season again with salt and freshly ground black pepper. Shape the mixture into four burger patties and refrigerate for at least 15 minutes.
4. Preheat the air fryer to 370°F. Transfer two of the veggie burgers to the air fryer basket and air-fry for 12 minutes, flipping the burgers gently halfway through the cooking time. Keep the burgers warm by loosely tenting them with foil while you cook the remaining two burgers. Return the first batch of burgers back into the air fryer with the second batch for the last two minutes of cooking to re-heat.
5. Serve on toasted whole-wheat pita bread, burger buns or brioche buns with some mayonnaise, tomato, avocado and lettuce.

Mushroom And Fried Onion Quesadilla

Servings: 2
Cooking Time: 33 Minutes

Ingredients:

- 1 onion, sliced
- 2 tablespoons butter, melted
- 10 ounces button mushrooms, sliced
- 2 tablespoons Worcestershire sauce
- salt and freshly ground black pepper
- 4 (8-inch) flour tortillas
- 2 cups grated Fontina cheese
- vegetable or olive oil

Directions:

1. Preheat the air fryer to 400°F.
2. Toss the onion slices with the melted butter and transfer them to the air fryer basket. Air-fry at 400°F for 15 minutes, shaking the basket several times during the cooking process. Add the mushrooms and Worcestershire sauce to the onions and stir to combine. Air-fry at 400°F for an additional 10 minutes. Season with salt and freshly ground black pepper.
3. Lay two of the tortillas on a cutting board. Top each tortilla with ½ cup of the grated cheese, half of the onion and mushroom mixture and then finally another ½ cup of the cheese. Place the remaining tortillas on top of the cheese and press down firmly.
4. Brush the air fryer basket with a little oil. Place a quesadilla in the basket and brush the top with a little oil. Secure the top tortilla to the bottom with three toothpicks and air-fry at 400°F for 5 minutes. Flip the quesadilla over by inverting it onto a plate and sliding it back into the basket. Remove the toothpicks and brush the other side with oil. Air-fry for an additional 3 minutes.
5. Invert the quesadilla onto a cutting board and cut it into 4 or 6 triangles. Serve immediately.

Cheesy Enchilada Stuffed Baked Potatoes

Servings: 4
Cooking Time: 37 Minutes

Ingredients:

- 2 medium russet potatoes, washed
- One 15-ounce can mild red enchilada sauce
- One 15-ounce can low-sodium black beans, rinsed and drained
- 1 teaspoon taco seasoning
- ½ cup shredded cheddar cheese
- 1 medium avocado, halved
- ½ teaspoon garlic powder
- ¼ teaspoon black pepper
- ¼ teaspoon salt
- 2 teaspoons fresh lime juice
- 2 tablespoon chopped red onion
- ¼ cup chopped cilantro

Directions:

1. Preheat the air fryer to 390°F.
2. Puncture the outer surface of the potatoes with a fork.
3. Set the potatoes inside the air fryer basket and cook for 20 minutes, rotate, and cook another 10 minutes.
4. In a large bowl, mix the enchilada sauce, black beans, and taco seasoning.
5. When the potatoes have finished cooking, carefully remove them from the air fryer basket and let cool for 5 minutes.
6. Using a pair of tongs to hold the potato if it's still too hot to touch, slice the potato in half lengthwise. Use a spoon to scoop out the potato flesh and add it into the bowl with the enchilada sauce. Mash the potatoes with the enchilada sauce mixture, creating a uniform stuffing.
7. Place the potato skins into an air-fryer-safe pan and stuff the halves with the enchilada stuffing. Sprinkle the cheese over the top of each potato.
8. Set the air fryer temperature to 350°F, return the pan to the air fryer basket, and cook for another 5 to 7 minutes to heat the potatoes and melt the cheese.
9. While the potatoes are cooking, take the avocado and scoop out the flesh into a small bowl. Mash it with the back of a fork; then mix in the garlic powder, pepper, salt, lime juice, and onion. Set aside.
10. When the potatoes have finished cooking, remove the pan from the air fryer and place the potato halves on

a plate. Top with avocado mash and fresh cilantro. Serve immediately.

Pinto Taquitos

Servings: 4
Cooking Time: 8 Minutes

Ingredients:

- 12 corn tortillas (6- to 7-inch size)
- Filling
- ½ cup refried pinto beans
- ½ cup grated sharp Cheddar or Pepper Jack cheese
- ¼ cup corn kernels (if frozen, measure after thawing and draining)
- 2 tablespoons chopped green onion
- 2 tablespoons chopped jalapeño pepper (seeds and ribs removed before chopping)
- ½ teaspoon lime juice
- ½ teaspoon chile powder, plus extra for dusting
- ½ teaspoon cumin
- ½ teaspoon garlic powder
- oil for misting or cooking spray
- salsa, sour cream, or guacamole for dipping

Directions:

1. Mix together all filling Ingredients.
2. Warm refrigerated tortillas for easier rolling. (Wrap in damp paper towels and microwave for 30 to 60 seconds.)
3. Working with one at a time, place 1 tablespoon of filling on tortilla and roll up. Spray with oil or cooking spray and dust outside with chile powder to taste.
4. Place 6 taquitos in air fryer basket (4 on bottom layer, 2 stacked crosswise on top). Cook at 390°F for 8 minutes, until crispy and brown.
5. Repeat step 4 to cook remaining taquitos.
6. Serve plain or with salsa, sour cream, or guacamole for dipping.

Falafel

Servings: 4
Cooking Time: 10 Minutes

Ingredients:

- 1 cup dried chickpeas
- ½ onion, chopped
- 1 clove garlic
- ¼ cup fresh parsley leaves
- 1 teaspoon salt
- ¼ teaspoon crushed red pepper flakes
- 1 teaspoon ground cumin
- ½ teaspoon ground coriander
- 1 to 2 tablespoons flour
- olive oil
- Tomato Salad
- 2 tomatoes, seeds removed and diced
- ½ cucumber, finely diced
- ¼ red onion, finely diced and rinsed with water
- 1 teaspoon red wine vinegar
- 1 tablespoon olive oil
- salt and freshly ground black pepper
- 2 tablespoons chopped fresh parsley

Directions:

1. Cover the chickpeas with water and let them soak overnight on the counter. Then drain the chickpeas and put them in a food processor, along with the onion, garlic, parsley, spices and 1 tablespoon of flour. Pulse in the food processor until the mixture has broken down into a coarse paste consistency. The mixture should hold together when you pinch it. Add more flour as needed, until you get this consistency.
2. Scoop portions of the mixture (about 2 tablespoons in size) and shape into balls. Place the balls on a plate and refrigerate for at least 30 minutes. You should have between 12 and 14 balls.
3. Preheat the air fryer to 380°F.
4. Spray the falafel balls with oil and place them in the air fryer. Air-fry for 10 minutes, rolling them over and spraying them with oil again halfway through the cooking time so that they cook and brown evenly.
5. Serve with pita bread, hummus, cucumbers, hot peppers, tomatoes or any other fillings you might like.

Eggplant Parmesan

Servings: 4

Cooking Time: 8 Minutes Per Batch

Ingredients:

- 1 medium eggplant, 6–8 inches long
- salt
- 1 large egg
- 1 tablespoon water
- ⅔ cup panko breadcrumbs
- ⅓ cup grated Parmesan cheese, plus more for serving
- 1 tablespoon Italian seasoning
- ¾ teaspoon oregano
- oil for misting or cooking spray
- 1 24-ounce jar marinara sauce
- 8 ounces spaghetti, cooked
- pepper

Directions:

1. Preheat air fryer to 390°F.
2. Leaving peel intact, cut eggplant into 8 round slices about ¾-inch thick. Salt to taste.
3. Beat egg and water in a shallow dish.
4. In another shallow dish, combine panko, Parmesan, Italian seasoning, and oregano.
5. Dip eggplant slices in egg wash and then crumbs, pressing lightly to coat.
6. Mist slices with oil or cooking spray.
7. Place 4 eggplant slices in air fryer basket and cook for 8 minutes, until brown and crispy.
8. While eggplant is cooking, heat marinara sauce.
9. Repeat step 7 to cook remaining eggplant slices.
10. To serve, place cooked spaghetti on plates and top with marinara and eggplant slices. At the table, pass extra Parmesan cheese and freshly ground black pepper.

Corn And Pepper Jack Chile Rellenos With Roasted Tomato Sauce

Servings: 3

Cooking Time: 30 Minutes

Ingredients:

- 3 Poblano peppers
- 1 cup all-purpose flour*
- salt and freshly ground black pepper
- 2 eggs, lightly beaten
- 1 cup plain breadcrumbs*
- olive oil, in a spray bottle
- Sauce
- 2 cups cherry tomatoes
- 1 Jalapeño pepper, halved and seeded
- 1 clove garlic
- ¼ red onion, broken into large pieces
- 1 tablespoon olive oil
- salt, to taste
- 2 tablespoons chopped fresh cilantro
- Filling
- olive oil
- ¼ red onion, finely chopped
- 1 teaspoon minced garlic
- 1 cup corn kernels, fresh or frozen
- 2 cups grated pepper jack cheese

Directions:

1. Start by roasting the peppers. Preheat the air fryer to 400°F. Place the peppers into the air fryer basket and air-fry at 400°F for 10 minutes, turning them over halfway through the cooking time. Remove the peppers from the basket and cover loosely with foil.
2. While the peppers are cooling, make the roasted tomato sauce. Place all sauce Ingredients except for the cilantro into the air fryer basket and air-fry at 400°F for 10 minutes, shaking the basket once or twice. When the sauce Ingredients have finished air-frying, transfer everything to a blender or food processor and blend or process to a smooth sauce, adding a little warm water to get the desired consistency. Season to taste with salt, add the cilantro and set aside.
3. While the sauce Ingredients are cooking in the air fryer, make the filling. Heat a skillet on the stovetop over medium heat. Add the olive oil and sauté the red onion and garlic for 4 to 5 minutes. Transfer the onion and garlic to a bowl, stir in the corn and cheese, and set aside.
4. Set up a dredging station with three shallow dishes. Place the flour, seasoned with salt and pepper, in the first shallow dish. Place the eggs in the second dish, and fill the third shallow dish with the breadcrumbs. When the

peppers have cooled, carefully slice into one side of the pepper to create an opening. Pull the seeds out of the peppers and peel away the skins, trying not to tear the pepper. Fill each pepper with some of the corn and cheese filling and close the pepper up again by folding one side of the opening over the other. Carefully roll each pepper in the seasoned flour, then into the egg and finally into the breadcrumbs to coat on all sides, trying not to let the pepper fall open. Spray the peppers on all sides with a little olive oil.

5. Air-fry two peppers at a time at 350°F for 6 minutes. Turn the peppers over and air-fry for another 4 minutes. Serve the peppers warm on a bed of the roasted tomato sauce.

Vegetable Hand Pies

Servings: 8

Cooking Time: 10 Minutes Per Batch

Ingredients:

- ¾ cup vegetable broth
- 8 ounces potatoes
- ¾ cup frozen chopped broccoli, thawed
- ¼ cup chopped mushrooms
- 1 tablespoon cornstarch
- 1 tablespoon milk
- 1 can organic flaky biscuits (8 large biscuits)
- oil for misting or cooking spray

Directions:

1. Place broth in medium saucepan over low heat.
2. While broth is heating, grate raw potato into a bowl of water to prevent browning. You will need ¾ cup grated potato.
3. Roughly chop the broccoli.
4. Drain potatoes and put them in the broth along with the broccoli and mushrooms. Cook on low for 5 minutes.
5. Dissolve cornstarch in milk, then stir the mixture into the broth. Cook about a minute, until mixture thickens a little. Remove from heat and cool slightly.
6. Separate each biscuit into 2 rounds. Divide vegetable mixture evenly over half the biscuit rounds, mounding filling in the center of each.
7. Top the four rounds with filling, then the other four rounds and crimp the edges together with a fork.
8. Spray both sides with oil or cooking spray and place 4 pies in a single layer in the air fryer basket.
9. Cook at 330°F for approximately 10 minutes.
10. Repeat with the remaining biscuits. The second batch may cook more quickly because the fryer will be hot.

Veggie Fried Rice

Servings: 4

Cooking Time: 25 Minutes

Ingredients:

- 1 cup cooked brown rice
- ⅓ cup chopped onion
- ½ cup chopped carrots
- ½ cup chopped bell peppers
- ½ cup chopped broccoli florets
- 3 tablespoons low-sodium soy sauce
- 1 tablespoon sesame oil
- 1 teaspoon ground ginger
- 1 teaspoon ground garlic powder
- ½ teaspoon black pepper
- ⅛ teaspoon salt
- 2 large eggs

Directions:

1. Preheat the air fryer to 370°F.
2. In a large bowl, mix together the brown rice, onions, carrots, bell pepper, and broccoli.
3. In a small bowl, whisk together the soy sauce, sesame oil, ginger, garlic powder, pepper, salt, and eggs.
4. Pour the egg mixture into the rice and vegetable mixture and mix together.
5. Liberally spray a 7-inch springform pan (or compatible air fryer dish) with olive oil. Add the rice mixture to the pan and cover with aluminum foil.
6. Place a metal trivet into the air fryer basket and set the pan on top. Cook for 15 minutes. Carefully remove the pan from basket, discard the foil, and mix the rice. Return the rice to the air fryer basket, turning down the temperature to 350°F and cooking another 10 minutes.
7. Remove and let cool 5 minutes. Serve warm.

Sandwiches And Burgers Recipes

Best-ever Roast Beef Sandwiches

Servings: 6

Cooking Time: 30-50 Minutes

Ingredients:

- 2½ teaspoons Olive oil
- 1½ teaspoons Dried oregano
- 1½ teaspoons Dried thyme
- 1½ teaspoons Onion powder
- 1½ teaspoons Table salt
- 1½ teaspoons Ground black pepper
- 3 pounds Beef eye of round
- 6 Round soft rolls, such as Kaiser rolls or hamburger buns (gluten-free, if a concern), split open lengthwise
- ¾ cup Regular, low-fat, or fat-free mayonnaise (gluten-free, if a concern)
- 6 Romaine lettuce leaves, rinsed
- 6 Round tomato slices (¼ inch thick)

Directions:

1. Preheat the air fryer to 350°F .
2. Mix the oil, oregano, thyme, onion powder, salt, and pepper in a small bowl. Spread this mixture all over the eye of round.
3. When the machine is at temperature, set the beef in the basket and air-fry for 30 to 50 minutes (the range depends on the size of the cut), turning the meat twice, until an instant-read meat thermometer inserted into the thickest piece of the meat registers 130°F for rare, 140°F for medium, or 150°F for well-done.
4. Use kitchen tongs to transfer the beef to a cutting board. Cool for 10 minutes. If serving now, carve into ⅛-inch-thick slices. Spread each roll with 2 tablespoons mayonnaise and divide the beef slices between the rolls. Top with a lettuce leaf and a tomato slice and serve. Or set the beef in a container, cover, and refrigerate for up to 3 days to make cold roast beef sandwiches anytime.

Black Bean Veggie Burgers

Servings: 3

Cooking Time: 10 Minutes

Ingredients:

- 1 cup Drained and rinsed canned black beans
- ⅓ cup Pecan pieces
- ⅓ cup Rolled oats (not quick-cooking or steel-cut; gluten-free, if a concern)
- 2 tablespoons (or 1 small egg) Pasteurized egg substitute, such as Egg Beaters (gluten-free, if a concern)
- 2 teaspoons Red ketchup-like chili sauce, such as Heinz
- ¼ teaspoon Ground cumin
- ¼ teaspoon Dried oregano
- ¼ teaspoon Table salt
- ¼ teaspoon Ground black pepper
- Olive oil
- Olive oil spray

Directions:

1. Preheat the air fryer to 400°F.
2. Put the beans, pecans, oats, egg substitute or egg, chili sauce, cumin, oregano, salt, and pepper in a food processor. Cover and process to a coarse paste that will hold its shape like sugar-cookie dough, adding olive oil in 1-teaspoon increments to get the mixture to blend smoothly. The amount of olive oil is actually dependent on the internal moisture content of the beans and the oats. Figure on about 1 tablespoon (three 1-teaspoon additions) for the smaller batch, with proportional increases for the other batches. A little too much olive oil can't hurt, but a dry paste will fall apart as it cooks and a far-too-wet paste will stick to the basket.
3. Scrape down and remove the blade. Using clean, wet hands, form the paste into two 4-inch patties for the small batch, three 4-inch patties for the medium, or four 4-inch patties for the large batch, setting them one by one on a cutting board. Generously coat both sides of the patties with olive oil spray.
4. Set them in the basket in one layer. Air-fry undisturbed for 10 minutes, or until lightly browned and crisp at the edges.
5. Use a nonstick-safe spatula, and perhaps a flatware fork for balance, to transfer the burgers to a wire rack. Cool for 5 minutes before serving.

Asian Glazed Meatballs

Servings: 4

Cooking Time: 10 Minutes

Ingredients:

- 1 large shallot, finely chopped
- 2 cloves garlic, minced
- 1 tablespoon grated fresh ginger
- 2 teaspoons fresh thyme, finely chopped
- 1½ cups brown mushrooms, very finely chopped (a food processor works well here)
- 2 tablespoons soy sauce
- freshly ground black pepper
- 1 pound ground beef
- ½ pound ground pork
- 3 egg yolks
- 1 cup Thai sweet chili sauce (spring roll sauce)
- ¼ cup toasted sesame seeds
- 2 scallions, sliced

Directions:

1. Combine the shallot, garlic, ginger, thyme, mushrooms, soy sauce, freshly ground black pepper, ground beef and pork, and egg yolks in a bowl and mix the ingredients together. Gently shape the mixture into 24 balls, about the size of a golf ball.
2. Preheat the air fryer to 380°F.
3. Working in batches, air-fry the meatballs for 8 minutes, turning the meatballs over halfway through the cooking time. Drizzle some of the Thai sweet chili sauce on top of each meatball and return the basket to the air fryer, air-frying for another 2 minutes. Reserve the remaining Thai sweet chili sauce for serving.
4. As soon as the meatballs are done, sprinkle with toasted sesame seeds and transfer them to a serving platter. Scatter the scallions around and serve warm.

Turkey Burgers

Servings: 3

Cooking Time: 23 Minutes

Ingredients:

- 1 pound 2 ounces Ground turkey
- 6 tablespoons Frozen chopped spinach, thawed and squeezed dry
- 3 tablespoons Plain panko bread crumbs (gluten-free, if a concern)
- 1 tablespoon Dijon mustard (gluten-free, if a concern)
- 1½ teaspoons Minced garlic
- ¾ teaspoon Table salt
- ¾ teaspoon Ground black pepper
- Olive oil spray
- 3 Kaiser rolls (gluten-free, if a concern), split open

Directions:

1. Preheat the air fryer to 375°F .
2. Gently mix the ground turkey, spinach, bread crumbs, mustard, garlic, salt, and pepper in a large bowl until well combined, trying to keep some of the fibers of the ground turkey intact. Form into two 5-inch-wide patties for the small batch, three 5-inch patties for the medium batch, or four 5-inch patties for the large. Coat each side of the patties with olive oil spray.
3. Set the patties in in the basket in one layer and air-fry undisturbed for 20 minutes, or until an instant-read meat thermometer inserted into the center of a burger registers 165°F. You may need to add 2 minutes to the cooking time if the air fryer is at 360°F.
4. Use a nonstick-safe spatula, and perhaps a flatware fork for balance, to transfer the burgers to a cutting board. Set the buns cut side down in the basket in one layer (working in batches as necessary) and air-fry for 1 minute, to toast a bit and warm up. Serve the burgers warm in the buns.

White Bean Veggie Burgers

Servings: 3

Cooking Time: 13 Minutes

Ingredients:

- 1⅓ cups Drained and rinsed canned white beans
- 3 tablespoons Rolled oats (not quick-cooking or steel-cut; gluten-free, if a concern)
- 3 tablespoons Chopped walnuts
- 2 teaspoons Olive oil
- 2 teaspoons Lemon juice
- 1½ teaspoons Dijon mustard (gluten-free, if a concern)

- ¾ teaspoon Dried sage leaves
- ¼ teaspoon Table salt
- Olive oil spray
- 3 Whole-wheat buns or gluten-free whole-grain buns (if a concern), split open

Directions:

1. Preheat the air fryer to 400°F.
2. Place the beans, oats, walnuts, oil, lemon juice, mustard, sage, and salt in a food processor. Cover and process to make a coarse paste that will hold its shape, about like wet sugar-cookie dough, stopping the machine to scrape down the inside of the canister at least once.
3. Scrape down and remove the blade. With clean and wet hands, form the bean paste into two 4-inch patties for the small batch, three 4-inch patties for the medium, or four 4-inch patties for the large batch. Generously coat the patties on both sides with olive oil spray.
4. Set them in the basket with some space between them and air-fry undisturbed for 12 minutes, or until lightly brown and crisp at the edges. The tops of the burgers will feel firm to the touch.
5. Use a nonstick-safe spatula, and perhaps a flatware fork for balance, to transfer the burgers to a cutting board. Set the buns cut side down in the basket in one layer (working in batches as necessary) and air-fry undisturbed for 1 minute, to toast a bit and warm up. Serve the burgers warm in the buns.

Chicken Apple Brie Melt

Servings: 3

Cooking Time: 13 Minutes

Ingredients:

- 3 5- to 6-ounce boneless skinless chicken breasts
- Vegetable oil spray
- 1½ teaspoons Dried herbes de Provence
- 3 ounces Brie, rind removed, thinly sliced
- 6 Thin cored apple slices
- 3 French rolls (gluten-free, if a concern)
- 2 tablespoons Dijon mustard (gluten-free, if a concern)

Directions:

1. Preheat the air fryer to 375°F .
2. Lightly coat all sides of the chicken breasts with vegetable oil spray. Sprinkle the breasts evenly with the herbes de Provence.
3. When the machine is at temperature, set the breasts in the basket and air-fry undisturbed for 10 minutes.
4. Top the chicken breasts with the apple slices, then the cheese. Air-fry undisturbed for 2 minutes, or until the cheese is melty and bubbling.
5. Use a nonstick-safe spatula and kitchen tongs, for balance, to transfer the breasts to a cutting board. Set the rolls in the basket and air-fry for 1 minute to warm through. (Putting them in the machine without splitting them keeps the insides very soft while the outside gets a little crunchy.)
6. Transfer the rolls to the cutting board. Split them open lengthwise, then spread 1 teaspoon mustard on each cut side. Set a prepared chicken breast on the bottom of a roll and close with its top, repeating as necessary to make additional sandwiches. Serve warm.

Chicken Spiedies

Servings: 3

Cooking Time: 12 Minutes

Ingredients:

- 1¼ pounds Boneless skinless chicken thighs, trimmed of any fat blobs and cut into 2-inch pieces
- 3 tablespoons Red wine vinegar
- 2 tablespoons Olive oil
- 2 tablespoons Minced fresh mint leaves
- 2 tablespoons Minced fresh parsley leaves
- 2 teaspoons Minced fresh dill fronds
- ¾ teaspoon Fennel seeds
- ¾ teaspoon Table salt
- Up to a ¼ teaspoon Red pepper flakes
- 3 Long soft rolls, such as hero, hoagie, or Italian sub rolls (gluten-free, if a concern), split open lengthwise
- 4½ tablespoons Regular or low-fat mayonnaise (not fat-free; gluten-free, if a concern)
- 1½ tablespoons Distilled white vinegar
- 1½ teaspoons Ground black pepper

Directions:

1. Mix the chicken, vinegar, oil, mint, parsley, dill, fennel seeds, salt, and red pepper flakes in a zip-closed plastic bag. Seal, gently massage the marinade ingredients into the meat, and refrigerate for at least 2 hours or up to 6 hours. (Longer than that and the meat can turn rubbery.)
2. Set the plastic bag out on the counter (to make the contents a little less frigid). Preheat the air fryer to 400°F.
3. When the machine is at temperature, use kitchen tongs to set the chicken thighs in the basket (discard any remaining marinade) and air-fry undisturbed for 6 minutes. Turn the thighs over and continue air-frying undisturbed for 6 minutes more, until well browned, cooked through, and even a little crunchy.
4. Dump the contents of the basket onto a wire rack and cool for 2 or 3 minutes. Divide the chicken evenly between the rolls. Whisk the mayonnaise, vinegar, and black pepper in a small bowl until smooth. Drizzle this sauce over the chicken pieces in the rolls.

Thai-style Pork Sliders

Servings: 4
Cooking Time: 15 Minutes

Ingredients:

- 11 ounces Ground pork
- 2½ tablespoons Very thinly sliced scallions, white and green parts
- 4 teaspoons Minced peeled fresh ginger
- 2½ teaspoons Fish sauce (gluten-free, if a concern)
- 2 teaspoons Thai curry paste (see the headnote; gluten-free, if a concern)
- 2 teaspoons Light brown sugar
- ¾ teaspoon Ground black pepper
- 4 Slider buns (gluten-free, if a concern)

Directions:

1. Preheat the air fryer to 375°F .
2. Gently mix the pork, scallions, ginger, fish sauce, curry paste, brown sugar, and black pepper in a bowl until well combined. With clean, wet hands, form about ⅓ cup of the pork mixture into a slider about 2½ inches in diameter. Repeat until you use up all the meat—3 sliders for the small batch, 4 for the medium, and 6 for the large. (Keep wetting your hands to help the patties adhere.)
3. When the machine is at temperature, set the sliders in the basket in one layer. Air-fry undisturbed for 14 minutes, or until the sliders are golden brown and caramelized at their edges and an instant-read meat thermometer inserted into the center of a slider registers 160°F.
4. Use a nonstick-safe spatula, and perhaps a flatware fork for balance, to transfer the sliders to a cutting board. Set the buns cut side down in the basket in one layer (working in batches as necessary) and air-fry undisturbed for 1 minute, to toast a bit and warm up. Serve the sliders warm in the buns.

Perfect Burgers

Servings: 3
Cooking Time: 13 Minutes

Ingredients:

- 1 pound 2 ounces 90% lean ground beef
- 1½ tablespoons Worcestershire sauce (gluten-free, if a concern)
- ½ teaspoon Ground black pepper
- 3 Hamburger buns (gluten-free if a concern), split open

Directions:

1. Preheat the air fryer to 375°F .
2. Gently mix the ground beef, Worcestershire sauce, and pepper in a bowl until well combined but preserving as much of the meat's fibers as possible. Divide this mixture into two 5-inch patties for the small batch, three 5-inch patties for the medium, or four 5-inch patties for the large. Make a thumbprint indentation in the center of each patty, about halfway through the meat.
3. Set the patties in the basket in one layer with some space between them. Air-fry undisturbed for 10 minutes, or until an instant-read meat thermometer inserted into the center of a burger registers 160°F (a medium-well burger). You may need to add 2 minutes cooking time if the air fryer is at 360°F.
4. Use a nonstick-safe spatula, and perhaps a flatware fork for balance, to transfer the burgers to a cutting

board. Set the buns cut side down in the basket in one layer (working in batches as necessary) and air-fry undisturbed for 1 minute, to toast a bit and warm up. Serve the burgers in the warm buns.

Sausage And Pepper Heros

Servings: 3

Cooking Time: 11 Minutes

Ingredients:

- 3 links (about 9 ounces total) Sweet Italian sausages (gluten-free, if a concern)
- 1½ Medium red or green bell pepper(s), stemmed, cored, and cut into ½-inch-wide strips
- 1 medium Yellow or white onion(s), peeled, halved, and sliced into thin half-moons
- 3 Long soft rolls, such as hero, hoagie, or Italian sub rolls (gluten-free, if a concern), split open lengthwise
- For garnishing Balsamic vinegar
- For garnishing Fresh basil leaves

Directions:

1. Preheat the air fryer to 400°F.
2. When the machine is at temperature, set the sausage links in the basket in one layer and air-fry undisturbed for 5 minutes.
3. Add the pepper strips and onions. Continue air-frying, tossing and rearranging everything about once every minute, for 5 minutes, or until the sausages are browned and an instant-read meat thermometer inserted into one of the links registers 160°F.
4. Use a nonstick-safe spatula and kitchen tongs to transfer the sausages and vegetables to a cutting board. Set the rolls cut side down in the basket in one layer (working in batches as necessary) and air-fry undisturbed for 1 minute, to toast the rolls a bit and warm them up. Set 1 sausage with some pepper strips and onions in each warm roll, sprinkle balsamic vinegar over the sandwich fillings, and garnish with basil leaves.

Dijon Thyme Burgers

Servings: 3

Cooking Time: 18 Minutes

Ingredients:

- 1 pound lean ground beef
- ⅓ cup panko breadcrumbs
- ¼ cup finely chopped onion
- 3 tablespoons Dijon mustard
- 1 tablespoon chopped fresh thyme
- 4 teaspoons Worcestershire sauce
- 1 teaspoon salt
- freshly ground black pepper
- Topping (optional):
- 2 tablespoons Dijon mustard
- 1 tablespoon dark brown sugar
- 1 teaspoon Worcestershire sauce
- 4 ounces sliced Swiss cheese, optional

Directions:

1. Combine all the burger ingredients together in a large bowl and mix well. Divide the meat into 4 equal portions and then form the burgers, being careful not to over-handle the meat. One good way to do this is to throw the meat back and forth from one hand to another, packing the meat each time you catch it. Flatten the balls into patties, making an indentation in the center of each patty with your thumb (this will help it stay flat as it cooks) and flattening the sides of the burgers so that they will fit nicely into the air fryer basket.
2. Preheat the air fryer to 370°F.
3. If you don't have room for all four burgers, air-fry two or three burgers at a time for 8 minutes. Flip the burgers over and air-fry for another 6 minutes.
4. While the burgers are cooking combine the Dijon mustard, dark brown sugar, and Worcestershire sauce in a small bowl and mix well. This optional topping to the burgers really adds a boost of flavor at the end. Spread the Dijon topping evenly on each burger. If you cooked the burgers in batches, return the first batch to the cooker at this time – it's ok to place the fourth burger on top of the others in the center of the basket. Air-fry the burgers for another 3 minutes.
5. Finally, if desired, top each burger with a slice of Swiss cheese. Lower the air fryer temperature to 330°F and air-fry for another minute to melt the cheese. Serve the burgers on toasted brioche buns, dressed the way you like them.

Thanksgiving Turkey Sandwiches

Servings: 3

Cooking Time: 10 Minutes

Ingredients:

- 1½ cups Herb-seasoned stuffing mix (not cornbread-style; gluten-free, if a concern)
- 1 Large egg white(s)
- 2 tablespoons Water
- 3 5- to 6-ounce turkey breast cutlets
- Vegetable oil spray
- 4½ tablespoons Purchased cranberry sauce, preferably whole berry
- ⅛ teaspoon Ground cinnamon
- ⅛ teaspoon Ground dried ginger
- 4½ tablespoons Regular, low-fat, or fat-free mayonnaise (gluten-free, if a concern)
- 6 tablespoons Shredded Brussels sprouts
- 3 Kaiser rolls (gluten-free, if a concern), split open

Directions:

1. Preheat the air fryer to 375°F .
2. Put the stuffing mix in a heavy zip-closed bag, seal it, lay it flat on your counter, and roll a rolling pin over the bag to crush the stuffing mix to the consistency of rough sand. (Or you can pulse the stuffing mix to the desired consistency in a food processor.)
3. Set up and fill two shallow soup plates or small pie plates on your counter: one for the egg white(s), whisked with the water until foamy; and one for the ground stuffing mix.
4. Dip a cutlet in the egg white mixture, coating both sides and letting any excess egg white slip back into the rest. Set the cutlet in the ground stuffing mix and coat it evenly on both sides, pressing gently to coat well on both sides. Lightly coat the cutlet on both sides with vegetable oil spray, set it aside, and continue dipping and coating the remaining cutlets in the same way.
5. Set the cutlets in the basket and air-fry undisturbed for 10 minutes, or until crisp and brown. Use kitchen tongs to transfer the cutlets to a wire rack to cool for a few minutes.
6. Meanwhile, stir the cranberry sauce with the cinnamon and ginger in a small bowl. Mix the shredded Brussels sprouts and mayonnaise in a second bowl until the vegetable is evenly coated.
7. Build the sandwiches by spreading about 1½ tablespoons of the cranberry mixture on the cut side of the bottom half of each roll. Set a cutlet on top, then spread about 3 tablespoons of the Brussels sprouts mixture evenly over the cutlet. Set the other half of the roll on top and serve warm.

Lamb Burgers

Servings: 3

Cooking Time: 17 Minutes

Ingredients:

- 1 pound 2 ounces Ground lamb
- 3 tablespoons Crumbled feta
- 1 teaspoon Minced garlic
- 1 teaspoon Tomato paste
- ¾ teaspoon Ground coriander
- ¾ teaspoon Ground dried ginger
- Up to ⅛ teaspoon Cayenne
- Up to a ⅛ teaspoon Table salt (optional)
- 3 Kaiser rolls or hamburger buns (gluten-free, if a concern), split open

Directions:

1. Preheat the air fryer to 375°F .
2. Gently mix the ground lamb, feta, garlic, tomato paste, coriander, ginger, cayenne, and salt (if using) in a bowl until well combined, trying to keep the bits of cheese intact. Form this mixture into two 5-inch patties for the small batch, three 5-inch patties for the medium, or four 5-inch patties for the large.
3. Set the patties in the basket in one layer and air-fry undisturbed for 16 minutes, or until an instant-read meat thermometer inserted into one burger registers 160°F. (The cheese is not an issue with the temperature probe in this recipe as it was for the Inside-Out Cheeseburgers, because the feta is so well mixed into the ground meat.)
4. Use a nonstick-safe spatula, and perhaps a flatware fork for balance, to transfer the burgers to a cutting board. Set the buns cut side down in the basket in one layer (working in batches as necessary) and air-fry undisturbed for 1 minute, to toast a bit and warm up. Serve the burgers warm in the buns.

Chicken Club Sandwiches

Servings: 3

Cooking Time: 15 Minutes

Ingredients:

- 3 5- to 6-ounce boneless skinless chicken breasts
- 6 Thick-cut bacon strips (gluten-free, if a concern)
- 3 Long soft rolls, such as hero, hoagie, or Italian sub rolls (gluten-free, if a concern)
- 3 tablespoons Regular, low-fat, or fat-free mayonnaise (gluten-free, if a concern)
- 3 Lettuce leaves, preferably romaine or iceberg
- 6 ¼-inch-thick tomato slices

Directions:

1. Preheat the air fryer to 375°F .
2. Wrap each chicken breast with 2 strips of bacon, spiraling the bacon around the meat, slightly overlapping the strips on each revolution. Start the second strip of bacon farther down the breast but on a line with the start of the first strip so they both end at a lined-up point on the chicken breast.
3. When the machine is at temperature, set the wrapped breasts bacon-seam side down in the basket with space between them. Air-fry undisturbed for 12 minutes, until the bacon is browned, crisp, and cooked through and an instant-read meat thermometer inserted into the center of a breast registers 165°F. You may need to add 2 minutes in the air fryer if the temperature is at 360°F.
4. Use kitchen tongs to transfer the breasts to a wire rack. Split the rolls open lengthwise and set them cut side down in the basket. Air-fry for 1 minute, or until warmed through.
5. Use kitchen tongs to transfer the rolls to a cutting board. Spread 1 tablespoon mayonnaise on the cut side of one half of each roll. Top with a chicken breast, lettuce leaf, and tomato slice. Serve warm.

Inside-out Cheeseburgers

Servings: 3

Cooking Time: 9-11 Minutes

Ingredients:

- 1 pound 2 ounces 90% lean ground beef
- ¾ teaspoon Dried oregano
- ¾ teaspoon Table salt
- ¾ teaspoon Ground black pepper
- ¼ teaspoon Garlic powder
- 6 tablespoons (about 1½ ounces) Shredded Cheddar, Swiss, or other semi-firm cheese, or a purchased blend of shredded cheeses
- 3 Hamburger buns (gluten-free, if a concern), split open

Directions:

1. Preheat the air fryer to 375°F .
2. Gently mix the ground beef, oregano, salt, pepper, and garlic powder in a bowl until well combined without turning the mixture to mush. Form it into two 6-inch patties for the small batch, three for the medium, or four for the large.
3. Place 2 tablespoons of the shredded cheese in the center of each patty. With clean hands, fold the sides of the patty up to cover the cheese, then pick it up and roll it gently into a ball to seal the cheese inside. Gently press it back into a 5-inch burger without letting any cheese squish out. Continue filling and preparing more burgers, as needed.
4. Place the burgers in the basket in one layer and air-fry undisturbed for 8 minutes for medium or 10 minutes for well-done. (An instant-read meat thermometer won't work for these burgers because it will hit the mostly melted cheese inside and offer a hotter temperature than the surrounding meat.)
5. Use a nonstick-safe spatula, and perhaps a flatware fork for balance, to transfer the burgers to a cutting board. Set the buns cut side down in the basket in one layer (working in batches as necessary) and air-fry undisturbed for 1 minute, to toast a bit and warm up. Cool the burgers a few minutes more, then serve them warm in the buns.

Provolone Stuffed Meatballs

Servings: 4

Cooking Time: 12 Minutes

Ingredients:

- 1 tablespoon olive oil
- 1 small onion, very finely chopped
- 1 to 2 cloves garlic, minced
- ¾ pound ground beef
- ¾ pound ground pork
- ¾ cup breadcrumbs
- ¼ cup grated Parmesan cheese
- ¼ cup finely chopped fresh parsley (or 1 tablespoon dried parsley)
- ½ teaspoon dried oregano
- 1½ teaspoons salt
- freshly ground black pepper
- 2 eggs, lightly beaten
- 5 ounces sharp or aged provolone cheese, cut into 1-inch cubes

Directions:

1. Preheat a skillet over medium-high heat. Add the oil and cook the onion and garlic until tender, but not browned.
2. Transfer the onion and garlic to a large bowl and add the beef, pork, breadcrumbs, Parmesan cheese, parsley, oregano, salt, pepper and eggs. Mix well until all the ingredients are combined. Divide the mixture into 12 evenly sized balls. Make one meatball at a time, by pressing a hole in the meatball mixture with your finger and pushing a piece of provolone cheese into the hole. Mold the meat back into a ball, enclosing the cheese.
3. Preheat the air fryer to 380°F.
4. Working in two batches, transfer six of the meatballs to the air fryer basket and air-fry for 12 minutes, shaking the basket and turning the meatballs a couple of times during the cooking process. Repeat with the remaining six meatballs. You can pop the first batch of meatballs into the air fryer for the last two minutes of cooking to re-heat them. Serve warm.

Chicken Gyros

Servings: 4

Cooking Time: 14 Minutes

Ingredients:

- 4 4- to 5-ounce boneless skinless chicken thighs, trimmed of any fat blobs
- 2 tablespoons Lemon juice
- 2 tablespoons Red wine vinegar
- 2 tablespoons Olive oil
- 2 teaspoons Dried oregano
- 2 teaspoons Minced garlic
- 1 teaspoon Table salt
- 1 teaspoon Ground black pepper
- 4 Pita pockets (gluten-free, if a concern)
- ½ cup Chopped tomatoes
- ½ cup Bottled regular, low-fat, or fat-free ranch dressing (gluten-free, if a concern)

Directions:

1. Mix the thighs, lemon juice, vinegar, oil, oregano, garlic, salt, and pepper in a zip-closed bag. Seal, gently massage the marinade into the meat through the plastic, and refrigerate for at least 2 hours or up to 6 hours. (Longer than that and the meat can turn rubbery.)
2. Set the plastic bag out on the counter (to make the contents a little less frigid). Preheat the air fryer to 375°F .
3. When the machine is at temperature, use kitchen tongs to place the thighs in the basket in one layer. Discard the marinade. Air-fry the chicken thighs undisturbed for 12 minutes, or until browned and an instant-read meat thermometer inserted into the thickest part of one thigh registers 165°F. You may need to air-fry the chicken 2 minutes longer if the machine's temperature is 360°F.
4. Use kitchen tongs to transfer the thighs to a cutting board. Cool for 5 minutes, then set one thigh in each of the pita pockets. Top each with 2 tablespoons chopped tomatoes and 2 tablespoons dressing. Serve warm.

Philly Cheesesteak Sandwiches

Servings: 3

Cooking Time: 9 Minutes

Ingredients:

- ¾ pound Shaved beef
- 1 tablespoon Worcestershire sauce (gluten-free, if a concern)
- ¼ teaspoon Garlic powder
- ¼ teaspoon Mild paprika
- 6 tablespoons (1½ ounces) Frozen bell pepper strips (do not thaw)
- 2 slices, broken into rings Very thin yellow or white medium onion slice(s)
- 6 ounces (6 to 8 slices) Provolone cheese slices
- 3 Long soft rolls such as hero, hoagie, or Italian sub rolls, or hot dog buns (gluten-free, if a concern), split open lengthwise

Directions:

1. Preheat the air fryer to 400°F.
2. When the machine is at temperature, spread the shaved beef in the basket, leaving a ½-inch perimeter around the meat for good air flow. Sprinkle the meat with the Worcestershire sauce, paprika, and garlic powder. Spread the peppers and onions on top of the meat.
3. Air-fry undisturbed for 6 minutes, or until cooked through. Set the cheese on top of the meat. Continue air-frying undisturbed for 3 minutes, or until the cheese has melted.
4. Use kitchen tongs to divide the meat and cheese layers in the basket between the rolls or buns. Serve hot.

Eggplant Parmesan Subs

Servings: 2

Cooking Time: 13 Minutes

Ingredients:

- 4 Peeled eggplant slices (about ½ inch thick and 3 inches in diameter)
- Olive oil spray
- 2 tablespoons plus 2 teaspoons Jarred pizza sauce, any variety except creamy
- ¼ cup (about ⅔ ounce) Finely grated Parmesan cheese
- 2 Small, long soft rolls, such as hero, hoagie, or Italian sub rolls (gluten-free, if a concern), split open lengthwise

Directions:

1. Preheat the air fryer to 350°F .
2. When the machine is at temperature, coat both sides of the eggplant slices with olive oil spray. Set them in the basket in one layer and air-fry undisturbed for 10 minutes, until lightly browned and softened.
3. Increase the machine's temperature to 375°F (or 370°F, if that's the closest setting—unless the machine is already at 360°F, in which case leave it alone). Top each eggplant slice with 2 teaspoons pizza sauce, then 1 tablespoon cheese. Air-fry undisturbed for 2 minutes, or until the cheese has melted.
4. Use a nonstick-safe spatula, and perhaps a flatware fork for balance, to transfer the eggplant slices cheese side up to a cutting board. Set the roll(s) cut side down in the basket in one layer (working in batches as necessary) and air-fry undisturbed for 1 minute, to toast the rolls a bit and warm them up. Set 2 eggplant slices in each warm roll.

Reuben Sandwiches

Servings: 2

Cooking Time: 11 Minutes

Ingredients:

- ½ pound Sliced deli corned beef
- 4 teaspoons Regular or low-fat mayonnaise (not fat-free)
- 4 Rye bread slices
- 2 tablespoons plus 2 teaspoons Russian dressing
- ½ cup Purchased sauerkraut, squeezed by the handful over the sink to get rid of excess moisture
- 2 ounces (2 to 4 slices) Swiss cheese slices (optional)

Directions:

1. Set the corned beef in the basket, slip the basket into the machine, and heat the air fryer to 400°F. Air-fry undisturbed for 3 minutes from the time the basket is put in the machine, just to warm up the meat.

2. Use kitchen tongs to transfer the corned beef to a cutting board. Spread 1 teaspoon mayonnaise on one side of each slice of rye bread, rubbing the mayonnaise into the bread with a small flatware knife.
3. Place the bread slices mayonnaise side down on a cutting board. Spread the Russian dressing over the "dry" side of each slice. For one sandwich, top one slice of bread with the corned beef, sauerkraut, and cheese (if using). For two sandwiches, top two slices of bread each with half of the corned beef, sauerkraut, and cheese (if using). Close the sandwiches with the remaining bread, setting it mayonnaise side up on top.
4. Set the sandwich(es) in the basket and air-fry undisturbed for 8 minutes, or until browned and crunchy.
5. Use a nonstick-safe spatula, and perhaps a flatware fork for balance, to transfer the sandwich(es) to a cutting board. Cool for 2 or 3 minutes before slicing in half and serving.

Inside Out Cheeseburgers

Servings: 2
Cooking Time: 20 Minutes

Ingredients:

- ¾ pound lean ground beef
- 3 tablespoons minced onion
- 4 teaspoons ketchup
- 2 teaspoons yellow mustard
- salt and freshly ground black pepper
- 4 slices of Cheddar cheese, broken into smaller pieces
- 8 hamburger dill pickle chips

Directions:

1. Combine the ground beef, minced onion, ketchup, mustard, salt and pepper in a large bowl. Mix well to thoroughly combine the ingredients. Divide the meat into four equal portions.
2. To make the stuffed burgers, flatten each portion of meat into a thin patty. Place 4 pickle chips and half of the cheese onto the center of two of the patties, leaving a rim around the edge of the patty exposed. Place the remaining two patties on top of the first and press the meat together firmly, sealing the edges tightly. With the burgers on a flat surface, press the sides of the burger with the palm of your hand to create a straight edge. This will help keep the stuffing inside the burger while it cooks.
3. Preheat the air fryer to 370°F.
4. Place the burgers inside the air fryer basket and air-fry for 20 minutes, flipping the burgers over halfway through the cooking time.
5. Serve the cheeseburgers on buns with lettuce and tomato.

Mexican Cheeseburgers

Servings: 4
Cooking Time: 22 Minutes

Ingredients:

- 1¼ pounds ground beef
- ¼ cup finely chopped onion
- ½ cup crushed yellow corn tortilla chips
- 1 (1.25-ounce) packet taco seasoning
- ¼ cup canned diced green chilies
- 1 egg, lightly beaten
- 4 ounces pepper jack cheese, grated
- 4 (12-inch) flour tortillas
- shredded lettuce, sour cream, guacamole, salsa (for topping)

Directions:

1. Combine the ground beef, minced onion, crushed tortilla chips, taco seasoning, green chilies, and egg in a large bowl. Mix thoroughly until combined – your hands are good tools for this. Divide the meat into four equal portions and shape each portion into an oval-shaped burger.
2. Preheat the air fryer to 370°F.
3. Air-fry the burgers for 18 minutes, turning them over halfway through the cooking time. Divide the cheese between the burgers, lower fryer to 340°F and air-fry for an additional 4 minutes to melt the cheese. (This will give you a burger that is medium-well. If you prefer your cheeseburger medium-rare, shorten the cooking time to about 15 minutes and then add the cheese and proceed with the recipe.)

4. While the burgers are cooking, warm the tortillas wrapped in aluminum foil in a 350°F oven, or in a skillet with a little oil over medium-high heat for a couple of minutes. Keep the tortillas warm until the burgers are ready.

5. To assemble the burgers, spread sour cream over three quarters of the tortillas and top each with some shredded lettuce and salsa. Place the Mexican cheeseburgers on the lettuce and top with guacamole. Fold the tortillas around the burger, starting with the bottom and then folding the sides in over the top. (A little sour cream can help hold the seam of the tortilla together.) Serve immediately.

Salmon Burgers

Servings: 3

Cooking Time: 8 Minutes

Ingredients:

- 1 pound 2 ounces Skinless salmon fillet, preferably fattier Atlantic salmon
- 1½ tablespoons Minced chives or the green part of a scallion
- ½ cup Plain panko bread crumbs (gluten-free, if a concern)
- 1½ teaspoons Dijon mustard (gluten-free, if a concern)
- 1½ teaspoons Drained and rinsed capers, minced
- 1½ teaspoons Lemon juice
- ¼ teaspoon Table salt
- ¼ teaspoon Ground black pepper
- Vegetable oil spray

Directions:

1. Preheat the air fryer to 375°F .

2. Cut the salmon into pieces that will fit in a food processor. Cover and pulse until coarsely chopped. Add the chives and pulse to combine, until the fish is ground but not a paste. Scrape down and remove the blade. Scrape the salmon mixture into a bowl. Add the bread crumbs, mustard, capers, lemon juice, salt, and pepper. Stir gently until well combined.

3. Use clean and dry hands to form the mixture into two 5-inch patties for a small batch, three 5-inch patties for a medium batch, or four 5-inch patties for a large one.

4. Coat both sides of each patty with vegetable oil spray. Set them in the basket in one layer and air-fry undisturbed for 8 minutes, or until browned and an instant-read meat thermometer inserted into the center of a burger registers 145°F.

5. Use a nonstick-safe spatula, and perhaps a flatware fork for balance, to transfer the burgers to a wire rack. Cool for 2 or 3 minutes before serving.

Crunchy Falafel Balls

Servings: 8

Cooking Time: 16 Minutes

Ingredients:

- 2½ cups Drained and rinsed canned chickpeas
- ¼ cup Olive oil
- 3 tablespoons All-purpose flour
- 1½ teaspoons Dried oregano
- 1½ teaspoons Dried sage leaves
- 1½ teaspoons Dried thyme
- ¾ teaspoon Table salt
- Olive oil spray

Directions:

1. Preheat the air fryer to 400°F.

2. Place the chickpeas, olive oil, flour, oregano, sage, thyme, and salt in a food processor. Cover and process into a paste, stopping the machine at least once to scrape down the inside of the canister.

3. Scrape down and remove the blade. Using clean, wet hands, form 2 tablespoons of the paste into a ball, then continue making 9 more balls for a small batch, 15 more for a medium one, and 19 more for a large batch. Generously coat the balls in olive oil spray.

4. Set the balls in the basket in one layer with a little space between them and air-fry undisturbed for 16 minutes, or until well browned and crisp.

5. Dump the contents of the basket onto a wire rack. Cool for 5 minutes before serving.

Chicken Saltimbocca Sandwiches

Servings: 3

Cooking Time: 11 Minutes

Ingredients:

- 3 5- to 6-ounce boneless skinless chicken breasts
- 6 Thin prosciutto slices
- 6 Provolone cheese slices
- 3 Long soft rolls, such as hero, hoagie, or Italian sub rolls (gluten-free, if a concern), split open lengthwise
- 3 tablespoons Pesto, purchased or homemade (see the headnote)

Directions:

1. Preheat the air fryer to 400°F.
2. Wrap each chicken breast with 2 prosciutto slices, spiraling the prosciutto around the breast and overlapping the slices a bit to cover the breast. The prosciutto will stick to the chicken more readily than bacon does.
3. When the machine is at temperature, set the wrapped chicken breasts in the basket and air-fry undisturbed for 10 minutes, or until the prosciutto is frizzled and the chicken is cooked through.
4. Overlap 2 cheese slices on each breast. Air-fry undisturbed for 1 minute, or until melted. Take the basket out of the machine.
5. Smear the insides of the rolls with the pesto, then use kitchen tongs to put a wrapped and cheesy chicken breast in each roll.

Chili Cheese Dogs

Servings: 3

Cooking Time: 12 Minutes

Ingredients:

- ¾ pound Lean ground beef
- 1½ tablespoons Chile powder
- 1 cup plus 2 tablespoons Jarred sofrito
- 3 Hot dogs (gluten-free, if a concern)
- 3 Hot dog buns (gluten-free, if a concern), split open lengthwise
- 3 tablespoons Finely chopped scallion
- 9 tablespoons (a little more than 2 ounces) Shredded Cheddar cheese

Directions:

1. Crumble the ground beef into a medium or large saucepan set over medium heat. Brown well, stirring often to break up the clumps. Add the chile powder and cook for 30 seconds, stirring the whole time. Stir in the sofrito and bring to a simmer. Reduce the heat to low and simmer, stirring occasionally, for 5 minutes. Keep warm.
2. Preheat the air fryer to 400°F.
3. When the machine is at temperature, put the hot dogs in the basket and air-fry undisturbed for 10 minutes, or until the hot dogs are bubbling and blistered, even a little crisp.
4. Use kitchen tongs to put the hot dogs in the buns. Top each with a ½ cup of the ground beef mixture, 1 tablespoon of the minced scallion, and 3 tablespoons of the cheese. (The scallion should go under the cheese so it superheats and wilts a bit.) Set the filled hot dog buns in the basket and air-fry undisturbed for 2 minutes, or until the cheese has melted.
5. Remove the basket from the machine. Cool the chili cheese dogs in the basket for 5 minutes before serving.

Fish And Seafood Recipes

Garlic And Dill Salmon

Servings: 2
Cooking Time: 8 Minutes

Ingredients:

- 12 ounces salmon filets with skin
- 2 tablespoons melted butter
- 1 tablespoon extra-virgin olive oil
- 2 garlic cloves, minced
- 1 tablespoon fresh dill
- ½ teaspoon sea salt
- ½ lemon

Directions:

1. Pat the salmon dry with paper towels.
2. In a small bowl, mix together the melted butter, olive oil, garlic, and dill.
3. Sprinkle the top of the salmon with sea salt. Brush all sides of the salmon with the garlic and dill butter.
4. Preheat the air fryer to 350°F.
5. Place the salmon, skin side down, in the air fryer basket. Cook for 6 to 8 minutes, or until the fish flakes in the center.
6. Remove the salmon and plate on a serving platter. Squeeze fresh lemon over the top of the salmon. Serve immediately.

Crab Cakes On A Budget

Servings: 4
Cooking Time: 12 Minutes

Ingredients:

- 8 ounces imitation crabmeat
- 4 ounces leftover cooked fish (such as cod, pollock, or haddock)
- 2 tablespoons minced green onion
- 2 tablespoons minced celery
- ¾ cup crushed saltine cracker crumbs
- 2 tablespoons light mayonnaise
- 1 teaspoon prepared yellow mustard
- 1 tablespoon Worcestershire sauce, plus 2 teaspoons
- 2 teaspoons dried parsley flakes
- ½ teaspoon dried dill weed, crushed
- ½ teaspoon garlic powder
- ½ teaspoon Old Bay Seasoning
- ½ cup panko breadcrumbs
- oil for misting or cooking spray

Directions:

1. Use knives or a food processor to finely shred crabmeat and fish.
2. In a large bowl, combine all ingredients except panko and oil. Stir well.
3. Shape into 8 small, fat patties.
4. Carefully roll patties in panko crumbs to coat. Spray both sides with oil or cooking spray.
5. Place patties in air fryer basket and cook at 390°F for 12 minutes or until golden brown and crispy.

Butternut Squash–wrapped Halibut Fillets

Servings:3
Cooking Time: 11 Minutes

Ingredients:

- 15 Long spiralized peeled and seeded butternut squash strands
- 3 5- to 6-ounce skinless halibut fillets
- 3 tablespoons Butter, melted
- ¾ teaspoon Mild paprika
- ¾ teaspoon Table salt
- ¾ teaspoon Ground black pepper

Directions:

1. Preheat the air fryer to 375°F .
2. Hold 5 long butternut squash strands together and wrap them around a fillet. Set it aside and wrap any remaining fillet(s).
3. Mix the melted butter, paprika, salt, and pepper in a small bowl. Brush this mixture over the squash-wrapped fillets on all sides.
4. When the machine is at temperature, set the fillets in the basket with as much air space between them as possible. Air-fry undisturbed for 10 minutes, or until the squash strands have browned but not burned. If the

machine is at 360°F, you may need to add 1 minute to the cooking time. In any event, watch the fish carefully after the 8-minute mark.

5. Use a nonstick-safe spatula to gently transfer the fillets to a serving platter or plates. Cool for only a minute or so before serving.

Black Cod With Grapes, Fennel, Pecans And Kale

Servings: 2

Cooking Time: 15 Minutes

Ingredients:

- 2 (6- to 8-ounce) fillets of black cod (or sablefish)
- salt and freshly ground black pepper
- olive oil
- 1 cup grapes, halved
- 1 small bulb fennel, sliced ¼-inch thick
- ½ cup pecans
- 3 cups shredded kale
- 2 teaspoons white balsamic vinegar or white wine vinegar
- 2 tablespoons extra virgin olive oil

Directions:

1. Preheat the air fryer to 400°F.
2. Season the cod fillets with salt and pepper and drizzle, brush or spray a little olive oil on top. Place the fish, presentation side up (skin side down), into the air fryer basket. Air-fry for 10 minutes.
3. When the fish has finished cooking, remove the fillets to a side plate and loosely tent with foil to rest.
4. Toss the grapes, fennel and pecans in a bowl with a drizzle of olive oil and season with salt and pepper. Add the grapes, fennel and pecans to the air fryer basket and air-fry for 5 minutes at 400°F, shaking the basket once during the cooking time.
5. Transfer the grapes, fennel and pecans to a bowl with the kale. Dress the kale with the balsamic vinegar and olive oil, season to taste with salt and pepper and serve along side the cooked fish.

Salmon Puttanesca En Papillotte With Zucchini

Servings: 2

Cooking Time: 17 Minutes

Ingredients:

- 1 small zucchini, sliced into ¼-inch thick half moons
- 1 teaspoon olive oil
- salt and freshly ground black pepper
- 2 (5-ounce) salmon fillets
- 1 beefsteak tomato, chopped (about 1 cup)
- 1 tablespoon capers, rinsed
- 10 black olives, pitted and sliced
- 2 tablespoons dry vermouth or white wine 2 tablespoons butter
- ¼ cup chopped fresh basil, chopped

Directions:

1. Preheat the air fryer to 400°F.
2. Toss the zucchini with the olive oil, salt and freshly ground black pepper. Transfer the zucchini into the air fryer basket and air-fry for 5 minutes, shaking the basket once or twice during the cooking process.
3. Cut out 2 large rectangles of parchment paper – about 13-inches by 15-inches each. Divide the air-fried zucchini between the two pieces of parchment paper, placing the vegetables in the center of each rectangle.
4. Place a fillet of salmon on each pile of zucchini. Season the fish very well with salt and pepper. Toss the tomato, capers, olives and vermouth (or white wine) together in a bowl. Divide the tomato mixture between the two fish packages, placing it on top of the fish fillets and pouring any juice out of the bowl onto the fish. Top each fillet with a tablespoon of butter.
5. Fold up each parchment square. Bring two edges together and fold them over a few times, leaving some space above the fish. Twist the open sides together and upwards so they can serve as handles for the packet, but don't let them extend beyond the top of the air fryer basket.
6. Place the two packages into the air fryer and air-fry at 400°F for 12 minutes. The packages should be puffed up and slightly browned when fully cooked. Once cooked, let the fish sit in the parchment for 2 minutes.
7. Serve the fish in the parchment paper, or if desired, remove the parchment paper before serving. Garnish with a little fresh basil.

Tuna Patties With Dill Sauce

Servings: 6

Cooking Time: 10 Minutes

Ingredients:

- Two 5-ounce cans albacore tuna, drained
- ½ teaspoon garlic powder
- 2 teaspoons dried dill, divided
- ½ teaspoon black pepper
- ½ teaspoon salt, divided
- ¼ cup minced onion
- 1 large egg
- 7 tablespoons mayonnaise, divided
- ¼ cup panko breadcrumbs
- 1 teaspoon fresh lemon juice
- ¼ teaspoon fresh lemon zest
- 6 pieces butterleaf lettuce
- 1 cup diced tomatoes

Directions:

1. In a large bowl, mix the tuna with the garlic powder, 1 teaspoon of the dried dill, the black pepper, ¼ teaspoon of the salt, and the onion. Make sure to use the back of a fork to really break up the tuna so there are no large chunks.
2. Mix in the egg and 1 tablespoon of the mayonnaise; then fold in the breadcrumbs so the tuna begins to form a thick batter that holds together.
3. Portion the tuna mixture into 6 equal patties and place on a plate lined with parchment paper in the refrigerator for at least 30 minutes. This will help the patties hold together in the air fryer.
4. When ready to cook, preheat the air fryer to 350°F.
5. Liberally spray the metal trivet that sits inside the air fryer basket with olive oil mist and place the patties onto the trivet.
6. Cook for 5 minutes, flip, and cook another 5 minutes.
7. While the patties are cooking, make the dill sauce by combining the remaining 6 tablespoons of mayonnaise with the remaining 1 teaspoon of dill, the lemon juice, the lemon zest, and the remaining ¼ teaspoon of salt. Set aside.
8. Remove the patties from the air fryer.
9. Place 1 slice of lettuce on a plate and top with the tuna patty and a tomato slice. Repeat to form the remaining servings. Drizzle the dill dressing over the top. Serve immediately.

Super Crunchy Flounder Fillets

Servings:2

Cooking Time: 6 Minutes

Ingredients:

- ½ cup All-purpose flour or tapioca flour
- 1 Large egg white(s)
- 1 tablespoon Water
- ¾ teaspoon Table salt
- 1 cup Plain panko bread crumbs (gluten-free, if a concern)
- 2 4-ounce skinless flounder fillet(s)
- Vegetable oil spray

Directions:

1. Preheat the air fryer to 400°F.
2. Set up and fill three shallow soup plates or small pie plates on your counter: one for the flour; one for the egg white(s), beaten with the water and salt until foamy; and one for the bread crumbs.
3. Dip one fillet in the flour, turning it to coat both sides. Gently shake off any excess flour, then dip the fillet in the egg white mixture, turning it to coat. Let any excess egg white mixture slip back into the rest, then set the fish in the bread crumbs. Turn it several times, gently pressing it into the crumbs to create an even crust. Generously coat both sides of the fillet with vegetable oil spray. If necessary, set it aside and continue coating the remaining fillet(s) in the same way.
4. Set the fillet(s) in the basket. If working with more than one fillet, they should not touch, although they may be quite close together, depending on the basket's size. Air-fry undisturbed for 6 minutes, or until lightly browned and crunchy.
5. Use a nonstick-safe spatula to transfer the fillet(s) to a wire rack. Cool for only a minute or two before serving.

Mahi-mahi "burrito" Fillets

Servings:3

Cooking Time: 10 Minutes

Ingredients:

- 1 Large egg white
- 1½ cups (6 ounces) Crushed corn tortilla chips (gluten-free, if a concern)
- 1 tablespoon Chile powder
- 3 5-ounce skinless mahi-mahi fillets
- 6 tablespoons Canned refried beans
- Vegetable oil spray

Directions:

1. Preheat the air fryer to 400°F.
2. Set up and fill two shallow soup plates or small pie plates on your counter: one with the egg white, beaten until foamy; and one with the crushed tortilla chips.
3. Gently rub ½ teaspoon chile powder on each side of each fillet.
4. Spread (or maybe smear) 1 tablespoon refried beans over both sides and the edges of a fillet. Dip the fillet in the egg white, turning to coat it on both sides. Let any excess egg white slip back into the rest, then set the fillet in the crushed tortilla chips. Turn several times, pressing gently to coat it evenly. Coat the fillet on all sides with the vegetable oil spray, then set it aside. Prepare the remaining fillet(s) in the same way.
5. When the machine is at temperature, set the fillets in the basket with as much air space between them as possible. Air-fry undisturbed for 10 minutes, or until crisp and browned.
6. Use a nonstick-safe spatula to transfer the fillets to a serving platter or plates. Cool for only a minute or so, then serve hot.

Classic Crab Cakes

Servings:4

Cooking Time: 10 Minutes

Ingredients:

- 10 ounces Lump crabmeat, picked over for shell and cartilage
- 6 tablespoons Plain panko bread crumbs (gluten-free, if a concern)
- 6 tablespoons Chopped drained jarred roasted red peppers
- 4 Medium scallions, trimmed and thinly sliced
- ¼ cup Regular or low-fat mayonnaise (not fat-free; gluten-free, if a concern)
- ¼ teaspoon Dried dill
- ¼ teaspoon Dried thyme
- ¼ teaspoon Onion powder
- ¼ teaspoon Table salt
- ⅛ teaspoon Celery seeds
- Up to ⅛ teaspoon Cayenne
- Vegetable oil spray

Directions:

1. Preheat the air fryer to 400°F.
2. Gently mix the crabmeat, bread crumbs, red pepper, scallion, mayonnaise, dill, thyme, onion powder, salt, celery seeds, and cayenne in a bowl until well combined.
3. Use clean and dry hands to form ½ cup of this mixture into a tightly packed 1-inch-thick, 3- to 4-inch-wide patty. Coat the top and bottom of the patty with vegetable oil spray and set it aside. Continue making 1 more patty for a small batch, 3 more for a medium batch, or 5 more for a larger one, coating them with vegetable oil spray on both sides.
4. Set the patties in one layer in the basket and air-fry undisturbed for 10 minutes, or until lightly browned and cooked through.
5. Use a nonstick-safe spatula to transfer the crab cakes to a serving platter or plates. Wait a couple of minutes before serving.

Italian Tuna Roast

Servings: 8

Cooking Time: 21 Minutes

Ingredients:

- cooking spray
- 1 tablespoon Italian seasoning
- ⅛ teaspoon ground black pepper
- 1 tablespoon extra-light olive oil
- 1 teaspoon lemon juice
- 1 tuna loin (approximately 2 pounds, 3 to 4 inches thick, large enough to fill a 6 x 6-inch baking dish)

Directions:

1. Spray baking dish with cooking spray and place in air fryer basket. Preheat air fryer to 390°F.
2. Mix together the Italian seasoning, pepper, oil, and lemon juice.
3. Using a dull table knife or butter knife, pierce top of tuna about every half inch: Insert knife into top of tuna roast and pierce almost all the way to the bottom.
4. Spoon oil mixture into each of the holes and use the knife to push seasonings into the tuna as deeply as possible.
5. Spread any remaining oil mixture on all outer surfaces of tuna.
6. Place tuna roast in baking dish and cook at 390°F for 20 minutes. Check temperature with a meat thermometer. Cook for an additional 1 minutes or until temperature reaches 145°F.
7. Remove basket from fryer and let tuna sit in basket for 10minutes.

Shrimp Patties

Servings: 4

Cooking Time: 10 Minutes

Ingredients:

- ½ pound shelled and deveined raw shrimp
- ¼ cup chopped red bell pepper
- ¼ cup chopped green onion
- ¼ cup chopped celery
- 2 cups cooked sushi rice
- ½ teaspoon garlic powder
- ½ teaspoon Old Bay Seasoning
- ½ teaspoon salt
- 2 teaspoons Worcestershire sauce
- ½ cup plain breadcrumbs
- oil for misting or cooking spray

Directions:

1. Finely chop the shrimp. You can do this in a food processor, but it takes only a few pulses. Be careful not to overprocess into mush.
2. Place shrimp in a large bowl and add all other ingredients except the breadcrumbs and oil. Stir until well combined.
3. Preheat air fryer to 390°F.
4. Shape shrimp mixture into 8 patties, no more than ½-inch thick. Roll patties in breadcrumbs and mist with oil or cooking spray.
5. Place 4 shrimp patties in air fryer basket and cook at 390°F for 10 minutes, until shrimp cooks through and outside is crispy.
6. Repeat step 5 to cook remaining shrimp patties.

Almond-crusted Fish

Servings: 4

Cooking Time: 10 Minutes

Ingredients:

- 4 4-ounce fish fillets
- ¾ cup breadcrumbs
- ¼ cup sliced almonds, crushed
- 2 tablespoons lemon juice
- ⅛ teaspoon cayenne
- salt and pepper
- ¾ cup flour
- 1 egg, beaten with 1 tablespoon water
- oil for misting or cooking spray

Directions:

1. Split fish fillets lengthwise down the center to create 8 pieces.
2. Mix breadcrumbs and almonds together and set aside.
3. Mix the lemon juice and cayenne together. Brush on all sides of fish.
4. Season fish to taste with salt and pepper.
5. Place the flour on a sheet of wax paper.
6. Roll fillets in flour, dip in egg wash, and roll in the crumb mixture.
7. Mist both sides of fish with oil or cooking spray.
8. Spray air fryer basket and lay fillets inside.
9. Cook at 390°F for 5minutes, turn fish over, and cook for an additional 5minutes or until fish is done and flakes easily.

Shrimp & Grits

Servings: 4

Cooking Time: 5 Minutes

Ingredients:

- 1 pound raw shelled shrimp, deveined (26–30 count or smaller)
- Marinade
- 2 tablespoons lemon juice
- 2 tablespoons Worcestershire sauce
- 1 tablespoon olive oil
- 1 teaspoon Old Bay Seasoning
- ½ teaspoon hot sauce
- Grits
- ¾ cup quick cooking grits (not instant)
- 3 cups water
- ½ teaspoon salt
- 1 tablespoon butter
- ½ cup chopped green bell pepper
- ½ cup chopped celery
- ½ cup chopped onion
- ½ teaspoon oregano
- ¼ teaspoon Old Bay Seasoning
- 2 ounces sharp Cheddar cheese, grated

Directions:

1. Stir together all marinade ingredients. Pour marinade over shrimp and set aside.
2. For grits, heat water and salt to boil in saucepan on stovetop. Stir in grits, lower heat to medium-low, and cook about 5minutes or until thick and done.
3. Place butter, bell pepper, celery, and onion in air fryer baking pan. Cook at 390°F for 2minutes and stir. Cook 6 or 7minutes longer, until crisp tender.
4. Add oregano and 1 teaspoon Old Bay to cooked vegetables. Stir in grits and cheese and cook at 390°F for 1 minute. Stir and cook 1 to 2minutes longer to melt cheese.
5. Remove baking pan from air fryer. Cover with plate to keep warm while shrimp cooks.
6. Drain marinade from shrimp. Place shrimp in air fryer basket and cook at 360°F for 3minutes. Stir or shake basket. Cook 2 more minutes, until done.
7. To serve, spoon grits onto plates and top with shrimp.

Spicy Fish Street Tacos With Sriracha Slaw

Servings: 2

Cooking Time: 5 Minutes

Ingredients:

- Sriracha Slaw:
- ½ cup mayonnaise
- 2 tablespoons rice vinegar
- 1 teaspoon sugar
- 2 tablespoons sriracha chili sauce
- 5 cups shredded green cabbage
- ¼ cup shredded carrots
- 2 scallions, chopped
- salt and freshly ground black pepper
- Tacos:
- ½ cup flour
- 1 teaspoon chili powder
- ½ teaspoon ground cumin
- 1 teaspoon salt
- freshly ground black pepper
- ½ teaspoon baking powder
- 1 egg, beaten
- ¼ cup milk
- 1 cup breadcrumbs
- 1 pound mahi-mahi or snapper fillets
- 1 tablespoon canola or vegetable oil
- 6 (6-inch) flour tortillas
- 1 lime, cut into wedges

Directions:

1. Start by making the sriracha slaw. Combine the mayonnaise, rice vinegar, sugar, and sriracha sauce in a large bowl. Mix well and add the green cabbage, carrots, and scallions. Toss until all the vegetables are coated with the dressing and season with salt and pepper. Refrigerate the slaw until you are ready to serve the tacos.
2. Combine the flour, chili powder, cumin, salt, pepper and baking powder in a bowl. Add the egg and milk and mix until the batter is smooth. Place the breadcrumbs in shallow dish.

3. Cut the fish fillets into 1-inch wide sticks, approximately 4-inches long. You should have about 12 fish sticks total. Dip the fish sticks into the batter, coating all sides. Let the excess batter drip off the fish and then roll them in the breadcrumbs, patting the crumbs onto all sides of the fish sticks. Set the coated fish on a plate or baking sheet until all the fish has been coated.
4. Preheat the air fryer to 400°F.
5. Spray the coated fish sticks with oil on all sides. Spray or brush the inside of the air fryer basket with oil and transfer the fish to the basket. Place as many sticks as you can in one layer, leaving a little room around each stick. Place any remaining sticks on top, perpendicular to the first layer.
6. Air-fry the fish for 3 minutes. Turn the fish sticks over and air-fry for an additional 2 minutes.
7. While the fish is air-frying, warm the tortilla shells either in a 350°F oven wrapped in foil or in a skillet with a little oil over medium-high heat for a couple minutes. Fold the tortillas in half and keep them warm until the remaining tortillas and fish are ready.
8. To assemble the tacos, place two pieces of the fish in each tortilla shell and top with the sriracha slaw. Squeeze the lime wedge over top and dig in.

Easy Scallops With Lemon Butter

Servings:3
Cooking Time: 4 Minutes

Ingredients:

- 1 tablespoon Olive oil
- 2 teaspoons Minced garlic
- 1 teaspoon Finely grated lemon zest
- ½ teaspoon Red pepper flakes
- ¼ teaspoon Table salt
- 1 pound Sea scallops
- 3 tablespoons Butter, melted
- 1½ tablespoons Lemon juice

Directions:

1. Preheat the air fryer to 400°F.
2. Gently stir the olive oil, garlic, lemon zest, red pepper flakes, and salt in a bowl. Add the scallops and stir very gently until they are evenly and well coated.
3. When the machine is at temperature, arrange the scallops in a single layer in the basket. Some may touch. Air-fry undisturbed for 4 minutes, or until the scallops are opaque and firm.
4. While the scallops cook, stir the melted butter and lemon juice in a serving bowl. When the scallops are ready, pour them from the basket into this bowl. Toss well before serving.

Stuffed Shrimp

Servings: 4
Cooking Time: 12 Minutes Per Batch

Ingredients:

- 16 tail-on shrimp, peeled and deveined (last tail section intact)
- ¾ cup crushed panko breadcrumbs
- oil for misting or cooking spray
- Stuffing
- 2 6-ounce cans lump crabmeat
- 2 tablespoons chopped shallots
- 2 tablespoons chopped green onions
- 2 tablespoons chopped celery
- 2 tablespoons chopped green bell pepper
- ½ cup crushed saltine crackers
- 1 teaspoon Old Bay Seasoning
- 1 teaspoon garlic powder
- ¼ teaspoon ground thyme
- 2 teaspoons dried parsley flakes
- 2 teaspoons fresh lemon juice
- 2 teaspoons Worcestershire sauce
- 1 egg, beaten

Directions:

1. Rinse shrimp. Remove tail section (shell) from 4 shrimp, discard, and chop the meat finely.
2. To prepare the remaining 12 shrimp, cut a deep slit down the back side so that the meat lies open flat. Do not cut all the way through.
3. Preheat air fryer to 360°F.

4. Place chopped shrimp in a large bowl with all of the stuffing ingredients and stir to combine.
5. Divide stuffing into 12 portions, about 2 tablespoons each.
6. Place one stuffing portion onto the back of each shrimp and form into a ball or oblong shape. Press firmly so that stuffing sticks together and adheres to shrimp.
7. Gently roll each stuffed shrimp in panko crumbs and mist with oil or cooking spray.
8. Place 6 shrimp in air fryer basket and cook at 360°F for 10minutes. Mist with oil or spray and cook 2 minutes longer or until stuffing cooks through inside and is crispy outside.
9. Repeat step 8 to cook remaining shrimp.

Fried Oysters

Servings:12

Cooking Time: 8 Minutes

Ingredients:

- 1½ cups All-purpose flour
- 1½ cups Yellow cornmeal
- 1½ tablespoons Cajun dried seasoning blend (for a homemade blend, see here)
- 1¼ cups, plus more if needed Amber beer, pale ale, or IPA
- 12 Large shucked oysters, any liquid drained off
- Vegetable oil spray

Directions:

1. Preheat the air fryer to 400°F.
2. Whisk ⅔ cup of the flour, ½ cup of the cornmeal, and the seasoning blend in a bowl until uniform. Set aside.
3. Whisk the remaining ⅓ cup flour and the remaining ½ cup cornmeal with the beer in a second bowl, adding more beer in dribs and drabs until the mixture is the consistency of pancake batter.
4. Using a fork, dip a shucked oyster in the beer batter, coating it thoroughly. Gently shake off any excess batter, then set the oyster in the dry mixture and turn gently to coat well and evenly. Set the coated oyster on a cutting board and continue dipping and coating the remainder of the oysters.
5. Coat the oysters with vegetable oil spray, then set them in the basket with as much air space between them as possible. Air-fry undisturbed for 8 minutes, or until lightly browned and crisp.
6. Use a nonstick-safe spatula to transfer the oysters to a wire rack. Cool for a couple of minutes before serving.

Firecracker Popcorn Shrimp

Servings: 6

Cooking Time: 8 Minutes

Ingredients:

- ½ cup all-purpose flour
- 2 teaspoons ground paprika
- 1 teaspoon garlic powder
- ½ teaspoon black pepper
- ¼ teaspoon salt
- 2 eggs, whisked
- 1½ cups panko breadcrumbs
- 1 pound small shrimp, peeled and deveined

Directions:

1. Preheat the air fryer to 360°F.
2. In a medium bowl, place the flour and mix in the paprika, garlic powder, pepper, and salt.
3. In a shallow dish, place the eggs.
4. In a third dish, place the breadcrumbs.
5. Assemble the shrimp by covering them in the flour, then dipping them into the egg, and then coating them with the breadcrumbs. Repeat until all the shrimp are covered in the breading.
6. Liberally spray the metal trivet that fits in the air fryer basket with olive oil mist. Place the shrimp onto the trivet, leaving space between the shrimp to flip. Cook for 4 minutes, flip the shrimp, and cook another 4 minutes. Repeat until all the shrimp are cooked.
7. Serve warm with desired dipping sauce.

Better Fish Sticks

Servings:3

Cooking Time: 8 Minutes

Ingredients:

- ¾ cup Seasoned Italian-style dried bread crumbs (gluten-free, if a concern)
- 3 tablespoons (about ½ ounce) Finely grated Parmesan cheese
- 10 ounces Skinless cod fillets, cut lengthwise into 1-inch-wide pieces
- 3 tablespoons Regular or low-fat mayonnaise (not fat-free; gluten-free, if a concern)
- Vegetable oil spray

Directions:

1. Preheat the air fryer to 400°F.
2. Mix the bread crumbs and grated Parmesan in a shallow soup bowl or a small pie plate.
3. Smear the fish fillet sticks completely with the mayonnaise, then dip them one by one in the bread-crumb mixture, turning and pressing gently to make an even and thorough coating. Coat each stick on all sides with vegetable oil spray.
4. Set the fish sticks in the basket with at least ¼ inch between them. Air-fry undisturbed for 8 minutes, or until golden brown and crisp.
5. Use a nonstick-safe spatula to gently transfer them from the basket to a wire rack. Cool for only a minute or two before serving.

Coconut-shrimp Po' Boys

Servings: 4

Cooking Time: 5 Minutes

Ingredients:

- ½ cup cornstarch
- 2 eggs
- 2 tablespoons milk
- ¾ cup shredded coconut
- ½ cup panko breadcrumbs
- 1 pound (31–35 count) shrimp, peeled and deveined
- Old Bay Seasoning
- oil for misting or cooking spray
- 2 large hoagie rolls
- honey mustard or light mayonnaise
- 1½ cups shredded lettuce
- 1 large tomato, thinly sliced

Directions:

1. Place cornstarch in a shallow dish or plate.
2. In another shallow dish, beat together eggs and milk.
3. In a third dish mix the coconut and panko crumbs.
4. Sprinkle shrimp with Old Bay Seasoning to taste.
5. Dip shrimp in cornstarch to coat lightly, dip in egg mixture, shake off excess, and roll in coconut mixture to coat well.
6. Spray both sides of coated shrimp with oil or cooking spray.
7. Cook half the shrimp in a single layer at 390°F for 5minutes.
8. Repeat to cook remaining shrimp.
9. To Assemble
10. Split each hoagie lengthwise, leaving one long edge intact.
11. Place in air fryer basket and cook at 390°F for 1 to 2minutes or until heated through.
12. Remove buns, break apart, and place on 4 plates, cut side up.
13. Spread with honey mustard and/or mayonnaise.
14. Top with shredded lettuce, tomato slices, and coconut shrimp.

Quick Shrimp Scampi

Servings: 2

Cooking Time: 5 Minutes

Ingredients:

- 16 to 20 raw large shrimp, peeled, deveined and tails removed
- ½ cup white wine
- freshly ground black pepper
- ¼ cup + 1 tablespoon butter, divided
- 1 clove garlic, sliced
- 1 teaspoon olive oil
- salt, to taste
- juice of ½ lemon, to taste
- ¼ cup chopped fresh parsley

Directions:

1. Start by marinating the shrimp in the white wine and freshly ground black pepper for at least 30 minutes, or as long as 2 hours in the refrigerator.
2. Preheat the air fryer to 400°F.
3. Melt ¼ cup of butter in a small saucepan on the stovetop. Add the garlic and let the butter simmer, but be sure to not let it burn.
4. Pour the shrimp and marinade into the air fryer, letting the marinade drain through to the bottom drawer. Drizzle the olive oil on the shrimp and season well with salt. Air-fry at 400°F for 3 minutes. Turn the shrimp over (don't shake the basket because the marinade will splash around) and pour the garlic butter over the shrimp. Air-fry for another 2 minutes.
5. Remove the shrimp from the air fryer basket and transfer them to a bowl. Squeeze lemon juice over all the shrimp and toss with the chopped parsley and remaining tablespoon of butter. Season to taste with salt and serve immediately.

Sea Bass With Potato Scales And Caper Aïoli

Servings: 2
Cooking Time: 10 Minutes

Ingredients:

- 2 (6- to 8-ounce) fillets of sea bass
- salt and freshly ground black pepper
- ¼ cup mayonnaise
- 2 teaspoons finely chopped lemon zest
- 1 teaspoon chopped fresh thyme
- 2 fingerling potatoes, very thinly sliced into rounds
- olive oil
- ½ clove garlic, crushed into a paste
- 1 tablespoon capers, drained and rinsed
- 1 tablespoon olive oil
- 1 teaspoon lemon juice, to taste

Directions:

1. Preheat the air fryer to 400°F.
2. Season the fish well with salt and freshly ground black pepper. Mix the mayonnaise, lemon zest and thyme together in a small bowl. Spread a thin layer of the mayonnaise mixture on both fillets. Start layering rows of potato slices onto the fish fillets to simulate the fish scales. The second row should overlap the first row slightly. Dabbing a little more mayonnaise along the upper edge of the row of potatoes where the next row overlaps will help the potato slices stick. Press the potatoes onto the fish to secure them well and season again with salt. Brush or spray the potato layer with olive oil.
3. Transfer the fish to the air fryer and air-fry for 8 to 10 minutes, depending on the thickness of your fillets. 1-inch of fish should take 10 minutes at 400°F.
4. While the fish is cooking, add the garlic, capers, olive oil and lemon juice to the remaining mayonnaise mixture to make the caper aïoli.
5. Serve the fish warm with a dollop of the aïoli on top or on the side.

Coconut Shrimp

Servings: 4
Cooking Time: 12 Minutes

Ingredients:

- 1 pound large shrimp (about 16 to 20), peeled and de-veined
- ½ cup flour
- salt and freshly ground black pepper
- 2 egg whites
- ½ cup fine breadcrumbs
- ½ cup shredded unsweetened coconut
- zest of one lime
- ½ teaspoon salt
- ⅛ to ¼ teaspoon ground cayenne pepper
- vegetable or canola oil
- sweet chili sauce or duck sauce (for serving)

Directions:

1. Set up a dredging station. Place the flour in a shallow dish and season well with salt and freshly ground black pepper. Whisk the egg whites in a second shallow dish. In a third shallow dish, combine the breadcrumbs, coconut, lime zest, salt and cayenne pepper.
2. Preheat the air fryer to 400°F.
3. Dredge each shrimp first in the flour, then dip it in the egg mixture, and finally press it into the breadcrumb-

coconut mixture to coat all sides. Place the breaded shrimp on a plate or baking sheet and spray both sides with vegetable oil.

4. Air-fry the shrimp in two batches, being sure not to over-crowd the basket. Air-fry for 5 minutes, turning the shrimp over for the last minute or two. Repeat with the second batch of shrimp.

5. Lower the temperature of the air fryer to 340°F. Return the first batch of shrimp to the air fryer basket with the second batch and air-fry for an additional 2 minutes, just to re-heat everything.

6. Serve with sweet chili sauce, duck sauce or just eat them plain!

Crispy Smelts

Servings:3

Cooking Time: 20 Minutes

Ingredients:

- 1 pound Cleaned smelts
- 3 tablespoons Tapioca flour
- Vegetable oil spray
- To taste Coarse sea salt or kosher salt

Directions:

1. Preheat the air fryer to 400°F.
2. Toss the smelts and tapioca flour in a large bowl until the little fish are evenly coated.
3. Lay the smelts out on a large cutting board. Lightly coat both sides of each fish with vegetable oil spray.
4. When the machine is at temperature, set the smelts close together in the basket, with a few even overlapping on top. Air-fry undisturbed for 20 minutes, until lightly browned and crisp.
5. Remove the basket from the machine and turn out the fish onto a wire rack. The smelts will most likely come out as one large block, or maybe in a couple of large pieces. Cool for a minute or two, then sprinkle the smelts with salt and break the block(s) into much smaller sections or individual fish to serve.

Miso-rubbed Salmon Fillets

Servings:3

Cooking Time: 5 Minutes

Ingredients:

- ¼ cup White (shiro) miso paste (usually made from rice and soy beans)
- 1½ tablespoons Mirin or a substitute (see here)
- 2½ teaspoons Unseasoned rice vinegar (see here)
- Vegetable oil spray
- 3 6-ounce skin-on salmon fillets (for more information, see here)

Directions:

1. Preheat the air fryer to 400°F.
2. Mix the miso, mirin, and vinegar in a small bowl until uniform.
3. Remove the basket from the machine. Generously spray the skin side of each fillet. Pick them up one by one with a nonstick-safe spatula and set them in the basket skin side down with as much air space between them as possible. Coat the top of each fillet with the miso mixture, dividing it evenly between them.
4. Return the basket to the machine. Air-fry undisturbed for 5 minutes, or until lightly browned and firm.
5. Use a nonstick-safe spatula to transfer the fillets to serving plates. Cool for only a minute or so before serving.

Tex-mex Fish Tacos

Servings:3

Cooking Time: 7 Minutes

Ingredients:

- ¾ teaspoon Chile powder
- ¼ teaspoon Ground cumin
- ¼ teaspoon Dried oregano
- 3 5-ounce skinless mahi-mahi fillets
- Vegetable oil spray
- 3 Corn or flour tortillas
- 6 tablespoons Diced tomatoes
- 3 tablespoons Regular, low-fat, or fat-free sour cream

Directions:

1. Preheat the air fryer to 400°F.
2. Stir the chile powder, cumin, and oregano in a small bowl until well combined.

3. Coat each piece of fish all over (even the sides and ends) with vegetable oil spray. Sprinkle the spice mixture evenly over all sides of the fillets. Lightly spray them again.

4. When the machine is at temperature, set the fillets in the basket with as much air space between them as possible. Air-fry undisturbed for 7 minutes, until lightly browned and firm but not hard.

5. Use a nonstick-safe spatula to transfer the fillets to a wire rack. Microwave the tortillas on high for a few seconds, until supple. Put a fillet in each tortilla and top each with 2 tablespoons diced tomatoes and 1 tablespoon sour cream.

Pecan-crusted Tilapia

Servings: 4

Cooking Time: 8 Minutes

Ingredients:

- 1 pound skinless, boneless tilapia filets
- ¼ cup butter, melted
- 1 teaspoon minced fresh or dried rosemary
- 1 cup finely chopped pecans
- 1 teaspoon sea salt
- ¼ teaspoon paprika
- 2 tablespoons chopped parsley
- 1 lemon, cut into wedges

Directions:

1. Pat the tilapia filets dry with paper towels.
2. Pour the melted butter over the filets and flip the filets to coat them completely.
3. In a medium bowl, mix together the rosemary, pecans, salt, and paprika.
4. Preheat the air fryer to 350°F.
5. Place the tilapia filets into the air fryer basket and top with the pecan coating. Cook for 6 to 8 minutes. The fish should be firm to the touch and flake easily when fully cooked.
6. Remove the fish from the air fryer. Top the fish with chopped parsley and serve with lemon wedges.

Fish Sticks For Kids

Servings: 8

Cooking Time: 6 Minutes

Ingredients:

- 8 ounces fish fillets (pollock or cod)
- salt (optional)
- ½ cup plain breadcrumbs
- oil for misting or cooking spray

Directions:

1. Cut fish fillets into "fingers" about ½ x 3 inches. Sprinkle with salt to taste, if desired.
2. Roll fish in breadcrumbs. Spray all sides with oil or cooking spray.
3. Place in air fryer basket in single layer and cook at 390°F for 6 minutes, until golden brown and crispy.

Crunchy And Buttery Cod With Ritz® Cracker Crust

Servings: 2

Cooking Time: 10 Minutes

Ingredients:

- 4 tablespoons butter, melted
- 8 to 10 RITZ® crackers, crushed into crumbs
- 2 (6-ounce) cod fillets
- salt and freshly ground black pepper
- 1 lemon

Directions:

1. Preheat the air fryer to 380°F.
2. Melt the butter in a small saucepan on the stovetop or in a microwavable dish in the microwave, and then transfer the butter to a shallow dish. Place the crushed RITZ® crackers into a second shallow dish.
3. Season the fish fillets with salt and freshly ground black pepper. Dip them into the butter and then coat both sides with the RITZ® crackers.
4. Place the fish into the air fryer basket and air-fry at 380°F for 10 minutes, flipping the fish over halfway through the cooking time.
5. Serve with a wedge of lemon to squeeze over the top.

Fried Shrimp

Servings:3

Cooking Time: 7 Minutes

Ingredients:

- 1 Large egg white
- 2 tablespoons Water
- 1 cup Plain dried bread crumbs (gluten-free, if a concern)
- ¼ cup All-purpose flour or almond flour
- ¼ cup Yellow cornmeal
- 1 teaspoon Celery salt
- 1 teaspoon Mild paprika
- Up to ½ teaspoon Cayenne (optional)
- ¾ pound Large shrimp (20–25 per pound), peeled and deveined
- Vegetable oil spray

Directions:

1. Preheat the air fryer to 400°F.
2. Set two medium or large bowls on your counter. In the first, whisk the egg white and water until foamy. In the second, stir the bread crumbs, flour, cornmeal, celery salt, paprika, and cayenne (if using) until well combined.
3. Pour all the shrimp into the egg white mixture and stir gently until all the shrimp are coated. Use kitchen tongs to pick them up one by one and transfer them to the bread-crumb mixture. Turn each in the bread-crumb mixture to coat it evenly and thoroughly on all sides before setting it on a cutting board. When you're done coating the shrimp, coat them all on both sides with the vegetable oil spray.
4. Set the shrimp in as close to one layer in the basket as you can. Some may overlap. Air-fry for 7 minutes, gently rearranging the shrimp at the 4-minute mark to get covered surfaces exposed, until golden brown and firm but not hard.
5. Use kitchen tongs to gently transfer the shrimp to a wire rack. Cool for only a minute or two before serving.

Beer-breaded Halibut Fish Tacos

Servings: 4

Cooking Time: 10 Minutes

Ingredients:

- 1 pound halibut, cut into 1-inch strips
- 1 cup light beer
- 1 jalapeño, minced and divided
- 1 clove garlic, minced
- ¼ teaspoon ground cumin
- ½ cup cornmeal
- ¼ cup all-purpose flour
- 1¼ teaspoons sea salt, divided
- 2 cups shredded cabbage
- 1 lime, juiced and divided
- ¼ cup Greek yogurt
- ¼ cup mayonnaise
- 1 cup grape tomatoes, quartered
- ½ cup chopped cilantro
- ¼ cup chopped onion
- 1 egg, whisked
- 8 corn tortillas

Directions:

1. In a shallow baking dish, place the fish, the beer, 1 teaspoon of the minced jalapeño, the garlic, and the cumin. Cover and refrigerate for 30 minutes.
2. Meanwhile, in a medium bowl, mix together the cornmeal, flour, and ½ teaspoon of the salt.
3. In large bowl, mix together the shredded cabbage, 1 tablespoon of the lime juice, the Greek yogurt, the mayonnaise, and ½ teaspoon of the salt.
4. In a small bowl, make the pico de gallo by mixing together the tomatoes, cilantro, onion, ¼ teaspoon of the salt, the remaining jalapeño, and the remaining lime juice.
5. Remove the fish from the refrigerator and discard the marinade. Dredge the fish in the whisked egg; then dredge the fish in the cornmeal flour mixture, until all pieces of fish have been breaded.
6. Preheat the air fryer to 350°F.
7. Place the fish in the air fryer basket and spray liberally with cooking spray. Cook for 6 minutes, flip and shake the fish, and cook another 4 minutes.
8. While the fish is cooking, heat the tortillas in a heavy skillet for 1 to 2 minutes over high heat.
9. To assemble the tacos, place the battered fish on the heated tortillas, and top with slaw and pico de gallo. Serve immediately.

Blackened Catfish

Servings: 4

Cooking Time: 8 Minutes

Ingredients:

- 1 teaspoon paprika
- 1 teaspoon garlic powder
- 1 teaspoon onion powder
- 1 teaspoon ground dried thyme
- ½ teaspoon ground black pepper
- ⅛ teaspoon cayenne pepper
- ½ teaspoon dried oregano
- ⅛ teaspoon crushed red pepper flakes
- 1 pound catfish filets
- ½ teaspoon sea salt
- 2 tablespoons butter, melted
- 1 tablespoon extra-virgin olive oil
- 2 tablespoons chopped parsley
- 1 lemon, cut into wedges

Directions:

1. In a small bowl, stir together the paprika, garlic powder, onion powder, thyme, black pepper, cayenne pepper, oregano, and crushed red pepper flakes.
2. Pat the fish dry with paper towels. Season the filets with sea salt and then coat with the blackening seasoning.
3. In a small bowl, mix together the butter and olive oil and drizzle over the fish filets, flipping them to coat them fully.
4. Preheat the air fryer to 350°F.
5. Place the fish in the air fryer basket and cook for 8 minutes, checking the fish for doneness after 4 minutes. The fish will flake easily when cooked.
6. Remove the fish from the air fryer. Top with chopped parsley and serve with lemon wedges.

Crunchy Clam Strips

Servings:3

Cooking Time: 8 Minutes

Ingredients:

- ½ pound Clam strips, drained
- 1 Large egg, well beaten
- ½ cup All-purpose flour
- ½ cup Yellow cornmeal
- 1½ teaspoons Table salt
- 1½ teaspoons Ground black pepper
- Up to ¾ teaspoon Cayenne
- Vegetable oil spray

Directions:

1. Preheat the air fryer to 400°F.
2. Toss the clam strips and beaten egg in a bowl until the clams are well coated.
3. Mix the flour, cornmeal, salt, pepper, and cayenne in a large zip-closed plastic bag until well combined. Using a flatware fork or small kitchen tongs, lift the clam strips one by one out of the egg, letting any excess egg slip back into the rest. Put the strips in the bag with the flour mixture. Once all the strips are in the bag, seal it and shake gently until the strips are well coated.
4. Use kitchen tongs to pick out the clam strips and lay them on a cutting board (leaving any extra flour mixture in the bag to be discarded). Coat the strips on both sides with vegetable oil spray.
5. When the machine is at temperature, spread the clam strips in the basket in one layer. They may touch in places, but try to leave as much air space as possible around them. Air-fry undisturbed for 8 minutes, or until brown and crunchy.
6. Gently dump the contents of the basket onto a serving platter. Cool for just a minute or two before serving hot.

Crispy Sweet-and-sour Cod Fillets

Servings:3

Cooking Time: 12 Minutes

Ingredients:

- 1½ cups Plain panko bread crumbs (gluten-free, if a concern)
- 2 tablespoons Regular or low-fat mayonnaise (not fat-free; gluten-free, if a concern)
- ¼ cup Sweet pickle relish
- 3 4- to 5-ounce skinless cod fillets

Directions:

1. Preheat the air fryer to 400°F.
2. Pour the bread crumbs into a shallow soup plate or a small pie plate. Mix the mayonnaise and relish in a small bowl until well combined. Smear this mixture all over

the cod fillets. Set them in the crumbs and turn until evenly coated on all sides, even on the ends.

3. Set the coated cod fillets in the basket with as much air space between them as possible. They should not touch. Air-fry undisturbed for 12 minutes, or until browned and crisp.

4. Use a nonstick-safe spatula to transfer the cod pieces to a wire rack. Cool for only a minute or two before serving hot.

Lobster Tails With Lemon Garlic Butter

Servings: 2

Cooking Time: 5 Minutes

Ingredients:

- 4 ounces unsalted butter
- 1 tablespoon finely chopped lemon zest
- 1 clove garlic, thinly sliced
- 2 (6-ounce) lobster tails
- salt and freshly ground black pepper
- ½ cup white wine
- ½ lemon, sliced
- vegetable oil

Directions:

1. Start by making the lemon garlic butter. Combine the butter, lemon zest and garlic in a small saucepan. Melt and simmer the butter on the stovetop over the lowest possible heat while you prepare the lobster tails.
2. Prepare the lobster tails by cutting down the middle of the top of the shell. Crack the bottom shell by squeezing the sides of the lobster together so that you can access the lobster meat inside. Pull the lobster tail up out of the shell, but leave it attached at the base of the tail. Lay the lobster meat on top of the shell and season with salt and freshly ground black pepper. Pour a little of the lemon garlic butter on top of the lobster meat and transfer the lobster to the refrigerator so that the butter solidifies a little.
3. Pour the white wine into the air fryer drawer and add the lemon slices. Preheat the air fryer to 400°F for 5 minutes.
4. Transfer the lobster tails to the air fryer basket. Air-fry at 370° for 5 minutes, brushing more butter on halfway through cooking. (Add a minute or two if your lobster tail is more than 6-ounces.) Remove and serve with more butter for dipping or drizzling.

Shrimp Po'boy With Remoulade Sauce

Servings: 6

Cooking Time: 8 Minutes

Ingredients:

- ½ cup all-purpose flour
- ½ teaspoon paprika
- 1 teaspoon garlic powder
- ½ teaspoon black pepper
- ¼ teaspoon salt
- 2 eggs, whisked
- 1½ cups panko breadcrumbs
- 1 pound small shrimp, peeled and deveined
- Six 6-inch French rolls
- 2 cups shredded lettuce
- 12 ⅛-inch tomato slices
- ¾ cup Remoulade Sauce (see the following recipe)

Directions:

1. Preheat the air fryer to 360°F.
2. In a medium bowl, mix the flour, paprika, garlic powder, pepper, and salt.
3. In a shallow dish, place the eggs.
4. In a third dish, place the panko breadcrumbs.
5. Covering the shrimp in the flour, dip them into the egg, and coat them with the breadcrumbs. Repeat until all shrimp are covered in the breading.
6. Liberally spray the metal trivet that fits inside the air fryer basket with olive oil spray. Place the shrimp onto the trivet, leaving space between the shrimp to flip. Cook for 4 minutes, flip the shrimp, and cook another 4 minutes. Repeat until all the shrimp are cooked.
7. Slice the rolls in half. Stuff each roll with shredded lettuce, tomato slices, breaded shrimp, and remoulade sauce. Serve immediately.

Coconut Jerk Shrimp

Servings:3

Cooking Time: 8 Minutes

Ingredients:

- 1 Large egg white(s)
- 1 teaspoon Purchased or homemade jerk dried seasoning blend (see the headnote)
- ¾ cup Plain panko bread crumbs (gluten-free, if a concern)
- ¾ cup Unsweetened shredded coconut
- 12 Large shrimp (20–25 per pound), peeled and deveined
- Coconut oil spray

Directions:

1. Preheat the air fryer to 375°F .
2. Whisk the egg white(s) and seasoning blend in a bowl until foamy. Add the shrimp and toss well to coat evenly.
3. Mix the bread crumbs and coconut on a dinner plate until well combined. Use kitchen tongs to pick up a shrimp, letting the excess egg white mixture slip back into the rest. Set the shrimp in the bread-crumb mixture. Turn several times to coat evenly and thoroughly. Set on a cutting board and continue coating the remainder of the shrimp.
4. Lightly coat all the shrimp on both sides with the coconut oil spray. Set them in the basket in one layer with as much space between them as possible. (You can even stand some up along the basket's wall in some models.) Air-fry undisturbed for 6 minutes, or until the coating is lightly browned. If the air fryer is at 360°F, you may need to add 2 minutes to the cooking time.
5. Use clean kitchen tongs to transfer the shrimp to a wire rack. Cool for only a minute or two before serving.

Crab Cakes

Servings: 2

Cooking Time: 10 Minutes

Ingredients:

- 1 teaspoon butter
- ⅓ cup finely diced onion
- ⅓ cup finely diced celery
- ¼ cup mayonnaise
- 1 teaspoon Dijon mustard
- 1 egg
- pinch ground cayenne pepper
- 1 teaspoon salt
- freshly ground black pepper
- 16 ounces lump crabmeat
- ½ cup + 2 tablespoons panko breadcrumbs, divided

Directions:

1. Melt the butter in a skillet over medium heat. Sauté the onion and celery until it starts to soften, but not brown – about 4 minutes. Transfer the cooked vegetables to a large bowl. Add the mayonnaise, Dijon mustard, egg, cayenne pepper, salt and freshly ground black pepper to the bowl. Gently fold in the lump crabmeat and 2 tablespoons of panko breadcrumbs. Stir carefully so you don't break up all the crab pieces.
2. Preheat the air fryer to 400°F.
3. Place the remaining panko breadcrumbs in a shallow dish. Divide the crab mixture into 4 portions and shape each portion into a round patty. Dredge the crab patties in the breadcrumbs, coating both sides as well as the edges with the crumbs.
4. Air-fry the crab cakes for 5 minutes. Using a flat spatula, gently turn the cakes over and air-fry for another 5 minutes. Serve the crab cakes with tartar sauce or cocktail sauce, or dress it up with the suggestion below.

Lightened-up Breaded Fish Filets

Servings: 4

Cooking Time: 10 Minutes

Ingredients:

- ½ cup all-purpose flour
- ½ teaspoon cayenne pepper
- 1 teaspoon garlic powder
- ½ teaspoon black pepper
- ¼ teaspoon salt
- 2 eggs, whisked
- 1½ cups panko breadcrumbs
- 1 pound boneless white fish filets
- 1 cup tartar sauce
- 1 lemon, sliced into wedges

Directions:

1. In a medium bowl, mix the flour, cayenne pepper, garlic powder, pepper, and salt.
2. In a shallow dish, place the eggs.
3. In a third dish, place the breadcrumbs.
4. Cover the fish in the flour, dip them in the egg, and coat them with panko. Repeat until all fish are covered in the breading.
5. Liberally spray the metal trivet that fits inside the air fryer basket with olive oil mist. Place the fish onto the trivet, leaving space between the filets to flip. Cook for 5 minutes, flip the fish, and cook another 5 minutes. Repeat until all the fish is cooked.
6. Serve warm with tartar sauce and lemon wedges.

Sesame-crusted Tuna Steaks

Servings:3

Cooking Time: 10-13 Minutes

Ingredients:

- ½ cup Sesame seeds, preferably a blend of white and black
- 1½ tablespoons Toasted sesame oil
- 3 6-ounce skinless tuna steaks

Directions:

1. Preheat the air fryer to 400°F.
2. Pour the sesame seeds on a dinner plate. Use ½ tablespoon of the sesame oil as a rub on both sides and the edges of a tuna steak. Set it in the sesame seeds, then turn it several times, pressing gently, to create an even coating of the seeds, including around the steak's edge. Set aside and continue coating the remaining steak(s).
3. When the machine is at temperature, set the steaks in the basket with as much air space between them as possible. Air-fry undisturbed for 10 minutes for medium-rare (not USDA-approved), or 12 to 13 minutes for cooked through (USDA-approved).
4. Use a nonstick-safe spatula to transfer the steaks to serving plates. Serve hot.

Cajun Flounder Fillets

Servings:2

Cooking Time: 5 Minutes

Ingredients:

- 2 4-ounce skinless flounder fillet(s)
- 2 teaspoons Peanut oil
- 1 teaspoon Purchased or homemade Cajun dried seasoning blend (see the headnote)

Directions:

1. Preheat the air fryer to 400°F.
2. Oil the fillet(s) by drizzling on the peanut oil, then gently rubbing in the oil with your clean, dry fingers. Sprinkle the seasoning blend evenly over both sides of the fillet(s).
3. When the machine is at temperature, set the fillet(s) in the basket. If working with more than one fillet, they should not touch, although they may be quite close together, depending on the basket's size. Air-fry undisturbed for 5 minutes, or until lightly browned and cooked through.
4. Use a nonstick-safe spatula to transfer the fillets to a serving platter or plate(s). Serve at once.

Fried Scallops

Servings:3

Cooking Time: 6 Minutes

Ingredients:

- ½ cup All-purpose flour or tapioca flour
- 1 Large egg(s), well beaten
- 2 cups Corn flake crumbs (gluten-free, if a concern)
- Up to 2 teaspoons Cayenne
- 1 teaspoon Celery seeds
- 1 teaspoon Table salt
- 1 pound Sea scallops
- Vegetable oil spray

Directions:

1. Preheat the air fryer to 400°F.
2. Set up and fill three shallow soup plates or small pie plates on your counter: one for the flour; one for the beaten egg(s); and one for the corn flake crumbs, stirred with the cayenne, celery seeds, and salt until well combined.
3. One by one, dip a scallop in the flour, turning it every way to coat it thoroughly. Gently shake off any excess flour, then dip the scallop in the egg(s), turning it

again to coat all sides. Let any excess egg slip back into the rest, then set the scallop in the corn flake mixture. Turn it several times, pressing gently to get an even coating on the scallop all around. Generously coat the scallop with vegetable oil spray, then set it aside on a cutting board. Coat the remaining scallops in the same way.

4. Set the scallops in the basket with as much air space between them as possible. They should not touch. Air-fry undisturbed for 6 minutes, or until lightly browned and firm.

5. Use kitchen tongs to gently transfer the scallops to a wire rack. Cool for only a minute or two before serving.

Fish-in-chips

Servings:4

Cooking Time: 11 Minutes

Ingredients:

- 1 cup All-purpose flour or potato starch
- 2 Large egg(s), well beaten
- 1½ cups (6 ounces) Crushed plain potato chips, preferably thick-cut or ruffled (gluten-free, if a concern)
- 4 4-ounce skinless cod fillets

Directions:

1. Preheat the air fryer to 400°F.
2. Set up and fill three shallow soup plates or small pie plates on your counter: one for the flour, one for the beaten egg(s), and one for the crushed potato chips.
3. Dip a piece of cod in the flour, turning it to coat on all sides, even the ends and sides. Gently shake off any excess flour, then dip it in the beaten egg(s). Gently turn to coat it on all sides, then let any excess egg slip back into the rest. Set the fillet in the crushed potato chips and turn several times and onto all sides, pressing gently to coat the fish. Dip it back in the egg(s), coating all sides but taking care that the coating doesn't slip off; then dip it back in the potato chips for a thick, even coating. Set it aside and coat more fillets in the same way.
4. When the machine is at temperature, set the fillets in the basket with as much air space between them as possible. Air-fry undisturbed for 11 minutes, until golden brown and firm but not hard.
5. Use kitchen tongs to transfer the fillets to a wire rack. Cool for just a minute or two before serving.

Maple Balsamic Glazed Salmon

Servings: 4

Cooking Time: 10 Minutes

Ingredients:

- 4 (6-ounce) fillets of salmon
- salt and freshly ground black pepper
- vegetable oil
- ¼ cup pure maple syrup
- 3 tablespoons balsamic vinegar
- 1 teaspoon Dijon mustard

Directions:

1. Preheat the air fryer to 400°F.
2. Season the salmon well with salt and freshly ground black pepper. Spray or brush the bottom of the air fryer basket with vegetable oil and place the salmon fillets inside. Air-fry the salmon for 5 minutes.
3. While the salmon is air-frying, combine the maple syrup, balsamic vinegar and Dijon mustard in a small saucepan over medium heat and stir to blend well. Let the mixture simmer while the fish is cooking. It should start to thicken slightly, but keep your eye on it so it doesn't burn.
4. Brush the glaze on the salmon fillets and air-fry for an additional 5 minutes. The salmon should feel firm to the touch when finished and the glaze should be nicely browned on top. Brush a little more glaze on top before removing and serving with rice and vegetables, or a nice green salad.

Flounder Fillets

Servings: 4

Cooking Time: 8 Minutes

Ingredients:

- 1 egg white
- 1 tablespoon water
- 1 cup panko breadcrumbs
- 2 tablespoons extra-light virgin olive oil
- 4 4-ounce flounder fillets
- salt and pepper

- oil for misting or cooking spray

Directions:

1. Preheat air fryer to 390°F.
2. Beat together egg white and water in shallow dish.
3. In another shallow dish, mix panko crumbs and oil until well combined and crumbly (best done by hand).
4. Season flounder fillets with salt and pepper to taste. Dip each fillet into egg mixture and then roll in panko crumbs, pressing in crumbs so that fish is nicely coated.
5. Spray air fryer basket with nonstick cooking spray and add fillets. Cook at 390°F for 3minutes.
6. Spray fish fillets but do not turn. Cook 5 minutes longer or until golden brown and crispy. Using a spatula, carefully remove fish from basket and serve.

Sweet Potato–wrapped Shrimp

Servings:3

Cooking Time: 6 Minutes

Ingredients:

- 24 Long spiralized sweet potato strands
- Olive oil spray
- ¼ teaspoon Garlic powder
- ¼ teaspoon Table salt
- Up to a ⅛ teaspoon Cayenne
- 12 Large shrimp (20–25 per pound), peeled and deveined

Directions:

1. Preheat the air fryer to 400°F.
2. Lay the spiralized sweet potato strands on a large swath of paper towels and straighten out the strands to long ropes. Coat them with olive oil spray, then sprinkle them with the garlic powder, salt, and cayenne.
3. Pick up 2 strands and wrap them around the center of a shrimp, with the ends tucked under what now becomes the bottom side of the shrimp. Continue wrapping the remainder of the shrimp.
4. Set the shrimp bottom side down in the basket with as much air space between them as possible. Air-fry undisturbed for 6 minutes, or until the sweet potato strands are crisp and the shrimp are pink and firm.
5. Use kitchen tongs to transfer the shrimp to a wire rack. Cool for only a minute or two before serving.

Horseradish Crusted Salmon

Servings: 2

Cooking Time: 14 Minutes

Ingredients:

- 2 (5-ounce) salmon fillets
- salt and freshly ground black pepper
- 2 teaspoons Dijon mustard
- ½ cup panko breadcrumbs*
- 2 tablespoons prepared horseradish
- ½ teaspoon finely chopped lemon zest
- 1 tablespoon olive oil
- 1 tablespoon chopped fresh parsley

Directions:

1. Preheat the air fryer to 360°F.
2. Season the salmon with salt and freshly ground black pepper. Then spread the Dijon mustard on the salmon, coating the entire surface.
3. Combine the breadcrumbs, horseradish, lemon zest and olive oil in a small bowl. Spread the mixture over the top of the salmon and press down lightly with your hands, adhering it to the salmon using the mustard as "glue".
4. Transfer the salmon to the air fryer basket and air-fry at 360°F for 14 minutes (depending on how thick your fillet is) or until the fish feels firm to the touch. Sprinkle with the parsley.

Shrimp Teriyaki

Servings:10

Cooking Time: 6 Minutes

Ingredients:

- 1 tablespoon Regular or low-sodium soy sauce or gluten-free tamari sauce
- 1 tablespoon Mirin or a substitute (see here)
- 1 teaspoon Ginger juice (see the headnote)
- 10 Large shrimp (20–25 per pound), peeled and deveined
- ⅔ cup Plain panko bread crumbs (gluten-free, if a concern)
- 1 Large egg
- Vegetable oil spray

Directions:

1. Whisk the soy or tamari sauce, mirin, and ginger juice in an 8- or 9-inch square baking pan until uniform. Add the shrimp and toss well to coat. Cover and refrigerate for 1 hour, tossing the shrimp in the marinade at least twice.
2. Preheat the air fryer to 400°F.
3. Thread a marinated shrimp on a 4-inch bamboo skewer by inserting the pointy tip at the small end of the shrimp, then guiding the skewer along the shrimp so that the tip comes out the thick end and the shrimp is flat along the length of the skewer. Repeat with the remaining shrimp. (You'll need eight 4-inch skewers for the small batch, 10 skewers for the medium batch, and 12 for the large.)
4. Pour the bread crumbs onto a dinner plate. Whisk the egg in the baking pan with any marinade that stayed behind. Lay the skewers in the pan, in as close to a single layer as possible. Turn repeatedly to make sure the shrimp is coated in the egg mixture.
5. One at a time, take a skewered shrimp out of the pan and set it in the bread crumbs, turning several times and pressing gently until the shrimp is evenly coated on all sides. Coat the shrimp with vegetable oil spray and set the skewer aside. Repeat with the remainder of the shrimp.
6. Set the skewered shrimp in the basket in one layer. Air-fry undisturbed for 6 minutes, or until pink and firm.
7. Transfer the skewers to a wire rack. Cool for only a minute or two before serving.

Tuna Nuggets In Hoisin Sauce

Servings: 4
Cooking Time: 7 Minutes

Ingredients:

- ½ cup hoisin sauce
- 2 tablespoons rice wine vinegar
- 2 teaspoons sesame oil
- 1 teaspoon garlic powder
- 2 teaspoons dried lemongrass
- ¼ teaspoon red pepper flakes
- ½ small onion, quartered and thinly sliced
- 8 ounces fresh tuna, cut into 1-inch cubes
- cooking spray
- 3 cups cooked jasmine rice

Directions:

1. Mix the hoisin sauce, vinegar, sesame oil, and seasonings together.
2. Stir in the onions and tuna nuggets.
3. Spray air fryer baking pan with nonstick spray and pour in tuna mixture.
4. Cook at 390°F for 3minutes. Stir gently.
5. Cook 2minutes and stir again, checking for doneness. Tuna should be barely cooked through, just beginning to flake and still very moist. If necessary, continue cooking and stirring in 1-minute intervals until done.
6. Serve warm over hot jasmine rice.

Salmon Croquettes

Servings: 4
Cooking Time: 8 Minutes

Ingredients:

- 1 tablespoon oil
- ½ cup breadcrumbs
- 1 14.75-ounce can salmon, drained and all skin and fat removed
- 1 egg, beaten
- ⅓ cup coarsely crushed saltine crackers (about 8 crackers)
- ½ teaspoon Old Bay Seasoning
- ½ teaspoon onion powder
- ½ teaspoon Worcestershire sauce

Directions:

1. Preheat air fryer to 390°F.
2. In a shallow dish, mix oil and breadcrumbs until crumbly.
3. In a large bowl, combine the salmon, egg, cracker crumbs, Old Bay, onion powder, and Worcestershire. Mix well and shape into 8 small patties about ½-inch thick.
4. Gently dip each patty into breadcrumb mixture and turn to coat well on all sides.
5. Cook at 390°F for 8minutes or until outside is crispy and browned.

Lemon-dill Salmon Burgers

Servings: 4
Cooking Time: 8 Minutes

Ingredients:

- 2 (6-ounce) fillets of salmon, finely chopped by hand or in a food processor
- 1 cup fine breadcrumbs
- 1 teaspoon freshly grated lemon zest
- 2 tablespoons chopped fresh dill weed
- 1 teaspoon salt
- freshly ground black pepper
- 2 eggs, lightly beaten
- 4 brioche or hamburger buns
- lettuce, tomato, red onion, avocado, mayonnaise or mustard, to serve

Directions:

1. Preheat the air fryer to 400°F.
2. Combine all the ingredients in a bowl. Mix together well and divide into four balls. Flatten the balls into patties, making an indentation in the center of each patty with your thumb (this will help the burger stay flat as it cooks) and flattening the sides of the burgers so that they fit nicely into the air fryer basket.
3. Transfer the burgers to the air fryer basket and air-fry for 4 minutes. Flip the burgers over and air-fry for another 3 to 4 minutes, until nicely browned and firm to the touch.
4. Serve on soft brioche buns with your choice of topping – lettuce, tomato, red onion, avocado, mayonnaise or mustard.

Five Spice Red Snapper With Green Onions And Orange Salsa

Servings: 2

Cooking Time: 8 Minutes

Ingredients:

- 2 oranges, peeled, segmented and chopped
- 1 tablespoon minced shallot
- 1 to 3 teaspoons minced red Jalapeño or Serrano pepper
- 1 tablespoon chopped fresh cilantro
- lime juice, to taste
- salt, to taste
- 2 (5- to 6-ounce) red snapper fillets
- ½ teaspoon Chinese five spice powder
- salt and freshly ground black pepper
- vegetable or olive oil, in a spray bottle
- 4 green onions, cut into 2-inch lengths

Directions:

1. Start by making the salsa. Cut the peel off the oranges, slicing around the oranges to expose the flesh. Segment the oranges by cutting in between the membranes of the orange. Chop the segments roughly and combine in a bowl with the shallot, Jalapeño or Serrano pepper, cilantro, lime juice and salt. Set the salsa aside.
2. Preheat the air fryer to 400°F.
3. Season the fish fillets with the five-spice powder, salt and freshly ground black pepper. Spray both sides of the fish fillets with oil. Toss the green onions with a little oil.
4. Transfer the fish to the air fryer basket and scatter the green onions around the fish. Air-fry at 400°F for 8 minutes.
5. Remove the fish from the air fryer, along with the fried green onions. Serve with white rice and a spoonful of the salsa on top.

Popcorn Crawfish

Servings: 4

Cooking Time: 18 Minutes

Ingredients:

- ½ cup flour, plus 2 tablespoons
- ½ teaspoon garlic powder
- 1½ teaspoons Old Bay Seasoning
- ½ teaspoon onion powder
- ½ cup beer, plus 2 tablespoons
- 12-ounce package frozen crawfish tail meat, thawed and drained
- oil for misting or cooking spray
- Coating
- 1½ cups panko crumbs
- 1 teaspoon Old Bay Seasoning
- ½ teaspoon ground black pepper

Directions:

1. In a large bowl, mix together the flour, garlic powder, Old Bay Seasoning, and onion powder. Stir in beer to blend.
2. Add crawfish meat to batter and stir to coat.
3. Combine the coating ingredients in food processor and pulse to finely crush the crumbs. Transfer crumbs to shallow dish.
4. Preheat air fryer to 390°F.
5. Pour the crawfish and batter into a colander to drain. Stir with a spoon to drain excess batter.
6. Working with a handful of crawfish at a time, roll in crumbs and place on a cookie sheet. It's okay if some of the smaller pieces of crawfish meat stick together.
7. Spray breaded crawfish with oil or cooking spray and place all at once into air fryer basket.
8. Cook at 390°F for 5minutes. Shake basket or stir and mist again with olive oil or spray. Cook 5 moreminutes, shake basket again, and mist lightly again. Continue cooking 5 more minutes, until browned and crispy.

Fish Sticks For Grown-ups

Servings: 4
Cooking Time: 6 Minutes

Ingredients:

- 1 pound fish fillets
- ½ teaspoon hot sauce
- 1 tablespoon coarse brown mustard
- 1 teaspoon Worcestershire sauce
- salt
- Crumb Coating
- ¾ cup panko breadcrumbs
- ¼ cup stone-ground cornmeal
- ¼ teaspoon salt
- oil for misting or cooking spray

Directions:

1. Cut fish fillets crosswise into slices 1-inch wide.
2. Mix the hot sauce, mustard, and Worcestershire sauce together to make a paste and rub on all sides of the fish. Season to taste with salt.
3. Mix crumb coating ingredients together and spread on a sheet of wax paper.
4. Roll the fish fillets in the crumb mixture.
5. Spray all sides with olive oil or cooking spray and place in air fryer basket in a single layer.
6. Cook at 390°F for 6 minutes, until fish flakes easily.

Fish Cakes

Servings: 4
Cooking Time: 10 Minutes

Ingredients:

- ¾ cup mashed potatoes (about 1 large russet potato)
- 12 ounces cod or other white fish
- salt and pepper
- oil for misting or cooking spray
- 1 large egg
- ¼ cup potato starch
- ½ cup panko breadcrumbs
- 1 tablespoon fresh chopped chives
- 2 tablespoons minced onion

Directions:

1. Peel potatoes, cut into cubes, and cook on stovetop till soft.
2. Salt and pepper raw fish to taste. Mist with oil or cooking spray, and cook in air fryer at 360°F for 6 to 8minutes, until fish flakes easily. If fish is crowded, rearrange halfway through cooking to ensure all pieces cook evenly.
3. Transfer fish to a plate and break apart to cool.
4. Beat egg in a shallow dish.
5. Place potato starch in another shallow dish, and panko crumbs in a third dish.
6. When potatoes are done, drain in colander and rinse with cold water.
7. In a large bowl, mash the potatoes and stir in the chives and onion. Add salt and pepper to taste, then stir in the fish.
8. If needed, stir in a tablespoon of the beaten egg to help bind the mixture.
9. Shape into 8 small, fat patties. Dust lightly with potato starch, dip in egg, and roll in panko crumbs. Spray both sides with oil or cooking spray.
10. Cook at 360°F for 10 minutes, until golden brown and crispy.

Shrimp

Servings: 4

Cooking Time: 8 Minutes

Ingredients:

- 1 pound (26–30 count) shrimp, peeled, deveined, and butterflied (last tail section of shell intact)
- Marinade
- 1 5-ounce can evaporated milk
- 2 eggs, beaten
- 2 tablespoons white vinegar
- 1 tablespoon baking powder
- Coating
- 1 cup crushed panko breadcrumbs
- ½ teaspoon paprika
- ½ teaspoon Old Bay Seasoning
- ¼ teaspoon garlic powder
- oil for misting or cooking spray

Directions:

1. Stir together all marinade ingredients until well mixed. Add shrimp and stir to coat. Refrigerate for 1 hour.
2. When ready to cook, preheat air fryer to 390°F.
3. Combine coating ingredients in shallow dish.
4. Remove shrimp from marinade, roll in crumb mixture, and spray with olive oil or cooking spray.
5. Cooking in two batches, place shrimp in air fryer basket in single layer, close but not overlapping. Cook at 390°F for 8 minutes, until light golden brown and crispy.
6. Repeat step 5 to cook remaining shrimp.

Blackened Red Snapper

Servings: 4

Cooking Time: 8 Minutes

Ingredients:

- 1½ teaspoons black pepper
- ¼ teaspoon thyme
- ¼ teaspoon garlic powder
- ⅛ teaspoon cayenne pepper
- 1 teaspoon olive oil
- 4 4-ounce red snapper fillet portions, skin on
- 4 thin slices lemon
- cooking spray

Directions:

1. Mix the spices and oil together to make a paste. Rub into both sides of the fish.
2. Spray air fryer basket with nonstick cooking spray and lay snapper steaks in basket, skin-side down.
3. Place a lemon slice on each piece of fish.
4. Cook at 390°F for 8 minutes. The fish will not flake when done, but it should be white through the center.

Curried Sweet-and-spicy Scallops

Servings:3

Cooking Time: 5 Minutes

Ingredients:

- 6 tablespoons Thai sweet chili sauce
- 2 cups (from about 5 cups cereal) Crushed Rice Krispies or other rice-puff cereal
- 2 teaspoons Yellow curry powder, purchased or homemade (see here)
- 1 pound Sea scallops
- Vegetable oil spray

Directions:

1. Preheat the air fryer to 400°F.
2. Set up and fill two shallow soup plates or small pie plates on your counter: one for the chili sauce and one for crumbs, mixed with the curry powder.
3. Dip a scallop into the chili sauce, coating it on all sides. Set it in the cereal mixture and turn several times to coat evenly. Gently shake off any excess and set the scallop on a cutting board. Continue dipping and coating the remaining scallops. Coat them all on all sides with the vegetable oil spray.
4. Set the scallops in the basket with as much air space between them as possible. Air-fry undisturbed for 5 minutes, or until lightly browned and crunchy.
5. Remove the basket. Set aside for 2 minutes to let the coating set up. Then gently pour the contents of the basket onto a platter and serve at once.

Sea Scallops

Servings: 4

Cooking Time: 8 Minutes

Ingredients:

- 1½ pounds sea scallops
- salt and pepper
- 2 eggs
- ½ cup flour
- ½ cup plain breadcrumbs
- oil for misting or cooking spray

Directions:

1. Rinse scallops and remove the tough side muscle. Sprinkle to taste with salt and pepper.
2. Beat eggs together in a shallow dish. Place flour in a second shallow dish and breadcrumbs in a third.
3. Preheat air fryer to 390°F.
4. Dip scallops in flour, then eggs, and then roll in breadcrumbs. Mist with oil or cooking spray.
5. Place scallops in air fryer basket in a single layer, leaving some space between. You should be able to cook about a dozen at a time.
6. Cook at 390°F for 8 minutes, watching carefully so as not to overcook. Scallops are done when they turn opaque all the way through. They will feel slightly firm when pressed with tines of a fork.
7. Repeat step 6 to cook remaining scallops.

Nutty Shrimp With Amaretto Glaze

Servings: 10

Cooking Time: 10 Minutes

Ingredients:

- 1 cup flour
- ½ teaspoon baking powder
- 1 teaspoon salt
- 2 eggs, beaten
- ½ cup milk
- 2 tablespoons olive or vegetable oil
- 2 cups sliced almonds
- 2 pounds large shrimp (about 32 to 40 shrimp), peeled and deveined, tails left on
- 2 cups amaretto liqueur

Directions:

1. Combine the flour, baking powder and salt in a large bowl. Add the eggs, milk and oil and stir until it forms a smooth batter. Coarsely crush the sliced almonds into a second shallow dish with your hands.
2. Dry the shrimp well with paper towels. Dip the shrimp into the batter and shake off any excess batter, leaving just enough to lightly coat the shrimp. Transfer the shrimp to the dish with the almonds and coat completely. Place the coated shrimp on a plate or baking sheet and when all the shrimp have been coated, freeze the shrimp for an 1 hour, or as long as a week before air-frying.
3. Preheat the air fryer to 400°F.
4. Transfer 8 frozen shrimp at a time to the air fryer basket. Air-fry for 6 minutes. Turn the shrimp over and air-fry for an additional 4 minutes. Repeat with the remaining shrimp.
5. While the shrimp are cooking, bring the Amaretto to a boil in a small saucepan on the stovetop. Lower the heat and simmer until it has reduced and thickened into a glaze – about 10 minutes.
6. Remove the shrimp from the air fryer and brush both sides with the warm amaretto glaze. Serve warm.

Shrimp "scampi"

Servings:4

Cooking Time: 5 Minutes

Ingredients:

- 1½ pounds Large shrimp (20–25 per pound), peeled and deveined
- ¼ cup Olive oil
- 2 tablespoons Minced garlic
- 1 teaspoon Dried oregano
- Up to 1 teaspoon Red pepper flakes
- ½ teaspoon Table salt
- 2 tablespoons White balsamic vinegar (see here)

Directions:

1. Preheat the air fryer to 400°F.
2. Stir the shrimp, olive oil, garlic, oregano, red pepper flakes, and salt in a large bowl until the shrimp are well coated.

3. When the machine is at temperature, transfer the shrimp to the basket. They will overlap and even sit on top of each other. Air-fry for 5 minutes, tossing and rearranging the shrimp twice to make sure the covered surfaces are exposed, until pink and firm.
4. Pour the contents of the basket into a serving bowl. Pour the vinegar over the shrimp while hot and toss to coat.

Fish Tacos With Jalapeño-lime Sauce

Servings: 4
Cooking Time: 7 Minutes

Ingredients:

- Fish Tacos
- 1 pound fish fillets
- ¼ teaspoon cumin
- ¼ teaspoon coriander
- ⅛ teaspoon ground red pepper
- 1 tablespoon lime zest
- ¼ teaspoon smoked paprika
- 1 teaspoon oil
- cooking spray
- 6–8 corn or flour tortillas (6-inch size)
- Jalapeño-Lime Sauce
- ½ cup sour cream
- 1 tablespoon lime juice
- ¼ teaspoon grated lime zest
- ½ teaspoon minced jalapeño (flesh only)
- ¼ teaspoon cumin
- Napa Cabbage Garnish
- 1 cup shredded Napa cabbage
- ¼ cup slivered red or green bell pepper
- ¼ cup slivered onion

Directions:

1. Slice the fish fillets into strips approximately ½-inch thick.
2. Put the strips into a sealable plastic bag along with the cumin, coriander, red pepper, lime zest, smoked paprika, and oil. Massage seasonings into the fish until evenly distributed.
3. Spray air fryer basket with nonstick cooking spray and place seasoned fish inside.
4. Cook at 390°F for approximately 5minutes. Shake basket to distribute fish. Cook an additional 2 minutes, until fish flakes easily.
5. While the fish is cooking, prepare the Jalapeño-Lime Sauce by mixing the sour cream, lime juice, lime zest, jalapeño, and cumin together to make a smooth sauce. Set aside.
6. Mix the cabbage, bell pepper, and onion together and set aside.
7. To warm refrigerated tortillas, wrap in damp paper towels and microwave for 30 to 60 seconds.
8. To serve, spoon some of fish into a warm tortilla. Add one or two tablespoons Napa Cabbage Garnish and drizzle with Jalapeño-Lime Sauce.

Catfish Nuggets

Servings: 4
Cooking Time: 7 Minutes Per Batch

Ingredients:

- 2 medium catfish fillets, cut in chunks (approximately 1 x 2 inch)
- salt and pepper
- 2 eggs
- 2 tablespoons skim milk
- ½ cup cornstarch
- 1 cup panko breadcrumbs, crushed
- oil for misting or cooking spray

Directions:

1. Season catfish chunks with salt and pepper to your liking.
2. Beat together eggs and milk in a small bowl.
3. Place cornstarch in a second small bowl.
4. Place breadcrumbs in a third small bowl.
5. Dip catfish chunks in cornstarch, dip in egg wash, shake off excess, then roll in breadcrumbs.
6. Spray all sides of catfish chunks with oil or cooking spray.
7. Place chunks in air fryer basket in a single layer, leaving space between for air circulation.

8. Cook at 390°F for 4minutes, turn, and cook an additional 3 minutes, until fish flakes easily and outside is crispy brown.

9. Repeat steps 7 and 8 to cook remaining catfish nuggets.

Shrimp Sliders With Avocado

Servings: 4

Cooking Time: 10 Minutes

Ingredients:

- 16 raw jumbo shrimp, peeled, deveined and tails removed (about 1 pound)
- 1 rib celery, finely chopped
- 2 carrots, grated (about ½ cup) 2 teaspoons lemon juice
- 2 teaspoons Dijon mustard
- ¼ cup chopped fresh basil or parsley
- ½ cup breadcrumbs
- ½ teaspoon salt
- freshly ground black pepper
- vegetable or olive oil, in a spray bottle
- 8 slider buns
- mayonnaise
- butter lettuce
- 2 avocados, sliced and peeled

Directions:

1. Put the shrimp into a food processor and pulse it a few times to rough chop the shrimp. Remove three quarters of the shrimp and transfer it to a bowl. Continue to process the remaining shrimp in the food processor until it is a smooth purée. Transfer the purée to the bowl with the chopped shrimp.
2. Add the celery, carrots, lemon juice, mustard, basil, breadcrumbs, salt and pepper to the bowl and combine well.
3. Preheat the air fryer to 380°F.
4. While the air fryer Preheats, shape the shrimp mixture into 8 patties. Spray both sides of the patties with oil and transfer one layer of patties to the air fryer basket. Air-fry for 10 minutes, flipping the patties over halfway through the cooking time.
5. Prepare the slider rolls by toasting them and spreading a little mayonnaise on both halves. Place a piece of butter lettuce on the bottom bun, top with the shrimp slider and then finish with the avocado slices on top. Pop the top half of the bun on top and enjoy!

Crabmeat-stuffed Flounder

Servings:3

Cooking Time: 12 Minutes

Ingredients:

- 4½ ounces Purchased backfin or claw crabmeat, picked over for bits of shell and cartilage
- 6 Saltine crackers, crushed into fine crumbs
- 2 tablespoons plus 1 teaspoon Regular or low-fat mayonnaise (not fat-free)
- ¾ teaspoon Yellow prepared mustard
- 1½ teaspoons Worcestershire sauce
- ⅛ teaspoon Celery salt
- 3 5- to 6-ounce skinless flounder fillets
- Vegetable oil spray
- Mild paprika

Directions:

1. Preheat the air fryer to 400°F.
2. Gently mix the crabmeat, crushed saltines, mayonnaise, mustard, Worcestershire sauce, and celery salt in a bowl until well combined.
3. Generously coat the flat side of a fillet with vegetable oil spray. Set the fillet sprayed side down on your work surface. Cut the fillet in half widthwise, then cut one of the halves in half lengthwise. Set a scant ⅓ cup of the crabmeat mixture on top of the undivided half of the fish fillet, mounding the mixture to make an oval that somewhat fits the shape of the fillet with at least a ¼-inch border of fillet beyond the filling all around.

4. Take the two thin divided quarters (that is, the halves of the half) and lay them lengthwise over the filling, overlapping at each end and leaving a little space in the middle where the filling peeks through. Coat the top of the stuffed flounder piece with vegetable oil spray, then sprinkle paprika over the stuffed flounder fillet. Set aside and use the remaining fillet(s) to make more stuffed flounder "packets," repeating steps 3 and

5. Use a nonstick-safe spatula to transfer the stuffed flounder fillets to the basket. Leave as much space between them as possible. Air-fry undisturbed for 12 minutes, or until lightly brown and firm (but not hard).

6. Use that same spatula, plus perhaps another one, to transfer the fillets to a serving platter or plates. Cool for a minute or two, then serve hot.

Recipe Index

C

D

E

F

N

O

P

Q

R

S

T

V

W

Y

Z

CPSIA information can be obtained
at www.ICGtesting.com
Printed in the USA
LVHW061236290521
688874LV00003B/455

9 781802 447675